THE POETRY OF EMILIO PRADOS

A Progression towards Fertility

TELEPEN
6 00 307975 2

The Poetry of Emilio Prados

A Progression towards Fertility

P. J. ELLIS

CARDIFF
UNIVERSITY OF WALES PRESS

1981

British Library Cataloguing in Publication Data
Ellis, P. J.
The poetry of Emilio Prados.
1. Prados, Emilio – Criticism and interpretation
I. Title
861'.62 PQ6629.R37Z/

ISBN 0-7083-0786-8

Text set in 11/12 pt Linotron 202 Baskerville, printed and bound in Great Britain at The Pitman Press, Bath

Cyflwynir
y gwaith hwn
i'm rhieni annwyl,
gyda diolch

FOREWORD

This study is based on a thesis offered in 1976 in candidature for a PhD at the University College, Cardiff. It deals chiefly with poetry Prados wrote during the years 1923 to 1953, the period marked by the publication of a personal choice from his own work, *Antología* (Losada, Buenos Aires, 1954). References to the poetry are taken from *Antología* and the two volumes of *Poesías completas*, which appeared in 1975 and 1976 respectively, edited by Carlos Blanco Aguinaga and Antonio Carreira, in Aguilar's *Biblioteca de autores modernos*. References to Prados poems contained in the anthology or the *Poesías completas* are given as part of the text. Those contained in the anthology are denoted by the page number alone, thus: 'Víspera' (9). Those which appear in the *Poesias completas* are referred to by volume and page number, thus: 'Juego de memoria' (I,97). When poems appear both in the selection and the complete edition of the poetry, the anthology's reference is first and separated from that of the *Poesías completas* by a colon, thus: 'Nocturno fiel' (11:I,373). This method is followed even when, as often occurs, Prados has attached a new title to an identical or similar text. As a rule, it is the *Antología* version which is preferred.

Since the completion of this work, the Prados papers, previously deposited in the Library of Congress, have been returned to the possession of the poet's family.

ACKNOWLEDGMENTS

This work has been undertaken and completed as a result of the co-operation and kindness of many. I should like to take this opportunity of thanking Mr H. Eccles and Mr H. Lawson who, when I was a pupil of the Wallasey Grammar School, kindled and sustained my interest in Spanish. My thanks are also due to those who particularly encouraged me while at Emmanuel College, Cambridge. I am indebted in more recent years to the department of Education and Science for their financial support; to the Department of Hispanic Studies at University College, Cardiff for the warmth of their welcome; to Professor Shergold in particular, for his prompt acquisition on my behalf of the Prados papers from Washington; to Professor C. B. Morris, for his practical and bibliographical help; to Sr José Luis Cano and Professor Carlos Blanco Aguinaga for their advice in the troublesome task of tracing some of Prados's publications; and to Professor José Manuel Blecua, who was kind enough to lend me several elusive editions from his private library. I am also grateful to Sra María Rosario Prados de Araoz and Mr L. Carroll Chipman, Prados's literary inheritors, for their promptness in granting me permission to reproduce his work; and to the staff of the University of Wales Press for their meticulous care and tactful guidance.

My special thanks are due to Professor José María Aguirre. His patient, painstaking and constructive criticism has been a constant source of encouragement.

CONTENTS

INTRODUCTION

Thus, language, in its origin and essence, is simply a system of signs or symbols that denote real occurrences or their echo in the human soul.

(Carl Gustav Jung, *Symbols of Transformation*)

"But 'glory' doesn't mean 'a nice knock-down argument,'" Alice objected.

"When *I* use a word," Humpty Dumpty said in rather a scornful tone, "it means just what I choose it to mean—neither more nor less."

"The question is," said Alice, "whether you *can* make words mean different things."

"The question is," said Humpty Dumpty, "which is to be master—that's all."

Alice was too much puzzled to say anything, so after a minute Humpty Dumpty began again. "They've a temper, some of them—particularly verbs, they're the proudest—adjectives you can do anything with, but not verbs—however, *I* can manage the whole lot! Impenetrability! That's what *I* say!"

(Lewis Carroll, *Alice's Adventures in Wonderland*)

In amongst the private papers of Emilio Prados are to be found what he cheerfully called: 'Apuntes para nada menos que una "Declaración estética" . . .'[1] These notes contain statements concerning the poet's views on the nature and purpose of his art: in particular dealing with what he sees as his own relationship to it. At first sight there is little to encourage the aspiring critic or reader. Rather, on the contrary, do they suggest that in Prados's view the mysterious, the esoteric, the inaccessible together constitute the very stuff of poetry:

> Para mí, la poesía, siempre es un secreto que no trato de descubrir sino que, como a una flecha, dejo que vaya ahondando más y más en mis entrañas; porque mientras esté el secreto clavado en ellas existirá conmigo la poesía, pero si me lo arranco, si lo descubro, presiento que la poesía se me convertirá, para siempre, en angustia.

Although such comments do little to elucidate the complexities of his work, they furnish us, nevertheless, with valuable insight into the way in which its author viewed its contents. They suggest, primarily, that as far as Prados is concerned poetry is as much a matter of withholding as of disclosing truth. And by the same token they warn us to approach his work with extreme caution. It has been necessary, as a matter of policy, to approach the poetry with a certain suspicion—to expect to find a reality behind the immediate appearance, a secret within the experience shared.

What is certain is that the reader of Prados's poems enters into an extremely private, intimate world. In much of the *Antología*, for example, little attention is paid to anyone except a single central figure, first met there as the young sailor of 'Víspera'. It is with the voyage of such a protagonist that this analysis deals. It has not been written in an attempt to relate the evolution of the central figure to the life of Emilio Prados. Rather is it intended to define, at various points in his development, the protagonist's view of himself and of his world.

It is perhaps because this view is so fraught with problems that it is wise to resign oneself to the 'secretiveness' and complexity of the poems. Only after lengthy analysis of the early poetry does something of his dilemma begin to emerge. The opening chapters suggest that, hidden beneath a welter of symbols and images lies an exposition of the central figure's main difficulties and of the sense of failure and insecurity consequent upon them. Subsequent chapters attempt to trace stages and turning points along the pathway towards a more settled experience. Piaget wrote: 'In reality, the most profound tendency of all human activity is progression towards equilibrium'.[2] However debatable such an assertion might be, nevertheless it stands as an apposite summary of the kind of quest charted in Prados's work. A recent critic has concluded that: '. . . unlike Jiménez and Cernuda, Prados makes no progess with his problems'.[3] It is hoped to suggest in the course of this study that such a statement is not altogether true.

Finally, in such an introduction as this, we feel obliged to crave the patient sympathy of our reader. Others have referred to Prados's poetry in terms of its ability to communicate freely and simply. We must confess that we have not always found it so. Rather have we battled with poems which stubbornly refuse to yield up their mystery; and with a 'yo' who shared the same reluctance. Perhaps in attempting to bring him out into the open we have torn too fiercely at the fabric of the poetry into which his experience is so inter-woven. Perhaps we have been impertinent in daring to analyse the central *persona* with a directness which he himself avoids. Be all that as it may, this study is born of the conviction that without just such an enquiry the life-blood, the central issue of these poems may escape the notice even of their admirers.

1 For the entire document, and a note on its source, see Appendix I.

2 J. Piaget, *Six Psychological Studies,* translated by A. Tenzer (London, 1968), p. 70.

3 G. G. Brown, *A Literary History of Spain: The Twentieth Century* (London, 1972), p. 105.

A Biographical Note[1]

Emilio Prados was born on 4 March 1899, in Málaga. From the first, and in spite of his mother's unfailing care and the advantages of a comfortable middle-class family, his was a childhood punctuated with illness. Such physical frailty was to have a profound effect on the formation of his character. Even in his youth it tended to set him at a distance from his fellows. His school-friend Aleixandre remembers him as a happy child—but at times also remote, lost in a day-dream of private thoughts: 'se le podía ver callado, absorto, devanando en su cabecilla, bajo un árbol del patio, mirando sin ver . . .'[2]

Ill-health also meant lengthy stays in 'los montes de Málaga'. If that introspectiveness and sensitivity which Aleixandre noted was an important feature of later years, so too was the love of nature which these visits fostered. Even as long afterwards as 1961, when Prados wrote 'Recuerdos de mi vida' his almost Wordsworthian experiences remain vibrant in the memory:[3]

> Después de 'La Venta', la carretera seguía llana y bordeada de magníficos alcornoques de tronco color de sangre y hoja espesa—verde oscura. Toda esta parte del camino estaba tan llena de silencio y majestad que nadie hablaba. Yo, la verdad es, que sentía un miedo espantoso en ello, pero me callaba también y nunca lo dije.

The extent of the impact of such scenery can be gauged from this more generalised comment:

> Al contacto directo con la naturaleza no contemplada, sino vivida, aprendida en su cuerpo verdadero, las anteriores observaciones y experiencias de mi soledad, hallaron su verificación normal. Inconscientemente aún, pude sentir la unificación de mis dos mundos: el que ocultaba en mi refugio incomprendido, primero, y el de la verdad tangible que la realidad me entregaba en lo natural hacia mis doce años de edad. La impresión fue tan fuerte que, aún en mis poemas actuales "Río natural", "Circuncisión del sueño', viven la misma tierra, el agua, el aire y el cielo que comencé a sentir entonces.

However, much of the material relating to the years immediately following these suggests that the impressions thus gained of the beauty and worth of the natural order served only to aggravate, rather than resolve, his sense of isolation. Even as early as the visits to 'los montes' and school-days in Málaga, which he dated from 1906 to 1914, there is evidence of deep-seated unrest. Looking back he asks:

> (¿Tendré que recordar toda mi vida en la escuela, el Instituto etc. con el cúmulo de inmoralidades que la llenaban? Mala enseñanza, injusticia de ella (como en la Historia, Religión, Psicología, Educación física, Literatura, Dibujo artístico etc.) y aún mayor lucha con la perversión de los compañeros?—perversión sexual, poco deseo de estudio, mofa y golpes contra los que se negaban a seguirlos en sus brutalidades.).

It is interesting to note the moral nature of his criticisms (as well as the implicit qualification of Aleixandre's picture of Prados as a socially integrated child).[4] What his school-mates regarded as signs of virility, he saw as breaches of morality. The resulting tension and ostracism are not difficult to imagine:

> Las faltas a clase estaban consideradas como un signo de virilidad. Alguna vez que yo intenté vencer al grupo que delante de la puerta de la clase obstaculizaba la entrada a ella fui arrojado por las escaleras a empellones, rodando hasta el patio en medio de los gritos de mofa y la risa general. Casi diariamente había algún incidente grave entre los compañeros. La moral no existía. Se debía faltar a clase o no se era hombre . . .
>
> Yo recuerdo estos años con verdadero terror, aun todavía. Jamás secundé la acción de mis compañeros. Y, como les reprochaba lo que hacían, se me hizo allá la vida imposible. Por otra parte, como tenía miedo de contar nada de esto en mi casa o a los profesores o a los amigos de mi familia, se me fue formando el carácter cada vez más desperadamente extraño y solitario.

What does seem certain is that Prados was an unusual and unconventional individual—expelled, for example, from the University of Seville shortly after suffering the same fate in the Universidad Central (1919). Referring to such institutions, he underlines what he saw as '. . . grandes contradicciones entre lo aconsejado y las realizaciones más cumplidas, por mí, del consejo recibido.'

It is also interesting to note that this sense of isolation is directly related to the body. After describing the enjoyment derived in childhood from the natural world he adds:

> Un punto solamente quedaba sin solucionar para mí, . . ., haciendo que por él siga sintiéndome constantemente 'cuerpo perseguido'.

In a letter to Cela, also preserved among the Prados papers, a similar point is made:

> Por una causa o por la otra desde mi nacimiento de entonces al de hoy, vivo en un "cuerpo perseguido" al que busco la paz que debe para verse él mismo y entregarse a los demás con ella. Desde que tuve recuerdo, sentí que la sensación de tiempo y de espacio separaban mi vida de la de los que me rodeaban, me querían, me observaban, me preguntaban con temor sin entenderme. Premonición, en sueño y en vigilia, lo que llaman "pavor nocturno"—que no eran tales pavores para mí—y otras formas que aún creo sobrenaturales, me han dado desde niño hasta el momento, un mundo de criaturas errantes, como yo mismo soy con ellas, mundo al que sé que me debo y al que sacrificaré por hallar toda mi vida.[5]

The years at the Residencia, the friendship with Lorca, convalescence at home, Switzerland and, from 1921 to 1923 in Freiburg, were important ones.[6] His reading during these years included the Greek and Latin classics, Manrique, *La Celestina*, the Arabic poetry of southern Spain, Mallarmé, Gide, Valéry.[7] In his own account he lists the following as read while in Germany: 'Poetas persas y orientales/Lafcadio Hearne (Leyendas de Oriente)/Goete (*sic*) y los románticos . . . Heine'.

But the ideas formed during this period of intensive reading (he mentions 'mi afán de grandes lecturas') were to meet with a disappointing response. 1930 is remembered in the following way:

> Después de grandes crisis religiosas, políticas, literarias, voy a Madrid con la idea de fundar el grupo de "surrealistas" . . .[8]

Prados's energy had already found its expression in literary work, most notably in founding the remarkable *Litoral* in 1927. But his arrival on the Madrid scene was not enthusiastically welcomed. Of 1931 he writes:

> Desde esa fecha gran ilusión ante una nueva formación del pensamiento español y gran decepción nueva al ver como las cosas iban ocurriendo . . .[9]

Abortive attempts at sculpture, collage and painting were to end in disorientation. The war years were spent actively in Málaga, Madrid, Valencia and Barcelona, but by 1939 he was forced to escape to Paris. There kindness extended by the Mexican embassy swayed him in his decision to emigrate to Mexico.

But the sense of disorientation which the activity of war had suspended returned soon after his arrival in Mexico, where he engaged in various 'empresas editoriales' and what he describes as an 'infinidad de proyectos irrealizables'. His final years were ones of quietness, reading and writing. Ernestina de Champourcin quotes him as having once said: 'Leo la Biblia y me pongo a escribir'.[10] This simplicity is reflected in Blanco's picture of the poet's later years, during which he adopted two homeless children while working in the Instituto Luis Vives.[11] José Luis Cano, writing in *Ínsula*, mentions a letter received from his exiled friend shortly before his death, which took place in Mexico City on 24 April 1962. Prados wrote: 'Tienes que irte acostumbrando a mi ausencia real . . . Estoy solito, pero con paz interior.'[12]

The extraordinary nature of the man emerges from a reading of the tributes paid to him on his death. Landa wrote, in an article on 'Emilio Prados como maestro', that 'Prados era un santo'.[13] Referring perhaps to an incident similar to those described by the poet in his 'Recuerdos de mi vida,' Muñoz Rojas, a school-friend, recalls his claim that he had fallen, a claim, it would seem, dismissed by his companions at the time:

> La verdad es que Emilio Prados llevaba la razón. A mí me ha costado mucho tiempo averiguarlo. Emilio se había caído esta y otras muchas veces, de algún lugar del cielo.[14]

García Ascot saw his passing in these terms: '. . . ha muerto nuestra juventud.'[15]

His personal sense of destiny, his curiously objective view of his own life mark this note of 1962:

> . . . cumplo 63 años, edad a la que murió mi padre y que siempre he considerado que para mí sería igualmente el fin de mi estancia consciente en mi cuerpo, cuyo nombre heredado del de mi padre me une aun más a él y a su recuerdo.[16]

Within just over a week, far from the shores of his native Málaga, he had indeed died.

[1] It would be extremely difficult to improve on Professor Blanco's sensitive and detailed review of Emilio Prados's life, in *Emilio Prados, Vida y obra, bibliografía, antología* (New York, 1960). The brief account included here is based on it. There is, however, one respect in which it complements Blanco's work. In addition to the comments of friends and literary critics, reference is made to the poet's own recollections of his life, taken chiefly from the unpublished 'Recuerdos de mi vida (1899 . . .)'. These are to be found

in Caja 20 of Prados's papers as deposited in the Library of Congress and catalogued by Professor Blanco in *Lista de los papeles de Emilio Prados* (The Johns Hopkins Press, Baltimore, 1967). They are reproduced in Appendix I.

2 Vicente Aleixandre, 'Emilio Prados, en su origen', *Ínsula*, no. 187 (1962), pp. 1–2.

3 See Appendix II. Unless otherwise stated, the quotations in Spanish used in this biography are taken from the same source.

4 For more of Aleixandre's account of Prados's childhood, see his *Los encuentros* (Madrid, 1968), pp. 115–20, quoted in Blanco Aguinaga, *Vida y obra*, p. 9.

5 From the folder described in *Lista de los papeles de Emilio Prados,* under Caja 20.3.

6 An interesting source of information on this period is the *Diario íntimo,* (Málaga, 1966).

7 C. Blanco Aguinaga, *Vida y obra,* p. 11.

8 Also from the letter to Cela—dated, incidentally, 4 June 1958, and written in Mexico.

9 From another set of hand-written autobiographical notes, Caja 20.3.

10 E. de Champourcin, 'Ha muerto un poeta', in *Litoral* (July 1970), pp. 57—61.

11 C. Blanco Aguinaga, *Vida y obra,* pp. 25—26.

12 J. L. Cano, 'Presencia viva de Emilio', *Ínsula*, no. 187 (1962), p. 3.

13 R. Landa, 'Emilio Prados como maestro', *Ínsula*, no. 242 (1967), p. 14.

14 J. A. Muñoz Rojas, 'Las caídas de Emilio', *Ínsula*, no. 187 (1962), p. 2.

15 J. García Ascot, 'Para Emilio', *Ibid.*

16 A note taken from the Prados papers, Caja 20.2, dated 16 April 1962.

CHAPTER ONE

The Problems of the Protagonist in the Early Poetry

. . . l'enfant, amoureux de cartes et d'estampes, . . .
(Charles Baudelaire, *Les Fleurs du mal*)

—Por Dios te ruego, marinero, digasme ora esse cantar.—
Respondiole el marinero, tal respuesta le fue a dar:
—Yo no digo esta cancion sino a quien conmigo va.
(Romance del conde Arnaldos)

Un paysage quelconque est un état de l'âme, et qui lit dans tous deux est émerveillé de retrouver la similitude dans chaque détail.
(Henri-Frédéric Amiel, *Fragments d'un Journal intime*).

Introduction

The aim of this chapter is to identify the emotional problems facing the central figure in Prados's early work.[1] This is no simple task. The protagonist is elusive, concealed in a world of private symbols and allusions. A first reading suggests that if there is indeed any personal dilemma to be recognised, then here is poetry designed to cloud rather than clarify its nature and extent.

Many critics of the day, certainly, saw little more than novelty and skill in these youthful publications. Porlán y Merlo praises the good taste and sound technique *Tiempo* displays. But the newcomer is introduced as a descriptive writer whose preoccupations are with mood and landscape.[2] Salazar y Chapela leaves a similar impression in his review of *Vuelta*:

> Resumen: Un poeta andaluz, malagueño, . . . próximo a esas islas maravillosas, de colores, que fingen las luces malagueñas (¡son tantas!), sobreponiente en sus atardeceres largos, blandos, patéticos.[3]

More recent criticism has modified such judgement. Professor Blanco Aguinaga sees the intense communion of the central *persona* with the natural world as something more than mere descriptive writing. There is, he claims, a concern with the reality and mystery which lie beyond what the eye observes:

> La Naturaleza es para el poeta un espectáculo vivísimo, penetrado de misteriosa y sutil actividad sólo apreciable para quien mira intensamente todas las formas de su cuerpo.[4]

C. B. Morris makes a similar point:

> Prados did not set himself to paint nature but to ponder and absorb its mysteries, to sink into what Carlos Blanco Aguinaga has aptly called his 'pure repetitive contemplation'.[5]

There is a sense, however, in which the modern critic is at a disadvantage in attempting to assess Prados's early poetry. The dominant theme of his mature output—the natural world and his relationship to it—is not necessarily the mainspring of *Tiempo* or the *Canciones del farero*. Perhaps this is why Gerardo Diego's contemporary appraisal of *Vuelta* is so illuminating. Here was a notable exception to those who, like Porlán y Merlo and Salazar y

Chapela, saw Prados at the outset of his career simply as an accomplished word-artist. Writing in 1927 he comments:

> No sé si me equivocaré; pero creo ver en Prados una influencia, una preocupación del gusto intelectual y abstracto de la poesía en boga, realizada por otros con una admirable perfección que a él le está vedada por incompatibilidad de temperamento.

More significantly, at the heart of the book he shrewdly detects 'sentimientos de humanidad . . . seguimientos y ausencias en el vacío tras de una presa esterilizada y enigmática'.[6] He discerns that hidden beneath the fashionable tendencies of the day lies the portrayal of some definite, inner and personal situation. Without an understanding of this situation the inner logic of later books cannot be appreciated, while the clearly-defined trajectory which the work of Prados as a whole describes loses that coherence and inevitability which are two of its most distinctive features.

For the purposes of this chapter, therefore, attention will be directed not so much to the nature of the protagonist's communion with the mystery of the world around him as to the nature of the protagonist himself. Setting aside biographical considerations, its aim is to discuss not Prados but rather the 'yo' who is at the heart of the poetry. The natural world he inhabits will be of interest insofar as it sheds light on the attitudes and experience of the central *persona*. It is the opening *Tiempo* section of the 1954 anthology which provides the most convenient and accessible starting point for the observation of this central figure.[7]

The distinctive features of Tiempo

Perhaps the most striking characteristic common to the poems Prados chose to represent the poetry of the early twenties is the uniformity of their time setting. The central figure inhabits a world which seems to exist only between the hours of dusk and dawn. The four longer poems of 'El corazón diario', the first part of *Tiempo*, demonstrate the strength of his devotion to the evening, the night and the early morning. Three of them 'Víspera', 'Noche en urna' and 'Tránsito en el jardín' begin with an evocation of the dusk and end with descriptions of the dawn. The fourth, 'Fin del día, en la escuela', concentrates, as the title suggests, on the moments which precede nightfall. Its history is an interesting one. Much of 'Fin del día, . . .' appears as a separate work, 'Juego de memoria', in *Vuelta*

(I,97).[8] There is, however, another version of 'Juego de memoria' in the Prados papers.[9] Significantly, in view of the title of the poem in *Tiempo*, this unpublished version, called 'Escuela del tiempo', carries a sub-title: 'Mediodía de agosto'. Its five stanzas contain little or no reference to evening:

Sobre el pupitre, el lápiz y el cuaderno sin lunas.
El aire, suspendido, péndulo del ensueño.
El milagro, en el mapa, ahuecando sus flores.
El cristal, ocultado, hecho sangre del día.

Tiende el dedo el puntero sobre la verde esfera
y señala su fruta cuajada en mariposa.
Deshila la armonía sus delgados compases
y estudia sus lecciones de pluma la memoria.

Alumno y sol de lata, en recuerdo mecánico,
mueven su juego antiguo bajo un jardín de agua.
Hállase el viejo oficio: marinero de parques
en bergantín velero de reflejos y plantas.

Giran las frescas brújulas sus posibilidades
y percibe el deseo la flor de su manzana;
pero el reloj se quiebra de un golpe sobre el viento
y brota del presente la luz de la campana.

Se despierta el momento con un barco en la mano
y gira su mirada prendida entre veletas.
El sol, sigue clavado redondo sobre el cielo
y en él cuelga la burla su máscara deshecha.

Comparison with 'Fin del día, . . .' (18–20) shows that stanzas 2,3,4 and 5 of 'Escuela del tiempo' correspond to stanzas 5,6,7 and 8 of 'Fin del día, . . .'. In addition, the opening stanza of the anthology poem is almost identical to that of 'Escuela del tiempo'. The unpublished poem's subtitle, the first stanza's reference to day and the final stanza's to the sun align it with the day-time.

In the *Antología* version, however, all this has changed. The lines which are woven into the text place 'Escuela del tiempo' in an entirely new perspective:

Un jardín aletea bajo el verde crepúsculo,
medio deshilachado por insectos y frutas.
Herido por el pájaro huye sobre el reflejo
y, en los flecos del agua, se enreda con la espuma.

Se para, vuelve atrás y, el cansancio del día,
refrescando sus luces, se cura con el baño.

Después, salta de nuevo en busca de la noche,
deshojando de peces y faisanes sus tallos.

La varilla del mar, a un lado del crepúsculo,
sostiene amaestrados al vapor y a la estrella.
Y el jardín, imitando su postura en el viento,
sobre un rayo de sombra sus alas también pliega . . . (19)

The closing lines of 'Fin del día, . . .' seal its identification with the evening:

¡Cierra el silencio al día!
(¡Mi cuerpo es el silencio! . . .)
¡Se me quiebra en la frente la flor de todo el sueño! (20)

The reference to the 'verde crespúsculo', the description of the rapid descent from twilight to darkness, the idea of silence 'shutting out' the day all demonstrate that the time setting has been radically altered with the result that the poem conforms to the overall pattern of *Tiempo*.

Equally revealing is this poem in *Otras canciones*, the second part of *Tiempo*:

La caja del alma guarda
su fragata hipnotizada.

Tiembla el pez en su equilibrio.
Cuelga el agua del Espacio,
su manso aliento dormido.

Devana el pez al silencio.
Se queda el agua en su alma
y nace hueco el reflejo . . .

Despacio se ondula el agua.
Muda, en su sereno anhelo,
se presiente la campana . . .

La caja del alma guarda
el ancla de la campana. (25:I,133)

The poem is also to be found amongst the early manuscripts contained in Caja 2.3. The text has reached its published form in the anthology virtually unscathed. But its connotation has been fundamentally revised by the simple expedient of a change of title. In its earlier form it was called 'Mediodía'. The version in the *Antología* is headed 'Espejismos del sueño'. And the disguise is complete: unlike the poems referred to above there is no mention of the time of day or of the sun, while the type of dreaming it describes has already been encountered in poems set at evening.

To a certain extent this trend merely confirms a general tendency in Prados's early poetry. Taken as a whole, poems dealing with the dusk to dawn cycle predominate. Given the nature of its subject matter, it is hardly surprising that night-time should be a main feature of *Canciones del farero*. The titles of some of the poetry intended for *Vuelta* point to a similar concern, titles such as 'Anochecer', 'Entrada al sueño', 'Crepúsculo' and 'Obscuridad'. But had he so wished Prados might have drawn on several poems dealing with the protagonist's day-time experience. A number use the title 'Mediodía', including one which ends with the lines: '(El barco quieto en el mar. / El sol sobre el olivar.)'. Among the group from the Prados papers, *Primeros originales de Vuelta—El misterio del agua*, a poem is given the heading 'Perfil del tiempo—Mediodía', and opens with the lines:

Mar infinito,
mar solo . . .

Un pez cruza lento el agua.

. . . el sol; más sol
en la arena . . .[10]

The conversation described in 'El primer diálogo' in *Tiempo* (1925) is 'regado por el sol' (I,28).[11] With the anthology group, however, the exclusion of such references is total. Poems dealing with midday or in which the sun rather than the moon predominates are neglected. Interest has been confined to the hours of the dusk, the night and the dawn.

A second distinctive feature of the *Tiempo* group is that it deals with seascape rather than landscape. Of the twenty-two poems contained in *El corazón diario* and *Otras canciones*, twenty refer specifically to the sea. The pattern of life established in the longer poems, the background against which the passage of time is set are those of the kind of fishing community in which Prados felt particularly at home.[12] The sea is also the setting for shorter poems dealing with the intricate world it contains, where the fish, the reflection of light, of the moon and the stars enjoy their private, but significant 'juegos de la noche'. The only poems from the material Prados intended for *Vuelta* which find a place in *Antología* ('7 de octubre' (13:I,144), 'Espejismos del sueño' (25:I,133) and 'Nivel del puerto' (26:I,115)) and those whose 'narrative' is of this type.

In the ordinary way this kind of concentration would not merit special attention. Prados is not alone amongst contemporaries such as Aleixandre and the more extrovert Alberti in drawing on material based on a marine setting at the outset of his career. What makes this limitation interesting in terms of the *Antología* is that, once again, it is a self-imposed one. Though the majority of early poems refer to the sea, a significant minority do not. There is a group of poems set in the city of Málaga. They contain detailed description of the life of workshops and small factories. 'Siesta interior', for example begins with these lines:

> Todo el taller tiembla ahogado
> dentro de un vaso de agua.
> Los telares olvidados . . .
> El tapiz a medio hacer,
> el aprendiz desmayado. (I,86)

Such specifically 'land-based' poems do not figure in *Antologia*.

A third factor governs the selection of *Tiempo*. Any poem mentioning the 'tú' is ignored. Such poems are by no means infrequent in the early work. True, they are not marked by the intimacy of their tone. In *Vuelta*, for example, the object of his interest is described as an 'alto navío al viento', a strangely remote and distant goddess (I,136). It is also true that the relationship does not always prove to be a happy or successful one. In 'Negación', from *Tiempo* (1925), we read:

> El idilio de cera
> ha durado bastante.
> Pesa ya demasiado
> la tierra de la noche,
> sobre la irrealidad de nuestro instante. (I,18)

Nevertheless it remains true to say that any relationship with the 'tú', whatever its quality might have been, is considered irrelevant to the anthology selection.

Examination of 'Palma del recuerdo' (14:I,385) underlines the ruthlessness with which all these criteria are applied. In an earlier form, contained amongst *Vuelta* papers in Caja 2.2, it is called 'Perfil del momento'. But there are more significant changes in the text. The *Tiempo* version appears on the right:

Nace la flor.	¿Nace la flor? . . .
Sobre el cielo:	
aroma,	(Sobre el cielo,

color
y luz, cruzan despacio
sus pétalos.
Y la azucena mecida,
baja el pensamiento a
verla . . .
(Surge el beso) . . .
(Sobre el sueño,
cae la Eternidad
cautiva.)

aroma, color y luz,
cruzan despacio
sus pétalos . . .)
—Cuanda el cielo se
marchita,
¿se va la flor? . . .
(Sobre el sueño,
cae la Eternidad
cautiva.)

There are two main modifications in the later version. The allusion to the 'azucena mecida' is omitted, as is the line containing the reference to the kiss. Though in themselves inconclusive, such changes provide further indication of the direction followed in the shaping of the *Tiempo* selection. The removal of the honeysuckle from the early version does not alter the fact that it is still concerned with the land rather than the sea. But at the same time such a step makes the presentation of the land as a physical, tangible reality far less obvious. The use of 'flor' suggests a less specific and 'concrete' landscape. In the context of the rest of the group it is more closely connected in the reader's mind with the inner, spiritual flower, the 'flor de todo el sueño' mentioned in the closing lines of 'Fin del día, en la escuela' (18). The elimination of the line '(Surge el beso) . . .' has a different effect. It represents the exclusion of anything which might be construed as applying to the 'tú'. The kiss pre-supposes the 'tú'. But the beloved is to remain tantalisingly and mysteriously absent.

Before asking why such restrictions have been imposed, a fourth factor governing selection for *Tiempo* needs to be considered. The reader's interest is concentrated on one central figure. The original poems of this period contain a number of characters. A Dª. Gertrudis day-dreams wistfully as she gazes at the sea and the boats (I,72). In 'Encaje negro', an old lady, reminiscent of Lorca's 'monja gitana', maintains a lonely vigil of prayerful 'ensueños' (I,359). *Canciones del farero* deals with the dreams and situation of a lonely light-house keeper. None of these appear in *Tiempo*. Instead the reader is presented with a lonely protagonist: the young sailor of 'Víspera', the sailor figure of the 'viaje de sueño' described in 'Noche en urna' and the schoolboy 'marinero de parques' of 'Fin del día . . .'. Attention is drawn not to a series of random reactions to the seascape or the particular times of day which have been singled out, but rather to the unified presentation of one central figure, the youthful swimmer-sailor with whom the 'yo' of these poems is identified.

The layout of the selection further demonstrates this deliberate concentration of interest. At the very beginning of the entire *Antología* the focus of concern is not the 'misterio de la naturaleza' but the 'marinero'. In no other arrangement of these poems, for example in Caja 1.2, does 'Víspera' occupy such a cardinal position. Again the poem's history is noteworthy. It first appeared in *Litoral* in November, 1926. Here are its closing lines in that version:

> Otro barco en mi pecho su movimiento imita,
> —doble siempre mi alma en su imagen dispersa—
> sus barandas arregla para la despedida
> y su timón prepara para el alba que espera.

The preceding stanzas have described the activities of the sailor in the evening. Their identification with the 'marinero' is strong. But in the *Tiempo* selection it is strengthened by the addition of these lines:

> —¡Saldrá la luz? . . .
> —¿Silencio! . . .
> (Llora el barco sus anclas.)
> ¿Despierto el marinero, rompe el sol sus amarras! (10)

The dawn towards which the young sailor moves is even more firmly associated with the fate of the central 'yo' who comments on the action in the stanza 'Otro barco . . .'. The boat in which he sails is even more certainly a boat related in some way to the central *persona* of the poetry. The journey mentioned is more than the journey of some unidentified fisherman. The intention of the poem is to establish that the journey of the central figure or the 'yo', who in these poems assumes the form of the adolescent sailor, is beginning. And it is to be a progression which will carry him right up to *Río natural* and beyond.

There are other examples of this concentration of interest in the 'yo', the central figure. 'Tránsito en el jardín' appears prior to the *Tiempo* selection in a group entitled *Ausencias*. There it ends with these lines:

> y otra vez quedó el árbol
> en pie sobre mi espíritu

con su fruto cuajado
sin cortar en la rama. (I,143)

They are not alone in echoing the work of Antonio Machado who, at the turn of the century had written in poem XVIII '(El poeta)' from *Soledades:*

¡Qué hermosamente el pasado
fingía la primavera,
cuando del árbol de otoño
estaba el fruto colgado,
mísero fruto podrido,
que en el hueco acibarado
guarda el gusano escondido![13]

But in the later version Prados goes beyond reference to this mysterious tree, adding the following:

¿Pero el día ha nacido! . . .
(¡Adónde va mi cuerpo? . . .)
¿Pisa la luz mi orilla y huye mi sombra al sueño! (23)

They have the effect of indicating that central to the poem is its relation to the situation and condition of the protagonist. The sailor, the schoolboy—the 'yo'—is not an incidental bystander merely observing the miracle of nature. Rather, from the first, it is with this composite figure that the poems are primarily concerned.

The anthology, *Tiempo*, then, presents a central figure placed in a uniform setting both of time and place. It is not a random choice. It would seem (at least on first inspection) to have been designed to confirm and clarify a pattern in the wealth of experience covered in the early poetry. It is for that reason that it was introduced as a convenient starting-point for a discussion of the protagonist's situation. And indeed it is against this background of common features that he will be investigated. At the same time, however, attention will be drawn to work which lies outside the criteria for the 1954 selection. Hidden there are vital clues to *Tiempo*'s overall significance. For the pattern Prados has imposed on his poems, while ordered and consistent, has not necessarily secured the most obvious exposition of the problems with which the central figure was struggling. These problems are the chief business of this chapter. But before they can be studied a further point needs to be made concerning Prados's technique in these early poems.

Words and symbols in the early poetry

Having outlined the journey of the boat during the night, the 'yo' makes a very interesting observation towards the end of 'Víspera'. The boat and its destination have been portrayed in some detail:

> Las anclas justifican el molde de su ausencia,
> aún sujetas al suelo entre rosas profundas.
> La enmohecida hélice sus pétalos ordena
> y, la máquina fiel, su corazón ajusta.
>
> Las brújulas se inquietan por su largo descanso,
> su inquietud multiplica los puntos cardinales
> y, muestra al marinero, en su oráculo falso,
> el balcón y la rosa final de su viaje . . .
>
> Toda la noche cuelga como un gran mapa negro.
> El cartón de la luna gira su blanca esfera
> y, en ella busca el barco, con su largo puntero,
> el puerto más cercano y el agua más serena . . . (10)

Suddenly the perspective of this description changes:

> Otro barco en mi pecho su movimiento imita,
> —¿siempre es doble mi alma en su imagen dispersa!—:
> sus barandas arregla para la despedida
> y su timón prepara hacia el alba que espera.

In a poem of sufficient importance to open the *Antología* the reader is invited to see its content on two levels: an evocation of the harbour and the boat, certainly, but also as a reflection, a masked revelation of the position of and the course to be followed by the protagonist. The implication is that the boat and the sailor are relevant as a source of information about the central figure's experience.

This reference to 'doble' is not unique. 'Acertijo', another early poem, depicts the inside of a workshop during a hot summer siesta.[14] The scene is almost entirely static. The apprentices gaze longingly at the inaccessible 'novia del oficial'. She is described in some detail:

> La novia del oficial
> lleva prendida en el pelo
> una rosa de azafrán.
> Una rosa de azafrán,
> de azúcar y terciopelo . . .

The poem seems fairly complete in itself. But it does not end there. Instead, after a few more lines of a similar type, the poet gives a key to the action and description which have preceded:

Es el oficial el Tiempo
y es su novia la mañana,
los aprendices los vientos
y es el sol la rosa grana
que va preso en sus cabellos.

Behind the surface or the prose meaning lies a carefully plotted inner sense, which the poet in this case has chosen to reveal.

A further reference to the word 'doble' will be quoted in order to show that this way of viewing the objective reality, as a kind of figure of a subjective mood or thought, is a common feature of Prados's youthful writing. *Vuelta* contains a poem entitled 'Cambio' (I,103). Most of the poem is concerned with the 'tú' both within the dream and outside it. Discussion of the dream and the 'tú' belongs to the next chapter: what is important here is that a personal relationship is seen in terms of some aspect of the visible world that surrounds the protagonist. He comments:

Así, doble el paisaje
y doble el mar y el barco,
sobre la palma abierta de la hora
y en mi luna brillante,
fue doble en mi memoria
—voz sin fin de lo eterno—
tu imagen sobre el día
—pluma verde en mi alma—.

Much of this chapter will be spent in assessing what is the situation which lies beneath the appearance, the claustrophobic world of the fish, the moon, the boat and sea amongst which the 'yo' dwells.

If the 'yo' is to be believed when he says in 'Víspera' that his soul is always 'doble', and that the boat referred to in the main body of the poem is related to another 'boat'—one which represents some aspect of his personal experience—then it should not be surprising to find certain words assuming a code-like and esoteric significance. The analyses which follow attempt to identify certain key-words with precise units of experience. Zardoya's comment: 'Todos los elementos del paisaje se corresponden con los estados espirituales', does not miss the mark by very much—even though examination of the text will show that 'spiritual' is not always an accurate description of the protagonist's experience.[15]

In this matter of the use of a private or semi-private vocabulary, a comparison can be drawn with the poetry of Prados's friend and contemporary, Lorca.[16] It is hardly surprising that in view of the close links which for a time existed between them similarities should be noticeable. A poem from *Tiempo*, 'Tránsito', illustrates this. The lines which begin and end the poem could have been written by Lorca himself:

Los naranjales del sol
mueven sus ramas doradas.
. . . .
Los naranjales del sol
—sin fruta—mueven sus ramas. (I,20–1)

Such lines are reminiscent of the 'Canción del naranjo seco'. The setting of Prados's poem, in its use of the imagery of embroidery and religion, invites comparison with 'La monja gitana':

Cuando se asome la noche
verá la luna endulzada,
que la llevan las estrellas
al blanco mantel del alba,
bordado con seda fría,
en bastidor de campanas,
por cinco monjas novicias,
—rosas de la madrugada—
que en el convento del día
flotan como cinco barcas.[17]

The similarity of the poetic world the two poets inhabit can be further gauged by comparing a stanza from 'Víspera' with two lines of a Lorca poem, 'Dos marinos en la orilla'.[18] He writes:

Olvida siendo marino
los bares y las naranjas.

Recounting the thoughts of the young sailor in his poem, Prados adds the following detail:

Fuera del camarote: la cubierta dormida,
meciendo sus naranjas entre miedo y tristeza . . .
Por las calles del puerto, aún las luces oscilan
y, en los bares lejanos, las voces cabecean. (9:I,91)

With greater economy and discipline Lorca is using a similar group of recurrent words and symbols in his work. The fish, the boat, the sea, the moon, the bird are those which, along with more detailed vocabulary related to the sea, like anchors and compasses, one most readily associates with *Tiempo*. Other common words, such as the clock and the tower, are not infrequently mentioned in *Tiempo* or Lorca.

The recurrent use of some of these words is a reminder that this was a generation for which the psychology of Freud was opening up new horizons. In his review of *Río natural* Vicente Nuñez alludes to the influence of 'la Psicología y el Freudismo analíticos' on Prados and his contemporaries.[19] The vogue enjoyed in the twenties by such publications as translations like that of *The Interpretation of Dreams* can be estimated by the frequency of references to them in magazine and newspaper reviews of the day. José Sacristán, writing in *La Pluma* on 'La doctrina de Freud en los pueblos latinos' in 1922, prophesied that the availability of translations of Freud's work would cause excitement and uproar 'entre hombres de letras y profesionales de la psiquiatría'.[20] This prophecy was accurate. Writing in 1923 he describes the new cult as 'la discutidísima psicología freudista'.[21] And by this time, according to Blanco's biography of Prados's life from 1915 to 1918, Prados was already familiar with French translations of Freud to which Miguel, his brother, had introduced him.[22] Viewed in such a light, repeated allusions to what Freud regarded as symbols relating to the sub-conscious and especially to the sexual realm cannot be regarded as casual or coincidental. It would also be surprising if reference to works dealing with contemporary views on the meaning of certain erotic symbols did not illustrate and confirm our analysis of Prados's symbolic language.

The presence of this kind of language is openly acknowledged by Blanco Aguinaga. In his analysis of the first section of the *Antología* he refers to the 'sensualismo evidente de esta poesía '. Commenting on the imagery, he takes for granted the existence of 'simbolismo erótico'. Indeed it is so much in evidence that he hardly deems it necessary to elaborate on 'los muchas detalles obvios de este simbolismo'.[23] Having established the centrality of the 'yo' in *Tiempo*, it will be shown that such symbolism relates to his problems and feelings, rather than the 'incesante actividad amorosa' of the natural world to which critics have tended to confine their attention. Our intention is to ascertain how such symbols shed light on the protagonist's situation during the early years, by reference to *Tiempo* and to poetry outside it. It is only when the poems are seen as a diary—a view encouraged by the sub-title 'Corazón diario'—that these difficult early poems begin to make some sense.[24]

The sailor and the boat

Discussion of the choice of poems for *Tiempo* led to the conclusion that interest had been deliberately concentrated on a single main figure, the young mariner. 'Protagonist' or 'central figure' are perhaps more apt than 'hero'. The young captain of 'Víspera' does display some 'heroic' qualities: but they are extremely deceptive. He is described as an 'ágil nadador joven'. As Bachelard points out, swimming is, in literature, the heroic activity par excellence. Comparing the esteem enjoyed by the hero who can fly and the hero who can swim he writes:

> Dans l'eau, la victoire est plus rare, plus dangereuse, plus méritoire que dans le vent. Le nageur conquiert un élément plus étranger à sa nature. le jeune nageur est un héros précoce.[25]

Guillén's poem 'Arranques. Por el agua' affords a further example of such an association of the god-like child hero and the sea.[26] But when the young man's swimming is examined more closely, thoughts of heroism are totally out of place. He is far removed from the sea-captain of Alberti's *Marinero en tierra*, the daring 'homme libre'. Here is the second stanza of 'Víspera':

> Enhebrada se queda la aguja del viaje
> junto a la carta azul, el compás y la lente;
> mientras el capitán, entre dos blancos mares,
> ágil nadador joven, limpia espuma desteje. (9:I,91)

All activity is restricted to the protagonist's day-dreaming as he sits amongst the charts and other navigational aids. He is travelling not across the real blue sea, but 'blancos mares' of his own imagining.

This preference for dream rather than the reality of the voyage, his indolence and passivity, account in part for the considerable note of anguish running through *Tiempo* and the early poetry in general, and it will be examined in this section of the chapter. To define more accurately the nature of the 'yo', it is helpful to look at descriptions of the boat from which he is inseparable.

An inspection of the poetry suggests that the boat is in some way linked with the central figure's emotional condition. It is with the heart, rather than with any intellectual or metaphysical consideration that it is associated. In 'Inscripción en la arena' (13:I,383) we read:

> Duerme el cielo, duerme el mar
> y, en medio, mi corazón:
> barco de mi soledad . . .

A poem from Caja 2.2 provides a second example. It includes these lines:

> (Barco sobre el horizonte,
> un corazón que se esconde). (I,356)

And in 'Palma del ensueño' is seen the closest possible association of boat and heart:

> Duerme la calma en el puerto
> bajo su colcha de laca,
> mientras la luna en el cielo
> clava sus anclas doradas.
>
> ¿Corazón,
> rema! (21:I,17)

But there is a more specific link between the 'yo' and the boat. Predictably it is the original material rather than the *Antología* that establishes it. The boat is related to the cause of fluctuation and anguish in the protagonist's emotions: the body.

Several poems suggest a relationship between the activity of this boat and the sexual response of the protagonist's body.[27] The early poem, 'Alta mar', makes little sense unless it is viewed in this light:

> El pez,
> el barco
> y el pájaro.
>
> El horizonte, redondo,
> bien cerrado.
>
> Pájaro—veleta al viento.
> Y pez—veleta en el agua—.
>
> El barco, llora sus anclas.
>
> El pez,
> el barco
> y el pájaro. (I,32)

On several occasions Freud refers to the erotic symbolism of the fish. Cirlot comments: 'According to Loeffler, the bird, like the fish, was originally a phallic symbol, . . .'[28] The inclusion of the boat within the list which opens and closes the poem suggests that it belongs to a similar realm—even though, as will be shown, the nature of its activity is very different from that of the fish and the bird. There is a parallel here with Lorca, again. In 'Romance sonámbulo', he uses the boat, with the horse, as sexual symbols:

Verde que te quiero verde.
Verde viento. Verdes ramas.
El barco sobre la mar
y el caballo en la montaña.[29]

A further poem from Caja 2.2 shows that comparison is intended between the fish and the boat:

El pez
cruza con una flor de tabaco
sobre el agua.
El marinero reposa.
(Vapor dormido en el puerto,
ancla y corazón despiertos.) (I,355)[30]

In both 'Alta mar' and the poem quoted above, however, the juxtaposition of the boat and other erotic symbols is an uncomfortable one. 'Alta mar' shows the bird and the fish engaged in energetic movement. They are like weathercocks as the wind blows on them. The presence of the wind has always been a token of fertility and sexual desire. It is the wind that pursues Preciosa in Lorca's 'Preciosa y el aire'. In 'Veleta' the wind is pictured specifically in terms of seed-bearing, bringing with it the promise of requited love in the flower of the orange tree:

Viento del Sur,
moreno, ardiente,
llegas sobre mi carne,
trayéndome semilla
de brillantes
miradas, empapado
de azahares.[31]

But the sailor's boat differs markedly from such windblown creatures. 'El barco, llora sus anclas'. It suffers from an agonising inability to move. In the poem quoted above where the fish moves 'con una flor de tabaco / sobre el agua', the plight of the boat is very different: '(Vapor dormido en el puerto, / ancla y corazón despiertos)'. Between these two lies the sailor. He is resting. His awareness of the fish awakens the heart—suggests the possibility of sexual activity—but the 'anchor', the inability of the body to respond to such an awareness, removes the possibility.

In 'Víspera', too, the boat is described as being asleep:

> Fuera del camarote: la cubierta dormida,
> meciendo sus naranjas entre miedo y tristeza . . . (9:I,91)

The cargo of the boat is made up of oranges. The 'business' of the body is partly to respond to desire. But our sailor's boat feels such a cargo to be an onerous responsibility. The knowledge that his body is unable to respond in a normal way (represented by the fish and the bird in other poems) fills him with fear and sadness. In short, his body is a burden to him. The day-dream, an intellectual realisation that desire and fulfilment in the realm of the body do exist are present: the reality in his experience is not.

The impossible voyage

'Víspera' ends with these lines:

> —¿Saldrá la luz? . . .
> —¡Silencio! . . .
> (Llora el barco sus anclas.)
> ¡Despierto el marinero, rompe el sol sus amarras! (10)

It is evident, therefore, that under certain conditions the boat does enjoy some kind of movement. Sometimes, as in the above example, it affords the central figure a certain amount of satisfaction. Such occasions will be discussed later. More often the voyage undertaken is a deceptive and fruitless one, a 'viaje de ensueño'.

From the first the boat's instruments in 'Víspera ' were associated with deception. The maps and compasses surrounding the sailor lure him towards impossible and unreal paths:

> Sobre su frente un atlas abre su mariposa
> y en el papel el barco juega a flores distantes,
> trazando itinerarios sobre las planas olas
> que, el pincel del ensueño, tiñe con falso esmalte.

In a state of semi-consciousness he is tricked into believing that the boat is moving, or at least capable of movement. But the journey is confined to the map, the illusory product of a day-dream.

That the promise which stems from this kind of day-dreaming remains unfulfilled is obvious later in the poem. The outcome of the voyage is described:

> Las brújulas se inquietan por su largo descanso,
> su inquietud multiplica los puntos cardinales
> y, muestra al marinero, en su oráculo falso,
> el balcón y la rosa final de su viaje . . .
>
> Toda la noche cuelga como un gran mapa negro.
> el cartón de la luna gira su blanca esfera
> y, en ella busca el barco, con su largo puntero,
> el puerto más cercano y el agua más serena . . . (10)

The ship's instruments are shown in their true colours: they are an 'oráculo falso'. They tempt him with the prospect of 'el balcón y la rosa final de su viaje'. As night falls there is a promise of fulfilment of the desire to experience desire. But the boat's journey ends not in the light of dawn, but in the light of the moon.

That the moon, and a cardboard moon at that, is the natural home of the boat or the body of the protagonist is of great significance. As far as the boat is concerned, 'el puerto más cercano y el agua más serena' is the moon. Díaz-Plaja had been quick to notice how important the symbol of the moon was in the new poetry.[32] It represented death and sterility. Its relevance to the question of the frustration of sexual emotions is clear in this Lorca poem:

> Nadie come naranjas
> bajo la luna llena.
> Es preciso comer,
> fruta verde y helada.[33]

Its presence is disturbing, unwelcome.

That the moon is being used as an expression of the protagonist's condition is illustrated in another 'false journey'. In 'Noche en urna' he is described in these terms:

> Cuerpo en pena del alma, una sombra en el muelle,
> razonando sigilos, repasa las penumbras:
> hurta sus mercancías al sueño, se detiene,
> se ausenta y, vuelta al pensamiento, en él se oculta. (15:I,366)

The expression 'cuerpo en pena'—an inversion of the more common 'alma en pena'—emphasises the central figure's dissatisfaction with the body to which he is confined. The stanza as a whole again evokes that unsettled, fitful state in which he is half-conscious, half-asleep. It is a reminder that it is only in the area of 'pensamiento' that any movement takes place—and it is in this area, therefore, that the central figure takes refuge: '. . . en él se oculta.' The illusory journey begins:

> Ahueca sus caudales y, en cáscara de barco,
> se le va el corazón por mapa de recuerdos

But again he is dealing with the 'map' rather than the reality, with 'recuerdos' rather than present, personal experience.

In the course of these wanderings, however, there seems to be a moment of satisfaction. The boat appears finally to have come to rest. The 'sombra en el muelle' is even decribed as 'fecundada'. Some direction has been found:

> La sombra, fecundada, el rumbo de la huída
> ve por fin y, ocultándose, al puerto oculta en ella.

There is a temporary forgetting of the 'puerto'—the moon of 'Víspera'. But it is to be only temporary. When the 'yo' emerges from this 'ensueño' the same frightening reality confronts him as he observes the night-sky:

> Al espejo los juegos y el milagro preguntan
> la polar de algún nombre que oriente sus verdades . . .
> Miro yo y en él veo, dibujado en la luna
> —corazón de su mundo—, mi cuerpo sin imagen.[34]

No matter where the voyage leads, he is reminded on waking of the affinity between his body and the moon.

It is because of this that in early poems the movement of the boat is most typically aimless and ineffectual, wandering in search of a 'port' where he can find rest and acceptance. The 'yo' seeks a satisfactory relationship with the 'tú'. The disappointment and shame which accompany the failure of this attempt is well illustrated in a poem appearing in the *País* section of Prados's papers. The symbol of the fish plays an important part in the little drama that follows:

> Mi barco entraba en el puerto . . .
>
> (Todos los peces saltaban
> solo por ver cómo entraba.)
>
> Mi barco se sofocaba . . .

(Los peces lo abanicaban.)

Mi barco se derretía . . .

(Los peces se sonreían.)

Cuando mi barco se fue
no lo siguió ningún pez. (I,61)

The boat does not feel at ease in the port, just as the 'yo' is unable to make successful physical contact with the 'tú'. It 'suffocates' and 'melts away'. The fish, reminders of the possibility of sexual fulfilment open to the normal individual, smile at one another in amusement at the boat's predicament. The boat suffers the indignity of leaving the port alone. The relevance of this poem to the protagonist's difficulties is clear. Indeed, so clear is it that it would be surprising to find such a poem in the *Antología*.

The acuteness with which the 'yo' experiences his dilemma is emphasised by antithesis between the voyage he feels he should be undertaking and the kind of progress he does in fact make. There is a mental assent to what he should be as a lover, an ability perhaps to play the part, but inability in his body to respond in the 'normal' way.

A further poem in the *País* group exemplifies this. It opens with a description of another restless journey:

El vapor va por el mar
sin saber adónde va. (I,66)

The boat (metonymic for the sailor steering it) is 'herido de mal de amor / en medio del corazón'. Why then, has it not found its port? Why has the sailor been unable to maintain a happy relationship with the 'tú'? The answer lies in the details which follow. When he left the beloved all he was able to leave with her was an orange, a parasol and a love-letter. But something was missing:

Pero en cambio no dejó
lo que el agua se llevó:

paloma, brazo y bandera,
brújula de flor y de canela.

Y sobre el dril de la manga,
bordado un recuerdo en ancla . . .

Por eso va por el mar
sin saber adónde va.

The references to the anchor, which has already been identified as a symbol of the impotence of the protagonist's body, gives the clue to what was missing. He gave her all the symbols, the tokens of love: the orange, a traditional symbol, the parasol, a Freudian one.[35] But he was unable to give her 'lo que el agua se llevó', in terms of the poem, the boat, or in terms of the private language of these poems, his body.

The net result of this condition is a distasteful indolence and frustration. In his analysis of Prados's poetry Debicki points to the use of 'sintagmas no progresivos' as being a typical aspect of his technique.[36] The poetry seems to stagnate because of extensive repetition of parallel syntactical structures. Debicki takes this as an indication of the poet's involvement with the natural world. But such repetition has other effects. It reflects the stagnation and sterility which the problem of the body produces. The whole point of some of such early poems is that precisely nothing happens in them.

This is specially noticeable in poems dealing with 'juegos de la noche' (the title of the opening poem of *Otras canciones*). They portray the intricate patterns woven by the fish, the stars, the moon and the land's reflection on the water. 'Nocturno fiel' is a good example of activity which leads in the end nowhere—except to a kind of death which will be identified later. These are the closing stanzas:

Luna en el cielo.
Luna en el suelo.

Canta el olivar dormido
en los brazos del silencio . . .

Luna en el suelo.
Luna en el cielo.

Cierra la muerte sus alas
sobre la espalda del viento.

Luna en el cielo.
Luna en el suelo. (12:I,373)

'Fiel errante' re-works the symbols of the fish, the sun, the sand and the water (I,368). Reproduced here is a variant from Caja 2.3, where it is called 'Perfil del tiempo':

Mar infinito,
mar solo . . .

Un pez cruza lento el agua . . .

. . . el sol, más sol
en la arena.

Mi corazón se levanta
y cruza solo mi pena.

. . . Y el sol,
más sol en la arena.

Once more the realm of the 'corazón' asserts itself. The sun and the fish remind the central figure of the level of the body. The heart is aroused, but such awakening can give rise only to pain. The poem ends with the nagging reminder with which it began: the sun shines, but only on the arid sterility of the sand.

The light-house keeper

This examination of the protagonist of the early years would be incomplete without reference to the central *persona* of *Canciones del farero*.[37] None of its poems appear in the *Tiempo* selection—possibly because the standpoint of the keeper differs in perspective from the figure whom Prados singled out for attention there. However, in method and in its underlying tensions it is similar to, though more obvious than, the poetry of *Tiempo*.

Its central theme has been hinted at in analysis of the poem 'El vapor va por el mar'. The book shows how the central figure's predicament results in feelings of unreality, artificiality and isolation. 'La rosa verde del mar,' leaves this impression very clearly (I,50). It describes two different worlds: that of the 'farero' inside the light-house and that of the sea outside it. Without, the boats and the fish carry on their day-to-day activities:

Por fuera de mi ventana,
sobre el mar, corren los barcos.
De día con su bandera,
y de noche con su luz.

Here is the normal pattern of life, fertile and healthy. The symbolism of the boat and the fish indicates the area of life to which the poem refers. But inside the light-house, i.e. within the limits of the central *persona*'s experience, the picture is very different:

(El gato ronda la jaula
y el pez vuela por el agua)

Both the bird and the fish (the two erotic symbols noted in 'Alta mar') are present. But they are present in totally artificial situations. The bird (to judge from the activities of the cat) is enclosed in the cage: the fish is confined to an aquarium.

The boat also appears in the keeper's quarters. But it is not the vigorous boat sailing on the open sea. It is a miniature, model boat which serves only to mimic the reality and remind him cruelly of the inadequacies of his own experience:

Durante las noches largas,
hago fragatas de vela,
con navaja
y con quinqué . . .

Even the light has a touch of the unreal, the artificial about it:

(Devana el faro la noche,
girando como un fantoche.)

The strange figure of the light-house keeper, then, helps in an understanding of the isolation of which the 'yo' of *Tiempo* complains for example in 'Inscripción en la arena' (13) and 'Espejismos' (20), poems which will be dealt with later. It is not that he does not wish to make contact with the 'other'. But just as the very nature and function of the light-house is to repel rather than attract, so it seems the lot of the protagonist to repel the reality, normal sexual emotions and reactions, that he feels at this stage he would like to attract. Nor is there any of the gentle resignation to solitude of Cernuda's 'Soliloquio del farero'.[38] Rather there is a restlessness, even despair, as the 'poet' (as he is called in the last poem of this little book) considers the dark reality facing him:

. . . el poeta cansado,
la pluma al mar ha tirado,
siempre mirando la luna,
su rueda de la fortuna.

Navegando a sotavento,
se marcha el barco del puerto. (I,55)

Time and the 'marinero'

The reader of *Tiempo* will be quick to point out that the whole story has not been told. There are occasions when the boat does move.

There are poems which communicate a sense of harmony and peace. The illusory 'viaje de sueño' is not the only escape from the inability to respond physically to the 'tú'. To understand why this should be closer attention must be paid to the relationship between time and the protagonist.

It has already been established that, as part of a deliberate attempt to concentrate attention on the protagonist in a set of carefully defined circumstances, only poems dealing with dusk, the night and dawn found their way into the *Antología*. A close reading of *Tiempo* suggests that the pattern of the central figure's emotional state is to some extent governed by the time of day—and that it is possible to ascribe with some accuracy certain attitudes and feelings to particular moments in the day-night cycle. Each of its phases seems to exert its own influence on him—or, using the language of *Tiempo*, on the mobility or immobility of the boat.

Inspection of *Tiempo* suggests that Prados has moulded his selection so that correspondences between times of day and the protagonist's emotional state should emerge clearly. 'Fin del día, en la escuela' is proof of this. The poem has already been examined from the point of view of the limitations Prados imposed upon himself in compiling *Tiempo*. It was observed that an early poem on which much of its content was based had been heavily disguised by the disappearance of its sub-title, 'Mediodía de agosto' and by placing it in the context of stanzas dealing with the evening. These stanzas, which were quoted as they appear in 'Fin del día, . . .' belong in fact to another poem, 'Juego de memoria' which is now quoted in its original form:

> El jardín aletea tras el verde crepúsculo,
> medio deshilachado por insectos y frutas.
> Herido por el pájaro, huye sobre el reflejo
> y en los flecos del agua se le enredan sus lunas.
>
> Se para. Vuelve atrás, y el cansancio del día,
> refrescando sus luces, cúrase con el baño;
> luego, salta de nuevo en busca de la noche,
> deshojando de peces y faisanes sus tallos.
>
> La varilla del mar, a un lado del crepúsculo,
> sostiene, amaestrados, al vapor y la estrella,
> y el jardín, imitando su postura, en el viento,
> sobre un rayo de sombras, sus alas al fin pliega.
>
> La noche se aproxima, descalza, de puntillas,

y ve al jardín dormido como un niño cansado,
y bajo su almohada le deja como premio,
una estrella sin puntas y un ruiseñor cantando.[39]

In earlier comments 'Fin del día. . . .', an amalgam of 'Escuela del tiempo, Mediodía de agosto' and 'Juego de memoria', was used to show the exclusiveness of Prados's concern in *Tiempo* with the dusk to dawn cycle. However, his adaptation of the two original poems can be viewed from another standpoint: the way in which its form underlines a connection between the time of day and its effect on the 'yo'. This is achieved by two main alterations. Firstly the fourth stanza of 'juego de memoria' is removed altogether. It is, significantly, an account of the way in which the approach of the evening affects the garden. As a result, it is uniquely with the impact of night-fall on the central figure that the *Tiempo* poem is concerned. The second alteration is the introduction of lines which were not to be found in either of the earlier sources. They are placed at the climax of the finished poem, at the point where time seems to have stood still. Furthermore, this climax has the effect of relating all the description which has preceded it to the central figure—and, to be precise, to his body:

Se despierta el momento con un barco en la mano
y gira su mirada prendida entre veletas:
el sol sigue clavado redondo sobre el cielo
y, en él, cuelga una burla su máscara deshecha . . .

¡Cierra el silencio al día!
(¡Mi cuerpo es el silencio! . . .)
¡Se me quiebra en la frente la flor de todo el sueño! (19–20)

Such changes transform what was previously 'descriptive' writing. The re-structuring of the material implies that there is some link between specific times of day, movements of the sun and moon, and fluctuations in the central figure's experience. The evening, the night, the dawn and the day will now be observed in relation to his varying response to them.

The evening

The evening stands as the point of entry into the world of *Tiempo*. It bears little similarity to the evening, 'querida en su entereza', which Guillén celebrates in his 'Santo suelo'.[40] Its most distinctive (but by no means unique) feature is referred to in 'Espejismos' (20:I,386) as 'equilibrio'. Such moments, when the movement of time seems to have been suspended, enable the central figure to enjoy an unusual sense of peace and harmony. In some examples of this state of 'equilibrium' the central point is associated with a tree. Thus the opening stanza of the evening poem 'Tránsito en el jardín' begins: 'Junto al árbol, la luz se pliega en mansas ondas,' (22:I,142). 'Crepúsculo' provides the evening with a similar setting:

La balanza de la sombra
pesa a la luna.

La tarde sujeta al árbol,
fiel de la noche y la espuma . . . (17:I,110)

But though the tree indicates that equilibrium has been attained, that the opposing forces of darkness and light are momentarily at peace, it is the moon's reaction to this state of affairs which shows why evening can afford the central figure some respite. During equilibrium, the oppressive awareness of the moon, described earlier in the chapter, is removed. This is why the personalised moon of 'Crepúsculo' so resents the setting up of the 'balanza de la sombra'. It means that for a short time, at least, it ceases to be a reminder of the death and sterility of his body.

'Vega en calma' confirms this view. Balance here is suggested by the use of antithesis; the sky and the earth, the thrush and the toad, the red and the grey:

Cielo gris.
Suelo rojo . . .

De un olivo a otro
vuela el tordo.

(En la tarde hay un sapo
de ceniza y de oro.)

Suelo gris.
Cielo rojo . . .

Quedó la luna enredada
en el olivar.

¡Quedó la luna olvidada! (11:I,30)

Once the state of balance has been attained, the moon is captured and forgotten. The use of 'olvidada' is significant: it implies what must be taken as a basic principle of interpretation in *Tiempo*, the presence of a human observer for whom the scene has some specific relevance. It implies, too, that only when the moon is forgotten can the protagonist enjoy the repose referred to in the poem's title.

It is in the context of this peace that the central figure is able to achieve the contemplation to which critics have drawn attention. The 'yo' is released from the barrier erected by his consciousness of the body's failure. He can have dealings with the infinite. The 'esponja' and the 'estrella' are reconciled:

> Las pisadas descalzas del reloj, en la torre,
> laten acompasando a la esponja y la estrella. (14:I,365)

For a moment, then, the 'cerrado equilibrio' which Guillén extols, the 'resplandor de una tarde perpetua', is the happy lot of the central figure.

'Perfil del tiempo' explains the 'mechanics' of this transformation, albeit short-lived, in the central figure's attitude towards his body. It begins with a description of the evening:

> La tarde y el abanico
> junto al pretil de la ausencia
> al borde de la armonía;
> sobre el brocal de la sombra
> peinan la pluma del día . . . (20:I,117)

The expressions: 'junto al pretil de', 'sobre el brocal de', 'al borde de' suggest the knife-edge, which is neither day or night, of 'equilibrio'. The picture is one of gentleness and repose: the evening and the fan 'peinan la pluma del día . . .'. Two lines in parenthesis, set apart from those quoted above, complete the poem:

> (Resbala el barco en el alma
> y el pensamiento en el agua . . .)

Once again, in the presence of the moon the activity of the boat is severely hampered. Its connotation as a symbol of his body is entirely negative. Its ability to enable the 'yo' to be united with the 'tú' physically is extremely limited. At the instant of 'balanza' all this changes. The body's physical deficiencies are forgotten—it is no longer what might be termed a 'barco negativo'. Its failure in one sphere of activity does not preclude the possibility of success in another. Viewed as a vehicle for transporting the 'yo' to the spiritual realm, his body is fully capable of making considerable headway. Within these confines, indeed, it could conveniently be referred to as 'positive', as being a 'barco positivo'. It is in these terms that the activity of the boat in the final couplet of 'Perfil del tiempo' is to be understood. The awareness of balance and the absence of the moon mean that spiritual activity can begin to take place: the 'boat' glides almost imperceptibly from the 'negative' role it plays in connection with physical activity to its 'positive' role in the realm of the soul.[41]

However, it is important to bear in mind that the kind of experience so far associated with the evening is never guaranteed. Its approach will always be viewed warily, partly because it contains the threat of the night and partly because the 'yo' is not certain whether it will produce the kind of balance described above or a sense of frustration stemming from the non-attainment of that higher level. Will he experience his body as the 'barco positivo' or the 'barco negativo'?

It is for this reason that 'Espejismos', the poem following 'Perfil del tiempo', begins with a question:

> ¿Barco en el mar o en el alma? (20:I,386)

Which level of reality is he going to experience? Is it the equilibrium which has been such a feature of the evening? Or is he to pass straight through to the night, the moon, the frustration of the 'barco negativo'? The bracketed questions which follow express the same dilemma:

> ¿Puerto del tiempo o del sueño? . . .
> . . . .
>
> ¿Soledad o soledad? . . .

Is he making for the 'puerto del tiempo', the home of his finite and unsatisfactory body, the 'barco negativo', or the 'puerto . . . del sueño', the natural habitat of his spiritual faculties, the 'barco positivo'? Is the 'soledad' he is about to experience that undesirable sense of isolation traced in *canciones del farero*? Or is it to be that delightful solitude enjoyed by the mystics?

The answer is a shattering one:

> (Repite el eco en la noche:
> "¡Soledad y soledad!" . . .)

It is the night which speaks. Nor is it the dark night of the soul: it is that time referred to earlier where the reality of what his body is—or is not—so oppresses the protagonist. The 'soledad' of the 'yo' can only be a double loneliness. He will be cut off from the 'tú' because of the impotence of his body. And he will be cut off from any other plane of activity in the spiritual realm because of the deadening consciousness of the presence of 'los límites de mi cuerpo'.

This use of questions is important in establishing the character of the central figure identified in *Tiempo*. In the anthology's opening section poems such as 'Palma del recuerdo', 'Espejismos', 'La hora mágica' and 'Tránsito en el jardín' all use questions as an inevitable stylistic reflection of his hesitancy and self-doubt. The skilful construction of 'Espejismos', with its parallel series of interrogatives, is brought to a dramatic climax by a contrasting moment of assertion. Its dramatic effect lies in the fact that its affirmation ("¡Soledad y soledad!" . . .) is totally negative. Debicki has already referred to Prados's predilection for this kind of interrogatory parallelism, and rightly concludes that: 'Las preguntas particulares vienen a ser ejemplos de una indagación fundamental'.[42] Such characteristics of Prados's style and tone will be taken up in later chapters.

The equilibrium of evening, then, and the peaceful 'alma' experience it brings with it, are intensely vulnerable. This is why the opening lines of 'Tránsito en el jardín', an attractive description of the evening, are marked by such fragility and delicacy of image:

> Toda la tarde es lirio de porcelana blanca;
> cálida y desvaída piel de lucero en cierne;
> voz de una despedida sin mano y sin campana,
> abanico caído sobre el agua luciente . . . (22:I,142)

Only too soon will the 'lirio de porcelana blanca' be destroyed by the 'puente y palma del mundo, hueca esfera del miedo, / la noche—negra pluma del pájaro del aire—,' to which the poem refers later on. It is the same pattern found in the closing lines of 'Crepúsculo'. The first four lines establish the equilibrium of the evening, the 'balanza de la sombra'. But the closing lines are a despairing cry that this moment should not evaporate:

> ¡Aguarda luz, no resbales,
> que se va a manchar tu río
> con las riberas del aire! (17:I,110)

The sun cannot, however, remain in perpetual suspension on the horizon. The protagonist is left alone to face the night.

The night

What has already characterised the night leads to a mistrust of Blanco's reference to the 'sombra amorosa de la noche'. It has been the setting for the illusory 'viaje de sueño', a journey which reminds the central figure of the sterility of his body. In consequence it evokes fear in him. 'Tránsito' refers to it as the 'hueca esfera del miedo'. In 'Noche en urna' the sounds or the absence of sound accompanying nightfall are described as the 'voz muda del miedo'. But there is another sinister aspect to the characterisation of the night, one which further explains its association in the protagonist's mind with impotence and sterility: the death of the wind.

The significance of the wind's absence can be judged from the early group of poems *Romances sin viento*.[13] Their key word is 'inútil'. They portray indolence and inertia, typified by the main figure's surroundings in the first of the group:

> Y mientras la inútil brújula
> del silencio lenta gira,
> por la sombra del desván
> los murciélagos patinan. (I,358)

The significance of the 'sin viento' of the general title becomes clearer in the equally gloomy second poem. Images and vocabulary overflow with references to sterility, barrenness and infertility:

> Se mudó de piel la luna
> imitando a la culebra
> y al códice de la noche
> envolvió con su luz seca.
>
> La momia de una campana
> sangre amarilla gotea,
> que en el viejo monasterio
> donde fue el pincel abeja,
> miniando sobre su alma
> se apaga un monje en su celda.
>
> El códice de la noche
> sus tapas doradas cierra. (I,358)

In the figure of the monk in his cell, totally cut off from the norm of sexuality, there is more than a faint reflection of the protagonist of *Canciones del farero* and *Tiempo*—though, predictably, the problem is less ambivalent in this discarded poem. The light itself is 'dry'; the bell is compared to a mummy; its blood is rust-yellow rather than vibrant with life.

The ambience of the third poem is one of decay, barrenness. The central figure is an old woman, engaged in dreams of less empty days:

Junto a una virgen de cera
—yema de un huevo de vidrio—
tiembla la almendra dorada
de una lámpara sin brillo.

Como una estrella de trapo
está el silencio caído
sobre almohada de miedo,
bordado en seda de olvido.
Y la sombra, como un gato
bajo la luz escondido,
en las paredes del aire
cuelga sus blandos maullidos.

Destilada del recuerdo
—blanco jazmín ya marchito—
teje una anciana su rezo
siendo de ensueños su ovillo.
Y en su pensamiento lento
se queda enredado el hilo,
empañando las imágenes
de sus espejos perdidos.

Tiembla la luz misteriosa . . . (I,359)

Once more the central figure is, like the monk of the second 'romance', cut off from normal life. She is dealing with 'espejos perdidos'. In each poem the common factor is the absence of fertility and the presence of barriers to any sexual relationship. They are, to use the group's title, 'sin viento'. This connotation is useful in interpreting the role of the wind in the night of *Tiempo*.

In the early poetry, the wind is most typically presented at night-time not as absent but rather as dying or as being killed. The wind's death in 'Noche en urna' preludes the journey which ultimately leaves the central figure contemplating the moon and the sterility of his own body:

Cuatro esbeltos luceros se llevan muerto al viento,
tendido sobre el eco como un pálido junco
y, el agua, busca ausencias para sus finos duelos,

tapada en los reflejos transparentes del luto. (15:I,365)

The presence of the moon is also prominent in 'Nocturno fiel', another poem which describes the death of the wind:

Luna en el suelo.
Luna en el cielo.

Cierra la muerte sus alas
sobre la espalda del viento.

Luna en el cielo,
Luna en el suelo. (12:I,373)

The doleful refrain 'Luna en el cielo. / Luna en el suelo.' points the irony of the title. The pleasant equilibrium of the evening has been lost: the 'fiel' of the night is a sinister one, for now the balance is between death, sterility on all sides, in the sky and on the ground. In other words, there is no relief from oppressive reminders of impotence and absence of sexual experience during the night. Little wonder, then, that the wind, traditionally the symbol of fertility and desire, should be suffocated beneath the wings of death.

However, there is an occasion when the 'yo' refers to a night into which he would not mind entering. It is a night without a moon—a night without reminders of his ineffectuality in the realm of the body. Into such a 'noche serena' he would go:

Quiero entrar en tu huerto,
noche,
adormece a tus guardas,
apaga la linterna de la luna,
encierra tus arañas
y dile al búho que me guíe
por tu espesa enramada. (I,12)

But it is only in later poetry, when some kind of answer to the problems of the body has been discovered, that such a night can be enjoyed.

The dawn

From this despair springs the hope of the dawn. The death of the night makes way for the life of the day. Reverting to the picture of the sailor and the ship, it heralds a less bitter voyage than the 'viaje de sueño' of the night. The rising of the sun is seen in terms of release, liberation. Thus 'Víspera' ends: '(Llora el barco sus anclas.) / ¡Despierto el marinero, rompe el sol sus amarras!' Bachelard's comment on death and the voyage is not without relevance here: '. . . la mort ne serait pas le dernier voyage. Elle serait le premier voyage.'[44] In a sense the experience of death in the night paves the way for the experience of the dawn.

A salient feature of the dawn is that it signifies the moon's death, the removal of the threat implicit in its presence. This is the dramatic significance of the events described in '7 de octubre':

El frío en la madrugada
pulió la piedra del agua . . .

Se quebró el barco en el cielo.
Ancló en el agua el lucero.

Rodando desde su altura,
cayó en la orilla la luna . . . (13:I,144)

Concurrent with the coming of the morning-star is the disappearance of the boat and the moon. The disturbing 'barco de mi soledad', the 'barco negativo' of the preceding poem in the selection, disintegrates. The demise of the moon parallels this development: the upsetting awareness of his body's deficiencies (the boat) and its outward symbol (the moon) diminishes with the arrival of the dawn.

Thus the dawn comes as a clearly defined moment of release from the paralysing grip of the night. Hence the exultant tone of the last lines of 'Tránsito en el jardín':

¡Pero el día ha nacido! . . .
(¿Adónde va mi cuerpo? . . .)
¡Pisa la luz mi orilla y huye mi sombra al sueño! (23)

Such moments become the ardent expectation of the protagonist. In the selection's first poem, writing of the 'otro barco en mi pecho' he observes: '. . . sus barandas arregla para la despedida / y su timón prepara hacia el alba que espera' (10:I,92).

One characteristic of the dawn in *Tiempo* is that it promotes the vigour and energy of youth. The day arrives, in 'Tránsito . . .', 'como nadador joven que arribara a la playa . . .'. Cernuda's 'joven marino', like Prados's 'marinero', belongs to the dawn:

No a estas horas,
No a estas horas de tregua cobarde,
Al amanecer es cuando debías ir hacia el mar, joven marino,
Desnudo como una flor;[45]

But this vigour does not seem to be translated into the channels traditionally associated, for example in the lyric 'Al alba venid, buen amigo', with this time of day.[45a] Certainly for the central figure of *Tiempo* the dawn does not signify a rendezvous with love. Indeed the content of his experience is extremely vague. Prados is fairly specific about events leading up to this 'sueño'. The last four stanzas of 'Noche en urna' describe the removal of the night from the sky, the entry of the 'mansa flor del tiempo' into the protagonist's soul and the approach of light. But at the point when 'toda la luz del sueño' steals upon his consciousness the poem ends:

Huye el tiempo y, el agua, vuela por detenerlo.
¿Entra bajo mi alma toda la luz del sueño! (16)

The experience seems to belong well outside the normal realm of mental activity. It is beyond expression. Or it is possibly, despite the anticipation surrounding it, insubstantial. Comparison with the dream described in Guillén's 'Alborada' makes this point. The experience, as intense and vivid as that of *Tiempo*, can also be related to the waking world:

Siento el mundo bajo el día,
Que me embarga
Los párpados. Bien me esconden
Las pestañas.

Ese piar renaciente
De las ramas
Da a mi sueño su envoltura
Buena, blanda . . .[46]

It is in no sense a dream of escape.

The dawn dream of *Tiempo* is dominated by this escapism: it is that which the central figure can enjoy only when an unwelcome reality has been temporarily put on one side. The final lines of 'Tránsito en el jardín' support this view. The dawn re-appears, and equilibrium is established, just as it was at evening. And the sense of balance attained is expressed, as it was in poetry dealing with the evening, by reference to a tree:

Y otra vez vuelve el día terso y bien enquillado,
como nadador joven que arribara a la playa . . .
Y otra vez queda el árbol en pie sobre mi espíritu
con la fruta madura sin cortar en su rama.

He has been removed to the level of the 'alma', and it is only in the resulting departure of the body from the scene that this nebulous dream can be enjoyed:

¡Pero el día ha nacido! . . .
(¿Adónde va mi cuerpo? . . .)
¡Pisa la luz mi orilla y huye mi sombra al sueño! (23)

Little more information about the dawn is divulged. It is a time of equilibrium and a time of escapism. But the remainder of the day is as irksome as the night.

The day

It is perhaps because little happens during it that so little reference is made to the day. The presentation of this area of time underlines the fragmentary nature of the protagonist's experience. For Guillén the midday was the apogee of a finely wrought, unified edifice. He wrote in 'Perfección':

Queda curvo el firmamento,
Compacto azul, sobre el día.
Es el redondeamiento
Del esplendor: mediodía.
Todo es cúpula . . .[47]

Compared with this, the activity or rather the inactivity of the boats and fish of Prados's verse seems not a little anaemic. In one poem from Caja 2.2. entitled 'Mediodía' the words 'perezoso' and 'soñoliento' are used. Its last two lines are: '(El barco quieto en el mar / El sol sobre el olivar)' (I,351). The whole point of the structure of 'Perfil del tiempo' was to emphasise the protagonist's inertia by its repetition of the lines '. . . el sol, más sol en la arena . . .'. Examination of the poem suggests an explanation for the return of this note of indolence. The presence of the sun during the day-time (apart from the escapist dream of the dawn) is as unwelcome as that of the moon during the night. An explanation is not hard to imagine. The sun is the most forceful symbol of fertility and virility. Its life and energy remind him remorselessly of the death that is in his body. Hence the telling lines: 'Mi corazón se levanta / y cruza solo mi pena '. During the day the central figure's heart is taunted and intimidated. It is not surprising that it is in a poem set in the day-time that the 'boat' of the protagonist is described as a 'corazón que se esconde' (I,356).

The dream

Neither by day nor by night, therefore, is the 'marinero' entirely free from consideration of the reality of his body. Only at certain moments, completely removed from his waking experience, can there be any release. This, in a sense, is the 'narrative' of the voyage undertaken by the young sailor of 'Víspera', a narrative which will be subject to considerable fluctuation in the course of the poetry's development.

It is a pattern which brings the dream into a position of prominence. At this stage it is not easy to define its nature or content. It has been suggested that apart from the 'viaje de ensueño' there is a dream which transports the 'yo' to a level which he calls that of the soul or the spirit. There is one early poem, contained in Caja 2.2, which provides some indication of what the higher 'sueño' might mean to the protagonist. It is called 'Canción marinera ':

Mi barco va por el viento
sin pensar en su timón:
se pasa del mar al cielo.

Mi sombra va por el suelo
colgada a mi corazón
y olvidada de mi cuerpo . . .
Del sueño se va al amor.

(Se olvida del tiempo el sol
y clava el día en lo eterno.)

The boat shifts from a physical, negative realm to the spiritual, positive realm—just as it did in 'Perfil del tiempo'. The body is left behind, the spiritual faculties begin to operate. The sphere of operation is hinted at: 'Del sueño se va [mi sombra] al amor.' It is in the *Cuerpo perseguido* and *Memoria del olvido* selections that this love is described in detail. A substitute for a fulfilment lacking in real life is sought there. *Tiempo* is mainly concerned with the problems facing the central figure when he does not or cannot escape from them. There are also glimpses of escape-routes. Fuller discussion of these is the concern of the next chapter.

El misterio del agua

Consideration of the poetry of the *Tiempo* era would be incomplete without reference to the long, complex and highly individual cycle,

El misterio del agua.[48] Blanco describes it as 'uno de los poemas más ricos de belleza plástica y conceptual de la lírica española moderna'.[49] It is also, because of its individuality, an extremely difficult poem. The characterisation of the elements—the day, water, time—is detailed, involved and more comprehensive than the two poems from Aleixandre's *Ámbito*, 'Mar y aurora' and 'Mar y noche' which closely resemble it and which appear to have been conceived at a similar period (*Ámbito* dating from 1924–7, *El misterio del agua* from 1926–7).[50] Here, for example, is the water of 'Milagro primero':

se descalza en el sueño
sus ligaduras últimas
y transportada
en éxtasis,
por mirar más
se funde en elle misma,
se deshace,
se vuela,
se desata . . . (32:I,196)

In amongst the vivid descriptions of the movement of the water are references to 'sueño' and 'éxtasis'—references which lead away from, rather towards the kind of 'plasticity' to which Blanco refers. There is, in addition, a curiously narcissistic motif running through the poetry, as in its description of 'tiempo':

¡Ay tiempo contra tiempo
sin piel; sangre en la sangre
de una misma sangre;
luz en la luz sin luz
de luz del aire! (36:I,199)

And in 'Milagro cuarto' the personification of the night and water extends to repeated mention of guilt and punishment—terms whose use is at least unusual in such a setting.

The narrative begins at dusk. In the opening poem, 'Tránsito del crepúsculo', the strength of the day-light has already begun to ebb: 'Se le va el pulso al día'. The second and third 'milagros' concentrate on the water as it is bathed in the reflection of the moon. The fourth describes the anguish of the water and the night as they are lost in darkness: the fifth the seeming release of dawn. From such an outline as this one of the cycle's most significant aspects is clear: it is heavily biased towards the dusk–night–dawn, rather than the dawn–day–dusk, part of the day. The reality with which the poet chooses to deal is that section of time when the moon, rather than the sun, predominates. It is, therefore, an echo, an image of the carefully restricted world of *Tiempo*. 'Víspera' warns us that: '—¡siempre es doble mi alma en su imagen dispersa!—:'. This analysis considers some of the ways in which the pattern of the central figure's behaviour in *Tiempo* is closely mirrored in *El misterio del agua*.

Prados's telling of this story is marked by the vigorous and dramatic quality of its imagery. The struggle and tension implicit in the contest between darkness and light is expressed in terms of 'wounding' and 'dying'. Here are lines from poem III of 'Milagro primero':

> No se resiste el día,
> al invisible dardo
> que busca su belleza
> y entero lo recibe
> en su cuerpo sin piel
> donde se clava . . . (34:I,197)

The 'body' of the day 'bleeds':

> ¡Herido se levanta el día!
> ¡Desnudo y desangrándose!
>
> Su pasión lo conduce
> en vilos de la muerte,
> mojado de presencias
> y abandonos del cielo,
> a otro nuevo martirio
> que su cuerpo presiente,
> . . . .

Such passages no doubt inspired Durán Gili's references to the poet's 'imágenes atrevidas'.[51] The natural cycle is depicted as being in conflict—even at times in turmoil.[52]

But there is another set of images which informs *El misterio del agua* with far greater consistency. The narrative is characterised by its use of sexual imagery. The poet emphasises the motif of penetration, and of objects of penetration, implicit in the contact between the sun and the water. In 'Milagro quinto' he writes:

> . . . .
>
> la luz penetra al cielo . . .

II

¡Entra la luz al cielo!
¡Abre el sueño su espalda!
¡Abre el amor sus alas!
No resiste la sombra
al dardo que, el instante,
invisible, le asesta
y, entero lo recibe
en su cuerpo sin piel
donde se clava . . . (52:I,228)

In 'Milagro primero' the day is described in a similarly erotic manner:

Como medio durmiendo,
curvado en abandono
—una pierna mecida
en últimos desmayos—: (31–2:I,195)

Particular attention will be given to the 'erotic' nature of the contact of the light with the water.

It has already been indicated that the cycle concerns itself with the natural world during the hours of evening, night and dawn. It begins, therefore, at a moment of decline. The light of day is losing its power:

¡Abre el cielo sus puertas!
¡Abre el amor sus alas!

Se le va el pulso al día.
Su corazón se agua
—se desnuda—,
se tiende deshilado,
huye por sombras,
se desabrocha en vahos . . .

In terms of the sexual symbolism referred to above, the light is losing its potency, its phallic strength:

Cae
en aire solamente,
en vilos de la fuga;
pero unido al descanso
—hundido en blanca ausencia—,
en anhelos de espalda
rendido a su blandura

adolescente
y claro.

Instead of fulfilment there is the exact opposite. The action of the narrative suggests that the light should penetrate the sea. In fact, it falls 'en aire solamente'. The phrases 'en vilos de' and 'en anhelos de' convey the suspension or postponement of satisfaction. The continued death of the light is recounted in the stanza which follows:

surge,
corta un latido
y más se desvanece,
se derrite de vida,
se desploma de luces . . .

It is a pattern of activity resonant with echoes of *Tiempo*. As light is confronted by the sea, it fades, 'se derrite de vida' (this, perhaps, being why love 'opens its wings', or 'escapes'). The central 'marinero', confronted by the presence of the woman, found himself incapable of response. In this *País* poem the entry of the 'boat' into the 'port' proved disastrous:

Mi barco se sofocaba . . .

(Los peces lo abanicaban).

Mi barco se derretía . . .

(Los peces se sonreían)
Cuando mi barco se fue
no le siguió ningún pez.

The light 'se derrite'; 'mi barco se derretía'.[53]

Eventually the light in *El misterio del agua* finds itself amidst 'silence':

Y, al fin, ya desprendido
—leve calor de pluma
sobre el cielo—:
se da
y queda en el aire,
bajo sus tibias nieblas,
mágico e invisible
perdido entre silencios . . . (32:I,196)

Silence surrounds a frustrating inactivity or death, followed, nevertheless, by the attainment of a moment of equilibrium. In Poem III Prados writes:

¡Sobre él mismo descansa!:
¡Sobre él mismo se queda
como un rumor vencido
absorto entre dos muertes! . . . (35:I,198)

There is a temporary ecstasy:

Cielo y cielo que mana
del cielo, hacia la fuente
del cielo, sobre el cielo
del cielo que sostiene!
cielo total y mínimo
ser total todo el cielo . . .

The slide towards complete inertia seems to have been halted.

The narrative surrounding the light in *El misterio del agua* is, then, a precise parallel to that of the central figure of *Tiempo*. In 'Fin del día, en la escuela' the moments preceding the day's equilibrium, 'la balanza de la sombra', are marked by sudden yet fruitless activity which peters out and finally comes to nought—the body is left, like the light, in 'silence':

Alumno y sol de lata, en recuerdos mecánicos,
mueven su juego antiguo bajo el jardín del agua,
dándome al fin oficio: "Marinero de parques
en bergantín velero de reflejos y plantas".
. . . .

Se despierta el momento con un barco en la mano
y gira su mirada prendida entre veletas:
el sol sigue clavada redondo sobre el cielo
y, en él, cuelga una burla su máscara deshecha . . .

¡Cierra el silencio al día!
(¡Mi cuerpo es el silencio! . . .)
¡Se me quiebra en la frente la flor de todo el sueño! (19–20)

From the silence there seemed to spring a momentary release. 'Crepúsculo' recorded a suspension of the central figure's consciousness of his moon-like sterility:

La balanza de la sombra
pesa a la luna.
La tarde sujeta al árbol,
fiel de la noche y la espuma . . . (17:I,110)

The same dusk pattern of fruitless activity—silence—equilibrium is common to the world of the 'yo' and of *El misterio del agua*.

But the moment of equilibrium noted in Poem III of 'Milagro primero' is short-lived. The light of the day is transformed into the night, described as 'Descentrada / y mal justificada'. It is a night which displays several unwelcome features.

There is a strong suggestion that it is linked with deceitfulness. By now it has impregnated the water with moon-light to such an extent that 'el tiempo' mistakes night for day, deceived by the 'mágico espejo' of the night—the moonlit water. Thus in 'Cuerpo de la noche', the 'milagro segundo', Prados writes:

Así, sin ser memoria,
tanta es la transparencia
y amor hacia la luz
que hundió la tarde en ella
que, el tiempo, confundido,
imagina presencia
del día, lo que es tránsito
que hacia el olvido lleva . . .
¡Entra a vivirlo! Y cae,
donde el agua lo espera
ahuecando amorosa
el cielo en que lo besa . . .

Y ¿qué mágico espejo
con esta imagen juega?
¡El agua! Sólo el agua!
¿Dóndo está el agua? . . .
¿Sueña? . . . (41–2:I,207)

It promotes activity which proves aimless, unreal, illusory, 'Soledad', the fourth miracle, underlines the distress experienced during the night: 'Penando está la noche'. It is restless, uneasy:

Pasa y va deteniéndose
por mirarse mejor a cada paso . . .
Parándose en su pena
y quedándose en elle en cada esquina
—ánima transparente—, (47:I,221)

It is also identified with feelings of guilt. There is a reference to:

. . . su alto grito
ya mudo y hecho espejo
para culpa.

The night is portrayed as a fugitive:

fugitiva se esconde
en filtraciones rápidas
quedándose tan sólo
en hálito de huella . . .

The natural world during the night is in a state of unrest, even turmoil. It is as if the removal of the sun and the substitution of the moon created a sense of oppression and unease:

Negra, negra, negrísima es la noche,
alta como una espada . . .
Semilla de su carne,
hoy sólo llanto y niebla
de un oscuro gemir vive la noche.

All these characteristics are typical of the activity and mood of the 'yo' of *Tiempo* during the night. In 'Noche en urna' this mysterious figure made his appearance:

Cuerpo en pena del alma, una sombra en el muelle,
razonando sigilos, repasa las penumbras:
hurta sus mercancías al sueño, se detiene,
se ausenta y, vuelta al pensamiento, en él se oculta.

Ahueca sus caudales y, en cáscara de barco,
se le va el corazón por mapa de recuerdos
—pirata de albedríos por él mismo apresado
en alta mar del ansia sin cadenas del cielo— . . .

The 'penando' of 'Soledad' is an echo of the earlier 'cuerpo en pena del alma'. The restlessness of the natural world is common to the scurrying, irregular movement of the 'yo'. There is in the mind of the 'yo' and in nature a sense of guilt: in 'Soledad' the cry of the night was 'hecho espejo para culpa', in 'Noche en urna' guilt is implicit in the images of stealing, piracy and furtiveness. The reference to the 'viaje de sueño' in the stanza following those quoted above reflects the deceitful aspect of the night in *El misterio del agua*. The lowest point reached by the night recorded in poem II of 'Soledad', will be discussed in the context of the experience of the other main 'character' in the cycle, water.

The dawn ('Milagro quinto') brings with it an end to the pain of the night. 'La luz penetra el cielo . . .'.[54] There is an exact reversal of the process of dusk. Poems I and III of the opening 'Milagro' read:

¡Abre el cielo sus puertas!
¡Abre el amor sus alas!
. . . .

No se resiste el día,
al invisible dardo
que busca su belleza
y entero lo recibe
en su cuerpo sin piel
donde se clava . . .

In the second poem of 'Amanecer' the two passages are brought together almost unchanged, except for the addition of the 'entering' of the light, and the exchange of 'darkness' for 'day' and of 'dream' for 'love':

¡Entra la luz al cielo!
¡Abre el sueño su espalda!
¡Abre el amor sus alas!

No resiste la sombra
al dardo que, el instante,
invisible, le asesta
y, entero lo recibe
en su cuerpo sin piel
donde se clava . . . (52:I,228)

There then emerges a moment of equilibrium—a parallel to that of the dusk. The language of the opening stanzas of the cycle is again repeated. 'Milagro primero', Poem III, states of the day:

Como un calor se filtra
—se baja por él mismo—,
se escapa de su frente
besándose hacia dentro
hasta darse de bruces
con su propia hermosura
cuerpo y cuerpo sin piel
de carne inexistente.

¡Sobre él mismo descansa!:
¡Sobre él mismo se queda
como un rumor vencido
absorto entre dos muertes! . . . (35:I,198)

The balance of the day at dawn is expressed in these terms:

Como un calor se eleva,
—emerge de ella misma—,

se escapa de su frente
volcándose hacia fuera,
hasta darse de bruces
entera en su hermosura,
húmeda y ya vencida
por el alba que llega.

¡Sobre el viento descansa!
¡Sobre ella misma queda!
¡Todo su cuerpo late
sostenido de estrellas! . . . (53:I,229)[55]

It is on the repetition of these two blocks of verse, at the beginning and end of the cycle, that its structure depends. For it is with the dawn that it draws to a close. This chronicle of the progress of the day ends before 'day-time' settles.

Before examining the significance of that omission, the water's response to the drama which unfolds about it needs to be considered again. Much of the poet's description of it draws attention to the sea's wave-motion. It seems to mesmerise itself by the repeated rising and breaking of its waves:

se funde en ella misma,
se deshace,
se vuela,
se desata . . .
Sube, abierta en un halo
y, se pierde de cuerpo
por luz,
en vapor de misterio,
en ronda de temblores . . . (32:I,196)

. . . .

Apenas se sostiene en ella misma;
no puede sostenerse:
se cae,
se medio hunde;
se da vencida,
se pierde entera,
se sumerge,
se acaba
. . . .
(39:I,205)

da contra los silencios
y se quiebra de estrellas,

se rompe,
se separa hacia arriba,
se cuelga horizontal,
se atiranta y se limpia,
se ahonda y pulimenta,
se hace cristal de viento,
se endurece . . . (45:I,213–4)

In consequence there is a feminine, playful aspect to the personification of the water. It is subject to changes of direction and activity (in contrast to the more constant movement of the 'masculine' light):

El agua viene alegre,
espera,
se retira,
. . . .
(44.I,213)

This attractiveness is, nevertheless, shown to be partly superficial and deceptive. Because it is observed during the night, it is inseparable from the ('feminine') light of the moon. In the second 'milagro' it is 'chorreando luna'. This is how the third, 'Pasión de la sombra', continues its description of the 'agua . . . alegre':

da su vidrio
y se oculta por fin
puliéndose en la noche
derramada en pupila;
empinándose en miedo,
conteniendo a sus peces en pena
como plumas sonámbulas
errando en el vacío;
cuidando de sus barcos oscuros,
resbalosos de sueño;
abierta en brillos
y, en su desmayo,
herida por el remo . . .

It contains elements of fear: its fish are 'en pena' . . . 'sonámbulas / errando en el vacío'; its boats are 'oscuros, / resbalosos de sueño'. Eventually it shares in the night's distress:

Y queda el agua en pie
y extremecida
en su tierra de luto
—cadenas la memoria,

prisiones la truncada
alta torre del cuerpo—:
la contrición en sombra
—aún húmeda en la sangre
del corazón del día—,
penando sobre el mundo
por castigo del tiempo . . . (48:I,222)

Water, like the night, is left 'penando'. The nadir, the moment of 'maximum' death, in the night-sea journey to which Jung refers, has been reached.[56]

Both the day and the water, then, during the night, suffer. The day–night suffers a sense of inadequacy and guilt because its power has deserted it. The water, in the absence of the intercourse which the sun supplies in the day-time, is bathed in moon-light, and mourns the loss of the sun. The kind of pattern noticed in *Tiempo* is echoed in *El misterio del agua*. There the mental activity of the 'yo' tried to compensate for the body's inadequacy in a kind of 'ensueño' (as in 'Víspera' and 'Noche en urna') to meet only with inevitable failure, akin to that of the water in the natural cycle as depicted in *El misterio del agua*.[57] Again there are details common to both the experiences of *Tiempo*'s protagonist and the participants of the later cycle. The water's 'fear' is a reflection of that of the 'yo'; the discomfort of the fish and the sluggishness of the boat (the 'peces en pena' and the 'barcos oscuros, / resbalosos de sueño') are direct reminders of the world of *Tiempo*. Its restricted, negative pattern is reproduced in five 'milagros'.

It has already been suggested that the period when, by implication, both day and water should find fulfilment—during the day-time—is not included. There is no account of a joyful, liberating 'sun–sea' intercourse. Rather is attention turned to the curious figure of 'tiempo':

Y el tiempo quedó pensando
que, de tanto en él pensar,
sin él se estaba quedando . . .

Luego se durmió en el mar
y el mundo lo fue olvidando. (54:I,230)

The day-time, the dawn, is as much of an anti-climax as the non-fulfilment of physical and mental desire found in *Tiempo*. In the realm of nature, it is time which is continually frustrated, bringing together the bodies of night and day, yet never witnessing their contact:

Un lucero
sólo velaba al misterio
que dejó morir la luz . . .
¡Eterna pasión del tiempo!

Instead of a climactic rapprochement of sea and water, the spectacle of a slumbering, introverted abstraction closes the cycle.

It is in some of the 'ausencias' (from which we took the lines quoted above) that the reflection of the preoccupations of *Tiempo* in the world of nature is clearest. Here is the first 'ausencia' to the second miracle:

¿Es toda el agua del mar,
el reflejo que, hoy, la luna
en ella, clavando está?
(Salta un pez . . .
 Se arruga el agua . . .)
¿Es toda el agua del mar
la blanca flor de la espuma? . . . (43:I,209)

These are the same questions which *El corazón diario*, in a different context, poses. Is the moon, sterility, death, to conquer and poison everything? A fish jumps—a fish which, were this a *Tiempo* poem, would remind us of the erotic norm inaccessible to the 'yo'. The doleful answer is the same as the one given the protagonist in 'Espejismos': '(Todo el mar es soledad.)' The water is as coldly isolated as was *Tiempo*'s central figure.

El misterio del agua, then, makes no direct reference to the anthology's central *persona*. It is an original and imaginative dramatisation of events in the natural world from dusk to dawn. In one sense, however, it contains nothing 'new'. The emotional pattern obtaining to its complex personification of the water, the day and time serves to reiterate—if only indirectly—the information supplied in poetry analysed in the earlier parts of this chapter. It certainly contains nothing to suggest that the 'yo' who will confront the reader of *Cuerpo perseguido* is very different from the one met in *Tiempo* or *Canciones del farero*.[58]

The language of doubt (1)

The extraordinary vacillations and self-concealment of the central *persona* are suitably reflected in the fabric of the writing. In the early poetry (and in particular in the *Antología* versions of it) the sense of hesitancy and deliberate opaqueness is heightened by his eccentric use of punctuation (standardised to a large extent in *Poesías completas*). This section examines some of the ways in which the punctuation colours the poetry.

Firstly there exists a tendency to over-punctuate. In *Antología* the poet consistently favours the inclusion rather than the omission of the comma. In 'Tránsito en el jardín' he writes:

> Prendido aún del cielo el pañuelo del día
> vierte, sobre el mar limpio, sus fáciles desmayos. (22)

In 'Noche en urna' the inclusion of commas around 'en la torre' has the effect of slowing up the movement of the line and of inviting the reader to consider the phrase, for a brief moment, independently of the rest of the sentence:

> Las pisadas descalzas del reloj, en la torre,
> laten acompasando a la esponja y la estrella. (14)

Later in the same poem he adds:

> Cuerpo en pena del alma, una sombra en el muelle,
> razonando sigilos, repasa las penumbras:
> hurta sus mercancías al sueño, se detiene,
> se ausenta y, vuelta al pensamiento, en él se oculta. (15)

A comparison of this text with earlier versions contained in the Prados papers (Caja 5.5) suggests that this version is closer to Prados's intention than the 'corrected' stanza as it appears in *Poesías completas* (I,366), which omits the comma after 'sigilos', 'y' and 'pensamiento'. It is noticeable too that the 1954 version captures more faithfully the hesitant, nervous wandering of the central figure.

If this kind of 'over-punctuation' is a matter of taste, then other anomalies in Prados's punctuation are less so. Among these is the separation of the verb from its subject and, at times, from its object. In 'Fin del día, en la escuela', 'el reloj' and 'lo quiebra' are articifically held apart:

> Las brújulas ensueñan sus posibilidades,
> percibiendo el deseo la flor de su manzana;
> pero el reloj, lo quiebra de un golpe, contra el tiempo,
> brotando en el presente desde una campanada. (19)

This is how 'Víspera' describes the movement of the boat:

. . . el barco juega a flores distantes,
trazando itinerarios sobre las planas olas
que, el pincel del ensueño, tiñe con falso esmalte. (9)

The removal of the commas enclosing 'el pincel del ensueño' (a step taken in the *Poesías completas* (I,91)) obviates both the broken rhythm and ambiguity created by their presence. While they remain, the reader is invited to play with the idea that it is the boat which is 'dream's brush'. This setting up of a deceptive apposition is also demonstrated in 'Noche en urna':

Cuatro esbeltos luceros se llevan muerto al viento,
tendido sobre el eco como un pálido junco
y, el agua, busca ausencias para sus finos duelos,
tapada en los reflejos transparentes del luto. (15)

The isolation of 'el agua' is matched by that of 'el fósforo' in the stanza which follows:

Pulimentan la piedra los pinceles del frío
y, el fósforo, resbala hueco, sobre la hora. (15)

These steps (though by no means entirely alien to normal Spanish practice) result in a clouding of the sense which runs parallel to Prados's treatment of thematic material. Again in 'Víspera' there is an example of the unnatural divorce of verb and object:

La campana acaricia, el silencio que ha roto
al cubrir las heridas de su piel bajo el eco. (10)

The reader is made, if momentarily, to play out the role of the protagonist—to doubt, to attempt to re-appraise, to vacillate. It is in this sense that consideration of this aspect of Prados's poetic technique is relevant to the question of how the central figure is to be understood.

The same stuttering nervousness results from Prados's frequent use of the comma after 'y'. Here are some examples:

La enmohecida hélice sus pétalos ordena
y, la máquina fiel, su corazón ajusta. (10)

Las brújulas se inquietan por su largo descanso,
su inquietud multiplica los puntos cardinales
y, muestra al marinero, en su oráculo falso,
el balcón y la rosa final de su viaje . . . (10)

¡Todo el cuerpo del día
se hace voz de la tarde

y, el pensamiento, tiempo
que sueña sobre el aire! (35–6)

It is interesting that Blanco, while claiming to reproduce the anthology version of 'El misterio del agua', omits the commas in the third passage quoted above—as indeed he does in those taken from 'Víspera' (I, LXIII). The ease with which they can be omitted, and the 'obviousness' of such a step, beg the question whether or not it is right to rationalise apparent anomalies.

A further unusual feature of punctuation in the anthology involves the use of the comma after 'que'. Here is a stanza from 'Noche en urna':

Se desclava la noche de la pared helada
que sostuvo sus brillos en silencioso encuentro.
Se derrama en el blanco recinto de mi alma
que, aguardaba tendida, su mansa flor de tiempo . . . (16)

This is punctuation to obscure, rather than clarify, the sense. In 'El misterio del agua' Prados writes:

Así, sin ser memoria,
tanta es la transparencia
y amor hacia la luz
que hundió la tarde en ella
que, el tiempo, confundido,
imagina presencia
de día, lo que es tránsito
que hacia el olvido lleva . . . (41)

In the same 'milagro' the water is described in these terms:

¡Cómo siente su espacio
sin piel, vivir la imagen
que del tiempo burló
y, al temeroso instante
que, aún no sabe si es tiempo,
bajo el tiempo soñarle! (42)

The use of the comma endows the lines with extra sense—that of the lines taken as a whole, and also that of the parenthesis which, for an illusory moment, can be taken out of context. Thus 'el tiempo' and 'aún no sabe si es tiempo', rather like waves of the sea, acquire momentarily their own individual importance—only to be engulfed by the larger sense of their context. The result is a constant shifting of angle and perspective—and a concomitant blurring of the sense. In discussing aspects of technique in the next chapter, it is hoped to show that this mysterious and personal attitude towards punctuation is in no way whimsical or arbitrary, but rather a part of the complicated defensive mechanism built into Prados's work during these early years, a mechanism responsible for the emergence of the distinctive voice of his poetry.

1 This chapter deals with poetry grouped in the *Antología* under the headings *Tiempo, Otras canciones* and *El misterio del agua*. These poems were written from 1923 to 1927. Most of Prados's work during those years, published and unpublished, has been gathered in the first volume of the *Poesías completas*, edited by C. Blanco Aguinaga and A. Carreira (Mexico, 1975), pp. 1–230.

2 R. Porlán y Merlo, 'Sobre *Tiempo*, poemas de Emilio Prados', *Mediodia*, no. 4 (September 1926), p. 16.

3 E. Salazar y Chapela, 'Sobre *Vuelta*', *El Sol* (3rd June, 1927), p. 2.

4 C. Blanco Aguinaga, *Emilio Prados: Vida y obra; Bibliografía, Antología*, p. 29.

5 C. B. Morris, *A Generation of Spanish Poets, 1920–1936*, (Cambridge, 1969), p. 149.

6 G. Diego, 'Emilio Prados: *Vuelta*', *Revista de occidente*, Vol. XVII, no. LI (1927), pp. 384–7.

7 The section entitled *Tiempo* in the *Antología* was not chosen exclusively from Prados's book of the same name. In further references *Tiempo* denotes the anthology's selection, *Tiempo (1925)* the original publication.

8 For an explanation of the reference system adopted for Prados's poetry, see Foreword.

9 These manuscripts have been catalogued by Carlos Blanco Aguinaga and described in *Lista de los papeles de Emilio Prados* (The Johns Hopkins Press, Baltimore, Maryland, 1967). This version of 'Juego de memoria ' appears in Caja 2.2. It is to this catalogue that any reference to 'cajas' applies.

10 A slightly different version of this poem appears in *Poesías completas*, where it is entitled 'Fiel errante' (I,368).

11 In his article 'La primera salida de Emilio Prados' Antonio Carreira makes the point that *Tiempo* (1925) is in fact a chronological record of a complete day—including the period between dawn and dusk. (A. Carreira, in *Homenaje universitario a Dámaso Alonso* (Madrid, 1970), p. 223.

12 His school-friend, Aleixandre, makes this point in his character-sketch of the young Prados, 'Emilio Prados, niño de Málaga', *Ágora*, no. 71/72 (1962).

13 A. Machado, *Obras: poesía y prosa*, edited by A. de Albornoz and G. de Torre (Buenos Aires, 1964), p. 71.

14 This poem does not appear in the *Poesías completas* but is to be found in Caja 2.3, with the sub-title: 'Misterio de la hora (Mediodía en el Sur, Fuenjirola. Verano).'

15 C. Zardoya, 'Emilio Prados, poeta de la melancolía', in *Poesía española contemporánea* (Madrid, 1961), pp. 431–5.

16 C. Blanco Aguinaga describes this friendship in his study *Emilio Prados: Vida y obra*, pp. 14–15. Perhaps it was not always as idyllic as he suggests. In *Diario Íntimo* Prados wrote of him: '¿Es que no me comprende todavía?' (*Diario Íntimo*, p. 31).

17 It is interesting to conjecture that Prados possibly wrote his poem before Lorca. *Tiempo* was published in 1925; *Romancero gitano* dates from 1924–7. For a note on the modernist motif of the moon seen as the sacramental host, strongly suggested in the Prados poem, see J. M. Aguirre, *Antonio Machado, Poeta simbolista* (Madrid, 1973), p. 203.

18 F. García Lorca, *Obras completas* (Madrid, 1957), p. 346.

19 V. Nuñez, 'Sobre Prados: *Río natural*', *Ínsula*, no. 142 (15th September, 1958), p. 7.

20 J. M. Sacristán, 'La doctrina de Freud en los pueblos latinos'. *La Pluma*, no. 23 (April, 1922), p. 238.

21 *Idem.*, 'Sobre Freud, S.: *Das Ich und das Es, Revista de Occidente,* V (October–December, 1923), pp. 263–6.

22 C. Blanco Aguinaga, *Emilio Prados: Vida y obra*, p. 12. In this connection, see also C. B. Morris, *Surrealism and Spain, 1920–1936,* Cambridge, 1972, pp. 36–37.

23 C. Blanco Aguinaga, *Vida y obra,* p. 30.

24 In this context Prados's undated comment, contained in Caja 19.1, is of great interest: 'Como todavía no es posible que hagamos nuestra autoconfesión o psicoanálisis, públicamente, creo que aun la poesía es un refugio. Un mundo en que la realidad se oculta en la aparencia. Otro mundo que en la actualidad habito. Algunas veces por él se llega a Dios.'

25 G. Bachelard, *L'Eau et les Rêves* (Paris, 1956), pp. 218–9.

26 J. Guillén, *Cántico* (Buenos Aires, 1950), p. 56.

27 It is of interest that Cirlot writes in this context: 'there is . . . a connexion between the boat and the human body'. (J. E. Cirlot, *A Dictionary of Symbols,* translated by J. Sage (London, 1962), p. 29).

28 *Idem,* p. 26. An example of Freud's opinion of the fish's symbolism is to be found in *The Complete Psychological Works of Sigmund Freud*, translated under the general editorship of J. Strachey, Vol. V (London, 1953), p. 357: 'Many of the beasts which are used as genital symbols in mythology and folk-lore play the same part in dreams: e.g. fishes, snails, cats, mice . . .'.

29 F. García Lorca, *Obras completas,* p. 358.

30 The antithesis between 'dormido' and 'despiertos' is interesting. The implication that the heart is awake to the possibility of sexual involvement while the body is unable to undertake it is consonant with the view put forward in this chapter.

31 F. García Lorca, *Obras completas,* p. 101.

32 G. Díaz-Plaja, 'La luna y la nueva poesía'. *La Gaceta literaria*, no. 61, July 1 (1929), p. 6.

33 F. García Lorca, 'La luna asoma', *Obras completas*, p. 321.

34 The image of the mirror is an interesting one in view of Blanco's note on the poet's mirror-gazing activities (*Vida y obra*, p. 15).

35 S. Freud, *The Complete Psychological Works*, Vol. V, p. 354: 'All elongated objects, such as sticks, tree-trunks and umbrellas (the opening of these last being compared to an erection) may stand for the male organ . . .'.

36 A. P. Debicki, *Estudios sobre poesía espa*ñola contemporánea (Madrid, 1968), p. 308.

37 E. Prados, *Canciones del farero* (Málaga, 1927).

38 L. Cernuda, *La realidad y el deseo* (México, 1958), p. 108.

39 These lines were published in *Mediodía*, Sevilla, no. VIII (1927), p. 10, with the foot-note: 'Del libro inédito *Poesía de cámara*'.

40 J. Guillén, *Cántico* (Buenos Aires, 1950), p. 364.

41 J. M. Aguirre, in his article 'La poesía primera de Luis Cernuda' makes this comment on 'el proceso del adormecimiento': '. . . en el cotidiano momento anterior al sueño los sentidos del poeta, "con el cuerpo ausente", pueden aprehender la totalidad del momento. Este es "Un abismo deleitoso.".' These words might almost have been written of the feelings of our 'marinero'. (In *Hispanic Review,* XXXIV (1966), p. 126).

42 A. P. Debicki, *Estudíos sobre poesía española contemporánea*, p. 314.

43 These poems, dedicated to Antonio Marichalar, appeared in *Verso y prosa*, a literary supplement to *La Verdad,* Murcia, no. 1, January, 1927.

44 G. Bachelard, *L'Eau et les Rêves*, p. 100.

45 L. Cernuda, 'El joven marino', *La realidad y el deseo*, p. 125.

45a D. Alonso and J. M. Blecua, *Antología de la poesía española* (Madrid, 1964), p. 16.

46 J. Guillén, *Cántico*, p. 50.

47 *Ibid.*, p. 240.

48 No full version of the cycle appears until the publication of the *Antología*. At least one

shorter section was, however, published during the twenties. 'El agua viene alegre' ('Milagro tercero') was first read in *Verso y prosa*, Murcia, no. 9 (September, 1927), p. 1.

49 C. Blanco Aguinaga, *Vida y obra*, p. 40.

50 V. Aleixandre, *Obras completas* (Madrid, 1968), pp. 129–132. There are several indications that at least in terms of poetic vocabulary it is with Aleixandre that Prados most closely aligns himself. Words such as 'pulida', 'clavado' and 'se hunde' are common to *El misterio del agua* and the two Aleixandre poems mentioned. Again in *Ámbito*, for example, a poem is entitled 'Pájaro de la noche' (*Idem.*, p. 125), while Prados, in 'Tránsito en el jardín', describes the night as the 'negra pluma del pájaro del aire' (23:I,143). *Nacimiento último* contains a poem dated 1927 and entitled: 'Emilio Prados (Retrato en redondo)' (*Idem.*, p. 629). Early poems by Aleixandre like 'Alba' and 'Noche final' reveal a common interest in the process and effects of time.

51 M. Durán Gili, *El superrealismo en la poesía española contemporánea* (Mexico, 1950), p. 88.

52 Blanco suggests that *El misterio del agua*, with its emphasis on 'el espectáculo', possesses distinctly theatrical qualities, (*Vida y obra*, footnote p. 97). In the same note he refers to the influence on Prados of the 'auto sacramental'. This line of thought opens up the possibility of the existence of an element of allegory in the cycle. It also raises the tantalising question: if *El misterio del agua* is some kind of allegory, then what do its participants represent? In the absence of clarification from the poet, our comments are confined in the main to ways in which the nature poem is an image or echo of the private situation of the 'yo' in *Tiempo*.

53 Jung's research illustrates the close association of light with sexuality in a way relevant to *El misterio del agua*. In *Symbols of Transformation* we read: 'Finally, we have to consider Øαλός, "bright, shining'. The Indo-European root is bhale, "to bulge, swell". Who does not think of Faust's "It glows, it shines, increases in my hand!" / This is "primitive" libido symbolism, which shows how direct is the connection between libido and light.' (*The Collected Works of C. G. Jung*, Volume V, p. 220.

54 Significantly the light did not penetrate the *water* at dusk. It fell 'en aire solamente'. The penetration of *water* by *light* does not take place. Similarly the 'yo' was unable to 'penetrate' the 'tú' (possibly represented by the female symbol, water). Penetration could only take place in the dream, in fantasy (the realm of 'el cielo'?)—a point elaborated in *Cuerpo perseguido*.

55 This passage suggests that dawn is not a time of vigorous fulfilment for the light. It is rather one of escape, of yielding ('vencida') and rest: '¡Sobre el viento descansa!'. The same is true, essentially, of the protagonist of *El corazón diario*. At the dawn of 'Tránsito en el jardín' he too escapes, yields, rests: '¡Pero el día ha nacido! . . . / (¿Adónde va mi cuerpo? . . .) / ¡Pisa la luz mi orilla y huye mi sombra al sueño!' (23).

56 C. G. Jung, *Symbols of Transformation*, p. 218.

57 Jung notes that: 'In dreams and fantasies the sea or a large expanse of water signifies the unconscious'. (*Symbols of Transformation*, p. 219). He also identifies it with a maternal, feminine symbol (*Idem.*, p. 218). If we were to attempt a precise interpretation of a possible allegory in the cycle, then perhaps the water would correspond to the mental activity of the 'yo', where his experience of the other, the feminine 'tú', is lodged, and which is confined to the 'viaje de sueño' of the night. The light would represent the activity of the body. The setting would be the sea. The 'producer' would be time ('rige / toda la bella empresa' (37:I,201). The mystery of the water would be the mystery of the 'yo', of the libido, of the relationship between mental and physical desire.

58 We would do well to remember here, and indeed in *Tiempo*, that exact and unbending 'rules' in the interpretation of Prados's symbolism are both unwise and impracticable. 'Symbols are not signs or allegories for something known; they seek rather to express something that is little known or completely unknown'. (C. G. Jung, *Symbols of Transformation*, p. 222).

CHAPTER TWO

The Emergence of the Dream and the Dream Figure

Care-charmer Sleep, son of the sable night,
Brother to death, in silent darkness born,
Relieve my languish, and restore the light,
With dark forgetting of my cares return.
(Samuel Daniel, *Sonnets to Delia*)

—Yo soy un sueño, un imposible
vano fantasma de niebla y luz;
soy incorpórea, soy intangible;
no puede amarte. —¡Oh, ven; ven tú!
(Gustavo Adolfo Bécquer, *Rimas*)

Et ma moitié: c'est une femme . . .
Une femme que je n'ai pas.
(Tristan Corbière, 'Paria', *Amours jaunes*)

Aimai-je un rêve?
(Stephane Mallarmé, 'Eglogue, Le Faune',
L'Après-midi d'un faune)

Introduction

The world of Prados's early poetry was extremely confined. Its setting was never far removed from the sea. Interest was limited in *Tiempo* to a single main character, while in books from which the selection was drawn the situations and problems faced by subsidiary figures were akin to his. There was no 'tú'. There was nobody with whom the central *persona* might share or in whom he might find respite. Only occasionally, when he was lifted to what he took to be the level of the soul, was the pressure of such confinement diminished.

The poetry analysed in this chapter, dating from the late twenties, can in part be seen as a direct progression from that of the *Tiempo* era.[1] It is a reaction to similar problems. It also outlines further and more subtle ones, related to the question of the protagonist's experience of his body. Furthermore, in response to his dilemma, as outlined in *Tiempo*, it contains attempts to resolve his feelings of isolation and impotence by means of the dream—the same dream to which *El misterio del agua*, in its indirect and deceptive fashion, has already formed an introduction. This chapter is concerned with the way in which the poetry reflects these strands of the central figure's experience.

Problems of interpretation in Memoria de poesía *and in* Cuerpo perseguido

In the past, the main line of criticism has asserted that the major development marked by these poems is the appearance of the 'tú'. Blanco makes this comment: '. . . lo que separa a esta segunda época de la primera es que, con *Cuerpo perseguido*, hace su aparición en la obra de Prados la criatura humana'.[2] He speaks of the central figure's 'relaciones con la persona amada'.[3] He is obliged, of course, to define his terms—love becomes 'la búsqueda de las correspondencias'[4]—and by the same token tacitly admit the strangely nebulous quality of the poetry. But, nevertheless, the reader is encouraged to regard the relationship described in *Cuerpo perseguido* in terms of the lover and his beloved. Anomalies are ascribed to the influence of 'el concepto platónico del amor . . .'.[5] Monterde's view of the relationship is even more straightforward. Of *Cuerpo perseguido*, 'donde el cuerpo, la persona, se sobrepone al paisaje', he comments: 'Con el cuerpo, la carne, hace acto de presencia la nota sensual; . . .'.[6]

But the experience of *Cuerpo perseguido* cannot be so easily categorised. Examples which follow are intended to do nothing more than suggest that this poetry cannot be regarded as 'straightforward' or 'normal'. They are intended also to suggest that neither the platonic view of love nor the conventional relationship of lover and beloved provide a relevant framework for discussion.

The protagonist's attitude to the role of his body in the 'yo-tú' relationship well illustrates the baffling paradoxes of *Cuerpo perseguido*. In some poems it seems he desires to escape from the physical reality altogether. 'Posesión luminosa' describes his thoughts as he considers the beloved:

> Igual que este viento, quiero
> figura de mi calor
> ser y, despacio, entrar
> donde descanse tu cuerpo
> del verano; irme acercando
> hasta él sin que me vea;
> llegar, como un pulso abierto
> latiendo en el aire; ser
> figura del pensamiento
> mío de ti, en su presencia;
> abierta carne del viento,
> estancia de amor en alma . (82:I,324)

It is hard to imagine what kind of a lover would be satisfied with such approaches. The central figure wishes to become ethereal, invisible.

But before categorising this as platonic love, it must be remembered that the selection contains also poems of a very different character.[7] At times the physical contact of the lovers seems to be, in parts of poems at least, intense. 'Forma de la huída' contains these lines:

> Prendidos por la cintura
> nuestros cuerpos amarrados,
> ¡qué haz de piernas, de cabellos,
> de brazos, de ojos! . . . (99:I,338)

In 'Alba rápida' there seems to be an earnest plea that the body's involvement in whatever is taking place should not be jeopardised:

> Sujetadme el cuerpo, ¡pronto!
> ¡que se me va!, ¡que se pierde

su reino entre mis caballos!
. . . .
¡Pronto, que el reino se acaba!
¡Ya se le tronchan las fuentes!
¡Ay, limpias yeguas del aire!
¡Ay, banderas de mi frente!
¡Qué galopar en mis ojos! (79:I,326–7)

The attitude towards the body of the 'tú' is just as equivocal. In some poems the 'tú' is a vague, insubstantial figure. The level of the body is ignored:

No te veía, pero te sentía
caer, desde tu pensamiento,
derramada en mi espalda,
como un calor de pájaro en el cielo . . . (60:I,235)

Other poems refer specifically to it:

Como un río, mi sangre,
va cruzando tu cuerpo.
¡Qué posesión perfecta
de todo tu camino! (94:I,329)

And the protagonist's concern is, at times, how he should make contact with 'tú' on the level of the body:

¿Qué podrá ser tocarte?
¿Será tu piel el viento? (88:I,286)

In this, and in further aspects of the 'tú', comparison with Salinas underlines the tenuousness of the central figure's allegiance to any physical reality. True, for the older poet the physical presence of the 'tú' and the 'yo' was a starting-point for a richly varied tapestry of emotional and mental activity; but it was never taken for granted. In *La Voz a ti debida* he wrote:

Tú vives siempre en tus actos.
Con la punta de tus dedos
pulsas el mundo, le arrancas
auroras, triunfos, colores,
alegrías: eres tú música.[8]

Another poem begins:

Ayer te besé en los labios.
Te besé en los labios. Densos,
rojos . . .

Though Salinas might be taken up with the essential 'voice', nevertheless poems such as the charming 'El teléfono', from *Fábula y signo* maintain a distinct landscape, a precise physical situation (even when it is a situation of physical separation—'diez ríos, tres idiomas, dos fronteras: cuatro días de ti a mí')[9]

Further complications arise in poems in which Prados's protagonist limits his interest to the nature of his own body. This is in itself something of a mystery to him:

Yo no sé si esta mano
que ahora va por mi frente
como una esponja en la memoria,
va por mí y es mi mano
o está cruzando el cielo
o va por los espejos
sin fuerza ni albedrío. (71:I,272)

It is as if there were problems and questions which lay outside the issue of the relationship with the 'tú'.

There are further reasons why the relationship of 'yo' and 'tú' poses unusual problems of interpretation when 'normal' criteria are applied to it. 'Posesión luminosa' is an example of this. The first half of the poem has already been quoted. The second deals with the contact between the lover and the beloved. He wishes to 'enter' the 'tú'. In other words, it would seem that he wishes to adopt the normal masculine role:

. . . Y yo ir entrando
igual que un agua serena,
inundarte todo el cuerpo,
hasta cubrirte y, entero
quedarme ya así por dentro,
. . . .
(82:I,324)

But this changes in mid-stream. It is the 'tú' who in the closing lines is within the 'yo', who describes himself:

viéndote temblar, luciendo,
brillar en medio de mí,
encendiéndote en mi cuerpo,
iluminando mi carne
toda ya carne de viento.

There seems to be a reluctance to commit himself to a feminine or masculine stance. He is neither consistently passive nor active in the relationship. 'Amor' is further evidence of ambivalence in this area:

> ¡Tu espalda con mi pecho,
> mi pecho con tu espalda!
> ¡qué alegre tajo el cielo
> nos cruza en la garganta! (100:I,333)

Akin to this phenomenon is the unnerving way in which the distinction between the two figures as individuals seems to be altogether lost. The fourth poem in 'Cinco de abril' exemplifies this:

> Mi cuerpo, por mis ojos
> transparentan mi cuerpo:
> tu cuerpo por mis ojos,
> por mi cuerpo y el cielo. (102)

The effect is intensified by introducing a confused grammatical structure (inexplicably revised in *Poesías completas* (I,314)). 'Mi cuerpo', a singular noun, is the subject of 'transparentan', a plural verb. The third and fourth of the lines quoted are even more ambiguous, precariously suspended from the insecure basis of the first and second, and, with the ellipsis of 'transparentan', suggesting that what is true of 'mi cuerpo' is equally true of 'tu cuerpo'.

In the third poem of *Cuerpo perseguido* this process is taken a step further. The 'tú' has now disappeared altogether. The 'yo' seems to be reacting only to himself:

> El umbral de mi sangre
> abierto está en mi sangre.
> Ya sin cuerpo mi cuerpo
> atraviesa mi cuerpo . . . (70–1:I,269)

Such lines cast doubt on what the protagonist means by 'cuerpo' and 'sangre'. And as long as such experiences as this and those already mentioned are possible then it is also important to be open-minded as to what might be meant by the 'tú' and the 'yo'.

It is with such 'mysteries' that this chapter is concerned. Enough has already been said to suggest that Aparicio Díaz is right to describe Prados's poetry as 'un incesante replegamiento sobre sí mismo'.[10] It is an introverted and self-enclosed world, here just as much as in *Tiempo*. Enough has been said to question Andújar's reference to the 'perenne capacidad comunicativa' of Prados's poetry. He warns that only with the passage of time will the reader be able to approach this poetry without the hindrances of personal memories, preferences and fancies:

> Quizá, entonces, languidezca la tesis de que sus pausados y mágicos sueños . . . su monólogo interior, el "clamor de lo eterno" que solía rondar, sean propiedad tapiada de las "minorías cultas", aptas para descifrar sus "dificultades" y "laberintos".[11]

Such encouragement does not eliminate the real problems facing the reader of *Cuerpo perseguido* and *Memoria de poesía*. This attempt to explain some of their inconsistencies and surprises will begin, where the protagonist begins, with an exposition of the problems he himself faces.

Problems facing the central figure

In the 1931 version of *Cuerpo perseguido* an introductory note is inserted. It contains this description of the poems:

> . . . deben ser considerados como un solo poema, manifestación última, incompleta, de mi cuerpo en tránsito constante, al lograr desprenderse, al fin, igual que de una piel inútil, de su trémula estancia por la huida.[12]

Both this 'justificación' and the selection's title in the *Antología*, *Cuerpo perseguido*, suggest that the poetry will record significant attitudes to the body. The reference to 'una piel inútil' is a reminder that the output of the later twenties is not to be completely divorced from that of the preceding years. How closely *Tiempo* and *Cuerpo perseguido* are linked is clear from the poem which opens *Memoria del olvido*, the first section of *Cuerpo perseguido* in the anthology. Its prominent position and its subject matter, the problems facing the protagonist and how he hopes to solve them, make it a convenient starting point for this analysis.

Before any mention is made of the 'tú' the central figure is careful to give a thorough exposition of the situation he faces. The first stanza confirms the emphasis in the 'justificación'—and in *Tiempo*—on the body. Hitherto he has been fully aware of his 'existence' only when he has been able to forget his body:

> Yo me he perdido porque siento
> que ya no estoy sino cuando me olvido;
> cuando mi cuerpo vuela y ondula
> como un estanque entre mis brazos. (69:I,279)

These lines summarise all that has been said in *Tiempo*. The moments of '*olvido*' are those mentioned briefly at the close of the longer poems, as in 'Tránsito en el jardín', where the protagonist exlaims: '¡Pero el día ha nacido! . . . / (¿Adónde va mi cuerpo? . . .) / ¡Pisa la luz mi orilla y huye mi sombra al sueño!' (23). They are moments when he loses direct consciousness of the body, in a way similar to that outlined in lines three and four of the stanza quoted above.

There are two strands of thought in the second stanza. Though their meaning is not immediately apparent it is clear that lines one and two contain some kind of admission of defeat, while lines three and four hint at the presence of a factor which might compensate for this defeat:

Yo sé que mi piel no es un río
y que mi sangre rueda serena;
pero hay un niño que cuelga de mis ojos
nivelando mi sueño como el mundo.

The import of this verdict on his 'skin' depends on what is meant by the words 'piel', 'río' and 'sangre'. This can be determined by reference to other Prados poems. 'Piel', the first of this group, is fairly straightforward. In *El misterio del agua* it is used as a parallel expression for the body. The second 'milagro' pictures the water in these terms:

El agua está en su lecho
delirante y desnuda,
sin cuerpo, palpitante,
brotando de ella misma
. . . .
(42:I,208)

In the stanza that follows reference is made to the fact that just as it is without body, it is also without skin:

¡Cómo siente su espacio
sin piel, vivir la imagen
que del tiempo burló . . .

'Piel', therefore, shares the same sense as 'cuerpo'. It suggests that troublesome area of experience identified in the first chapter.

'Río', by its very nature a symbol of fertility, is used elsewhere in contexts which suggests that it has erotic connotations for the protagonist. 'Atardecer. Quietud' describes a moment of joyful activity. The river is used in a way which equates it with the traditional erotic symbols of the fountain and the tree. The river itself is 'en pie en mi cuerpo':

> . . . mi sangre
> ¡qué rojo tallo de pulsos
> alza dentro de mi carne!
> ¡Qué fuente! ¡qué claro río
> en pie en mi cuerpo se abre,
> igual que se abre en el cielo
> este árbol! . . . (89:I,282)

The meaning of 'mi piel no es un río', then, is beginning to emerge. It is in line with the general tone, one of the admission of defeat, to which reference was made earlier. He is confessing to the inadequacy of his body. The second line, 'y que mi sangre rueda serena', is a re-statement of the same idea. The blood, the symbol of passion, is not easily roused. Although there might be a desire for desire, there is no effective impetus towards the 'tú' on the physical level. Together the lines state that in the realm of the body limitations and inadequacies persist. It is not the fertile river he feels it should be.

Before dealing with the remaining lines of the second stanza, where the 'yo' refers to a potentially compensating factor, the 'niño que cuelga de mis ojos', other veiled references to the question of the sterility of his body will be examined. These are to be found in stanzas three, four and five:

> Cuando mi rostro suspira bajo la noche
> cuando las ramas se adormecen como banderas,
> si cayera una piedra sobre mis ojos
> yo subiría del agua sin palomas.
>
> Yo subiría del fondo de mi frente
> hasta habitar mi cuerpo como un ídolo:
> hasta brotar en medio de mi carne
> otra vez sobre el mundo sin cigueña.
>
> Pero el Japón no tiene más que un niño
> y mis ojos aún sueñan bajo la luna.
> Cuando se seque el viento entre las flores,
> así terminaré mi olvido.

Again, as in the second stanza, there are two strands of thought. One describes the reality facing the protagonist. The other is hypothetical. It deals with what might happen if certain things took place. Analysis of the 'hypothetical' material contained in these lines together with that of the reference to the mysterious child-figure, will be postponed until the reality, the actual problem facing him, has been fully established. Unless this is done, then the relevance of the new developments contained in *Cuerpo perseguido* and later books will be less obvious.

The third stanza of the poem, then, depicts the central figure sighing in the night, the branches hanging limply about him in the darkness. Cernuda, like Prados, found no comfort in those branches which sang 'en el aire dormido'.[13] Here is the reality of Prados's situation. It has not changed from the one observed in *Tiempo*. The reader has already made the acquaintance of this semi-conscious, listless figure in 'Noche en urna', where he was described as 'Cuerpo en pena del alma, una sombra en el muelle'. His nocturnal activities also reflect those of the 'yo' of the *Cuerpo perseguido* poem: they lead to sighing, to the oppressive awareness of the nature of his body, that it is similar to that of the moon. Indeed in the last stanza he states openly: 'mis ojos aún sueñan bajo la luna'.

That this is the case in 'Yo me he perdido . . .' is confirmed by the line: 'cuando las ramas se adormecen como banderas'. The night is characterised, as it was in *Tiempo*, by the removal of the fertilising wind. Where there should be life, there is an absence of movement. It is for this reason that the infertile 'piel' of the central figure causes him such discomfort.

He moves on to explain what would happen if a 'stone' were to fall on his eyes. His situation would be radically altered: 'Yo subiría del agua sin palomas.' He would be rescued from the 'agua sin palomas'. Here, again, the symbolism of the water and the dove is helpful. Water, which 'gives birth' to the day and to the sun has always been inseparable from life, fertility. Lorca writes in *Otras canciones*:

> Y la canción del agua
> es una cosa eterna.
>
> . . . .
>
> Es el amor que corre
> todo manso y divino,
> es la vida del mundo,
> la historia de su alma.[14]

References to doves in other Prados poems align them with fulfilling contact with the 'tú':

tu mano y la mía en el alba . . .
¡Qué limpias sueñan!
¡Qué blancas,
juntas por el cielo vuelan
como palomas! (95:I,336)

Thus the dove, an established erotic symbol, is seen in the context of flight, equivalent in the dream, according to Freud, to the sexual act. The point the protagonist is making is a simple one: the reality is that at the time of writing the poem he is without the kind of life that the symbol of the dove suggests.

There is one more reference to the problems facing the 'yo'. The first two lines of the final stanza provide a telling insight into his predicament:

Pero el Japón no tiene más que un niño
y mis ojos aún sueñan bajo la luna.

The reference to Japan is unique in *Antología*. It is, however, closely linked with the sun: it is known as the land of the rising sun. The problem is that the 'yo' feels himself to be far more akin to the moon than the sun. The only chance he had of becoming fertile is for him to become more like the sun. But instead of feeling at home with 'Japan's child' he finds himself reluctantly drawn towards the moon. He is re-stating the argument of the third stanza. He longs, like Lorca in 'Cantos nuevos', for an experience free from the moon's interference:

Yo tengo sed de aromas y de risas,
sed de cantares nuevos
sin lunas y sin lirios,
y sin amores muertos.[15]

Several poems in *Cuerpo perseguido* illustrate the impossibility of such happiness, at least while the protagonist is awake. Before returning to 'Yo me he perdido . . .', to the positive statements it makes about ways out of the difficulty, these poems will be examined. Before discussing the quest for the 'piedra' embarked on from the very outset of the anthology selection the problems this quest is meant to solve must be exactly established. The theme of impotence in poems other than 'Yo me he perdido . . .' will be dealt with first. Attention will subsequently be drawn to difficulties associated less directly with the sense of sexual inadequacy which has so distressed the protagonist.

'Bosque de la noche', from the *Memoria de poesía* group, provides further information about the 'suspiro' mentioned in 'Yo me he perdido . . .'. In Chapter 1 the 'yo' was seen to use the symbol of the boat as an expression of the body: the boat's immobility signified his inability to respond physically in the presence of normal stimuli. In 'Bosque de la noche' this disappointing response is not described in terms of the boat, as it was in *Tiempo*, but rather in terms of the natural world. The common feature of such poetry is the motif of immobility, stagnation—a motif inseparable here from feelings of impotence and frustration.

Examination of the poem justifies such statements. Again, reference to other poems sheds light on the experiences represented by certain words. Its central image is the 'manzana de ébano'. A similar expression appears in an early version of *El misterio del agua*, to be found in *Caja* 2.3:

La manzana está negra.
¡Córtala!

Tiene vida en el hueso.
¡Ábrela!
¿Y la culebra?

—Arriba,
en la frente del agua . . .

(Quedó dormido el ojo
desangrándose en sombras
en la mano del alma.) (I:381)

The presence of the adder, as well as the shrill commands of the second and fourth lines, confirm the sinister tone of the title: 'Maldición de la noche'. And in amongst these darker elements is the 'manzana negra', the 'manzana de ébano' of 'Bosque de la noche'. In itself this is enough to cast doubt on Debicki's view of the poem, in which he sees: 'una unión . . . armoniosa entre el hombre y el mundo', and an attempt to show that the human and natural levels are 'intercambiables'.[16]

It is not enough, however, simply to say that the poem is related to an unhappy experience. It includes indications of why the protagonist is unsettled during the night. Each of the four stanzas contains a similar message, arrived at through different permutations of key-words in Prados's private language. It is the 'mirada' that is of central importance. It denotes the presence of the protagonist. It indicates the direction in which his thoughts are moving. In the first stanza they are directed towards the wind:

Se alzó,—manzana de ébano—,
la mirada en el viento
y se quedó en el alma
meciéndose en su rama. (58:I,242)

A simplification of the content might read: 'se alzó la mirada en el viento y se quedó en el alma'. The 'mirada' can be drawn initially (as it is in the remaining stanzas) to the level of the soul or to that of the body (represented, as it has been so far, by the wind and the water). Here it is on the level of the body that the protagonist wishes to exist. But he meets with failure. The resulting experience is one of frustration—the unwelcome 'manzana de ébano'.

In the second stanza he is drawn initially to the level of the soul. But the result is non-activity: the 'mirada' is left to rock gently in the water:

Se alzó—manzana de ébano—
el alma sobre el viento
y quedó la mirada
meciéndose en el agua.

He is forced to return to the physical level where, as *Tiempo* showed, any real progress is impossible.[17]

Even when the water and the wind come together, as they do in the third stanza, the result is unsatisfactory:

Se alzó—manzana de ébano—
el agua sobre el viento
y se quedó en el alma
mecida en su mirada.

The conjunction of the water and the wind represents the most promising possibilities in the realm of physical fertility. But it is a situation which amounts to ineffectual narcissistic contemplation rather than contact with the 'tú'.

The fourth stanza demonstrates how much more easily the central figure can operate on the level of the intellect than of the body, suggested here by allusion to the wind:

Se alzó—manzana de ébano—
el alma en la mirada
y se quedó en el viento
meciéndose en su rama . . .

The fertility he knows on a spiritual or intellectual plane is impossible to reproduce on the physical plane. None of the variations of 'alma / viento / agua' produces anything more than the 'manzana de ébano', the 'maldición de la noche'.

The sum-total of the poem is non-progression and frustration on all sides. His enjoyment of the ability of his mind and soul is marred by the realisation that what the wind and the water represent is out of reach. The overall structure of the poem is further evidence of this. Far from conveying the sense of harmony Debicki sees, it is intentionally fragmented and unresolved. The four combinations of the same key-words stubbornly refuse to organise themselves into any recognisable pattern. This can best be illustrated by contrast with a poem which seems to bear some resemblance of form to 'Bosque de la noche':

Llegó desnudo el viento
a mirarse en el agua.

Iba desnuda el agua
a mirarse en el cielo.

Bajó desnudo el cielo
a mirarse en el viento . . .

Quedó hueca la noche,
redonda de misterio. (77:I,332)

The resemblance is superficial. The satisfying circular pattern of the first three stanzas quoted, together with the wholeness and order suggested by the adjective 'redonda', have no counterpart in the *Memoria de poesía* poem. Like the central figure in Cernuda's 'El viento y el alma', the protagonist of 'Bosque de la noche' is apart from the fertility enjoyed by the natural world. Of the wind Cernuda writes:

. . . sus sones
Elementales contagian
El silencio de la noche.

Solo en tu cama le escuchas
Insistente en los cristales
Tocar, llorando y llamando
Como perdido sin nadie.[18]

The wind is insistent, seeking respite: but the central figure remains alone. For the 'yo' of *Memoria de poesía*, too, the night is a labyrinth of confused, restless and frustrating experience.

Not all the problems of *Cuerpo perseguido* and *Memoria de poesía* relate to frustration and impotence, at least in such a direct way. The poem 'Quisiera estar por donde anduve' explains some of the factors which make him dissatisfied with his present condition and which spur him on in the quest for the 'piedra' which will be dealt with in the next section of the chapter.

Two main points emerge from the poem. The first is that in some way or another the central figure wishes to return to a state which is no longer his:

> Quisiera estar por donde anduve
> como la rama, como el cuerpo;
> como en el sueño, como por la vida;
> igual que sin la frente, sin la sombra;
> como en mis labios, como en el aire,
> donde no sé si estuve o voy a estar o estoy
> o el árbol me ha traído,
> como no sé si soy o voy a ser o quizá sea
> o todo es como el cielo. (70:1,269)

Here, then, is one way that the central figure has developed which has proved unsatisfactory. Far from showing, as Debicki suggests, the 'compenetración de los mundos natural y humano', these lines reveal that, as far as the 'yo' is concerned, the inter-relationship of his own life and that of the world around him has broken down.[19] Fellowship between the two has been disrupted.

In investigating this unwelcome development it is interesting to refer to comments made by Prados on his poetry of this era, and to the important contemporary prose poems, *Las tres noches del hombre*. In these prose poems the state of harmony sought in 'Quisiera estar . . .' finds a close parallel. The *Cuerpo perseguido* poem sets out the protagonist's longing for a time when he was unaware of any distinction between his body and the fertile 'bodies' of natural objects around him. It was a time when the branch of a tree and the tree of his own body were not distinct in character; when his hand shared the same qualities as the life-filled water; when his lips were in some sense like the air, free to enjoy contact with the objects of its love. In *Las tres noches del hombre* this condition is one enjoyed by the child: 'Mira [el niño] hacia los cuerpos que le rodean y siente la compañía y el calor de ellos'.[20] The problem facing the central figure of *Cuerpo perseguido* is, in part, that he has left the world of childhood. Adolescence, with the inevitable insurgence of desire and intense consciousness of the body, put a stop to the fellowship with the natural world enjoyed in infancy. As *Tiempo* suggests, what the protagonist learnt about the tendencies of his own body would be enough to make him feel isolated from the rest of the natural world.

The significance of Prados's comments on the closely related *Memoria de poesía* is obvious:

> Salvados fuera y dentro de mí por su batalla estos fragmentos fronterizos de mi adolescencia, luz y muerte, hoy se encuentran acaso materiales dislocados sin orden, buscando un equilibrio que no han tenido, ni tendrán, ni llevan. (I,233)

The barrier which has arisen and which is vaguely mentioned in 'Quisiera estar . . .' is one which was erected in or after adolescence. It was only with adolescence that he came to appreciate any discrepancy between reality and desire.

The definition of the problems of the protagonist in terms of the process of 'growing up' represents a filling out of information provided in *Tiempo*, and opens the way for important developments in later poetry, including the search for the lost garden of childhood. This grieving for something which he once had is related to the second main point of 'Quisiera estar por donde anduve'. He writes:

> Quisiera hallar mi ley,
> igual que hallo mi oficio como el aire,
> igual que mi blancura,
> como una luz, como una herida,
> lo mismo que un cansancio igual que un ángel. (71:I,269)

The settled disposition of childhood has given way to a situation in which he feels he is without a 'ley'. There is a fundamental questioning of the most elementary truths about himself, giving rise to doubts and insecurities which litter *Cuerpo perseguido*. Before describing his search for a way of escape, the exact nature of these difficulties, hardly apparent in *Tiempo*, must be discussed.

Some of the lines quoted already have drawn attention to the fact that the protagonist has an extremely unusual way of looking at himself. In the opening poem, he considers the effect the 'piedra' would have on him. If it were to fall on his eyes, then:

> Yo subiría del fondo de mi frente
> hasta habitar mi cuerpo como un ídolo:
> hasta brotar en medio de mi carne
> otra vez sobre el mundo sin cigueña. (69:I,279)

It is the way in which he seems to see himself as being made up of two quite distinct parts which arouses curiosity here. On the one hand there is the 'frente'. This is the habitual abode of the 'yo'—he would rise 'del fondo de mi frente', where he apparently is at the moment of writing. On the other hand there is his body, 'mi carne'. His 'flesh' appears here to be only potentially the dwelling place of the 'yo'—and at the time of writing these words he is entirely separate from it.

In *Cuerpo perseguido* it is this attitude to the body which prevails. Often the protagonist's body (and, sometimes, that of the 'tú') is unwilling or unable to act in concert with the central figure's wishes. He seems to be a mere observer of what happens to it. Some poems find him unsure of whether he owns his body at all:

Yo no sé si esta mano
que ahora va por mi frente
como una esponja en la memoria,
va por mí y es mi mano
o está cruzando el cielo
o va por los espejos
sin fuerza ni albedrío. (71:I,272)

At times it is as if the body belonged to somebody else. In 'Recuerdo' he comments:

Como un barco, mi carne
flotaba por la música.
El silencio, en mi espalda
clavó sus largas plumas . . . (85:I,331)

Parts of the body are described as 'floating' or 'hanging', outside his control:

Mi cabeza y el viento
cuelgan bajo el insomnio . . .

Igual que un cirio el mundo
te busca por mi frente.

Sin cabeza mi cuerpo
vuela por la luna . . . (105:I,328)

He is even able to talk in terms of leaving the body behind, of 'abandoning' it, as he does in the *Memoria de poesía* section of *Memoria del olvido* as it appeared in 1940:

Abandoné la forma de mi cuerpo;
la carne de mi hastío . . .
. . . .
Quedé como un fantasma hueco
. . . . (II,265)

Lest these be thought random examples, and since this is a development of some significance, further material relating to this phenomenon will be quoted. It is taken from a series of 'retratos'. These prose-poems are roughly contemporary with the poetry of *Cuerpo perseguido* and, interestingly enough, a little earlier than the similar 'textos oníricos' contained in Hinojosa's *La flor de California* (1928) and the more straightforward prose poems included in Aleixandre's *Pasión de la tierra* (1928–9).[21]

In the following example the body of the central figure is dead. But in this most unusual composition the life of the being whose body it was continues unabated. There is a total absence of reference to the 'alma' which might accompany any possible platonic division into body and soul. Rather is it the 'yo' (or in this case the 'él') that is living on:

> No estaba muerto como todos creían, aunque ya todo el río le había cruzado el pecho; . . . Pero había comenzado a sepultarse, porque ya olía; porque ya no se reconocía él mismo en los espejos.
>
> Un día al levantarse se olvidó de su piel, dormida entre las sábanas. Ya de vuelta, a la tarde trajo colgando de sus hombros, como milagros de cartón, un árbol, cuatro barcos, un cuchillo, la luna, dos escapularios, tres niños, una piedra, y luego en su cuarto comenzó a podrirse despacio por las sienes.[22]

The example which follows illustrates the central figure's indifference to his body's fate, his impatient and entirely objective appraisal of it. The first sentence gives the impression that he regrets that he is 'burying himself'. It is as if the loss of the body disturbed him. But in fact what he regrets is the 'burying' of the 'real me' in the 'carne tan negra':

> Lo que a mí me pesa es que me estoy sepultando. Eso es, que me voy hundiendo. Y en qué carne tan negra; en qué cartón tan duro. El rostro, arriba, se niega, tendido de perfil, plano, como una luna redonda de yeso. ¡Qué trabajo tan fuerte!
>
> Me estoy sepultando como raíces, como cabellos en el agua, como orugas. Y me sepulto tembloroso, eléctrico, sonámbulo, deshilachado, colgando en hebras negras desde el rostro, parado terco en la

corteza. Desde este rostro pegado arriba al fondo, como un plato vacío o como una charca de cera en la memoria.

A mí no me importa podrirme; por eso estoy vivo. Pero mi rostro que siempre fue un horario en síntesis no quiere descomponer en sus cinco sentidos. Por eso se sostiene intacto en su negación sorda, sin podrirse, sin querer pasar a mejor vida, quedándose quieto en lo alto, muerto, de perfil como una enorme moneda de yeso.[23]

The face is putting up a struggle against the putrefaction which threatens it: but it receives scant support from the 'yo', who is wholly indifferent to the fate of the body.

Such is its unreality that the body comes to take on the nature of glass. One 'retrato' contains this sentence: 'Me quedé tendido como un hueso de cristal blando, mate, flotando quieto en el aire enrarecido y tibio de la habitación'. And another passage describes the body in a similar way:

> Pasé mi brazo por debajo de mi cuerpo como para cerciorarme que terminaba dentro de mi sangre, pero no pude hallar el límite de mi piel ni pude tampoco palpar la superficie del lecho sobre el que yo me creía estar recostado. Intenté abrir los ojos pero fue inútil todo esfuerzo. Volví a pasar una vez y otra mi brazo por debajo de mi espalda pero todo en vano: mi cuerpo había huído, quizá se había quedado muerto sin sentido; pero mi pensamiento todavía se encontraba allí sobre el aire, inmóvil, intangible, flotando, como una nube, como un huso olvidado en el vacío.

The 'pensamiento' again predominates, unharmed in the face of the mixed fortunes which befall the body. In every case—and perhaps not surprisingly in view of what we know of the central figure's body—it is with the mind that the 'yo' identifies himself.

It is important to emphasise here that this appraisal of himself by the central figure does not belong to the realm of poetic contrivance. Indeed in order to appreciate such experiences it is useful, while being careful to avoid any ill-informed 'psycho-analysis' of the central figure, to relate them to evidence of similar phenomena in the outside world. R. D. Laing's book, *The Divided Self*, though it deals chiefly with schizophrenia, is at pains to show that symptoms of the schizophrenic condition exist in people whom one might describe as 'normal'. They manifest themselves in a way of experiencing reality which differs from that of the majority. The 'normal' person is, Laing claims, 'ontologically secure'. He is confident he exists and that there is a realness in the world about him. The 'ontologically insecure' person enjoys no such confidence.

The relevance of this distinction to the definition of the protagonist's problems may be judged by citing some of the descriptions he gives of his 'unreal man'. It has already been noted that the 'yo' sees himself in terms of glass, describing himself as 'hueco'—like Eliot's 'hollow' men or indeed Alberti's 'hombre hueco'. The implication is that he could be easily broken, that he is like a mirror which a word from the 'tú' would shatter and send him hurtling downwards 'hasta quebrarme contra al primer suelo'.[24] Laing writes of his subject:

> . . . a schizophrenic may say that he is made of glass, of such transparency and fragility that a look directed at him splinters him into bits and penetrates straight through him.[25]

The characteristic separation of the 'yo' or the 'real' self from the body, mentioned in earlier examples, is a further mark of the 'unreal' or 'ontologically insecure' person:

> He may feel more insubstantial than substantial, and unable to assume that the stuff he is made of is genuine, good, valuable. And he may feel his self as partially divorced from his body.[26]
>
> [Some] . . . persons do not seem to have a sense of that basic unity which can abide through the most intense conflicts with oneself, but seem rather to have come to experience themselves as primarily split into a mind and a body. Usually they feel most closely identified with the 'mind'.[27]

Such parallels, in conjunction with the evidence of the continued weaknesses described at the beginning of the chapter, hardly suggest that the protagonist is, as Blanco suggests, 'vibrante a la presencia de lo concreto'. Nor can the nature of the doubts expressed in the poetry be ascribed to the body-soul dualism which he sees there, conflicts which he claims arise because of:

> . . . su pasión de presencias y su amor a lo ausente, la memoria y el olvido, la luz y la sombra, su ilimitada capacidad de entrega y su incontrolable tendencia a huir a un sueño sólo suyo que pretendía imponerse a todo lo ajeno a sí; . . .[28]

This evidence, then, suggests that the protagonist is not involved simply in a struggle between 'cuerpo' and 'alma' which is troublesome because the desires of the flesh are so strong that they stand in the way of the satisfaction of higher appetites. Rather is there an anguished questioning of the nature of a body which seems only accidentally to belong to him, and, consequently, a questioning of the reality around him. The contrast with Guillén is again pointed. Few modern poets could have experienced such a degree of 'ontological security':

> Duden con elegancia los más sabios.
> Yo, no. ¡Yo sé muy poco!
> Por el mundo asistido,
> Me sé, me siento a mí sobre esta hierba
> tan solícitamente dirigida.
> ¡Jornalero real!
> También de mi jornada jornalero,
> Voy pisando evidencias,
> Verdores.[29]

Such a happy and unquestioning acceptance of experience is, at this stage at least, totally foreign to the central figure of *Cuerpo perseguido*.

The quest

Before analysing in more detail poems from the main body of the book it is worth defining the sense of quest, of searching for an answer to the questions raised by his own unusual nature. To do this 'Yo me he perdido . . .' must be re-examined.

There the protagonist points to one factor which would entirely re-shape his view of himself and of his world. He is in search of a mysterious stone:

> Cuando mi rostro suspira bajo la noche,
> cuando las ramas se adormecen como banderas,
> si cayera una piedra sobre mis ojos
> yo subiría del agua sin palomas. (69:I,279)

Ostensibly, at least, the quest for this 'piedra' is central to *Cuerpo perseguido*. In the *Antología* arrangement its discovery is an important feature of the climactic final poem:

> ¡La Noche! . . .
> (¿Es que tu carne . . .)
> ¡Silencio! . . .
> (¿Acaso el Aire . . .)
> ¡La Luz!
> ¡La Piedra! (115:I,275)

That this stone has to do with a search for identity is confirmed by the sequence referred to above, *Las tres noches del hombre*. These prose poems describe the development of the individual along the path toward knowledge, that is, a point where everthing 'se ha transformado por el amor, por entrega, y no hay muerte . . .'[30] These 'nights' are infancy, adolescence and mature adulthood. Though these writings contain many interesting features, the role of the stone in them is particularly relevant. For it is the stone to which the child looks to see the kind of all-embracing knowledge mentioned above:

> Y es el rocío el que le habla de su fábula, y hoy, llena el hueco del nombre grabado en la piedra ante la que se encuentra el muchacho.

The child is drawn by 'un nombre que fue tallado en la piedra '. It acts as the furnisher of the kind of information that most individuals take for granted. It directs the 'impulso amoroso' towards the 'nombre de mujer'. And it provides him with information about his body, for during childhood his is a 'cuerpo en noche oscura, puesto que de él nada sabe'. The knowledge of what the stone has to say also means, finally, that the central figure has found what 'los juegos y el milagro' of the 'Noche en urna' lacked, 'la polar de algún nombre que oriente sus verdades . . .' (16). At the close of 'Tres noches' Prados writes:

> Canta la esperanza desde la piedra blanca . . .
> El hombre mira a su alrededor. No hay límites. Vive el espacio infinito en el cual todo lo ama . . .
> Todas las cosas son su esencia viva eterna.

Of course, the contexts of these prose poems and *Cuerpo perseguido* are different: the terminology is different. But at the same time they do establish a clear link between the stone and a search for information about oneself and one's position in the universe. They also align such a search with an interest in the nature and development of the body and the individual's interest in it.[31]

The character of this quest is further indicated by the kind of things which the presence of its symbol, the stone, effects. The third and fourth stanzas of 'Yo me he perdido . . .' take up this theme:

> yo subiría del agua sin palomas.
>
> Yo subiría del fondo de mi frente
> hasta habitar mi cuerpo como un ídolo:
> hasta brotar en medio de mi carne
> otra vez sobre el mundo sin cigueña.

These lines suggest that the search is for something to rescue him from the sterility represented by the 'agua sin palomas'. It is also a search for the answer to the curious way in which he experiences himself. If he could find the stone then the 'yo' and the 'cuerpo' would not longer function separately: he could come to exist 'en medio de mi carne'.

The poem contains an acknowledgement that such an answer lies, potentially, within him. He could be like other people:

> . . . hay un niño que cuelga de mis ojos
> nivelando mi sueño como el mundo.

The possibility exists that he might come to know a fertility which would make him 'como el mundo'. What the 'child' is will be examined later in the chapter. For the moment it is best understood as a symbol of fertility the 'yo' experiences in the dream—far more in fact than what Blanco calls the '—inocencia natural del poeta, esperanza siempre *abierta*—, esta capacidad de asombro y de entrega de Prados . . .'.[32] With but little modification a parallel can be drawn between this sense of quest and the condition of the 'divided self' as described by Laing:

> If the patient contrasts his own emptiness, worthlessness, coldness, desolation, dryness with the abundance, worth, warmth, companionship that he may yet believe to be elsewhere (a belief which often grows to fantastically idealized proportions, uncorrected as it is by any direct experience), there is evoked a welter of conflicting emotions, from a desperate longing and yearning for what others have and he lacks, to frantic envy and hatred of all that is theirs and not his, or a desire to destroy all the goodness, freshness, richness in the world.
>
> This emptiness, this sense of inner lack of richness, substantiality and value . . . is a powerful prompter to make "contact" with reality. The soul or self thus desolate and arid longs to be refreshed and fertilized, but longs not simply for a relationship between separable things, but to be completely drenched and suffused by the other.[33]

In the case of our protagonist there is not as yet the 'frantic envy' or the 'desire to destroy' Laing mentions. These are to come to light in later developments. But other features are recognisable. *Cuerpo perseguido* records a search for a relationship with the other or the 'tú'. How this search is carried out must now be discussed.

The memory of oblivion

The poetry of *Cuerpo perseguido* has already been described as a quest. *Memoria del olvido*, the title given to the 1940 version of these poems, and to the first section of *Cuerpo perseguido*, also provides us with a useful approach to poetry of the period. For the 'olvido' is the starting-point for much of the experience described here.

It is a starting-point in both the senses in which it is used in *Cuerpo perseguido*. For the word can be understood in two ways. The first is related to what the protagonist sees as his normal condition, outside sleep. It is a state of ignorance—the state of the child and the adolescent in *Las tres noches del hombre*. *Memoria del olvido* contains these interesting lines:

> Hoy mis ojos se niegan
> a su oscuro trabajo
> por tierras de silencio.
> Mis dos miradas vivas
> trato de libertar
> de su prisión letárgica de olvido.[34]

'Olvido' is the imprisoning reality experienced when his eyes refuse to help with the 'dark' work of the dream.

Las tres noches del hombre contains an important reference to this oblivion. Prados writes there that in the third night of man he emerges from the confusion and uncertainty of adolescence into manhood. This is how the process is described: '. . . sale del olvido (noche oscura en que estaba).' 'Olvido', then, has a connotation of ignorance—hence the pejorative reference to it in the *Memoria del olvido* poem.[35] Certainly it has little to do with the everyday idea of 'forgetting' which Xirau mentions: 'El recuerdo del olvido puede ser temor a que el olvido nos constituya y puede ser también revelación que lo olvidado sea lo verdaderamente real'.[36] Rather is it a reference to the doubts and insecurities which the central figure feels about himself. The poetry is, then, in this first sense, the memory of this condition.

Secondly, 'olvido' is to be equated with the protagonist's self-confessed delight in escapism. The first lines of the *Antología* selection from *Memoria del olvido* confirm such a view and suggest what it is that he is escaping from. He is happy when 'mi cuerpo vuela y ondula'. Only when the irksome body has been dealt with can he feel that he exists. In itself it is negative and, as Xirau points out, 'una imagen de este olvido que es el dejar de ser'.

That this process of 'olvido' is part of a deliberate policy is clear from the poem placed second in the anthology's *Cuerpo perseguido*. It is an elaboration of the opening lines of 'Yo me he perdido . . .'. Sleep and the dream shut out the body: the world—and reminders of normality—are excluded:

> Cerré mi puerta al mundo;
> se me perdió la carne por el sueño . . . (70:I,270)

Exactly the same process was recorded in these lines already quoted from *Memoria del olvido*:

> Abandoné la forma de mi cuerpo,
> la carne de mi hastío.
> Por el fiel de mis ojos,
> corté en dos la balanza
> que me sostuvo en pie como hombre vivo.
>
> Quedé como un fantasma hueco
> —en pena de equilibrio—;
> como el traje de un sueño,
> en la corteza de mi propio abismo.[37]

There is a complete rejection of the oppression *Tiempo* describes. The quotation from *Memoria del olvido* emphasises the extent to which he resents his body, the 'carne de mi hastío', and seeks to see himself apart from it. In 'abandoning' the body he feels he is correcting the false impression that he is 'como hombre vivo'. He is in the same situation as Laing's subject:

> The body is felt more as one object among other objects in the world rather than as the core of the individual's own being. Instead of being the core of his true self, the body is felt as the core of a false self, which a detached, disembodied, "inner" self looks at with tenderness, amusement, or hatred as the case may be.[38]

But, as the poems following 'Cerré mi puerta . . .' in *Antología* indicate, this negative 'olvido' can be productive. Although it is artificial and unreal, it is also liberating. It is the 'olvido' where Cernuda envisages himself as being 'libre . . . / Disuelto en niebla, ausencia, / Ausencia leve como carne de niño . . .', 'Donde el deseo no exista.'.[39] It is the context for all the dream experience recorded in *Cuerpo perseguido*. The poetry is a record of what emerges from this deliberate elimination of the level of the body and the intense introspection which results.

The emergence of the dream

It is against this background of 'olvido' that the dream comes to assume great importance in *Cuerpo perseguido*. Only when its influence and role in the narrative of many of the poems is recognised does any coherent pattern formulate.

Changes in the protagonist's attitude to the time of day indicate the extent of this new dependence on the dream. The 'sueño' of *Tiempo*, experienced at dawn and evening, was a release from the body. It was an intense but short-lived experience. Day and night were marked by an illusory 'ensueño' or an equally undesirable insomnia. In *Memoria de poesía* and *Cuerpo perseguido* attention is shifted entirely to the night where he is likely to enjoy uninterrupted the life of the dream.

The dawn, for example, is no longer a haven. The poem 'Alba rápida' demonstrates that the arrival of the dawn constitutes a threat. It means the end of escape from the realm of the body: and it issues a direct challenge to what the 'yo' calls his 'reino', the night:

¡Pronto, de prisa, mi reino,
que se me escapa, que huye,
que se me va por la fuentes!
. . . .

¡Ya se le tronchan las fuentes!
¡Ay, limpias yeguas del aire!
¡Ay, banderas de mi frente!
¡Qué galopar en mis ojos!

Ligero, el mundo amanece . . . (78–9:I,326)

The 'world', the physical reality, represented by the erotic symbols of the flag and the horses, returns to plague him.

The night no longer presents the threat it once did. The transition from evening to night is anticipated with a degree of happy expectancy:

¡Qué grande sobre el viento se reparte
la noche ya segura de su palma!
¡Qué pura luz la anima a su viaje! . . .
¡Mi sangre es el caudal que la levanta! (57:I,249)

The same poem, 'Tránsito' in *Poesías completas,* 'Signo de la luz' in *Antología*, provides the explanation for this shift of emphasis. The insomnia which afflicted him has gone. He is able to sleep during the night:

¡Cómo en su nueva forma deseada
—en blando cristal hueco adormecido—
flotando sobre el cielo transparente,
halla mi sueño lecho en el crepúsculo!

This is the earliest intimation of the main method which the 'yo' will adopt to satisfy his quest for fertility and relationship. The night, then, while still posing problems in the absence of sleep, is the mine in which he will dig for the treasure of the dream.

'Enero 10' further establishes the link between the night and the dream which such sleep affords:

Se está quedando la noche
sin carne, temblando viva
como un ojo.
. . . .

¡Qué oscura yema de sueños
engendra con su agonía!
¡Qué alta fruta de milagros
deja en el cielo prendida,
como flor de oro y de sombras
por limpios vidrios cautiva! (83:I,290)

None of the experiences recorded in the poetry of these years can be properly understood without reference to the presence and absence of sleep and, within sleep, the presence or absence of the dream. The exploration of the world of the dream comes to assume tremendous importance.[40]

The nature and function of the dream

The main advantage of the dream to the 'yo' is that it provides him with an entirely different setting and perspective from those of waking life. This is the basis of 'Cerré mi puerta . . .'. It follows on naturally from the closing lines of 'Yo me he perdido . . .'. There the wind and flowers were reminders of the external world and of an elusive fertility. 'Cerré mi puerta . . .' records the central figure's instinctive reaction: to retire into a private world. Through 'sueño' he cuts himself off from the message of the flowers and the wind. The body is set on one side:

Cerré mi puerta al mundo;
se me perdió la carne por el sueño . . .
Me quedé interno, mágico, invisible,
desnudo como un ciego. (70:I,270)

This is the escapist 'olvido' referred to earlier. It is a means of realising the position which he has always felt himself to be in, even in waking life: the 'real' me, the mind, thought, assumes complete control. It is 'lo interno' rather than 'lo externo' that counts.

The comparison with the blind man is a telling one in this respect. The blind man is naked in the sense that he cannot see the clothes he wears. When the 'yo' sleeps he too becomes 'blind', he cannot see. But the clothing of which he is no longer aware is the 'unreal' body beneath which his 'real' self lies hidden. Thanks to the mental process recorded in the poem, the only reality is the 'carne del alma' of 'Fuentes del bautismo' (66). He has worked a kind of magic which defeats the laws normally governing his experience.

As a result he experiences a fulness and an illumination which compensate for the old feelings of inner emptiness and death:

Lleno hasta el mismo borde de mis ojos
me iluminé por dentro.

Trémulo, transparente,
me quedé sobre el viento,
igual que un vaso limpio
de agua pura,
como un ángel de vidrio
en un espejo. (70:I,270)

The reference to 'illumination' hints at the hopes the protagonist has for the dream. It is in the dream that he seeks to find the answers to problems outlined earlier—answers which will come when the protagonist turns in upon himself, 'por dentro'.

This withdrawal from everyday life again finds its parallel in Laing's research. It has been established that escape into sleep and the dream is a means of allowing the central figure to shed the 'unreal' level of the body. Laing comments:

> If the individual cannot take the realness, aliveness, autonomy and identity of himself and others for granted, then he has to become absorbed in contriving ways of trying to be real, of keeping himself or others alive, or preserving his identity, in efforts, as he will often put it, to prevent himself losing his self.[41]

This is the grounds for the protagonist's justification of the dream. He admits that he is a 'romántico de huídas'. But without such activities he would be as unreal as an immobile statue or a phantom:

> yo sé que soy romántico de huídas;
> que sueño porque un sueño es mi figura,
> pero si persiguiera yo a mi ausencia
> y a descansar saliera de otra hechura:
> inmóvil me hallaría en pie en mi cuerpo,
> como un fantasma mío de mi fuga. (74:I,313)

The pursuit of the dream, therefore, becomes the reality.

His description of himself in the second and third stanzas of 'Cerré mi puerta . . .' is full of interest. The use of the word 'trémulo' suggests something of that equilibrium that has always marked the presence or imminence of the dream. 'Transparente', the references to glass (the 'ángel de vidrio' and the mirror) are reminders of that sense of fragility and vulnerability that Laing noted as typical of the schizoid personality.

It might seem strange that this sense of fragility is not lost in the process of 'interiorization'. It might also seem puzzling that in these early stages he proceeds to compare himself with images of sterility and insubstantiality. The water is pure and invisible; the glass clean and invisible; the angel, by its very nature asexual, is made even more incorporeal by the reference to the glass and the mirror. In the dream he seems, deliberately and voluntarily, to be adopting the very position he has so resented.

The logic of such a step again becomes apparent on referring to Laing:

> It seems to be a general law that at some point these very dangers most dreaded can themselves be encompassed to forestall their actual occurrence. Thus, to forgo one's autonomy becomes the means of secretly preserving it; to play possum, to feign death, becomes a means of preserving one's aliveness . . .[42]

The protagonist has turned in on himself completely. Such introspection is as much a defence-mechanism as a way forward to whatever the 'inner' world may bring. By voluntarily anticipating the criticisms levelled at him that he is barren, unusual, infertile (and it would appear from later poetry that such criticisms were made) he seeks to free himself of the stigma which attaches to him. He is removing himself from the line of fire.

An incidental consequence of this is that he is moving towards a world which is increasingly esoteric and inaccessible. In the words of C. B. Morris, he is becoming 'the pivot of his own poetic activity'.[43] The following lines, taken from Caja 19.2, confirm this tendency:

> Amarrado en el centro de mi sangre
> prendido estoy, sujeto a mis entrañas.
> Cautivo, sin moverme, vivo en ellas,
> más ausente de mí por estar quieto.
>
> Cierro mis ojos por sentirme vivo.
> . . . .
>
> El mundo, fuera está. Cierro mis ojos.

A comparison with Guillén shows how isolating and escapist this process is. For Guillén the dream is an extension of waking life and of enjoyment of the world outside him. 'La rendición al sueño' describes the experience of the central *persona* as he falls asleep:

> Todo el cuerpo se sume,
> Con dulzura se sume entre las cosas.
> ¿No ser? Estar, estar profundamente,
> . . . .[44]

There is a deliberate rejection of the shifting and illusory world which the central figure of *Cuerpo perseguido* has embraced. Guillén writes, in staunchly anti-platonic fashion:

> No quiero soñar con fantasmas inútiles,
> No quiero caverna.
> Que el gran espacio sin luna
> Me aísle y defienda.[45]

In his isolated and insecure position, the central figure of 'Cerré mi puerta . . .' regards the real world about him as a liability. The dream world takes over as the 'reality'.

The positioning of 'Cerré mi puerta . . .' is of some significance. In both *Memoria del olvido* and *Cuerpo perseguido* it occupies second place. In the former it follows: 'Quisiera estar . . .', in the latter, 'Yo me he perdido . . .'. In both cases, and even though the arrangements differ widely in many respects, the poem succeeds outlines of the difficulties he faces. The narcissistic reaction it describes is the instinctive—and, at this stage in his development, usual—response to them. Later analysis will suggest that the 'tú', in the sense of a feminine figure apart from the 'yo', will have but a small part to play. Amidst his self-imposed isolation he can begin to regard himself without regret. To quote Cernuda again:

Se goza en sueño encantado,
Tras espacio infranqueable,
Su belleza irreparable
El Narciso enamorado.[46]

Furthermore, as the central figure becomes involved in this strange contact with himself, the need for that contact with the 'other' which he found impossible in *Tiempo* is obviated. Bachelard writes:

> L'image contemplée dans les eaux apparaît comme le contour d'une caresse toute visuelle. Elle n'a nul besoin de la main caressante . . . Rien ne subsiste de matériel dans cette image délicate et fragile. Narcisse retient son souffle:
>
> "Le moindre soupir
> Que j'exhalerais
> Me viendrait ravir
> Ce que j'adorais,
> . . . ."
>
> (Narcisse. Paul Valéry, *Mélanges*)[47]

The protagonist finds within the dream that he can be "lleno hasta el mismo borde de mis ojos'.

The 'sueño positivo'

In the previous chapter it was noted that the connotation of certain words seemed to be transformed when used in the context of the dream. 'Canción marinera' which appeared in Caja 2.2, is typical:

Mi barco va por el viento
sin pensar en su timón:
se pasa del mar al cielo.
Mi sombra se va por el suelo
colgada a mi corazón
y olvidada de mi cuerpo . . .
Del sueño se va al amor.

The boat, regarded in much of *Tiempo* as a symbol of the protagonist's fruitless body, has sailed from port to port in a vain attempt to find its true resting place. But the symbol of the boat is at times transferred from the physical realm. At the beginning of the poem it is in the sea: but 'se pasa del mar al cielo'. As it does, so the 'yo' is freed from the body and moves on to the dream and to love. His attention and energy are directed towards the life of the soul.

'Espejismos' (211:I,386) displayed a similar dualism. The central figure wants to know if the boat is to lie 'en el mar o en el alma'. Significantly from the point of view of *Cuerpo perseguido*, the third question posed was this: '¿Puerto del tiempo o del sueño?'. Time, like the sea, is the setting for unhappy, frustrating experience, the dream, its antithesis, is the setting for the productive life of the soul.

The outcome of 'Espejismos' is an unhappy one. The 'yo' is left in a chilling isolation. The boat is still a symbol of oppression. But there are other words which have this 'negative' connotation. A list of them would include: 'mundo', 'mar', 'barco', 'ancla', 'pez', 'luna', and 'ensueño'. Because they all relate to the level of the body they are regarded as being apart from the 'real' self. Other words, to do with the level of the 'alma', have a 'positive' connotation. They include 'cielo', 'pensamiento', 'balanza', 'árbol', 'sol' and 'sueño'. The experience of *Cuerpo perseguido*, limited as it is to the confines of the dream, means that words associated with 'negative', unwelcome experiences, are absorbed into the 'positive' realm of the dream, into his 'reino'.

The treatment of the 'negative' word, 'carne', is an example of this process. The word is used for the body in 'Fuentes de bautismo' (65:I,244). As far as the protagonist is concerned, the link between the sinfulness of the flesh and his own view of its undesirability is singularly appropriate. The poem explains how, just as the stain of sin is removed from the infant's soul by baptism (according to Catholic theology) so the bane of the 'real' 'yo', his body, is transferred to a realm controlled by the 'positive' 'alma':

Estamos en el agua:
¡en el sueño del alma!
¡en el alma del alma!
¡en la carne del alma!

Within this dream lies the new body, the 'carne del alma '.

A further example of this 'cuerpo vivo' has already been touched upon. It is contained in 'Signo de la luz'. In the course of the gentle descent into sleep, the memory or consciousness is transformed into what the protagonist calls a 'body':

¡Cómo se va saliendo por mi frente,
clara, serena, toda mi memoria
y, huyendo por el cielo derramada,
libre, su anhelo cambia en cuerpo vivo! . . . (57:I,249)

As he falls asleep he comes to experience what he desired when awake. This is the 'positive', inner, fertile life denied him in the presence of the physical body, which has been transformed into the 'cuerpo vivo' of the dream.

'Cuerpo' is used in a similar way in the middle stanza of 'Quisiera estar . . .' (70:I,269). The 'yo', faced with the discrepancy between what he is and what he would like to be, reacts by resorting to the 'huída' of the dream, represented as 'Signo de la luz' has shown, by 'sangre'. He comments:

El umbral de mi sangre
abierto está en mi sangre.
Ya sin cuerpo mi cuerpo
atraviesa mi cuerpo . . . (70–1:I,269)

The conscious awareness of the 'yo' gives way to another awareness, that of the dream. The 'body' he finds there is, like the 'cuerpo vivo' of the previous poem, alive and active. Within the dream he is able to assume those roles impossible to him outside it.

The 'pez', the unwelcome erotic symbol of *Tiempo*, undergoes the same transformation. It was the fish which mocked the sailor for his impotence and helplessness. But in 'Presencia inagotable', it has a different part to play. These fragmentary poems begin with a clear reference to the onset of sleep and to the adjustment of the sleeper to the preferred level, the 'presencia inagotable' of the dream, the soul:

El alma se ha dormido;
se ha perdido en el sueño . . .
Queda el hueco del alma,
velando sobre el agua. (75:I,343)

The salient feature of the cryptic narrative which follows is that the fish is now attracted to and adopted by the protagonist as he dreams:

Cuando se fue acercando
por ver el alma al agua,
el pez saltó del agua
y, cuando se fue el agua,
el pez siguió nadando
por el ojo hasta el alma.

The fish jumps from the water ('negativo') to the sky ('positivo'). The water disappears altogether and the way to the 'alma' level of the central observer of these nocturnal activities is clear. Because, then, of the dream, objects like the fish and the bird from *Canciones del farero*, blatant reminders of a fertility he did not possess, are no longer an embarrassment.

Coincident with the emergence of the dream is the re-alignment of a number of antitheses. This includes the platonic opposition of body and soul under which the protagonist has grouped the two halves of his 'divided self'. In some poems 'cuerpo' and 'alma' become synonymous. The subject of 'Nuevo nacimiento' (58) is the dream, by means of which he is 'born again' out of the despair of 'Bosque de la noche'. It takes place in the realm of the sky and in the presence of the bird (which is by now closer to a symbol of the higher 'spiritual' level than of the erotic as it was in the *Tiempo* period). As a result body and soul are reconciled. The 'image' of the dream belongs to neither and to both:

(La imagen se pasea,
dentro y fuera del alma,
dentro y fuera del cuerpo.)

The terms are no longer, as they were for example in 'Espejismos', antithetical. They are, in the presence of the dream, interchangeable.

Thus the relevance of the dream experience to the kind of problems outlined earlier in the chapter is obvious. The central figure regards himself as a 'divided' self. His body has been viewed as separate from the 'real' self. The dream is a way (even though it may be a trick) of overcoming the problem, of unifying what had before been disparate elements.

The relevance of the dream to the problem of infertility can be judged by reference to the image of the bird. Its presence in the dream testifies to the life and fertility he now finds there. There indeed is to be found Jiménez's 'semilla iluminada / de otro y más bello mundo'.[48] Jiménez writes in another poem:

Sé bien que soy tronco
del árbol de lo eterno.
Sé bien que las estrellas
con mi sangre alimento.

Que son pájaros míos
todos los claros sueños . . .[49]

Lorca uses the bird in connection with fertility in *Yerma*. This is how María describes the feeling of expecting a child:

María: ¿No has tenido nunca un pájaro vivo apretado en la mano?
Yerma: Sí.
María: Pues lo mismo . . ., pero por dentro de la sangre.[50]

The 'yo' of Prados's poetry has a similar experience. The image of the bird is to be found in several poems dealing with his emergence from the despair of the waking state. 'Nuevo ser' is an example of this. The 'yo', like María, has a bird within him:

(Un pájaro en mi pecho,
cruza abierto tu sangre.) (115:I,275)

Moments of happy contact between the 'tú' and the 'yo', where there is a suggestion of happiness and fulfilment, are regularly seen in terms of flight (though the exact nature of this contact with the 'tú' needs to be more carefully examined later):

¡Qué blanco
mechón de nieve, de voces,
de pulsos, de alas! . . .
. . . .

¡Qué quebrar de plumas
cruza la voz del Espacio! (99–100:I,338–9)

It is in the 'sueño positivo', then, that all this takes place.

Finally, in order to underline the radical effect of the dream on the condition of the central figure, a comparison will be drawn between passages which are entirely contradictory unless the factor of the dream is taken into account. Thus in the second stanza of 'Yo me he perdido . . .' the 'yo' has confessed that his skin 'no es un río' (69:I,279). In 'Ascensión', in which the penultimate stanza of the *Antología* version relates to what is described to the dream ('Tallos, pulsos, campanas / desencajan el sueño . . .') he adds:

Como un río, mi sangre,
va cruzando tu cuerpo. (94:I,329)

The failing river of earlier poetry has been transformed in the dream to a powerful torrent. And instead of becoming the 'agua sin palomas', as he did in another stanza of 'Yo me he perdido . . .', he writes of the dream experience of 'Pájaros':

Sueltas
tu mano y la mía en el alba . . .
¡Qué limpias sueñan!
¡Qué blancas,
juntas por el cielo vuelan
como palomas! (94–5:I,336)

Unless the intervention and effect of the dream are taken into account, such comments make little sense. It follows, in addition, that a consideration of the role of the dream will be of vital importance when the real nature of the 'tú' who appears in it is considered.

The 'tú' and the dream

The 'tú' is the most unusual feature of this poetry. Fundamental problems are raised. The quotations from poems dealing with the 'tú' with which the chapter began are enough to cast doubt on the pre-suppositions underlying such comments as these, on 'Posesión luminosa':

> En ningún momento se nos distrae aquí de la realidad física de este amor: el poeta quiere acercarse donde descanse *el cuerpo* de la amada, presencia que domina todo el poema, tanto en el vocabulario (*calor, el cuerpo*—asociado a *verano*—, *abierta, carne*, etc.) como en el sostenido símbolo erótica que significa ese 'entrar' en 'posesión'.[51]

A subsequent analysis will show that this figure towards which he moves is far from being a passionate love-object, while the nature of his advances are anything but sexual. The 'tú' is 'blando marfil de sueño, / nieve de carne, quietud / de palma, luna en silencio', while the 'yo' is as ethereal as 'un pulso abierto / latiendo en el aire', 'entering' the 'tú' 'igual que un agua serena' (82:I,324).

In the context of the dream, such vagueness must prompt the question whether or not the figure of the 'tú' exists apart from it. It is necessary, too, to preface comments on the 'tú' by reference to another area of vagueness. It is necessary to ask not only whether or not the protagonist's attention is being directed towards a physical presence, but also whether or not that presence is unquestionably that of a woman. It has already been said that these poems were decribed as 'fragmentos fronterizos de mi adolescencia . . . buscando un equilibrio que no han tenido, ni tendrán, ni llevan'. In *Las tres noches del hombre* it was the stone which was to reveal the direction which the sexual impulses were to take. But the 'yo' of 'Yo me he perdido . . .' is still without his 'piedra'. The text of *Las tres noches del hombre* originally read:

> A través, juntamente del nombre de mujer inscrito ante sus ojos comienza a sentir un impulso amoroso casi agradecido, ya que es, debido a ese nombre misterioso, a lo que él mismo va encontrándose.

What is significant is that the words 'de mujer', though still clearly legible, have been scored out. The 'yo' is unsure whether it is towards the man or the woman that he is attracted. Among the interminable questionings of '15 de julio' (88) and 'Imagen perseguida' (I,286) are those demonstrating his uncertainty in this realm. Apart from wondering whether or not he has a body, the 'yo' is interested in what 'nature' that body might have:

> Relaciona mi estancia.
> ¿Soy un hombre? En el sueño,
> tu ausencia aún no revela
> mi forma por tu espejo.

Whatever else it might accomplish, the dream does not reveal what is his nature outside it.

The 'retratos' are unusual in that, though they deal with an intimate relationship between the 'tú' and the 'yo', the sex of the 'tú' remains undisclosed. Even in such lengthy passages as these it remains open to doubt:

> Estábamos sentados frente a frente en mi cuarto. Apenas había luz. Nuestra conversación se había extinguido ya hacía rato y nosotros aun continuábamos mirándonos, pendiente uno de otro, como esperando que una palabra nueva viniera a deshacer toda la melancolía que nublaba nuestro pensamiento. Muy lentamentre y en silencio siempre, me levanté de mi butaca y me dirigí hacia el extremo de la habitación. Una vez allí comencé a desnudarme totalmente muy despacio. Ya desnudo me tendí de espaldas con los ojos cerrados sobre mi lecho. Tú desde el mismo sitio en el que anteriormente te encontrabas me ibas siguiendo atentamente con la vista, sin comprenderme pero observando sin embargo mis menores movimientos. Me ardía el corazón. Aquella quemadura me escocía en el pecho como una lanzada.[52]

Certainly the relationship is marked by a sense of secrecy, uncertainty and futility, as in this 'retrato':

> Habían roto nuestra conversación de un golpe. Nos retiramos, como dos trozos de un elástico en tensión, que cortan, y nos quedamos

recogidos, arriba en el recuerdo, medio apagados, por los aires rápidos, que el trajinar sordo de fuera, iba tratando de colgar a nuestra luciérnaga . . .

Nos movíamos para lo más inútil con verdadero afán de terminarlo todo a la costumbre, para eludir preguntas, para poder abandonarnos al cuidado de nuestra crisálida anhelante, y llevarla, completada por nosotros mismos, silenciosa y cumplida en su trabajo para la reanudación.

Poems of the most obvious sexuality in *Cuerpo perseguido* reveal similar ambiguity. 'Amor' is perhaps the best example. It begins with these lines:

¡Tu espalda con mi pecho,
mi pecho con tu espalda:
¡qué alegre tajo el cielo
nos cruza en la garganta! (100:I,333)

It is with such considerations in mind that analysis of the 'tú' must be undertaken.[53]

In discussing *Cuerpo perseguido*, Blanco claims that, in the last analysis, the central figure's problem is one of isolation. The kind of dream he is enjoying leads inevitably to the 'radical aislamiento en que se refugia la realidad interior de toda persona. Nadie, parece decirnos, penetra jamás el sueño de nadie'.[54] The dream is 'una huída a la que se entrega sólo uno de los dos amantes'.[55] It is hoped to show that far from cutting him off from the 'tú', the dream is the only means he has of making contact with 'lo otro'. Its inaccessibility, far from being a disappointment, is rather a necessary condition of its usefulness: it creates for him an independent and unassailable position, free from the undesirable yard-sticks the world seeks to impose. There, as Morris says, he is able to seek the body with the mind.

The narrative of the opening poems of *Cuerpo perseguido* in the anthology arrangement suggests that the presence of the 'tú' is first of all entirely dependent on the presence of the dream. That this is so has already been indicated by the *Memoria de poesía* poem 'Cita hacia dentro'. The central figure has already betrayed his predilection for the night. There he is, according to 'Signo de la luz', able to sleep and dream. More specific reasons are given in 'Cita hacia dentro':

Con el sol sobre el cielo,
hoy nunca te vería

que pesa más que el hombre
la luz que lo ilumina.

La noche, en cambio, tiene
al sol bajo sus aguas.
Sus páginas oscuras,
viven deshabitadas.

For the night is the home of the dream:

En el centro del mundo,
bajo el sueño—en sus alas—
te harás toda silencio,
apretada en mi alma. (61–2:I,236–7)

Poems I to IX of the 1954 *Cuerpo perseguido* are significant in this respect. They represent the conception and birth of the 'tú'. Beginning with 'Yo me he perdido . . .' the 'yo' describes the reality he faces—a reality which cuts him off from anyone outside himself. His immediate reaction is the 'huída' described in 'Cerré mi puerta al mundo . . .'. The 'yo' shuts out the world and enters the world of sleep, where the awareness of the body disappears. Poem III acts as a commentary on this move. It is an attempt to answer the enigma he feels himself to be outside sleep:

Quisiera hallar mi ley,
igual que hallo mi oficio como el aire,
igual que mi blancura,
como una luz, como una herida,
lo mismo que un cansancio igual que un ángel. (71)

Poem IV, set at dusk, suggests in its questionings and confusion the kind of doubts discussed earlier. The protagonist is in a limbo between sleep and the dream:

Yo no sé si esta mano
que ahora va por mi frente
como una esponja en la memoria,
va por mí y es mi mano
o está cruzando el cielo
o va por los espejos
sin fuerza ni albedrío.
¿Por qué umbral de mi frente
ha nacido al crepúsculo?
¿Es que mi cuerpo enciende
su dintel bajo el sueño? . . .
Porque busca mis párpados

y no encuentro sus puertas
y todo está cruzando
como una sola sombra.
¿Acaso esté sonámbulo? (71)

The predominant motif of 'Ya no sé . . .' can lead, as it did after 'Yo me he perdido . . .' only to the release of the protagonist from his problems. In the next poem night falls. It is entitled: 'Nocturno. 3 de enero', and begins:

Abierta la ventana,
se derramó en el cuarto
gota a gota, la luna,
como el agua en un vaso. (72)

The final stanza leaves the 'yo' in the same position as he was in poem II—entirely apart from the exterior reality:

Y, al fin, reinó la ausencia
—¡qué quietud en las fuentes!—
El tallo del recuerdo
brotó limpio en mis sienes. (73)

It is only at this crucial moment, when the process of separation from the exterior world is complete, and in the context of an inward-looking and narcissistic experience taking place solely 'en mis sienes', that the 'tú' is mentioned, in poem VI:

Mi frente está cansada como un río.
Yo pienso en ti porque soy como un cuerpo.
Tu mano me abanica lejos por la memoria.
La muerte está soñando mi piel por tu ceniza.

Notice where the 'tú' is to be met:

Yo te busco en mis párpados
igual que un espejo;
pero el mundo ha perdido
su razón por mi sangre
y, huyendo de tu cuerpo,
sueño que te persigo . . .

The closing couplet confirms doubts about the intensely physical aspect of the presence of the 'tú' to which Blanco alludes:

Ya no sé si es que cierro los ojos
o es que estoy silencioso a tu lado. (73)

The process described in the *Memoria del olvido* section of *Cuerpo perseguido*, then, has little to do with 'normal' order of things, the appearance in the dream of someone identifiable from real life. There is no parallel to Guillén's enthusiasm in 'Los brazos':

—¡Amor; henos aquí para que nos enlaces!—
Esa verdad tan plena que se convierte en sueño.[56]

In Prados's case it is the 'anhelo' of 'Signo de la luz' which is transformed into a 'cuerpo vivo'.

The next stage, outlined in VII, reverts to an experience similar to that of 'Cerré mi puerta . . .'. There he wrote: 'Se me perdió la carne por el sueño . . .'. Here the 'yo' asks: 'Tu carne ¿es aún más dulce bajo el sueño?'. It is hard to imagine a plainer reversal of the norm, where sleep removes the physical presence of other from the scene. But such a question is not surprising in the light of the lines which follow:

. . . Cerca como tu propia imagen,
lejos como tu propio cuerpo,
mi soledad me ha sorprendido
como una forma humana:
como un ser invisible. (73–4)

It is in solitude that the central figure meets with the 'forma humana'.

The release marked by the entry of the 'tú' is celebrated in the group's culminating poem, VIII. The central figure feels that in this self-enclosed state he has become fertile: he has produced the 'ser invisible'. As a result the presence of the child is no longer irksome. He has found new direction and release from the instability of the 'divided self':

la voz de un niño, puede
cambiarme por un pájaro . . .
Mi nombre ya no es tiempo.

¡Todo está ya cumplido! (74)

Strictly speaking he has become his own lover. The 'tú' exists within the dream and cannot meaningfully exist outside it. In the dream, however, there is an image which can not least be regarded as 'otro'. The dream becomes not only a private world, but a world he can share, if only with a creature of his own imagining. He is further isolating, defending himself. Laing observes: 'To consume oneself by one's own love prevents the possibility of being consumed by another'.[57] We are dealing with an inner, non-physical world, in which he becomes an 'ángel de vidrio', but in which he feels he experiences reality. In some notes in Caja 19.2, Prados comments:

> 'No hay falta de mundo angélico. Si se habla del cuerpo es porque el mundo angélico puede naturalmente estar dentro de un cuerpo.'

Within his body a new world forms, a world which is 'positive' and of which the protagonist is in control.

Some of what has already been said assumes that the 'tú' cannot be properly understood apart from the 'yo'—that the very existence of the 'tú' apart from him is questionable. Such a claim needs to be further substantiated. Comparison of poems dealing with the 'yo' exclusively and those dealing exclusively with the 'tú' is revealing. What stands out is their similarity. In '15 de julio' the 'yo' asks:

> ¿Qué podrá ser tocarte?
> ¿Será tu piel el viento?
> ¿Será sólo tu nombre
> mi corazón latiendo? (88:I,286–7)

A different poem, found in Caja 19.2, and making no mention of the 'tú', follows the same lines:

> Quiero besar en mí mis propios labios
> para saber como mi cuerpo empieza.
> Nada veo. Mis labios, al buscarme,
> huyen de mí que me deshago en ellos.
> Soy un fantasma.

Poems from *Formas de la huída* afford further examples of this pattern. This is how the 'yo' describes himself in 'Si entrar en la muerte fuera':

> . . . entero
> igual que la sombra pasa
> a la tarde, mi cuerpo
> subiéndose por mis pulsos,
> vivo, temblando, por ellos,
> desnudo, saldría de mí
> golpe tras golpe ascendiendo
> conmigo al hombro . . . (90:I,310)

The emergence of the body is linked with the pulses, the shoulder and an overall rising movement. In 'Ángeles' ('Recuerdo' in the anthology) exactly the same features are to be observed, but relating to the 'tú':

Desvanecida, ahogada,
tu cabeza flotando,
resbaló por tus hombros
hasta entrar en mis brazos.

Como un papel mi sangre
se escapó por el viento.
Desmayado, en mis manos
se derramó tu cuerpo.

De perfil, por sus aguas,
medio hundido en el río
de mis pulsos, tu rostro
navegó por tu olvido . . . (85:I,331)

The expressions 'tú' and 'yo' are used interchangeably. Two versions of 'Presente ausencia' also lead to this conclusion when placed side by side. The last three lines of the *Antología* version read thus:

Te hiciste toda pulso
derretido . . .

¡Se te perdió la carne por el sueño! (60)

The version found in Caja 2.8 and reproduced in the *Poesías completas* differs only in one word:

Te hiciste toda pulso
derretido:

Se me perdió la carne por el sueño. (I,235)

But it is possible to go further than this. Not only does the 'tú' seem inseparable from the 'yo': the 'tú' can be identified with specific aspects of the 'yo'. It has been maintained that the 'tú' does not exist as a separate individual apart from the dream. Poem IX of the anthology's 'Cinco de abril' section provides an opportunity to examine what is represented by the 'tú' figure which appears outside the dream. If, as evidence suggests, it does not refer to an individual, what, then, does it represent?

It is apparent from the opening couplet that the poem describes the condition of the central figure outside sleep: 'Mi cabeza y el viento / cuelgan bajo el insomnio . . .' (105). The lines which follow re-state the situation of the 'divided self' of 'Yo me he perdido . . .'

Igual que un cirio el mundo
te busca por mi frente.

Sin cabeza mi cuerpo
vuela bajo la luna . . .

The mind, the 'cabeza', and the body are totally divorced. The body is dead, it flies 'bajo la luna'. The 'yo' is isolated: '¡Soledad en mis ojos!'. But in the final couplet reference is made to the 'tú': 'Sobre mi frente errante / tus dos manos difuntas'. What are described as 'mi cuerpo' (i.e., that part of himself from which he has felt divorced) and 'tus . . . manos ' share the same characteristic—both are dead. Only the 'yo' who operates on the level of the mind is truly alive. The inference is an important one: that outside the dream the isolated and 'divided' protagonist looks on his body as the 'tú'—or, to use the terms of earlier analysis, a 'tú negativo'.

The dream is a way of reconciling the 'yo' and the 'tú'—of drawing the body into his own territory where he has power over it and where it becomes a part of himself. He is able to achieve what he longs for in the poem already quoted from Caja 19:

Quiero besar en mí mis propios labios
para saber como mi cuerpo empieza.
Nada veo. Mis labios, al buscarme,
huyen de mí que me deshago en ellos.
Soy un fantasma.

It is only in the light of such a pre-supposition, and by taking 'tu' and 'mi' to refer to the same central figure, that some of the anomalies mentioned at the beginning of the chapter can be explained.

It is because the poems do not deal with a simple man–woman relationship that the experience is described in such unusual ways. The 'tú' and 'yo' combine in ways impossible in ordinary human contact. Poem VIII of 'Memoria del olvido' in the 1954 grouping reads: 'Mi calor y tus ojos / vuelan ya confundidos.'. The 'ya' is significant: the dream has marked the long awaited reconciliation of the 'yo' and his body. Integration impossible on any physical level is also described in 'Amanecer'. The dream has taken over, the 'tú' has appeared:

¡Qué cerca! ¡Desde mi ojo a tu ojo
ni el canto de un alma!
. . . .

. . . ¡Qué juntos
nuestros perfiles en medio
del día! (93:I,323)

So marked is this inter-penetration that some poems depend on the fact that to seek the 'tú' is to seek the 'yo', to see the 'tú' is to see the 'yo'. The opening lines of 'Bajo el tiempo de un nombre' exemplify both the reconciliation of 'tú' and 'yo' in the dream and the extent to which the 'bodies' are indistinguishable:

Mi sueño anda rondando en otro sueño,
porque mi sueño es ya tu sueño . . .

Porque habito mi sueño por tu sueño,
habito por tu cuerpo por mi cuerpo.

Persiguiendo a tu mano
me he perdido en mi pecho . . .
El cielo, por tu sangre,
te busca por mi cuerpo. (96:I,288; I,271)

'El cielo sin estrellas' re-affirms this desire to 'contain' or to 'absorb' his own body by means of the dream. Such is his 'heaven':

Mi pecho sin estrellas
—párpados de tu ausencia sobre el aire—,
anda en busca del cielo
—presencia de tu cuerpo por mi carne—. (101:I,312)

When this is achieved, there is peace and fulfilment. It is what the subsequent poem in *Antología* describes. The two bodies (the body of the 'yo', or the mind, and the body of the 'tú', the body of the divided self) are both referred to as 'mi cuerpo'. The division has been healed:

Mi cuerpo, por mis ojos,
transparentan mi cuerpo:
tus cabellos mi sangre
—¡esa nube en el cielo!—;
mi corazón tus manos
—¡este árbol en el viento!—,
mis brazos tus raíces . . .
(En la noche, un lucero.)
Mi cuerpo, por mis ojos
transparentan mi cuerpo:
tu cuerpo por mis ojos
por mi cuerpo y el cielo. (101–2)

The unusual use of the plural verb 'transparentan' with the singular 'mi cuerpo' is not simply a verbal trick. It is intended to convey something of the co-habitation of mind and body which the dream makes possible.

This happy duality is often described in physical terms—as if there were two lovers coming together. But careful reading further removes the possibility that the relationship has much to do with a masculine–feminine union. There is an absence of the normal active and passive role. In 'Amor', both bodies are facing the same way—and both are concerned with the 'cielo' rather than sexual love:

¡Tu espalda contra mi pecho,
mi pecho con tu espalda:
¡qué alegre tajo el cielo
nos cruza en la garganta! (100:I,333)

Such considerations prompt us to mistrust Monterde and Andújar's references to 'la nota sensual' and 'el sofocado afán de la sangre'. There is but little in the way of physical description to suggest the 'atracción que tiene para los sentidos la presencia de un cuerpo amado'.[58] Indeed the kind of contact which purports to be the most direct and physical proves, on closer examination, to be most incorporeal and unreal in physical terms. The 'realidad física de este amor', to which Blanco has referred, is in fact highly questionable.[59] In fact, the narrative of the poem veers sharply away from any conventional erotic pattern. From the first, stress is laid on the *non*-physical nature of the 'yo'. He wants to be the 'figura del pensamiento / mío de ti . . .' (82:I,324). This is not the body and its desires: he describes himself as 'abierta carne del viento, / estancia de amor en alma'. The 'tú' is linked with the body, but in a detached and markedly cold way: 'Tú—blando marfil de sueño, / nieve de carne . . .'. Their contact is mysterious and ambivalent; the protagonist begins, as Blanco points out, by entering the 'tú', but ends the poem with the 'tú' inside *him*:

. . . .
quedarme ya así por dentro,
como el aire en un farol,
viéndote temblar, luciendo,
brillar en medio de mí,
enciendiéndote en mi cuerpo,
iluminando mi carne
toda ya carne de viento.

The poem makes far more sense when viewed as an example of the extremely personal use made by the central figure of the 'tú'-'yo' distinction. The 'yo' of the opening lines represents that part of the protagonist which he feels to be 'real'. The 'tú' is the remote, dead body—the 'luna en silencio' of the second stanza. The coming together of the 'yo' and the 'tú' in the dream represents that reconciliation of the dual nature of the divided self foreshadowed in 'Yo me he perdido . . .'. There he wrote that if he were to find the 'piedra', then:

> Yo subiría del fondo de mi frente
> hasta habitar mi cuerpo como un ídolo:
> hasta brotar en medio de mi carne
> otra vez sobre el mundo sin cigüeña.

The images of the lines from 'Posesión luminosa' quoted above, the air inside the lamp, the idea of light within the body provide an exact parallel with the 'Yo me he perdido . . .' statement.

The dream, then, represents the redemption—if only temporary—of that part of himself from which he feels cut off and which has earlier caused him such anguish, the body. During it he is able to enjoy a narcissistic world over which he has complete control. The experience is described in terms of an almost impossible vigour, as in the first poem of the anthology's 'Cinco de abril' section:

> Prendidos por la cintura
> nuestros cuerpos amarrados,
> ¡qué haz de piernas, de cabellos,
> de brazos, de ojos! . . . (99:I,338)

He becomes all-powerful—but only within the dream. A final parallel with Laing underlines the credibility of such a situation:

> The schizoid individual fears a real live dialectical relationship with real live people. He can relate himself only to depersonalized persons, to phantoms of his own phantasies (imagos), perhaps to things, perhaps to animals.[60]
>
> Since the self, in maintaining its isolation and detachment does not commit itself to a creative relationship with the other and is preoccupied with the figures of phantasies, thought, memories, etc. (imagos), which cannot be directly observable by or directly expressed to others, anything (in a sense) is possible . . . In phantasy, the self can be anyone, anywhere, do anything, have anything. It is thus omnipotent and completely free—but only in phantasy.[61]

The language of doubt (2)

The obtuse thematic content of *Tiempo* was reflected in eccentricities of grammar and punctuation peculiar to Prados's work. Examination of *Cuerpo perseguido* suggests that it is hard to imagine a closer identification of expression with sense. The central figure's intense self-doubt and introspection spill out into a number of hesitant mannerisms which together emerge as the distinguishing tone of this poetry. In his thesis, Sanchis-Banús refers to the frequency with which lines that 'revisten forma de pregunta o dubitación' punctuate the poems.[62] It is this which unites the various characteristics discussed here.

What distinguishes Prados from his contemporaries is not simply his consistent posture of doubt, but his persistent avowal that his only knowledge is a kind of 'not knowing'. With Prados, in contrast to Guillén, certainly, and even to Cernuda, with whom he has many affinities, expressions of doubt are taken to be the only certainties. This is why the 'yo no sé . . .' motif to which Morris and Blanco refer is so vital to the texture of *Cuerpo perseguido*. 'Yo no sé si esta mano' traces a deepening mistrust of his perception of himself and the world around him. It begins, by its deliberate inclusion of the 'yo', with what amounts to an emphatic assertion of doubt, as if to invite comparison with Guillén's characteristic 'yo sé . . .':

> Yo no sé si esta mano
> que ahora va por mi frente
> como una esponja en la memoria,
> va por mí y es mi mano
> o está cruzando el cielo
> o va por los espejos
> sin fuerza ni albedrío. (71:I,272)

It is by increasing the frequency of the repetition of 'no sé' through the poem and by qualifying it (as he does elsewhere) by the use of 'ya' that the poet skilfully conveys the sense of a vortex of doubt into which he is being sucked relentlessly. Twenty lines separate the first 'no sé' from the second, while the third follows on almost immediately. The result is an impression of an accelerating diminution of certainty:

> Yo ya no sé si el mundo
> vivirá por su ausencia,
> ni si la estrella roba
> su carne por mis ojos . . .

Ya no sé si la aurora,
la fuente o la tristeza
son mi cuerpo en mi mano,
mi soledad o el agua . . .

The descent into doubt is the dynamic which Prados uses to prevent hesitancy from degenerating into poetical structures that are aimless or flabby.

The conjunction of 'ya' and 'no sé . . .' reappears in 'Mi frente está cansada como un río.'. At the heart of the poem is not merely lack of certainty but the process of losing certainty. The sand seems to slip through the fingers as the poem is being read and as doubt is over-taken by insubstantiality. The first stanza declares that the protagonist is contemplating the 'tú'; the second begins less confidently:

Yo te busco en mis párpados
igual que en un espejo;

pero el mundo ha perdido
su razón por mi sangre (73:I,284)

From this significant 'pero' the whole movement of the poem is towards a sudden enshrouding in a mist of uncertainty:

. . . huyendo de tu cuerpo,
sueño que te persigo . . .

Ya no sé si es que cierro los ojos
o es que estoy silencioso a tu lado.

There is another feature to be noted in connection with the 'no sé . . .' motif. It sometimes acts as a key to a list of alternatives. The central *persona* knows not 'nothing' but rather at times does not know 'which'. Thus '15 de julio' begins:

No sé si mi memoria
es o fué bajo el tiempo,
o si en tu amor, desnuda
va a nacer sobre el cielo. (88:I:286)

And, in 'Oración', he writes:

Ahora, ya no sabría
si espalda o tristeza; (113:I,315)

The consequences of such a procedure are two-fold. It allows for the exploration of a number of possibilities without limiting the 'yo' to a particular conclusion. And it has the effect of allowing him to retain his 'misterio'. The tantalisingly obscure choice between concrete and abstract, 'espalda' and 'tristeza', typifies this. In providing an alternative, the poet seems to be making every attempt to explain and divulge his position. The very incompatibility of the choice offered, however, secures an exactly opposite result.

Allied to this abnormally frequent use of expressions of 'not knowing' is the central figure's obsession with questions. Again '15 de julio' is typical:

Relaciona mi estancia.
¿Soy un hombre? En el sueño,
tu ausencia aún no revela
mi forma por tu espejo.
¿Seré yo el agua? Dime:
¿por dónde va mi cuerpo?
¿Es mi país tu sangre
y yo en ti su reflejo?

There follows a pause in the questioning, a moment of apparent joy and relaxation:

¡Qué serenas auroras
tus pulsos sin recuerdo! . . .

But this peace is immediately disturbed by a further rush of interrogation:

¿Qué podrá ser tocarte?
¿Será tu piel el viento?
¿Será sólo tu nombre
mi corazón latiendo?

Such alterations of apparent certainty and repeated questioning are a feature of the 'empleo de interrogaciones' to which Sanchis Banús refers. In 'Atardecer.Quietud' the central *persona* seems to have attained a point of rest. But its repose is totally undermined by the insidious question which closes the poem:

Serena, igual que esta rama,
se alza en el viento mi sangre . . .
¿Hasta qué espacio, mis ojos
han de llegar por buscarte? (89:I,282)

Such a use of questions has a distinctive effect. They are often entirely radical in nature. They cast doubt on the whole framework of the experience recorded in the poem. It is only in the last word of the question from 'Atardecer.Quietud' that the all-important matter of the absence of the 'tú' comes to light. The question, then, dramatises the central dilemma observed in *Cuerpo perseguido* and it is this, its dramatising quality, which Prados uses to most advantage. 'Nuevos vínculos' contains a poem built around the same technique:

Mira caer mis párpados . . .
¡No los toques!
¡Respétalos! . . .
Rodea por mi cuerpo.
Mírame por la espalda:
como un espejo soy.
¿Espejo de tu cuerpo? (111:I,304)

The first six lines (having accepted the surrealistic image of the falling eye-lids) seem to move along a recognisable pattern. He invites the 'tú' to observe him from behind; he compares himself to a mirror—and there, suddenly, all certainty evaporates. Has he, he asks, any real existence apart from the 'tú'? Once more it is by means of the question that the central *persona* undermines what seemed to have been meaningful and recognisable assumptions.

It is not surprising that such expressions of doubt are accompanied by stylistic characteristics which arise from a sense of stagnation. In his analysis of the grammatical features of Prados's work Debicki refers to Dámaso Alonso's 'sintagmas no progresivos'.[63] In discussing *El misterio del agua* he suggests that the repeated use of words having the same syntactical function conveys a sense of oneness with nature, 'la búsqueda de una armonía perenne en el mundo natural cíclico'. Sanchis Banús argued that Prados's lengthy lists of nouns are part of a 'dinamismo creativo', creating 'la sensación de movimiento'. There are, however, cases where the emotional framework of the poetry is far too negative to allow of such an interpretation. Just as frequently it is meant to underline a feeling of intense stagnation—of being set in circumstances from which he cannot withdraw. Thus in the self-critical 'Porque me voy cierro los ojos,', not one but three possible descriptions of the 'yo' are listed:

pero no sé si estoy huyendo en vano por mí mismo
o voy desmelenado y sin corbata,

cautivo en mi silencio sin memoria
o ando cesante y sin espaldas,
sin párpados, perdido por mi sueño . . . (74:I,313)

The impression is not of an abundance of choice, but rather that the concept of choice is irrelevant. Thus in the first stanza of 'Quisiera estar . . .' Prados notes that he would like to be:

como en mis labios, como en el aire,
donde no sé si estuve o voy a estar o estoy
o el árbol me ha traído,
como no sé si soy o voy a ser o quizá sea
o todo es como el cielo. (70:I,269)

These lists imply that there are times when questions and self-doubt loom so large that one answer becomes as good as another, to the extent that any forward movement becomes difficult (hence the central figure's plea at the close of the poem that he should find 'mi ley'—some way of establishing certainty about himself).

Non-progression is also reflected in the structure of some poems. Several seem to offer a satisfying circular movement (described by Debicki under the heading 'esquemas paralelísticas'). Closer inspection reveals that this circularity is only apparent. 'Bosque de la noche' is the most sinister example. In each stanza there is a repetition of a pattern established in the first:

Se alzó, —manzana de ébano—,
la mirada en el viento
y se quedó en el alma
maciéndose en su rama. (58:I,242)

Various combinations of soul/water/glance are essayed. A sense of harmony is created by the re-appearance of these elements. But the pattern is never finally resolved. The promised circularity is never attained. As earlier analysis revealed, the fruit of this kind of activity is the cursed 'manzana de ébano'. With great ingenuity Prados has found a structural technique to reflect the inner frustration of the central *persona*.

It is again the structure of 'Nocturno fiel' which is mainly responsible for its claustrophobic atmosphere. Central to that structure is the repeated couplet:

Luna en el cielo.
Luna en el suelo. (11:I,373)

The repetition of 'moon' has an initially soothing effect. The lines placed between each repetition, however, form a nightmarish crescendo, culminating in the final stagnation of death:

> Cierra la muerte sus alas
> sobre la espalda del viento.

The chorus has become a doom-laden and inescapable ground bass. The same words are used, but they are gradually charged with increasing significance. The impression is of a quagmire of desolation from which the 'yo' struggles in vain to escape.

But it is not only in the conveying of a feeling of stagnation that Prados has excelled. Part of his originality lies in his ability to extend the language of doubt into areas of insubstantiality. While *Tiempo* is marked by its attachment to the sea and the coast, *Cuerpo perseguido* is concerned with a far more abstract range of expression. The appearance of the dream figure brings with it the language of the dream, the art of saying without explaining, of suggesting without making explicit.

One of the ways in which the insubstantiality of the dream is recorded is by the inter-changing of verb tenses. Debicki has already referred to the poetry's 'sentimiento general de intemporalidad'. Often it is by the juxtaposition of present and future tenses that he expresses the evanescence of the fragile 'tú'. In this example the use of the atemporal participle further distances the reader from any precise time or place:

> Como ahora te vas durmiendo
> despacio; perdiendo suelo
> de la vida por tus ojos;
> derramándote por ellos
> sobre tu memoria ; hundiéndote
> casi ahogada bajo el sueño
> por dentro de ti . . . Así un día
> te irás durmiendo . . .
> . . . te irás subiendo,
> perdiendo pie de tus ojos,
> volando, . . . (80:I,306)

Even as we read the 'tú' seems to be in the process of floating from our sight.

On other occasions the hypothetical, insubstantial nature of the protagonist's experience is reflected in his use of the conditional tense. In 'Forma de la huída' he explains:

Si en este espejo yo hubiera
dejado, al irme, encerrado
mi cuerpo tapiado en luz,
vivo —emplazado en sus aguas—:
ahora en él, como el recuerdo
de un muerto se va despacio
cuajando en la memoria,
mi carne se iría cuajando
lenta, de nuevo en su luna,
desnuda —en mi cuerpo hallado—
y a su orilla, desde el fondo
subiría, . . . (108:I,299)

It is the avoidance of the simple future and past which allows of a being which is at once 'forma' and 'huída'. A similar technique, using the subjunctive and the conditional with reference to the ineffable 'tú', is to be observed in 'Oración':

Si tu voz me llamara,
yo me saldría al sueño
rajándome los párpados
hasta encontra mi sangre, (112–3:I,315)

In 'Posesión luminosa' it is the use of the infinitive and the participle which distances the 'tú' from the tangible. As a result neither time nor personality assert themselves with any clear definition. After the opening 'quiero / ser' (itself a negation of the substantial) the finite verb is overshadowed by infinitives:

Igual que este viento, quiero
figura de mi calor
ser y, despacio, entrar
donde descanse tu cuerpo
del verano, irme acercando
hasta él sin que me vea;
llegar, como un pulso abierto
latiendo en el aire; ser
figura del pensamiento
mío de ti, en su presencia; (82:I,324)

The pointed omission of finite verbs from the second stanza underscores the fact that the 'possession' of which the poem speaks is indeed acorporeal and far from any 'normal' physical, erotic reality:

Tú —blando márfil de sueño,

nieve de carne, quietud
de palma, luna en silencio—,
sentada, dormida en medio
de tu cuarto. Y yo ir entrando
igual que un agua serena,
inundarte todo el cuerpo
hasta cubrirte . . . (82:I,324)

The neglect of the finite verb suggests the attempt to retain in the memory snatches of experience which will soon drift into oblivion. It is exactly the language of the dream.

There is another way in which this sense of the transient, the insubstantial is captured by Prados: the frequent use of 'ya'. With it comes a breathless awareness that happiness and ecstasy are, as in a dream, vulnerable and fleeting. In 'Rapto' the wind's activity is described:

Ya te ciñe el muslo, el pie,
la cintura, el brazo, el cuello,
la mano . . .
¡Ya! ¡Ya te lleva
sobre su lomo en pedazos! (64:I,260)

In the exuberant 'Alba rápida' it is the repetition of 'ya' which lends urgency to the account:

¡Qué caballos de blancura
mi sangre en el cielo vierte!
ya van por el viento, suben,
saltan por la luz, se pierden
sobre las aguas . . .
Ya vuelven
redondos, limpios, desnudos . . . (79:I,326)

The apostrophes, the 'puntos suspensivos' which are so prominent a feature of such poetry (see also, for example, 'Enero, 10' (83:I,290) and 'Cristal del universo' (77:I,314)) are evidence of a poet grappling with the expression of an experience which is at once intense and yet abstract, real and yet without tangible substance, radical in its significance to the protagonist, yet uncertain, brittle. It is only with the greater stability of later years that such imbalances are resolved, with consequent effects on the poetic language of Prados.

The dangers of the dream

The course adopted by the protagonist is fraught with difficulties. He is himself aware of the possibility that he will end up as the 'fantasma mío de mi fuga' (74:I,313). It produces both this fear and a sense of guilt. This last is the jarring note that accompanies the end of the dream. In 'Condenación' the protagonist confesses:

¡Qué presagios de culpa
tu sangre derramaba,
gota a gota en el viento,
como estrellas de agua!

Tus lágrimas de cera
cerraron mi garganta.
¡Qué honda noche sin venas
se abrió sobre tu espalda!

En tu lecho, la muerte
cruzó sus largas alas.
¡Qué lutos de silencio
mis labios rezumaban!

Tus ojos sobre el cielo
como negras espadas,
clavaron en la sombra
la cruz de tu mirada. (106–7:I,335)

Whatever the 'yo'–'tú' contact represents, it is certain from *Cuerpo perseguido* that the protagonist has yet to find a permanent solution to the problems of sterility and the divided self which will operate as effectively during waking life as in the dream. The 'piedra' of the selection's final poem seems to cover only sleep and the dream.

'Cuerpo perseguido'

In the light of this analysis the overall title of these poems assumes an important double meaning. For there is both a 'body' which the central figure is pursuing and a body which is being pursued. He is seeking that state where the mind, the soul, the 'real' self and the physical body from which he feels separated constitute a single unit. And he is also being pursued by the reminders of what he is—no longer the child, at home in the natural fertile world; constantly being reminded of what, as a man, he should be. As both pursuer and pursued, he walks an uncomfortable tight-rope leading into the precarious dream. The triumphant note on which the 1954 selection's *Cuerpo perseguido* closes, 'Nuevo ser', follows on directly and inexplicable from a poem entitled 'Desesperanza'. Such intense emotional fluctuations warn us that the battle of the 'yo' with his body is by no means won.

1 The two anthology sections dealt with here, *Memoria de poesía* and *Cuerpo perseguido* are dated 1926–7 and 1927–8 respectively. The book *Memoria del olvido*, in which all the *Cuerpo perseguido* poems appear, though in a different order, was published in 1940 (México, Editorial Séneca). Blanco and Carreira have produced a text by bringing together original manuscripts, *Memoria del olvido* and *Cuerpo perseguido*. This volume is called: *Cuerpo perseguido*, Edición, prólogo y notas de Carlos Blanco Aguinaga, con la colaboración de Antonio Carreira (Barcelona, 1971). See also *Poesías completas* (I,231–344).

2 C. Blanco Aguinaga, *Vida y obra*, p. 45.

3 *Idem.*, *Cuerpo perseguido*, p. 9.

4 *Idem.*, *Vida y obra*, p. 45.

5 *Ibid.*, p. 11.

6 F. Monterde, 'Obra de dos poetas españoles en América', *Cuadernos americanos*, no. 3 (México, 1955), pp. 284–6

7 Besides, platonic love is different again from the process described in 'Posesión luminosa'. In platonic love the 'vision of the beautiful' is encouraged by the lovers' contemplation of their bodies (the 'prescribed devotion to boyish beauties' (Plato, *Symposium*, translated by Michael Joyce (London, 1935), p. 85.)). In Prados's poem, the body does not seem even to be a starting-point.

8 P. Salinas, *Poesías*, (Barcelona, 1971), p. 219.

9 'Ayer te besé', *Idem.*, p. 278: 'El teléfono', *Idem.*, p. 199.

10 F. Aparicio Díaz, 'La soledad en Emilio Prados', *Caracola*, no. 49 (1956).

11 M. Andújar, 'Primeras palabras en torno a Emilio Prados', *Ínsula*, no. 187 (1962), p. 3: also in *Índice de artes y letras*, no. 168 (1962), p. 16.

12 This precedes the type-script copy of *Cuerpo perseguido* contained in Caja 1.10. For a note on this version, see C. Blanco Aguinaga, *Lista de los papeles de Emilio Prados* (Baltimore, 1967), p. 4.

13 In *Primeras poesías* (VII) we read: 'Mas no quiero estos muros, / Aire infiel a sí mismo, / Ni esas ramas que cantan / En el aire dormido.' (*La realidad* y *el deseo*, p. 14). There is the same association of the branches with inactivity, somnolence. Poem XIV from the same group of Cernuda poems refers again to branches. Once more the implication is the protagonist's inability to respond sexually—he is 'sin fuerza': 'Ingrávido presente. / Las ramas abren trémulas. / Cándidamente escapan / Estas horas sin fuerza.' (*La realidad* y *el deseo*, p.18).

14 F. García Lorca, 'Mañana', *Obras completas*, pp. 120–2.

15 *Ibid.*, p. 139.

16 A. P. Debicki, *Etudias sobre poesía española contemporánea*, pp. 317–18.

17 Here it is the water which is a symbol of the level of the body. We have already seen it used in *Tiempo* as a direct contrast to 'alma', as in 'Perfil del tiempo' (20:I,117) and 'Espejismos' (20:I,386).

18 L. Cernuda, *La realidad* y *el deseo*, 'El viento y el alma', p. 253.

19 A. P. Debicki, *Estudios sobre puesía española contemporánea*, p. 311.

20 The full text of *Las tres noches del hombre* is contained in Appendix III. It is an account of the emergence of an individual from childhood towards knowledge and the 'piedra'. The tableaux are reminiscent of the 'myth of the cave' from *The Republic*.

21 These prose poems are taken from Caja 1.7 and are contained in Appendix II. For the 'Textos oníricos', see C. B. Morris, *Surrealism and Spain, 1920–1936* (Cambridge, 1972), pp. 260–2. Poems such as 'Cabeza, en el recuerdo' (*Obras completas*, p. 120) and prose poems like 'Ansiedad para el día' (*Ibid.*, p. 228) are comparable to Prados's work of this period in both expression and, to some extent, content (especially in the treatment of the body). In the latter, for example, Aleixandre writes: '. . . una muchacha, una seca badana estremecida, quiere saber si aún queda la piel por los dos brazos.'

22 For the context to these quotations, see Appendix IV. Note here the recurrence of key-words found in the poetry of the time. I believe that the relevance and intrinsic interest of these excerpts justify fairly full quotation.

23 See Appendix IV, pp. 1–2. The closing lines of this quotation are further evidence of links between Prados and Lorca during these early years. In 'Muerte de Antoñito el Camborio' Lorca wrote: 'Tres golpes de sangre tuvo / y se murió de perfil. / Viva moneda que nunca / se volverá a repetir'. *Obras completas*, p. 376).

24 In Caja 19 there is a jotting which reads: 'Nunca he creído en mí cuando me veo frente a un cristal, pasando, o que me miran'. There is, of course, nothing unique or new in this. In Porphyry's biography of Plotinus we read: 'Plotinus, the philosopher our contemporary, seemed ashamed of being in the body. So deeply rooted was this feeling that he could never be induced to tell of his ancestry, his parentage or his birthplace. He showed, too, an inconquerable reluctance to sit to a painter or to a sculptor, . . .' (Plotinus, *The Enneads*, translated by S. McKenna (London, 1962), p. 1).

25 R. D. Laing, *The Divided Self* (Harmondsworth, 1970), p. 37.

26 *Ibid.*, p. 42.

27 *Ibid.*, p. 65.

28 C. Blanco Aguinaga, *Vida* y *obra*, p. 55.

29 J. Guillén, 'Tiempo Libre', *Cántico*, p. 157.

30 See Appendix IV for the context to the excerpts quoted here and below.

31 Consideration of the harrowing problems facing the protagonist leads us to see the stone in terms of the 'lapis Philosophorum' to which Jung refers, that which would heal not only the disharmonies of the physical world but the inner psychic conflict as well, the "affliction of the soul";'. (C. G. Jung, *Mysterium Coniunctionis*, in *The Collected Works*, Vol. XIV, p. 473. Possibly Prados also had in mind the reference in Revelation, Chapter 2, v. 17: 'To him who conquers I will give some of the hidden manna, and I will give him a white stone, with a new name written on the stone which no one knows except him who receives it'.

32 C. Blanco Aguinaga, *Vida* y *obra*, p. 58.

33 R. D. Laing, *The Divided Self*, p. 91.

34 *Memoria del olvido*, p. 129.

35 The influence of Plato can be discerned here. In arguing for the pre-existence of man, Plato sees the process of learning as one of remembering that which is forgotten at birth. At the stage represented by *Cuerpo perseguido* and *Memoria de poesía* the 'yo' is still in the position of having 'forgotten' the normal desires and appetites which accompany adolescence and manhood. Something has gone wrong with the mechanism which should remind him of them. The body remains only half-awakened.

36 R. Xirau, 'El poema de Emilio Prados, *Poetas de México y España* (Madrid, 1962), pp, 97–102.

37 *Memoria del olvido*, p. 131.

38 R. D. Laing, *The Divided Self*, p. 69.

39 L. Cernuda, *La realidad* y *el deseo*, p. 89.

40 Something of the lofty status enjoyed by the dream can be judged by these typically obscure and metaphysical notes from Caja 19: 'El sueño es comunicación a través de nuestra sangre, entre la vida y la muerte, es decir entre la vida y la vida en el tiempo llamado pretérito. La sangre es herencia; materia del universo. En la sangre heredamos el conocimiento del bien y del mal. Estamos obligados a aumentar su conocimiento para

dejar enriquecida nuestra herencia.' Though these thoughts relate to a later period, they are nevertheless an indication of Prados's attitude to the dream.

41 R. D. Laing, *The Divided Self*, pp. 42–3.

42 *Ibid.*, p. 51.

43 C. B. Morris, *A Generation of Spanish Poets*, p. 237.

44 J. Guillén, *Cántico*, p. 143.

45 *Idem.*, 'Quiero dormir', p. 137.

46 L. Cernuda, *La realidad* y *el deseo*, p. 18.

47 G. Bachelard, *L'Eau et les Rêves*, p. 35.

48 J. R. Jiménez, 'Alerta', *Tercera antología poética, (1898–1953)*, (Madrid, 1957), p. 960.

49 *Ibid.*, p. 548.

50 F. G. Lorca, *Obras completas*, p. 1190.

51 C. Blanco Aguinaga, *Vida* y *obra*, p. 50.

52 For the context to this and the quotation which follows, see Appendix IV.

53 Though we hope to avoid any pretence of a sophisticated psycho-analytic study of the central figure, it is again interesting to compare his attitudes and thought with those of individuals described in Laing's work. In *The Divided Self* (pp. 146–7) he quotes from and corroborates M. Boss's comments on Freud's view that in the disturbed personality persecution thoughts were caused by those homosexual tendencies which he found to be common to all paranoiacs. Boss states: 'We, however, see in both phenomena, in this sort of homosexuality and in the persecution ideas, nothing but two parallel forms of expression of the same schizophrenic shrinkage and destruction of human existence, namely two different attempts at regaining the lost parts of one's personality'. (M. Boss, *Meaning and Content of Sexual Perversions* (New York, 1949), pp. 122–4). The feeling of being 'persecuted' manifest in the 'retrato' cited above, taken in conjunction with the unusual type of love relationship suggested in some of the poetry of *Cuerpo perseguido* affords what is possibly an illuminating example of the kind of behaviour pattern Boss was describing.

54 C. Blanco Aguinaga, *Vida* y *obra*, p. 53.

55 *Ibid.*, p. 52.

56 J. Guillén, *Cántico*, p. 250.

57 R. D. Laing, *The Divided Self*, p. 51.

58 C. Blanco Aguinaga, *Vida* y *obra*, p. 49.

59 In a footnote Blanco describes the unusual phraseology of this poetry as an attempt to '"desrealizar" lo físico', (*Vida* y *obra*, p. 50). We see it rather as an expression of something which never has been truly 'physical'.

60 R. D. Laing, *The Divided Self*, p. 77.

61 *Ibid.*, p. 84.

62 J. Sanchis Banús, 'Temas y formas en la obra de Emilio Prados', Sorbonne thesis 1959, pp. 55–6.

63 A. P. Debicki, *Estudios sobra poesía española contemporánea*, p. 308.

CHAPTER THREE

A New Perspective

Car le mot, qu'on le sache, est un être vivant.
(Victor Hugo, *Les Contemplations*)

A call in the midst of the crowd,
My own choice, orotund sweeping and final.
. . . .
(I am large, I contain multitudes.)
(Walt Whitman, 'Song of Myself', *Leaves of Grass*)

Introduction

This chapter deals with poetry to be found under the titles *La voz cautiva* and *Andando, andando por el mundo.*[1] According to notes written in the course of the preparation of the *Antología*, Prados felt that with *Llanto en la sangre* they represent a fundamental development in his work. Of books written or published in the twenties he states: '. . . forman el ciclo anterior a los cambios sociales (y personales) y a la Guerra civil'. Those which follow (the subject of this chapter) relate: '. . . precisamente al desarrollo de estos cambios'.[2] According to Blanco these 'changes' mark a period when Prados was increasingly separating himself from both private problems and from the literary world. His time was spent with printers, fishermen, carpenters. He describes the early circulation of *Calendario incompleto del pan y del pescado* in these terms:

> Según va escribiendo los poemas de este libro, un tanto a la manera de los poetas revolucionarios (cuyo ejemplo mayor quizá sea por aquellos años el ya entonces legendario Mayakovski), los lee a los pescadores; sólo después, en 1936 (o 1937), cuando el publicar estos poemas sea un gusto histórico necesario, publicará una parte de libro en *Llanto en la sangre.*[3]

Paradoxically, in view of such isolationist and 'anti-literary' tendencies, certain aspects of Prados's development at this stage appear to bring him closer to his contemporaries.

The first of these aspects is the very fact of a dramatic change of direction. C. B. Morris, in comparing Lorca's *Romancero gitano* (1924–7) with his *Poeta en Nueva York* (1929–30), Cernuda's *Égloga, elegía, oda* (1927–8) with *Un río, un amor* (1929) and Alberti's *Cal y canto* (1926–7) with *Sobre los ángeles* (1927–8), maintains that during the last years of the twenties 'the work of several Spanish poets changed considerably'.[4] Comparison of *Cuerpo perseguido* (1927–8) and *Andando, andando por el mundo* (1930–5) suggests that Prados too may take his place in this overall pattern. There seems to be a radical move away from the 'yo' and the 'tú' towards a ground of moral and social concern more in common with some of his fellow poets (although, as this chapter seeks to show, such a move is more apparent than real).

There are several obvious ways in which this manifests itself. The poem 'Tengo miedo' contains these lines:

He pedido mi ingreso en la legión de los hombres perdidos;
de los hombres que suenan sus huesos solitarios
por los huecos caminos que los alejan de su frente . . . (I,401)

There is an involvement with the lot of certain types of social outcast:

Yo pertenezco al fondo de esas viejas lagunas
de esos hombres que marchan sin conocerse sobre el mundo;
a esos largos racimos que duelen contra el cáñamo,
que abandonan sus nombres como las hojas del aceite. (I,426–7)

In 'Llanto subterráneo' there are more examples of this kind of identification:

Junto al mar, ese canto que el silencio origina,
donde los niños lloran
y las cabezas de los hombres miran y mueren contra el vino,
yo he visto, he visto a veces cernerse un ancho pájaro en la bruma
como bajo los puentes hoy los ápteros brazos de los viejos obreros.
(I,424)

Another version of this poem contained in the Prados papers establishes his sense of identification even more clearly:

Al fin puedo cantar: "¡Estoy bajo los puentes,
con los ápteros brazos de los vicios obreros!"[5]

In place of the harbour setting of *Tiempo* and the abstraction of *Cuerpo perseguido* there appears an abrasive and disintegrated world of cement, lime and plaster. In *La voz cautiva* he addresses the fire thus:

Ataca, punza, desmorona la carne,
el canto y el cemento.
Sube, enróllate, aprieta con tu asfixiante estrago,
la cal y la mentira,
la fibrosa entraña
del caño de la vida,
la madera y el yeso . . . (119:I,506)

The suggestion of a rootless, disorientated society is contained in 'Primera salida':

Aquí los hombres mueven
las anchas cintas blancas de sus vidas
como vueltas raíces encrespadas sobre agitado cielo. (I,500)

The picture seems to be of an existence as empty as it is white, as troubled as the sky above.

It is most obviously in the case of Lorca that such a stance finds its like. He is even more direct and vituperative than Prados—but the target of attack appears to be related:

Yo denuncio a toda la gente
que ignora la otra mitad,
la mitad irredimible
que levanta sus montes de cemento
donde laten los corazones
de los animalitos que se olvidan
y donde caeremos todos
en la última fiesta de los taladros.
Os escupo en la cara.[6]

It is the 'Paisaje de la multitud' (a word which appears in the third line of the anthology's *Andando, andando* . . . section) 'que vomita' or, 'que orina'. In an interesting prefiguring of the 'cintas blancas' of 'Primera salida' Lorca delves, though in a direction not investigated by Prados, into similar symptoms of malaise:

Pero el hombre vestido de blanco
ignora el misterio de la espiga,
ignora el gemido de la parturienta,
ignora que Cristo puede dar agua todavía,
ignora que la moneda quema el beso de prodigio
y da la sangre del cordero al pico idiota del faisán.[7]

Side by side with such observations are passages in Prados's work which express distaste, a desire to 'opt out'—in 'Quisiera huir' he exlaims:

¡Quisiera huir: perderme lejos de su olvido! (125:I,403)

The title 'Andando, andando por el mundo' in itself implies that there is no resting place to be had. He is 'tired'—with a 'cansancio sordomudo' rather like Lorca's in 'Vuelta de paseo'.[8] While he stands apart in this way he is akin to Alberti in search of the lost Paradise:

. . . Hombres
fijos, de pie, a la orilla
parada de las tumbas,
me ignoran. Aves tristes,
cantos petrificados,

en éxtasis el rumbo,
ciegas. No saben nada.[9]

And in the restless figure of the poem 'Andando andando por el mundo' ('andando andando por las desiertas calles' (129:I,413)), bearing in mind the 'hollow man' of *Cuerpo perseguido*, is seen a curious reflection of the same poet's 'cuerpo deshabitado':

Quedó mi cuerpo vacío,
negro saco, a la ventana.
  Se fue.
  Se fue, doblando las calles.
Mi cuerpo anduvo, sin nadie.[10]

In amongst feelings of association and rejection Prados also shares with some of his contemporaries a consciousness of the importance of the 'voz' (a concept to be examined in more detail later). Many of the poems of the period have the flavour of prophetic utterance. It is the voice of experience, of the one who has seen things for what they are. Lorca in '1910. (Intermedio)' declares:

No preguntarme nada. He visto que las cosas
cuando buscan su curso encuentran su vacío.[11]

Prados writes also in the tradition of Machado as one who has 'understood':

He vivido, he soñado, he pensado que he muerto
como ese estiércol que fermenta bajo la luz fecunda de su aurora.
. . . .
andando andando sobre el mundo, se entiende: (130:I,43–4)

If Aleixandre seems more light-hearted in his quotation of Byron at the beginning of *Espadas como labios* (1930–1), where the poet is defined as 'a babbler', what follows, poems such as 'Mi voz' and 'La palabra', together with the 'naming' poems of *La destrucción o el amor* witness to the fact that Prados was not alone in his search for a role for the 'voz cautiva'.

Formal developments accompanying this new 'voice' again seem to draw Prados more closely to his colleagues. The following are lines from 'Hay voces libres . . .':

Hay límites
y hay cuerpos.
Hay voces libres

y hay voces con cadenas.
Hay barcos que cruzan lentos sobre los lentos mares
y barcos que se hunden medio podridos en el cieno profundo.
(128:I,429–430)

They sprawl untidily across the page, as untidy and as shapeless as the reality they seek to express. What is interesting is the extent to which similar expression was discovered by others. In 'Nacimiento último' Aleixandre proclaims:

he visto el mar, la mar, los mares, los no-límites.
. . . .
¿Hacia qué cielos o qué suelos van esos ojos no pisados
que tienen como yemas una fecundidad invisible?
¿Hacia qué lutos o desórdenes se hunden ciegas abajo esas manos abandonadas?[12]

The common pool of vocabulary 'límites, mar, se hunden' hinted at by such examples is less striking than the use of lists and repetition—by Prados, Aleixandre and Lorca in particular—to convey a heaping up of invective, an invective which, nevertheless remains, because of its sheer plainness, unrhetorical. In 'Hay voces libres . . .' twenty-one lines begin with 'Hay' or 'y hay'. The effect is of the remorseless, insistent drumming home of a message:

Hay voces libres
y hay voces con cadenas
y hay palabras que se funden al chocar contra el aire
y corazones que golpean en la pared como una llama. (128:I,430)

In Aleixandre's 'Bajo la tierra' there is a similar repetition:

Hay piedras que nunca serán ojos. Hay hierbas que son saliva triste.
Hay dientes en la tierra . . .
Debajo de la tierra hay, más honda, la roca,
la desnuda, purísima roca . . .
Hay agua bajo la tierra.[13]

Poeta en Nueva York teems with this kind of evocation of a barely organised or organisable chaos. In the space of a few stanzas of 'Oda al rey de Harlem' Lorca writes: 'La sangre no tiene puertas . . . Sangre furiosa . . . Sangre que busca . . . Sangre que mira . . . Es la sangre que viene,'.[14] The central stanzas of 'Vuelta de paseo' begin: 'Con el árbol . . . Con los animalitos . . . Con todo . . .'[15]

In his desire to state clearly and to re-define where necessary

Prados again draws upon a series of patterns which others had used. In 'Andando andando por el mundo' he affirms:

> no es el amor tan sólo lo que se para en nuestros ojos.
> (130:I,414)

In 'Danza de la muerte' Lorca had already written:

> No son los muertos los que bailan,
> estoy seguro.[16]

In 'Panorama ciego de Nueva York' he explains:

> No, no son los pájaros.
> No es un pájaro el que expresa la turbia fiebre de laguna,
> ni el ansia de asesinato . . .
> Es una cápsula de aire . . .[17]

Again in 'Bajo la tierra' it is Aleixandre who follows this technique of non-definition:

> No sois vosotros, los que vivís en el mundo,
> los que pasáis . . .[18]

Before moving on to examine the content of Prados's work during this period one further example of a shared starting point might be mentioned. The powerful 'Invocación al fuego' from *La voz cautiva* is another reminder that, despite the impression a reading of his biography may give, Prados is not entirely to be isolated from his contemporaries. Alberti's 'Los dos ángeles' would seem, in its use of the imperative, the short, urgent line and insistence on physical pain, to have in it the germ of Prados's later poem. Alberti wrote:

> Ángel de luz, ardiendo,
> ¡oh, ven!, y con tu espada
> incendia los abismos . . .
> . . . .
>
> Me duelen los cabellos
> y las ansias. ¡Oh, quémame!
> ¡Más, más, sí, sí, más! ¡Quémame![19]

Here is Prados addressing himself to the fire (compare Alberti's '¡Quémame!'):

> ¡Ven,
> que vengas,

que vuelvas,
rompedora de sombras! . . .
¡Oh!
¡Clávate en los pechos!
Tus buriles se pierdan por la sangre.
¡Más hondo!
¡Más arriba!
¡Libértala! (120:I,507)

Resemblances and cross-references such as these, superficial though they may be, are reminders that there is a sense in which Prados belongs to his generation.

Any conclusions drawn from such comparisons must be guarded. In referring to a 'change of direction' in the case of Prados, Alberti, Lorca or Cernuda, it must be remembered that though linked in time and in idiom they are each separate, unique. An analysis of Prados's output during the pre-war years cannot disregard the deliberately tortuous and ambiguous *persona* of *Tiempo* and *Cuerpo perseguido*. Recent criticism, mentioned at the beginning of this chapter, has tended to underline the relationship between his 'cambios sociales' and his poetry. Blanco records that, faced with a deteriorating political situation and eventually war, Prados began to dedicate himself to ideals of co-existence and harmony. Such a commitment to 'la realidad social que llama urgentemente a todos los hombres' was, says Blanco, by the same token a renunciation of earlier, more introspective attitudes. He has cut himself off from 'lo que acosa a él solamente'. It is hoped to suggest that it is misleading to infer that because, as the examples given above show, this poetry is more outward-looking that it is, therefore, 'poesía objetiva'.[20] Even the overtly social and political poetry dating from this period is not to be divorced from the central figure's private dilemma. The 'objective'–'subjective' dichotomy is an ambiguous and, in a sense, an irrelevant one.

'La voz cautiva'

It has already been hinted that differences exist between *La voz cautiva* and *Andando, andando por el mundo*. The latter could be characterised in part by its emphasis on the protagonist's consciousness that he belongs to his social environment, or at least to those parts of it which he chooses to describe:

> Yo pertenezco a esos anchos caminos donde los árboles se cuentan;

a ese olor que el estambre abandona en sus ruedas hilo a hilo que
canta. (I,426)

. . . .

Vivo bajo esa lama de los estanques,
en la paz de los bosques que se ignoran.
Como la luna resbala por la piedras
vivo en las multitudes herrumbrosas que acampan junto a un río.[21]

La voz cautiva is marked by his apartness from the social order: he stands, like some Old Testament prophet, in judgement upon it. Indeed, so veiled and, as Blanco puts it, 'general' are the allusions to society in *La voz cautiva* that the whole question of its relationship to social problems is an open one. The real emphasis in *La voz cautiva* is on that which is 'within' the protagonist himself, inner, invisible, yet at the same time real and vital.

Some of the original group's titles confirm this inwardness, e.g. 'Foco interior', 'Hacia adentro' and 'Interno sol'. The attention of the reader is directed, in 'Foco interior', to that which lies beneath the protagonist's breast:

Como el agua pregunta.
Como la misma lumbre se resbala.

Si tajaran el pecho;
si cercenaran la garganta:
¡qué hondo estanque redondo encontrarían! . . . (121:I,508)

In poems such as 'Vuelta' introspection is as intense as it has been anywhere in *Tiempo* or *Cuerpo perseguido*. The 'yo' pleads:

No, volvedme a mis noches;
a mi encerrado acento;
a las pesadas piedras que me esconden,
al oscuro terrón de mi silencio. (I,503)

The desire to be hidden, shut in—even buried away—from all that surrounds him suggests that issues other than social ones are at the heart of the poetry. It is with this in mind that the mysterious 'voz' and the reasons for its attractions will be examined.

Examination must begin by asking what the term 'voz' signifies. A poem entitled 'La voz cautiva' refers to it at some length.

Esta voz pesadumbre,
coagulación interna,
goterón errabundo golpe a golpe
donde un mar sin arena

impetuosamente irrumpe contra flores más altas;
contra cielos profundos
donde los párpados se hunden amontonados como estiércol,
incinerante llama que no sube,
se ahoga,
se agiganta palpitando su espectro
contra muros de yesos interiores.

Esta voz pesadumbre,
cuajarón o desierto,
piedra o lodo que en pena se atesora
por soledades hondas sin salida,
en sus prisiones cóncavas errante
huéspedes invocando vive. (I,487)

The description evokes an impression of uneasiness. The 'voz' is oppressed; it longs to be released from within the central figure. It needs to be rescued from oblivion and from the world's rejection of its message (later in the poem, he writes: 'Mírate. / Nadie escucha. / Fuera, suenan descargas . . .'). It possesses tremendous potential for good, as the second stanza quoted above shows: it is 'treasured up', and invites and awaits its guests.

If there is something frightening or sinister in the potential strength of the 'voice' in 'La voz cautiva', 'Foco interior' stresses the more tranquil aspect of its character:

Quieta el agua profunda de la sangre:
¡qué crisálida eleva de su centro!
¡qué luz votiva y cinta interrogante! . . .
Como un cisne, allí en medio
—¡qué fecunda palma!—,
vive la voz cautiva . . . (121:I,508)

That which is captive is, significantly, within the central figure. For although it is often referred to as having a wide-spread, universal effect (as in 'Invocación al fuego') it is nevertheless most easily understood as the 'voice' of the protagonist himself. The 'guests' it invites, the treasure it stores up, are those words which will constitute his poetry. In the revealing poem 'Vuelta' this alignment of the protagonist with the voice is at its clearest:

soy hombre entre cadenas;
soy voz entera que levanta;
sangrienta voz que se derrama,
carne que se conoce;
. . . . (I,503)

The importance of this new and ambitious role for poetry, in search of Jiménez's 'nombre exacto de las cosas', pre-figures important developments in later stages in the life of the 'yo'.[22]

Given that this is how the 'voz cautiva' is to be understood, an important question remains unanswered. What are the factors which, in a period when the 'yo' is supposed to show a revived interest in the outside world, cause him to turn in upon himself yet again, to seek out the 'foco interior' mentioned in the anthology?

Several possibilities suggest themselves. The first has already been mentioned in another context. These lines are from 'Vuelta':

¡Redobladme los hierros!
¡Que no escape!
¡Tenedme!
¡Sujetadme!
¿Qué tengo yo en el viento?
No, volvedme a mis noches;
a mi encerrado acento;
a las pesadas piedras que me esconden,
al oscuro terrón de mi silencio. (I,503)

There is a recognition that he has no interest in what the wind represents and reminds him of—fertility. He asks to be enclosed within the night, where *Cuerpo perseguido* found him. In the context of the outside world he is made aware of his own infertility (a theme which *Andando, andando* . . . drives home with some force). Within, these tensions cease to weigh upon him. Indeed, there is even the possibility of finding there the 'voice' which 'Foco interior' refers to specifically in terms of fertility: '—¡qué fecunda palma!—'. In this sense the pursuit of the 'voice' mirrors that of the dream of *Cuerpo perseguido*. It creates a situation where it is the central figure who is in a position to control and limit his experience.

There is a second reason for the central figure's pursuit of that which is 'within' him. It is the note of 'desengaño' which many poems sound. The world is presented as something which is illusory, deceptive. In this sense Prados continues to find himself in direct opposition to the confident, joyous Guillén. 'Meditación primera' finds the 'yo' unconvinced of the worth or reality of what surrounds him:

¿Por qué llamar amor y muerte
a lo que sólo es forma de un impotente anhelo?
Fríos fantasmas, ráfagas sin mundo,
huelen por la memoria de la sangre.

Y no es que el mundo encuentre divisiones de término
aun la piedra es la piedra y hay flores en la rama.
No ha llegado el gusano, que el corazón persiste;
pero un témpano asombra su permanente engaño.[23]

Human pain and misery lead him to the conclusion that this is, to quote 'Primera salida', a 'mundo falso'. Is there even such a thing as existence? This is the question raised by these lines, so reminiscent of Cernuda:

Aquí los hombres mueven
las anchas cintas blancas de sus vidas
como vueltas raíces encrespadas sobre agitados cielos.
¡Oh cabellera altísima de esta humana demencia
que ni el sabor conoce de una piel contra el suelo!
Estos cuerpos o fiebres en bandada,
que aun se mueven y rozan sin conocer sus límites,
como la sombra misma se hieren contra el agua.
¿Quizás su vida exista como tierra sin tacto?
—¡Quizás la vida exista como cruza esta nube!

A man's life is marked by reminders of transience, reminders which separate him from the permanent enjoyment of the higher life which the natural world, for example, enjoys. The civilised order, on the other hand, serves only to increase his sense of 'desengaño'. He sees it, as did Lorca, as a threat to the consideration of more important values. As has already been mentioned, 'la cal y la mentira' are referred to in 'Invocación al fuego'. In 'Para qué está tu sangre' the 'yo' invites the natural power of the 'voz', symbolised by the sun, to come and sweep away the artefacts of civilisation:

Caigan templos o llamas.
Cruja el papel ardiendo entre el escombro, la saliva, la piedra
y la mentira.
Ascienda el humo y claven los crujidos
sus lenguas el cielo de la hoguera.
Mira: la carne canta y se fecunda. (I,490)

There is, then, a sense of uselessness and futility in what he has come to see round about him. This expresses itself in fierce condemnation of the 'world'—a condemnation in which interestingly enough, in the light of what we learn of his condition in *Tiempo* and *Cuerpo perseguido*, the central figure accuses the world of sterility, infertility. 'Para qué está tu sangre' contains this assessment of it:

Está el mundo parado, perseguido;
todo el polen temblando está en sus bordes.
¿Quién levanta estos hierros?
¡Qué murallas!
¡Qué dolor sin lamento!
¡Qué fuerza atenazada en cordura!
¡Qué sangrienta templanza! (I,490)

In 'Vuelta' he writes:

Mira:
fuera el pavor se siente:
no anda el río;
el pájaro está en tierra muerto;
tronchado el árbol,
el hombre perseguido . . . (I,504)

So it is in part, also, his view of the world as impoverished, offering little in terms of permanence or fertility, which leads him to adopt such an inward-looking stance.

It would come as no surprise if this stance were to involve some version of the dream which appears in *Tiempo* and *Cuerpo perseguido*. But it does not. A further aspect of the protagonist's 'desengaño' concerns this vital area. '¿Para qué está tu sangre . . .' draws attention to the 'luz del mundo', the 'voice'—a life-giving force standing, once more, in opposition to the flimsy fabrication of society. The central figure, in contrast with the tortured protagonist of *Sobre los ángelos*, feels he has some kind of an answer to problems which surround him. But where is the light to direct its energies? A number of suggestions are rejected—and they include the dream:

. . . .
¿para qué está la sangre sino para arrastrar la sombra y la
ceniza?
Sí, voz,
que escuchen tu palabra:
¡luz del mundo!
Pero ¿dónde?
¿Hacia dónde esa mano se extiende sin memoria?
¿Otra vez vuelta al sueño?
¿Nuevamente a la fábula?
¿al mito?
¿a la mentira?
¡Oh, frío espanto!
¡Oh, témpanos de angustia! (I:490–1)[24]

As Cano points out, he is beginning to seek a release from the 'cárcel del sueño'.[25]

The poem 'Vuelta' confirms this view. The rejection of the dream is expressed by reference to the symbol of the flower. In 'Fin del día, en la escuela', it is the flower which is destroyed by the arrival of the dawn: '¡Se me quiebra en la frente la flor de todo el sueño!' (20). In the poem 'Vuelta', however, the protagonist in no way resents the elimination of the dream—indeed, he seems to encourage it. In discussing *Cuerpo perseguido* it was suggested that it was in the dream that the 'tú' was to be found by the protagonist. In 'Cita hacia dentro' he abandons the sun, the day, for the night where sleep, the dream and, thus, the 'tú' are to be encountered:

Deja el sol; deja el cuerpo,
ya vendrán otras albas . . .
¡Voy a coger el sueño!
¡Te espero en su terraza! (61:I,236)

Addressing the darkness, the 'tiniebla', in 'Vuelta' he pleads for an end to these same 'terraces' of the dream:

Suban;
suban tus brazos,
tus paredes.
Se apaguen tus terrazas.
Tus anchos ventanales y tus puertas
endurezcan sus hierros con la noche.
¡Oh tinieblas altísimas,
cerrad los curvos pétalos;
llevadme,
ocultadme en el centro
de la siniestra torre en esta cárcel! (I,502)

There is an important—though admittedly, at this stage, vague—change in the direction of the central figure's energies. The search is for an alternative which will remove him from the realm of the unreal, the transient.

It is, then, against a background of radical doubt and questioning that the 'voz' is sought. As the lines already quoted from '¿Para qué está tu sangre . . .' suggest, a number of the escape-routes used in the past are now being rejected. He is no longer content to return 'al sueño . . . a la fábula . . . al mito . . . a la mentira'. Yet despite the elusiveness of the voice as described there, the 'yo' nevertheless presses on to experience it more fully. In 'Primera salida' he explains:

> 'ese dolor me llama: / esa piedra fugaz o piel me incita.'
>
> (I,501)

The search for the 'voz' triggers off experiences which are as distinctive as the problems outlined above which inspire that search. The new note of insecurity, a lack of permanence, gives rise to an experience described in terms of the eternal—and which later poetry, such as *Mínima muerta* and *Jardín Cerrado*, will develop. But before finally considering the nature of this experience of the 'voz' reference must first be made to some of the factors which act as a barrier to its enjoyment.

To do this the poem 'La voz cautiva' must be re-examined. The initial stanzas refer to the hidden treasure of the voice within the 'yo'. But there is some kind of restriction on its activities. Speaking of the 'voz' he writes:

> ¿Adónde van sus golpes? . . .
> ¡Qué curvas se levantan!
> Ráfagas vuelan contra internos bosques.
> Se derrumban pilares.
> Quiebran puertas.
> ¡Siempre la horrible sombra de sus límites! (I,487–8)

'Espejismos' from *Tiempo* suggests what these 'limits' might be. There the 'yo' asks: '(¿En dónde cómenzarán / los límites de mi cuerpo?)' (21:I,386). Not only is the body limiting in the contact of love: it is limiting in its finiteness. Like the world it is of a nature opposite to that of the 'voz'. These lines, which close 'La voz cautiva', underline this point and at the same time indicate that some form of 'death' is needed before the central figure can experience the 'voz':

> ¡Oh voz pujante, ten tus ímpetus!
> ¡Qué pesadumbre voz contra el silencio!
> ¡Qué restallar de sangre contra duros barrotes!
>
> ¿Hasta cuándo?
> ¿Hasta cuándo este acento?
>
> ¡Ay voz! . . .
> ¡Ay voz! . . .
>
> FECUNDA MUERTE:
> LA PRISIÓN ES EL MUNDO (I,488)

The theme of 'desengaño' already mentioned is confirmation of the central figure's attitude towards these restricting forces. That which is transient, subject to constant change, cannot provide a basis for the type of experience he desires. That can only be achieved when there is a dying, a 'fecunda muerte' which will release the voice, the infinite which is at present, he believes, captive within him. If it is perhaps the youthful reading of Whitman which informs *Andando, andando por el mundo*, then it is of Prados's early enthusiasm for San Juan and his links with Jiménez that *La voz cautiva* (and even more, *Mínima muerte* and *Jardín cerrado*) is a reflection.[26]

'S.O.S.' is further proof that it is, above all, his finiteness which stands in the way of the experience of the liberation of the 'voice', the 'alta llama'. The reference to the 'larga cuchilla' suggests that it is only by a process of mortification that the 'voz' can be released:

Afilada cuchilla
¿qué largas venas abres?

Ya al viento:
¡volad ríos!

Muñecas, duras torres,
descolgad vuestras manos:
¡las campanas!

La tierra está en el suelo:
se oye crujir bajo los pies su entraña.

Larga cuchilla
¡raja por los ojos!
¡Liberta, liberta de su sombra
la alta llama! (I,505)

The finite level of the body and the senses (represented by 'los ojos') must be removed before the higher territory of the inner 'voice' can be explored.

It has been stated that *La voz cautiva* shares something of the introspection of *Tiempo* and *Cuerpo perseguido*. The new note which it sounds—its 'desengaño', its search for the 'voz' within the central figure—is reflected in a number of important ways, ways which prefigure many key developments in later poetry. Though together they do not form any cohesive pattern—indeed, *La voz cautiva* is one of the most disparate and incohesive sections of Prados's output—

they nevertheless serve as valuable pointers to lines of thought which will later preoccupy the protagonist.

The first of these is an involvement with the natural world. At times the 'yo' has gone so far as to accuse the outside world of sterility and barrenness—the river no longer flows, the bird is dead, the tree hewn down. But there is also a deep admiration of the natural cycle, an admiration which, in a poem like 'Hondo cielo', far outweighs such accusations. If in *Tiempo* nature was important as an expression of the central figure's emotional situation, here it is rather an embodiment of those qualities of permanence and harmony which he has come to seek in the 'voice'. Within its cycle, struggle and death yield life. The life of its individual parts is fleeting, but it is absorbed into a pattern which seems to have no end. 'Hondo cielo' describes the life of the deep ocean:

> "Nunca más, nunca más" es un signo allí desconocido
> como la historia de regiones que jamás existieron.
> "Donde" también sin sangre no encuentra su sentido,
> vuela o sueña la vida la altitud de sus límites
> sin que el ansia del borde hiera el goce del tacto.
>
> Ni el pedernal ni la inocencia pisan, sumergidos,
> la existencia real que animan con su verbo:
> la entraña de la piedra su inútil llama enfría sin encender su nombre
> y la culpa no existe donde el hombre está ausente . . .
> . . . .
> ¡Oh profundo secreto!
> ¡Hondo abismo! (I,513–4)

Its appeal lies in its timelessness, its limitlessness—qualities which separate it from human existence, and which will in future books—especially *Río natural*—increasingly attract the central figure. It is the sea to which Jiménez, in 'Para que yo te oiga', listened 'Con oído de dios'.[27]

A second development springs from this new preoccupation with the voice. In *Tiempo* the central figure was irresistibly—and involuntarily—drawn towards the moon. He was forced to admit that there was an affinity between his body and the moon. With *La voz cautiva* there is an indication of re-alignment. The 'voz' on a number of occasions, is related to the sun. 'Interno sol' refers to a new power within the body of the 'yo' which protects and helps give birth to the voice:

> Interno sol,

¿qué llamas contra el cuerpo?
¿Sordos golpes? ¿Pedradas?
¡Oh qué campana el pulso a gritos hieres!
¿Adónde vas?
¿Qué aliento nuevo empujas?
. . . .
¡Oh fuente, no te huyas!
Voz, resiste.
Interno sol, ocúltate en tus rayos. (I,498)

In 'Para qué está tu sangre . . .' the voice is again referred to in terms of light:

Sí, voz,
que escuchen tu palabra:
¡oh Luz del mundo! (I:490)

The protagonist is becoming increasingly aware of a potential for the existence of the infinite within himself, of a timeless fertility such as the sun represents.

This potential, however, has another symbol in *La voz cautiva*. It involves a third change of attitude on the part of the 'yo'. In poetry of earlier years the sea, by association with the fish and the busy boats which inhabited it, played a conventional role as a symbol of fertility—a fertility not shared by the central figure. One of the main characteristics of the *La voz cautiva* poem, 'Foco interior', is the use of images related to water—the 'estanque' or the 'agua profunda de la sangre'—to describe the inner consciousness of the protagonist himself:

Como el agua pregunta.
Como la misma lumbre se resbala.

Si tajaran el pecho;
si cercenaran la garganta:
¡qué hondo estanque redondo encontrarían! . . .

Quieta el agua profunda de la sangre:
¡qué crisálida eleva de su centro!
¡qué luz votiva y cinta interrogante! . . . (121:I,508)

Something of the infinite and fertile nature of the sea is being discovered within the 'yo'.

Of the poems discussed, only two find their place in *Antología*. Taken in conjunction with the poems from which they were chosen, however, they mark significant changes in attitude. They record a search for a sense of permanence and of the infinite within the 'yo'; and in the reference to the water and to the sun, they make use of a symbolic language which suggests that he is beginning to look at himself in a new way.

Andando, andando por el mundo

Monterde's verdict on *La voz cautiva* was that it marked an 'etapa de transición': and that in *Andando, andando por el mundo,* the poet 'recobra el paso anterior, el ritmo isócrono'.[28] As has been mentioned in the introduction to this chapter, strong links exist between the two sections. There are technical similarities—the use, for example, of lengthy lines of free verse, referred to by Monterde. There are also thematic links: they share that 'tono menor' which Allué y Morer sees as typical of Prados's work.[29] And in both society is a factor which the 'yo' is beginning to take into account.

In *Andando, andando por el mundo* however, his relationship with the world about him is more exactly defined. *La voz cautiva* presented it as the 'falso mundo', one of several reasons why the 'yo' sought an experience which would be 'real', permanent, eternal. Here its depiction has one clear effect: to act as a context for and reflection of the same intense personal problems as were outlined in *Tiempo*. What seems to be 'social comment' or 'objective' observation is, in fact, a recapitulation of those insidious anxieties and frustrations which *Tiempo* described. To use the language of the journey of the 'marinero', it signals a temporary return to the point where the voyage began.[30]

The section is most easily understood in terms of two underlying tensions. The first lies in an antithesis between what the 'yo' feels to be his sterility and the fertility which normal life, despite all its shortcomings, enjoys. The second is based on the antagonism he senses between himself and a society which regards him as abnormal, infertile. Analysis will begin by establishing the norm against which the protagonist judges himself, that healthy fertility which runs through the pattern of everyday life.

The four poems which constitute the section and the more extensive group of poems from which they were chosen are strewn with references to the fertility and life that exist potentially in the natural and the human realm. In *Tiempo* the presence of the bird and the fish made the sailor increasingly miserable. Erotic symbols were reminders of the careless enjoyment other members of the natural order could find in the realm of the body. That they should reappear in *Andando, andando por el mundo* suggests that such problems persist. But a new emphasis emerges: the awareness that others are alive to his inadequacies; and a growing realisation that both the dream of *Cuerpo perseguido* and the mysterious inner experience of *La voz cautiva* are an inadequate substitute for the fertility others share.

'Quisiera huir', the selection's opening poem, illustrates this. The poem contains one of the first references in the anthology which leads us to see the 'yo' as at least in some respects 'normal': he is talking with a friend. The conversation is reported:

> Un amigo me dice:
> "Hay cuerpos que aún se ofrecen
> como jugosas frutas sin sentido" . . .
> Otro amigo me canta:
> "¡Vuelan las aves, vuelan!" . . . (125:I,403)

The first friend's comments presuppose that the central figure has expressed his despair that any relationship with a woman could be formed—the unhappy conclusion to be derived from *Tiempo*. His companion's suggestion is that he should try to solve the problem by recourse to a purely physical relationship, the prostitute, the 'jugosas frutas sin sentido'. No reply is made. Even the bought body is capable of some kind of natural sexual activity: but the protagonist is not.

The second suggestion, the reference to the flight of the birds, has a similar connotation. The image of the bird in *Tiempo* and *Canciones del farero* was used as an erotic symbol. The initial, and only, reaction to these reminders of the norm, in this poem at least, is to escape into the unchallenging world of his own dream:

> Yo quiero huir, perderme lejos,
> allá en esas regiones en que unas anchas hojas
> tiemblan sobre el estanque de los sueños que inundan.

'Nunca más' also reports a conversation, and one which leads to a similar conclusion. Here the remarks are characterised by their inconsequentiality and aimlessness:

> Se habla, se habla y nunca llega a deshilarse la verdad de una historia:
> —. . . "¡Una vez . . ."
> —. . . "¡Fue allá lejos donde crece el tabaco . . ." (126:I,415)

It is the lines which follow which are of interest here. While this meaningless chatter is being carried on, the process of reproduction, represented here by the contact of the boat (a masculine symbol) with the sea, the 'légamo oscuro' (a feminine symbol) and the activities of the birds, is being far more vigorously pursued. The 'yo', however, is still without an 'amante':

> Pero los barcos vuelven a hundirse bajo el légamo oscuro
> y los pájaros siguen multiplicándose a espaldas de la noche
> como estrellas.
> ¿Dónde estará ese amante impreciso? . . .
> ¿Dónde estará esa palabra incorruptible? (126:I,415)

In 'El llanto subterráneo' the protagonist gives clear expression to his conviction that his nature differs markedly from that of the people and animals around him.[31] He admits that he cannot sing as do the birds:

> Y he deshilado el río de los mapas
> recostado en mi llanto como encima de un sueño.
> Blanca estuvo mi mano en su dulzura;
> mas no puedo cantar como esas aves.
> Ya no puedo cantar. (Canta quien puede).
> Ya no puedo cantar como esas aves . . .

The central figure is unable to share their joyful and natural experience: as he did in *Tiempo*, he can concern himself only with the illusion, the 'río de los *mapas*', languishing helplessly in the realm of the dream. The body has become again an object of fear and shame. In 'Tengo miedo' he outlines some of his reasons for feeling apart from the norm—including the heartless birds which, like the fish in *Tiempo*, mock his 'flesh':

> Tengo miedo a este brazo que en la tierra navega.
> Tengo miedo a esas aves que mi carne circundan.
> Tengo miedo a esa profunda estrella mojada por la muerte.
> Tengo miedo a estas hojas marchitas que rezuma mi boca.
> Tengo miedo a este cielo que me pudre las sienes.
> Tengo miedo a ese día que taladra mi sangre.

A further reason given relates to the question of his attitude to his body: his reluctance to behold it, his discomfort on seeing it. He writes:

> Tengo miedo . . .
> . . . .

A esa luz que me ordena desnudarme en la sombra tengo miedo.[32]

In 'Quisiera huir', in the same vein—but this time, it would seem, shielding himself from other people's reaction to his body—he confesses:

Estoy cansado de ocultarme en las ramas;
de perseguir mi sombra por la arena;
de desnudarme entre las rocas,
. . . . (125:I,403)

The continuation of 'Tengo miedo' makes such complaints more specific. The night is, as it was in *Tiempo*, irksome and sleepless:

Permanezco sin señas estrangulado por mi sangre
en las horas nocturnas que pueblan mis desiertos;
en las horas nocturnas que levantan mis pozos
como torres inversas al cuerpo que no encuentro.

The 'yo' is still alone, without true direction, 'sin sueño'. The 'towers' are inverted—the phallic symbol cruelly distorted. The fertile body is still 'un cuerpo que no encuentro'.

Tiempo used the symbol of the boat to refer to the body. 'Tengo miedo' begins by further reference to it:

He pedido mi ingreso en ese cuerpo voluntario,
en esa rumorosa claridad disidente,
en esa muerta nave que aún flota hundida
bajo el celeste asedio de las más altas naves.

The boat is, characteristically, 'dead'. It cannot compare with 'las más altas naves'. But the 'yo' still hopes to enter fully into it, to experience the reality it should, by rights, afford.

'Si yo pudiera' indicates the futility of such a hope. Such a desire is a mere dream-wish:

"Si yo pudiera un día
abandonar sobre este ardor lejano,
como un blanco navío,
el altísimo témpano que apuñala mi angustia . . ." (I,427)

Here the 'blanco navío' is, by implication, 'lejano'. Even more hopelessly, it is linked with 'el altísimo témpano de mi angustia'. The truth is more akin to Cernuda's experience who, in 'No intentemos el amor nunca', wrote of 'Barcos . . . / En un fondo de noche, / . . . Viajando hacia nada'.[33] There is none of the optimistic assurance of Guillén's 'Quiero dormir':

> Abandonándome a la cómplice
> Barca
> Llegaré por mis ondas y nieblas
> Al alba.[34]

The boat representing the protagonist's body has changed little from the one described in *Canciones del farero*, limping shamefacedly from one unwelcoming port to another.

Having reviewed the protagonist's attitude to the fertility of the natural and human order, and towards his own miserable condition, it is possible to examine the presentation of society in *Andando, andando por el mundo*. The picture is an unusual and unhappy one. But it is not one which can be understood in purely political or social terms. Of *La voz cautiva* and *Andando, andando* . . . Blanco writes:

> Sociedad-suciedad, parecen decirnos estos poemas: entrevistos el dolor del individuo y de la sociedad cuando los ideales de dos o tres años antes empiezan a falsearse en el creciente caos político español, no le es ya posible al poeta el canto libre como si viviese fuera del tiempo: . . .[35]

In the introduction to this chapter several examples were given of poems where the central figure seemed to be involving himself in the plight of members of certain elements of society. But lines quoted from 'Quisiera huir' and 'Nunca más' are enough in themselves to suggest something other than social problems. Why is it that the 'yo' portrays society in terms of 'suciedad'? Such references as there are to the social order are significant, in terms of the central figure, for reasons other than that they express any desire for the improvement of that order.

The protagonist is, in fact, highly selective as to those parts of society which he describes. Certain emphases are very strong. There is a concentration on a sense of dullness and indolence. Attention is repeatedly drawn to men engaged in some kind of fruitless activity:

> Andando andando sobre el mundo se llega,
> con el mundo se asciende a sus altos confines:
> andando andando donde duermen los hombres,
> donde cuelgan sus manos como largos balidos.

Andando andando por el dolor se entiende,
en las ínfimas salas en que crujen sus lechos;
andando andando por las desiertas calles
en las interminables colas que aguardan en los muelles. (129:I,413)

'El llanto subterráneo' refers to: 'los grandes puentes donde duele la vida / y unos hombres se acercan a morir en silencio' (I,422).

There is a related concentration on those who have been rejected by society, those who, according to 'Tengo miedo', find themselves alone:

He pedido mi ingreso en la legión de los hombres perdidos,
de los hombres que suenan sus huesos solitarios
en los huecos caminos que los alejan de su frente. (I,401)[36]

The desperate vagrants of 'El Llanto subterráneo' are also marked by their isolation:

—esos hombres que llegan sin amor y sin rostro,
uno a uno, millones desde los cuatro olvidos.
Desde los cuatro mares que los pescados lloran,
llegan y se arrodillan bajo los anchos puentes
—bajo esos anchos puentes donde duele la vida
y obedecen los muslos sin temblor y sin gozo
a la sombra que escupen de un ardor que no sienten.[37]

The descriptions evoke a sense of frustration, the waste, the non-realisation of potential. The phrase 'un ardor que no sienten' finds its echo in 'Como piedra olvidada', a poem in which similar ideas re-appear:

Como ese sabor acre que nos deja en los labios la miseria;
que comienza en los ojos igual que una cuchilla,
estos cuerpos sin sangre tendidos sobre la arena
desnudan gota a gota una conciencia que no duerme.

Sueñan cuerpos de niños y gritos de mujeres,
la vida que no sienten de una amarga sonrisa . . .
su sueño, un ancho lago, supurante memoria,
allá lejos donde el mar mece y mece sus constantes espinas.
(I,420)

Above all, those parts of society with which *Andando, Andando . . .* deals are being persecuted, harassed by other members of it. 'Si yo pudiera' mentions 'las multitudes herrumbrosas que acampan junto a un río' (I,426). They are those who, for some reason or another, are 'seres que velan sus rebaños y el ansia de otros muertos', 'rostros míseros que a la luna dormitan o que tal vez se mueren'.[38]

The reason why such emphases should exist is clear when this poetry is compared with that of *Tiempo*. There it was the landscape or seascape which served as a reflection of the central figure's condition. Here society is the new landscape. The 'yo' associates with these strands of society simply because he too is desolate, fruitless, rejected, persecuted. The following outburst, taken from 'El llanto subterráneo', makes this clear:

> ¿Soy otro peso errante sobre la misma esfera?
> ¿otro cuerpo que ofrece sus inútiles horas?
> ¿otra apesadumbrada voluntad que camina?
> ¿otro crimen reciente? . . .
> "¡Tal vez! ¡Tal vez . . ."
> ¿Quién canta? ¿Soy yo?: Tal vez soy yo. (Canta quien puede).
> Ahora cantan de mí como esas aves .
> Antes cantaba yo como ellas vuelan
> sobre la blanca espuma. Mi voz, también cantaba . . .
> Cantaba yo sobre la blanca espuma . . .
> Volaba yo, volaba yo como esas aves . . .
> Mas hoy perdí mi rostro, el pescado me duele,
> toda la arena clava su espina en mi silencio,
> y no puedo cantar, tan sólo escucho . . .[39]

The pathetic tragedy of those he observes is to be related to his own.

The structure of 'Si yo pudiera' bears this out. The poem is composed of two alternating types of material. The first begins with the words 'Yo pertenezco a . . .'. The second, in inverted commas and sandwiched between the first, consists of the expression of the desires of the central figure. There are four such stanzas, each beginning: 'Si yo pudiera . . .'. These are, significantly, entirely consonant with the protagonist's previous attitudes to his body. They are sufficiently important to be quoted in full here. The first reminds us of the tension between the central figure's 'mental' awareness of the possibility of physical contact ('esta razón que mi genio anima') and his inability to experience it (suggested by the image of opening the doors of his body):

> "Si yo pudiera un día, un día tan sólo,
> como esta razón que mi genio anima,
> abrir de par en par las puertas
> de mi cuerpo y las granjas . . ." (I,426)

In the second the moon returns, and in its presence the 'yo' seeks to shed the oppressive load, that 'ansia que circunda mi frente', described in the opening poem of *Cuerpo perseguido*:

> "Si yo pudiera como esos seres en olvido que pasan y repasan
>   su soledad bajo la luna,
> dejar sobre la nieve
> todo el ardor del ansia que circunda mi frente . . ."

The third, already cited, echoes the note of anguish and pain:

> "Si yo pudiera un día
> abandonar sobre este ardor lejano,
> como un blanco navío,
> el altísimo témpano que apuñala mi angustia . . ."

The final stanza of this type reiterates his longing to leave the world of the map, the chart of *Tiempo*, the dream of *Memoria del olvido*, with all their attendant pain and implicit sterility (represented by the reference to the 'bueyes'):

> "Si yo pudiera un día, un día tan sólo,
> abandonar sobre la tierra enteramente
> estos bueyes que hoy labran los bordes de mi sueño . . ."

This is a longing which in itself bears little relation to the social problems which Blanco describes. What then is the relevance of the second category of material in the poem, material which, as the following examples illustrate, does seem linked with the delineation of conditions faced by the lower strata of society?:

> Yo pertenezco al fondo de esas viejas lagunas,
> de esos hombres que marchan sin conocerse sobre el mundo;
> . . . .
>
> Yo pertenezco a esos hombres que mueren.
> . . . .
>
> vivo en las multitudes herrumbrosas que acampan junto a un
>   río.

Its presence is to be explained in the terms outlined above. The images of misery, despair gleaned by the 'yo' from the outside world are intended as a graphic revelation of his own condition: it is only because he is as he is, sterile, isolated, persecuted (as subsequent quotation will confirm) that such a selection is made. The section's portrayal of 'society' is of necessity limited. While the longing described in 'Si yo pudiera' remains unfulfilled, and as long as he is still plagued with anguish and fear, then his only real link with society will be, as in *Andando, Andando por el mundo*, a discriminatory identification with that part of it which in some way reflects his own dilemma.

In the light of such conclusions, it is possible to review the central figure's current situation. In a sense it is worse than in *Tiempo* or *Cuerpo perseguido*. For the mockery and reproach of 'normal' people has now been added to his previously self-inflicted torment. This is why he is portrayed typically in the group as an outsider, afraid to reveal his true self. This is how he describes himself in 'Estoy cansado' (a title borrowed from Cernuda's *Un río, un amor*):

> Estoy cansado de ocultarme en las ramas;
> de perseguir mi sombra por la arena;
> de desnudarme entre las rocas,
> de aguardar a las puertas de las fábricas
> y tenderme en el suelo con los ojos cerrados:
> estoy cansado de esta herida. (125:I,403)

The poem 'Yo estoy no es la adolescencia' is a savage attack— almost completely a-social in content— on that adolescence which, for the 'yo', brought only a consciousness of inadequacy. The nature of his body set him apart from his fellows—and persecuted by them. It contains this definition of adolescence:

> Es la indolencia,
> el primer navazajo que un río nos desmaya,
> la formación de un mapa y de un ejército,
> la voz,
> las persecuciones que transmutan sus términos,
> la tierra sin aliento que no será una estancia en un cuerpo
> seguro:
> ¡un grito! (I,418)

He is a figure forced to take refuge in the night:

> Andando andando esa otra piel más íntima;
> esas voces que alumbran los labios que no ignoran,
> esa carne que busca su refugio en la noche:
> andando andando por el sueño se entiende . . . (129:I,413)

Like Lorca, he walks 'llorando por la calle, / grotesco y sin solución'.[40] He finds himself, as did Cernuda, rejected: 'Como él mismo extranjero, / Como el viento huyo lejos.'[41] Such is the harsh reality which confronts the central figurc of *Andando, andando. . . .*

In view of the transitional nature of this poetry it is worth noting that, like *La voz cautiva*, it contains important indications of future developments. The lengthy 'Aquí estoy' looks forward to a time when he will enjoy a level of peace impossible at present—and makes this point by reference to those curves and circles which will come to play an integrated part in the protagonist's way of thinking only much later in his development. Such stanzas as these reflect, or indeed, pre-figure, Guillén's 'perfección del círculo':

> Están las tiernas ramas y las hojas que mecen
> mientras curva la tierra uniendo al horizonte . . .
> . . . .
>
> Me quedo en estas playas hasta esperar que lleguen
> de nuevo a ver mis manos la curva del espacio . . .[42]

The vision of the new day he hopes to see is expressed in terms of the ring:

> Un día será el mundo
> como un inmenso anillo abierto;
> . . . .
>
> un anillo de brazos unidos sobre la tierra,
> . . . .[43]

The optimism of these, the two final closing poems of one manuscript arrangement of *Andando, andando* . . . —'Aquí estoy' and 'Un día'—is, however, something of a post-script. The central figure is still, as the bulk of the poetry suggests, deeply disturbed. He still seeks some kind of a refuge where his private condition can either be absorbed and thus hidden, or simply forgotten. Although he seems to have stepped into the outside world, he has but a specialised and limited interest in the social order. He is still as Gerardo Diego reminds us, a 'cazador de nubes'. *Llanto en la sangre*, the next step in what Xirau calls Prados's 'obra continua', serves, in a sense, to postpone the possibility of any real step forward in the central figure's inner development. For there, too, he has found an ideal, though bloody, landscape for the profound struggle raging within him.

1 Most of the poetry quoted here is contained in *Poesías completas* I, pp. 399–447 and 485–514 and in the *Antología*. Some additional poems or variants are to be found in Appendix VI.

2 This classification of his output is recorded in Caja 2.5, and is reproduced in Appendix V.

3 C. Blanco Aguinaga, *Vida* y *obra*, p. 62.

4 C. B. Morris, *Rafael Alberti's Sobre los Ángeles: Four Major Themes* (Hull, 1966), p. 7.

5 See Appendix VI, p. 320.

6 F. G. Lorca, *Obras completas*, p. 516.

7 *Ibid.*, p. 521.

8 *Ibid.*, p. 471.

9 R. Alberti, *Poesía (1924–1967)* (Madrid, 1977), p. 317.

10 *Ibid.*, p. 133.

11 F. G. Lorca, *op. cit.*, p. 472.

12 V. Aleixandre, *Obras completas*, p. 257.

13 *Ibid.*, p. 450.

14 F. G. Lorea, *op. cit.*, p. 480.

15 *Ibid.*, p. 451.

16 *Ibid.*, p. 486.

17 *Ibid.*, p. 495.

18 V. Aleixandre, *op. cit.*, p. 450.

19 R. Alberti, *Poesía*, p. 339.

20 C. Blanco Aguinaga, *Vida* y *obra*, p. 63.

21 Appendix VI, p. 317.

22 Juan Cano Ballesta describes the voice of the poet as 'una poderosa fuerza interior, . . .' ('Poesia y revolución: Emilio Prados', in *Homenaje universitario a Dámaso Alonso* (Madrid), p. 241). In his article he argues that *La voz cautiva* represents the poet's dilemma when confronted with the question of 'la poesía comprometida'. We hope to suggest that also is it to be related to the protagonist's search for permanence, security and fertility.

23 See Caja 3.5.

24 For the slightly different version quoted here, see Caja 3.5.

25 J. L. Cano, *La poesía de la generación del 27*, p. 266.

26 C. Blanco Aguinaga, *Vida* y *obra*, p. 15.

27 J. R. Jiménez, *Tercera antología poética*, p. 994.

28 F. Monterde, 'Obra de dos poetas españoles en México', *Cuadernos americanos* no. 3 (México, 1955), pp. 284–6.

29 F. Allué y Morer, 'El poeta Emilio Prados', *Poesía española* (1962).

30 Juan Cano Ballesta, in his article 'Poesía y revolución: Emilio Prados', notes that *Andando, andando por el mundo* contains a degree of social involvement, 'sin ser en su conjunto un libro de preocupación social, . . .'.

31 The version included in Appendix VI, p. 318, differs from the one included in the *Poesías completas*.

32 For this variant of 'Tengo miedo', see Caja 3.6.

33 L. Cernuda, *La realidad y el deseo*, p. 52.

34 J. Guillén, *Cántico*, p. 436.

35 C. Blanco Aguinaga, *Vida* y *obra*, pp. 62–3.

36 It is interesting to compare the tone of these lines with these of Machado—lines which, incidentally might account for the title, *Andando, andando por el mundo*: 'He andado muchos caminos, / he abierto muchas veredas; / he navegado en cien mares, / y atracado en cien riberas. / En todas partes he visto / caravanas de tristeza, / soberbios y melancólicos / borrachos de sombra negra, . . .' (A. Machado, 'Soledades', *Obras: poesía y prosa*, p. 56).

37 See again the version contained in Appendix VI, p. 318. For Blanco's text, see I,424.

38 Appendix VI, p. 317.

39 This version differs slightly from the one reproduced in *Poesías completas* I,424, and is taken from Caja 3.6.

40 F. G. Lorca, 'Canción menor', *Obras completas*, p. 112.

41 L. Cernuda, 'Como el viento', *La realidad y el deseo*, p. 45. In connection with *Cuerpo perseguido* we have already quoted Laing's reference on the concurrence of homosexual tendencies and persecution ideas. Reference to this kind of attitude-pattern is not out of place here.

42 Appendix VI, pp. 320–2.

43 Appendix VI, p. 324.

CHAPTER FOUR

The Poetry of Commitment

I too haughty Shade also sing war, and a longer and greater one than any,
Waged in my book with varying fortune, with flight, advance and retreat, victory deferr'd and wavering,
(Yet methinks certain, or as good as certain, at the last,) the field the world,
For life and death, for the Body and for the eternal Soul,
. . . .

(Walt Whitman, 'As I ponder'd in Silence', *Leaves of Grass*)

The adversities to which we are accustomed do not disturb us.

(Claudian, *In Eutropium*, Book ii)

Introduction—war within and without

Prados, on his return from Germany in 1922, had been among the first of the poets of his generation to address himself to political problems. It was 1929 before Alberti began to take an active part in politics and 1932 before Lorca devoted his energies to La Barraca and thus, indirectly, to social problems. Prados's work does not reflect the intense anti-clericalism of Alberti, nor share the kind of commitment of which Cernuda wrote in *Octubre*; 'Confío . . . en una revolución que el comunismo inspire. La vida se salvará así'.[1] His name is, however, to be found amongst those of intellectuals who, in August, 1937, clearly identified themselves with the 'juventud de la República'. Writing in a 'ponencia colectiva' they explain their position with respect to 'la lucha actual del pueblo español contra el fascismo internacional'. Their concern for ordinary people has led them to a radical re-appraisal of their own aesthetic ideals:

> Lo puro, por antihumano, no podía satisfacernos en el fondo; . . . Con todo, y por instinto tal vez, más que por comprensión, cada vez estábamos más al lado del pueblo. El arte abstracto de los últimos años nos parecía falso . . .[2]

Something of this anti-intellectual feeling is reflected in poetry which Prados wrote at this time. In technique and expression it is simpler than the work which precedes it. What is less than clear is the extent to which the poet's commitment to the proletariat cause is reflected in its thematic content. How much of the poetry relates to the struggle of the people, and how much to the individual struggles of the 'yo'?

This has been a point at issue in such criticism as has been written on the war poetry of Prados. Blanco sees in it a total, and therefore, by implication, exclusive commitment to the people's cause. He comments: 'El dolor personal es ya grito de todos'.[3] But what, according to Blanco, is this 'dolor personal'? He describes it as 'cautiverio individual y social': it is personal only in that it relates to the moral principle of the rights and liberty of the individual, 'el derecho del hombre a su sueño y a su voz'. Lechner, on the other hand, senses a more intimate note. His comprehensive survey of the poetry of the Civil War singles out that of Prados as being radically different from that of the other 'poetas comprometidos'. In discussing, for example, 'Tres cantos en el destierro' he observes that they possess a 'tono elegíaco, nostálgico, como si el poeta cantara únicamente dolores personales, . . .'[4] It is its private, extra-circumstantial nature which prompt him to esteem it more highly than much of the contemporary 'poesía panfletaria'. But it is not simply the privateness of Prados's poetry which is its distinguishing feature. Other poets, such as Serrano Plaja in 'Virginia, el amor en la guerra', were voicing equally personal experience:

> Quisiera estar más triste por España
> que por la sorda pena que me invade.
> . . . .
>
> Mas no puedo.

His patriotism is engulfed in the sense of loss he feels in the realm of his relationship with his beloved.[5] Similarly, in his poem 'El otoño' Juan Gil-Albert confines his attention to non-political themes.[6] Manuel Altolaguirre's 'Última muerte', 'Ejemplo' and 'Canto de vida y esperanza' are sensitive, private and related only indirectly to any specifically public situation.[7] The intention of this study is to establish the precise relationship between the poetry written by Prados during these years and the condition of the central figure.

Poetry for the people

It is first necessary, however, to assert that in many ways these poems are akin to much of the literature born of the national struggle. Considerable technical adjustment had already been made in poetry leading up to that of the war years. There had been a movement towards simplification and towards a reflection of the anti-cultural, anti-bourgeois ideals of the 'ponencia'. Some of these changes were superficial. The laboured, chant-like repetitions of both 'No podréis' and 'Existen en la Unión Soviética' from *No podréis* (1930–2) are delivered in the complete absence of punctuation:

> Existen en la Unión Soviética
> millones de hombres que trabajan
> millones de hombres que arden iluminados lo mismo que la
> espiga de una llama
> Existen en la Unión Soviética
> millones de hombres que sonríen
> millones de hombres que duermen confiados
> . . . . (I,451)[8]

In terms of subject matter such lines represent little more than the common interest of poets of the day. Miguel Hernández's 'Rusia' and 'La Fábrica-Ciudad' in *El hombre acecha* are similar enough to suggest that originality was never the primary concern.[9] The same can be said of such straightforward tirades against the ruling classes as this:

> Llamad llamad inútilmente por el sueño
> Nadie os responderá
> Igual que espaldas vueltas
> Sus despojos cegados desemparan las voces que reclaman
> consuelo
> No tendréis paz
> No habrá ningún alivio para los que olvidaron que eran
> hombres (I,448)[10]

Comparison with César M. Arconada's 'Hasta dónde llegará la noche' reveals how embedded Prados was in a common thematic ground:

> ¿Hasta dónde llegarán los límites oscuros de esta noche de
> clases
> en la cual los ricos tienen y los pobres carecen,
> los poderosos mandan y los humildes sirven,
> los tontos brillan y los inteligentes son estériles como los
> altos riscos que no orea la mañana templada de los
> valles . . .?[11]

Nor are Prados's poems lamenting the loss of 'lo más florido del monte' alone in their idealisation of the life of the countryside and its workers. He writes, as did José María Quiroga Plá in 'Una mujer está cantando', or Serrano Plaja in 'Federación de los Trabajadores de la Tierra' with that sympathy for the peasant which was part of a widespread 'repudio del mundo técnico', to quote Lechner. Arconada summarised these sentiments in 'Vivimos en una noche oscura' when he wrote: 'Y porque creo en la Naturaleza, creo en ti, Pueblo.'[12] It was in poems like 'Los campesinos' that the Alberti of *Capital de la gloria*, though with greater polish and technical verve, voiced the same admiration.[13] Prados asks:

> ¿Dónde está? ¿Quién se ha llevado
> la lumbre de nuestros soles?
> ¿Dónde está quien ha dejado
> a la justicia sin nombre?

¡Ay, qué temblor de silencios
la piel del campo recorre! (I,528)

In a similar vein, other poems bemoan the painful misery and separation war brings:

Es muy duro el invierno,
los vientos fríos;
nieva sobre la sierra,
hiela en el río.

Trabajan las mujeres,
luchan los hombres;
separados sus cuerpos,
se unen sus voces. (I,684)

Such uncomplicated poetry has the effect of reaching and reflecting the concerns of ordinary people.

The involved elaboration of *Tiempo*, to which Gerardo Diego took exception, has been abandoned. The two 'canciones' which open the *Llanto en la sangre* section of the *Antología* demonstrate this. It is here, as Blanco suggests, that the affinity between Machado and Prados is unmistakeable. The first 'canción' begins in this way:

Si el hombre debe callar,
cállese y cumpla su sino
que, lo que importa, es andar . . .
Andar es sembrar camino
y morir es despertar. (133:I,749)

These lines from the *Campos de Castilla* have the same simplicity and share similar lines of thought:

Caminante, son tus huellas
el camino, y nada más;
caminante, no hay camino,
se hace camino al andar.
Al andar se hace camino,
y al volver la vista atrás
se ve la senda que nunca
se ha de volver a pisar.[14]

A further consequence of these tendencies is the standardisation of the poetry's symbolic language. A feature of the anthology has been the variable and esoteric private language used. The dawn, the sun, the night, the moon have taken on meanings specific to each new development in the protagonist's condition. In these poems there are no such complications. 'Marzo en el mar' is an example of this. It is inspired by the loss of the San Francisco off Málaga. The first and major section of the 'romance' records the disaster itself. It is seen through the eyes of the waiting son and wife of one of the victims. Within its framework, the poem is entirely predictable. The setting for their pathetic conversation is the night, cold and hungry:

Viento negro, viento negro
trae la mar alborotada.
Viento negro, viento negro
hincha las venas del agua.
Viento negro, viento negro
mueve la arena en la playa. (I,461)

The wind, the water, the sand have a purely narrative function. From this tragic loss the poet sees the possibility of hope rising from despair. Consequently the closing stanzas are filled with allusions to the dawn and to light:

Ya la mar abre su pecho
ante otras luces más claras.
Ya soplan los buenos vientos
para la tierra y el agua.
....

Viento limpio, sol de fuego
trae la sangre alborotada . . .

Viento limpio, mar de fuego,
¡nuevos tiempos se preparan!

Whatever the dawn might mean to Prados's 'yo' (in *Tiempo*, for example, where it brings anything but hope) is of secondary importance. As far as this poem is concerned, it fulfils the standard role as the night, the morning and the dawn in Arconada's 'Poema de vagabundos' (a title to remind us of the influence of Machado during these years). These lines typify Arconada's optimism and expression:

Mañana, al amanecer, la luz tendrá ese calor de carne virgen de las flores de los almendros, y el campo estará alegre de pájaros y olivos.
¿Marcháis? Que os guíe un buen sol y un fino viento, ¡Salud! ¡Buen caminar, buen amigo![15]

The dawn in the Prados poem is, equally, a symbol of resurgence and renewal.

Further evidence of 'standardisation' is to be found in 'Primavera en rumbo'. Here, again, the sun is not something to be feared. In 'Cita hacia dentro' the cry was that the 'tú' should escape with him from the early morning light, because 'no me dará [el sol] descanso / para alcanzar la dicha' (62:I,236). In the *Calendario del pan y el pescado* poem it has been accorded its normal role, a central agent in the life-giving process of nature:

Mayo su pecho levanta
hacia el sol que lo fecunda,
y aún caliente, entre las sombras,
alegre su carne oculta. (I,471)

It would be unfair, however, to dismiss these more obvious poems as being entirely unoriginal. While there is nothing to match Alberti's powerful re-working of the stock symbolic significance of the sun in 'Al sol de la guerra', for example, in some poems Prados produces telling effects by the deliberate disruption of established patterns.[16] 'Amanece' is such a case. Dawn breaks on a quiet village. The reader is led to expect a description of the ordered beginning of a new day:

Ni la perdriz en el monte,
ni el mirlo por las cañadas,
ni la mujer en el río,
ni el hombre por la besana.

(El agua clava al silencio
sobre la desierta plaza.)

Las seis. El pueblo palpita
su apretada luz de lágrimas. (I,532)

Such effects can only be gained when the poet aligns his symbolic world with that of his audience, when he is aiming at a 'popular' poetry.

The distinctive nature of Prados's war poetry

Prados's war poetry, however, does have features which set it apart from contemporary work. Chief amongst them is a vagueness and a width of perspective which few others attempted. Clariana noted this in his review of *Llanto en la sangre*. He refers to the *Calendario incompleto del pan y el pescado* in terms of 'la mayor imprecisón de la lucha y sus consignas'.[17] That this should be the view of a contributor to *Hora de España*, a publication whose poetry is in any case more sensitive and generalised than much that was being written at this time, only serves to underline an important preference for the general rather than the particular, a preference which manifests itself in several ways.

When criticism is made, it is of a very high moral tone. The point at issue is the extent of the injustice done, the abrogation of human rights, crimes perpetrated against the brotherhood of man. The poems are littered with abstractions:

Digan, digan ellos: ¡Digan!,
que ya iluminará el cielo
la verdad por que luchamos
y la verdad del suceso.
Si ahora a la justicia temen;
. . . .

Sepan que paz y trabajo
buscaba tan sólo el pueblo. (I,594–5)[18]

The poem 'Huelga en el campo' shows how offences against the individual are seen in abstract terms:

¿Quién pide a gritos justicia?
¿Quién a la justicia ofende?
¿Quién dejará sin castigo
al que ya al castigo teme?
Todo el campo se levanta ;
como una mancha de aceite
sobre las verdes campiñas
la huelga roja se extiende. (I,481)

It is the whole natural order, the 'campo', rather than individual passions which are portrayed as being aroused.

Other aspects confirm this concern with a broader perspective. The lengthy poem 'Tránsito' illustrates one of them.[19] The war is seen as part of a universal bias in man towards vanity and meaninglessness. In this respect, there is a re-statement of some of the ideas found in *Andando, andando por el mundo*. Noteworthy again is the preference for the abstract expression:

¿Y aun hay cuerpos tan torpes que se entregan y asombran

de que su propio engaño no resuelva sus culpas?
Cuerpo a cuerpo se pasa. Cuerpo a cuerpo se olvida
y cuerpo a cuerpo el mundo se desangra y padece.
Luchan los hombres, luchan por su nueva inocencia; (I,721)

'La voz certera', which complements the 'La voz de la duda' section of the poem, takes an even more remote view. The vanity and meaninglessness of war are reviewed against the backcloth of Time and Space:

Cortos años vivimos sobre este mismo Tiempo,
que es muy débil la cinta que sujeta a los hombres.

As the poem develops it becomes, increasingly, a statement on life in general, the human condition:

. . . es muy pequeño el hombre bajo el cielo que admira
y aunque a veces suponga que un dios corre en sus ríos
y le ordena las fuentes que penetran sus ojos
humildemente vuelve a su humano recinto
y a la penosa lucha de preparar su vuelo. (I,722)

Politics and parties are unmentioned: the people are, simply, 'Los que circunda el alba, frente a frente a su brillo'.

A third characteristic which contributes to broadening the perspective of the poetry is the mythologising of war. The title of the unpublished *Destino fiel* suggests the likelihood that such a process might take place. In the poem 'Presente oficio' the 'yo' outlines the position he ought to adopt in the face of war. But he does not address the enemy: there is no simple confrontation of 'pueblo' and 'amos'. Rather is there a calling upon the god of war, a third party, in the sight of whom the conflict is taking place. The war is placed in the context of an ageless struggle:

Guerra, yo no te canto.
¿Cómo podré cantar tu inmenso cuerpo?
. . . .
Hijos son de la paz, por la que mueren;
vivieron por la paz y en ella siguen.
Tu frágil arrebato
vencerá su ternura
que hoy, contenida, acecha,
escondida en sus hierros. (I,553–5)

'Meditación en la noche' confirms this point. Its invective is not being aimed against a specific target. The poet's quarrel is with war itself. There is an independent agent at work behind the visible conflict. The poem's imagery, the references to the universe and to the 'flecha de la historia' are indications of this:

> ¿En qué sueño, tú, guerra, te figuras
> que en alterado empeño has de lograrte
> trocando el caminar del Universo?
> . . . .
> ¿podrás cambiar la flecha de la historia ? (I,652)

In all this, of course, there is that element of rhetoric peculiar to any propagandist poetry. Nevertheless the net result is the same: to present the misery and threat of war in an extremely wide-ranging and generalised context.

A final facet of this abstraction of the war from the specific situation is concerned with the order of the natural world. The war is seen as much as a violation of the natural cycle as a struggle between opposing parties. This is specially so in 'Tres cantos en el destierro'. In its first section, 'El campo', the 'yo' looks to a time when this cycle was unbroken and to a time when it will be restored. Little reference is made to war, to particular battles or incidents. The central figure chooses to remember rather Andalucía, greater and more lasting than its present troubles (its occupation by Franco being referred to in the last two lines quoted):

> Te veré nuevamente volver de tus despojos
> levantando hacia el cielo tus olivares quemados;
> arrastrando los lentos caudales de tus ríos
> por tu pecho surcado de profundas trincheras.
>
> Volverá nuevamente el hombre a tu pupila
> a gozar libremente las luces de tu aurora
> y de nuevo las aves mirarán sus trabajos
> y volarán serenas por las altas montañas.
>
> Tierra, tierra, lejana, cantaré nuevamente
> pero no ya este llanto que me da tu recuerdo.
> Te cantaré, ya canto la luz que ahora te falta:
> la luz porque padeces, hermosa Andalucía. (I,672)[20]

Before any mention is made of war in the poem which follows, 'El mar', attention is drawn to the life-force of the sea itself. Its opening questions include: 'quién bajo el sueño de tus pesadas aguas / remueve tus pescados y tus algas profundas?'. War is seen as an impertinence, misguided in the thought that she might be able to disrupt the unending cycle of maritime life. The poem concentrates not on war, but on the sea, its power and vastness. Arturo Serrano Plaja's 'Invocación del mar', though by no means entirely specific in character, ends with these lines:

Sólo el sordo trabajo
salobre de las olas,
incesante, perdura.
Como el caliente corazón del hombre
el mar tiene su propio movimiento.[21]

While emphasising the sea's permanence and force, they do not, however, to the same extent as 'Tres cantos en el destierro', stress a personal and intimate theme, the relationship between the 'yo' and the sea:

¡Ay lejano mar solo!: mis ojos te han perdido,
pero no así la sangre, que constante te llama.
Conozco tus trabajos y el viento que te enciende:
¡cuántas veces mi cuerpo con tu paz recibiste! (I,674)

Even when addressing the city, in the group's third poem, the emphasis lies not so much on the destructiveness of war as on the central figure's desire to experience more fully that life-giving strength (akin to that of nature itself) which imbues the city with power and, ultimately, victory:

Ahora que estoy lejano, quisiera conocerte,
como dentro del árbol ya conoce la savia
el fruto porque enciende la flor de su destino:
así quiere mi sangre conocer tu victoria. (I,675)

All this suggests a re-alignment of forces. In *Tiempo* he could associate himself only with the negative, sterile aspects of natural life. In *Llanto en la sangre*, however, he joins forces with nature and the people in order to oppose the ruling minority. 'Agosto en el campo', from *Llanto en la sangre*, illustrates this well:

Cómo se aprietan las manos
bajo sus recios tendones,
prendiendo rencor y fuerza
entre sus vivos barrotes,
cuando ven cruzar a agosto,
fecundo en fruta y sudores,
bien endulzado en sus uvas
y amargo en sus sinsabores,

llevando por tierra y viento
su riqueza y sinrazones
hasta otras manos lejanas
que los trigos no conocen,
que al corazón se resisten
y a la conciencia se oponen. (I,483)

The identification of the protagonist with the peasant workers is complete: they in turn are inseparable from the earth which they cultivated, the natural cycle on which they depend: and all are united against the common enemy, the parasitic 'manos lejanas'. The victory of the socialist is inevitable because the battle is not a question of the force of arms. The battle lies between the time-honoured, just order of good, of nature, and the upstart, destructive non-participants in that order. It is, to use the language of *La voz cautiva*, the opposition of the 'voz del universo' to the corrupt civilised world. In the poem 'Cinta del tiempo' victory is seen as part of the general law of the triumph of good over evil. 'Youth' is the executor of a divine and abiding mission:

¡Oh juventud dichosa, tan fielmente escogida
por el amor y el Tiempo para flor de sus glorias,
mira cómo naufraga la humanidad sin brújula!
Cumpla tu brazo armado la misión que le imponen. (I,695)

We are not attempting to suggest that all Prados's war poetry rises above that level which Lechner terms 'poesía panfletaria'. But such features indicate that the war had wider implications for Prados, in terms of the central figure of his poetry, than for many of his contemporaries. Lechner's comment summarises much of what has been established: 'La guerra está ausente de sus versos y las pocas veces que figura en ellos es en forma alusiva o, cuando más, en su forma más abstracta: "la guerra"'.[22] It would come as a surprise to find that Prados had written Darín's 'Romance de la Ley de Fugas', an account of the murder of five married workers, Pla y Beltrán's strident '¡Imitaremos vuestro ejemplo!', where the poet expresses his desire to advance 'con el fusil al hombro', or even the skilfully worked detail of Alberti's 'Un fantasma recorre Europa . . .'.[23] Prados's work bears a close relationship to intimate struggles which have been and will be the fabric from which his poetry is fashioned. It cannot be viewed apart from problems in the realm of the body which have emerged as the unifying theme of his work.

The personal struggle

For in this abstraction and vagueness, as well as in the identification of the 'yo' with nature is implicated the presence of a private struggle, a struggle which is more than the 'dolor personal' of which Blanco speaks, concerned with the right of the individual to his 'sueño'. Rather is it the pain, mental and physical, which his body causes him. A two-fold process has taken place. Firstly the 'yo' found that the kinds of problems posed by his own inner life, amounting in themselves to a war within, provided him with ready-made language to express another and less personal hostility. And secondly, while the war poems were being written, this central figure still faced private problems similar to those already described. Images of conflict and pain relating to the Civil War come to coincide with expressions of his own dilemma. The war provides the protagonist with another landscape by means of which he can expose, and at the same time conceal, his own predicament. There are three levels on which this process takes place: that of vocabulary, specific words; content, thematic material; and structure, the lay-out of the material.

The vocabulary of such compositions as 'Estancia en la muerte con Federico García Lorca' is what first draws the reader's attention to links between this and earlier poetry. It has obvious affinities with *Tiempo*. There, in 'Fin del día en la escuela', Prados wrote:

> Sobre la verde esfera tiende un puntero el índice
> y señala una ruta cuajada en mariposas.
> Deshila la armonía sus delgados compases
> y estudia sus lecciones de sueño la memoria . . . (19)

These lines are echoed in the later poem:

> Yo sé que junto al agua el imán de tu brújula
> hace girar sus índices hacia el dulce horizonte
> donde el pan y el azúcar con el carbón y el aire
> alzan bella la aurora por que el hombre trabaja. (I,663)

In itself there is little significance in this. It would be surprising if the words a poet used could be parcelled off into neat chronological compartments. What is surprising is that they re-occur in groups, and that they are used in particular contexts. Usually—as in the case of the Lorca poem, where the 'yo' is searching for the 'piel violenta' of the dead poet—this context relates to the body.

Further examples, from 'Tres cantos en el destierro', confirm this. In the first poem of the anthology's *Memoria de poesía* section there was an implied relationship between the words 'frente', 'memoria' and 'cuerpo':

¡Cómo se va saliendo por mi frente,
clara, serena, toda mi memoria
y, huyendo por el cielo derramada,
libre, su anhelo cambia en cuerpo vivo! . . . (57:I,249)

In 'Tres cantos en el destierro' the tone of the poetry is intimate—its content concerned as much with his own thought-processes as with the question of war. In amongst such considerations of his own situation exactly the same combination of words reappears:

Un año llevo andando por mis constante sueños.
Constantemente miro mis lejanas riberas
y más alzo mi cuerpo por hallar mi memoria
y romper en recuerdo la unidad que limita. (I,671)

It is noticeable that the body, 'mi cuerpo', is, once more, central to this description of the course of action he is at present adopting.

A comparison of *Llanto de octubre*, the title of a section of *Llanto en la sangre*, and 'Oración' from *Cuerpo perseguido* points to the same kind of similarity in phrasing. In 'Oración' the 'yo' admits:

Yo no sé si esta yedra
que cuelga por mi nuca,
es que una frente mana
por detrás de mi sombra,
. . . . (113:I,315)

The *Llanto de octubre* group contains this lament:

¡Ay, que no encuentren reposo
las corrientes de mi cuerpo!;
¡que las fuentes de la angustia
se despeñen por mis huesos
y las yedras del temblor
suban gritando a mis nervios
. . . . (I,517)

A final example suggests that this curious overlapping of vocabulary used in what seems at first sight to be very different contexts is in no sense coincidental. Here are the opening lines of *Llanto de octubre*, poem 2:

Tengo mi frente en el fuego
y está mi ventana abierta,
pero mis sienes no quieren
más viento que su tristeza. (I,519)

This is how the *Cuerpo perseguido* poem, 'Nocturno, 3 de enero', begins:

Abierta la ventana,
se derramó en el cuarto
gota a gota, la luna,
como el agua en un vaso.

Mi frente sin memoria
—¡Qué llanura de viento!—,
desclavada a mi sangre
flotó libre en el cielo. (72:I,341)

The 'frente', the 'ventana abierta', the wind and, by implication, the blood ('mis sienes' in the first quotation, 'sangre' in the second) are common to both. It is also noteworthy that here, as in some of the other cases mentioned above, such echoes are clustered round the image of the body—the 'brújulas' which in *Tiempo* were related to the central figure's useless imaginary activity in the sexual realm, the 'constantes sueños' of 'Tres cantos en el destierro', together with its direct references to 'mi cuerpo', the 'corrientes de mi cuerpo' of 'Llanto de octubre', and, in 'Tengo mi frente en el fuego' the forehead, the temples and the inevitable wind. Though in no way conclusive, such coincidences are enough to suggest that it is unwise to consider the poetry of the war years in isolation from that of a previous date.

There is also an overlap of thematic material. The question of the 'reality' of the body, a pervasive theme in *Cuerpo perseguido*, is again posed. It is most easily recognisable in the 'Canción de consuelo', contained in *Destino fiel*. The poem is set, like Alberti's '1º de mayo en la España leal de 1938', in the form of a dialogue.[24] But this is a dialogue between two contrasting views of death. Of course it is death in the context of war: but the comments have a wider application. Really the point at issue is the nature of the body. The situation is incidental, the imminence of death only serves to concentrate the mind of the protagonist. The one argues that were he to die all memory of him would disappear:

Cuando yo me muera
¿quién me llorará?

Perdido en el campo
¿quién me buscará? (I,689)

The other voice maintains that death is by no means the end and that from the death of the body will spring life:

Si tu cuerpo da en llorar
y por su dolor te olvida
¿qué fuente podrá elevar
la oscura voz de tu vida?

Si en él la guerra ha dejado
tu amor con dolor vencido,
ni estás solo ni olvidado
ni para el mundo perdido.

These are in fact the same opinions as those expressed in *Cuerpo perseguido*:

Pero . . . ¡qué golpe de tierra
será mi muerte! ¡Qué negro
árbol tenderá en el suelo,
seco!
¿Qué martillazo de sombra
hundirá sordo en el tiempo!
. . . .
¡Qué dolor de desprendido
me irá clavando el silencio!
Pero ¡qué luz me hará, firme,
pájaro y árbol ya eterno! (90–1:I,310–11)

The 'yo' swings wildly between the fear that death is just Machado's 'golpe de ataúd en tierra', and the hope that in death he will know eternal life.[25] But in the course of the dialogue there are striking reminders of the 'body' of earlier poetry. The unusual, 'unreal' 'fantasma de mi fuga' described in 'Porque me voy . . .' (74:I,313) is recalled by these lines:

¿Qué espera mi vida
si tan loco estoy
que si a ella me acerco
pienso que me voy,

y ando tan lejano
por mi pensamiento,
que sólo al dormirme
despierto me siento?

Si no hallo mi cuerpo
¿qué podré buscar,
si lo que él ha dado
solo he de esperar? (I,691)

The phrase: 'sólo al dormirme / despierto me siento . . .' immediately revives the world of *Cuerpo perseguido* where 'siento / que ya no estoy sino cuando me olvido;' (69:I,279). The niggling fear of madness, the insubstantiality of the body are sufficiently emphasised to suggest that this is more than a poem dealing simply with the theme of war and death. The lines of thought are entirely personal and follow closely those traced in earlier chapters.

A similar theme appears in the *Llanto en la sangre* poem, 'Cuerpo de tristeza'. This poem appeared in the *Romancero de la guerra civil española*. Lechner singles it out as one of three—all by Prados—which achieved what he calls the 'superación de la realidad inmediata de la guerra . . .'[26] The 'yo' betrays some of the symptoms of the 'disembodied self' of an earlier chapter. These include an objectivity, a separateness from the body, a desire to assess it completely apart from what he regards as his 'real' self:

Miro mi cuerpo, fantasma
de mi corazón doliente.
Miro mi cuerpo vencido
y no acierto a conocerme,
que ni es forma de mi olvido
ni sueño de mi presente
y como un traje vacío
cuelga de mi propia frente. (I,577)

The image of the 'traje vacío' is one of the most telling expressions so far of this fundamental divorce. It recalls, as did *Cuerpo perseguido*, Cernuda's 'cuerpos siempre pálidos, en su traje de olvido' and his 'cuerpo vacío', along with Alberti's strange 'cuerpo deshabitado'.[27] Such is Prados's unbelief in his body, an unbelief fostered by the war, that as he writes in 'Destino fiel', in the collection of that name, 'mi presencia busca por mi tacto' (I,733).

The life which the 'yo' in this condition faces is little short of death. Consequently, the protagonist is able to make veiled reference to the death which is in his own body in the guise of apparently generalised comments on the death that war brings about. 'La traición traicionada', another of the poems singled out by Lechner, is a good example of this dualism. The circumstances of war are, of course, implicit. But Lechner's comment again underlines its unusual character:

> . . . aunque escrito durante la guerra e inspirado por ella, difícilmente puede calificarse de poema comprometido debido a que constituye más bien un testimonio del dolor personal del poeta.[28]

This is how it begins:

> Como un espectro en la tierra,
> sin pie, sin luna, sin aire,
> apuñalado en mis sueños
> y estrangulado en mi sangre,
> vuelo el cuerpo que me han dado
> y el corazón que en él late;
> vuelo el dolor que me toca,
> que es más dolor que en mí cabe;
> vuelo mis ojos sin lumbre
> y el llanto que en ellos arde; (I,587)

Significantly, there is no reference to 'traición' in the sense of an act of treachery by one of his own side. The treason is his own private affair; it is directed against him personally. The crime which has been committed is related to the question of his body, the 'cuerpo que me han dado . . .'. The key issue of the poem is his own situation:

> vuelo el luto de mi sombra,
> sombra color de mi carne,
> tizón de mi desventura
> y ceniza de mis males,
> que como llama tendida
> sobre el suelo agonizante,
> equilibrio de mi angustia
> pide a la muerte triunfante:

Enough has been learnt of the protagonist to know that when he speaks in these terms he is referring to an 'angustia' which neither the presence nor the absence of the war affects. Allusions to 'mi lengua sangrante', 'mis venas' and 'mi voz' which follow in the text confirm the view that though the poem deals with problems stemming from the circumstance of war, they are nevertheless inseparable from the private dilemma confronting the central figure.

There are further evidences that in the situations which war brought about the protagonist was able, in a half concealed way, to express his own predicament. Thus the 'tú'–'yo' duality which was a feature of *Cuerpo perseguido* finds its echo in the 'Pérdida' section of his homage to Lorca. There is a 'tú' which the 'yo' cannot reach—just as there was in 'Rapto' a 'tú' beyond the grasp of the wind, a 'tú' inaccessible for the most part save in the dream. Compare, for example, the closing lines of 'Atardecer. Quietud' (83:I,282) with the lines from 'Pérdida' which follow:

> Serena, igual que esta rama,
> se alza en el viento mi sangre . . .
> ¿Hasta qué espacio, mis ojos
> han de llegar por buscarte?

Of Lorca, he writes:

> Mis brazos se prolongan,
> pero no encuentran nunca,
> ni el término del cuerpo,
> ni el dolor de sus límites.
>
> No te llegan las manos. (I,661-2)[29]

The search for the 'tú' differs little from that which is found in *Cuerpo perseguido*. Nor does the nature of the union of the 'tú' and the 'yo': here, as in *Cuerpo perseguido*, it takes place 'bajo el sueño del aire'.

It is the frequency of such personal allusions which marks this poetry off from that of Prados's contemporaries. Albornoz's edition of Machado's output during this years provides an interesting comparison.[30] The senior poet's poems are entirely taken up with specific events, places or people. There are poems on Madrid, on 'el crimen que fue en Granada' (another poem on the death of Lorca, but strictly narrative, and beginning with the lines: 'Se le vio, caminando entre fusiles, / por una calle larga, salir al campo frío . . .'), landscapes leading straight into direct references to the war, poems on Miaja, Lister, and so on. There is a 'personal' reaction, of course: but the concern is with public, shared experience. Prados's work is not short of similar examples. But in addition, and, often, inseparable from them, are poems of the type referred to above where special reference is made to the protagonist's body.

His particular attitude to the war leads to the conclusion that it has not come upon him as an outstanding catastrophe which completely fills the horizon. Some of the poetry's content indicates that, in the context of his 'dolor personal', it is viewed as another in a series of outward circumstances which have all along been at work to shed light on and affect his relationship to himself and to his body. He realises, consequently, that the end of the Civil War will not necessarily mean that his problems will all be resolved. In the first part of 'Tránsito' he writes:

> Cuando a la tierra vuelva la paz que tanto anhelo
> ¿volverán nuevamente las pequeñas desdichas
> y de nuevo los hombres separarán los labios
> sin comprender apenas el color de su sangre?
> . . . .
> . . . el rumor de la intriga, las pequeñas historias,
> bajo las hojas débiles que en los árboles gimen,
> se escuchan, con el sueño y el llanto que acarician
> . . . . (I,719–20)

The society which existed before the Civil War, which treated him with indifference and intolerance, caused him as much distress as the present situation does. The absence of war will not necessarily mean peace, as far as he is concerned. 'Sombra de abril' explains why this should be so. The concern of this extremely personal poem (it is taken from a pair entitled 'Dos poemas íntimos') is with the body. All the old problems—the difficulty of identifying himself with his body, the pain which it has brought him—are reviewed. It is in this context that the war is mentioned:

> Mi cuerpo vive y casi lo conozco;
> apenas percibir puedo su forma
> y sólo cuando cruza por mis sueños
> siento, por el dolor, que en él habito.
>
> No sé cómo se llama, ni he sabido
> cual es su nombre nunca, ni lo quiero;
> su nombre ha de formarse en su memoria;
> la memoria de mí, que nunca es mía.
>
> Pero nacido estoy, casi ya viejo
> después de tantos duros vendavales
> y en él se afila entera mi ternura,
> hoy por la guerra, al borde de la muerte,
> igual que antes miedosa mi esperanza
> se afilaba, al nacer, junto a mi vida.[31]

The perspective is again interesting. The war is the problem which afflicts him 'hoy'—but there have been, and will be, many other persecutors because the presence of the body is synonymous with torment and hardship for him:

> ¡Oh forma persistente que así enredas
> mi pensamiento al giro de las horas!
> ¿adónde has de llevar mi eterna lucha
> que siempre has de encontrarme desolado? . . .

In the course of the poem's development stress is laid on how April, rather than the war, finds him:

> Abril, en guerra o en paz, siempre me encuentras
> desconocido en medio del combate,
> junto a las hojas de mi muerte, trémulo,
> . . . .
>
> Siempre al llegar, ves que mi cuerpo sigue
> la romántica forma de su ausencia,
> que un desmedido afán le llama olvido.
> Yo, siempre en mi dolor, sin conocerme.

His situation, his 'combate', is the same in war as it is in peace. He is still, as he was in *Cuerpo perseguido*, 'desconocido', 'en mi dolor, sin conocerme'. In the reference to 'la romántica forma de mi ausencia' there is a direct reminder of the 'romántico de huídas' who remains very much at the core of the poetry.

Because so much of the intimate material which has found its way into the poetry of the war years is involved with his attitude to his body, it has also been marked by expressions of pain and discomfort. Before the Civil War broke out he had been afflicted by his awareness of himself and of what he felt he 'should' be. Indeed, it is possible to point to poems dealing with these more private concerns which suggest that the fact of war—however deplorable in terms of human suffering—affords a certain amount of respite to the protagonist. The body has brought death, isolation, rejection, illusion: war stands as a temporary release from them.

'La traición traicionada' is a good example of this principle—despite the abstract quality of its language. From the outset the 'yo' sees himself as dead, as 'un espectro en la tierra'. And it is from this stand-point that the central figure, instead of bemoaning the intervention of the war, exults in it. Because he is already dead, he cannot be affected by its presence:

> Vete, muerte, muerte, vete,
> que en ti no puedo encontrarme. (I,588)

The logic behind such an exultation is not difficult to follow. For the ordinary, healthy, 'normal' person, war is a threat to the physical existence of the body. She is a 'traitress' because she threatens that which is his right. Under the conditions of war the value of the body depreciates dramatically: it is at the mercy of any stray bullet or misinterpreted command. For the 'yo', however, the position is different. Before war began he had already been betrayed, as was suggested in an earlier reference to this poem. He had already been cheated of what the war was now depriving the ordinary man—the appreciation of his body. In a sense, therefore, the treacherous war had eliminated—if only for a while—the disparity he had felt to exist between himself and his fellows. Such knowledge grows like a seed within him:

¡Ay, traición, qué hermoso cuerpo
con tus balas levantaste!
¡Mal tallo para ti lleva
la simiente que sembraste!

War, which should have re-inforced the original act of treason perpetrated against him, the 'cuerpo que me han dado', has in his case over-reached herself. In jeopardising the body of every man she has removed one of his main burdens—his apartness from other men.

'Destino fiel' is another poem which suggests that in war there is a swallowing up of the death which is his body. Surrounded by the activity of war he finds a sense of purpose so real as to be called an 'hermoso cuerpo' in 'La traición traicionada' and, here, 'mi piel':

¿Qué tengo yo que en medio de esta hoguera
donde la muerte ataca de continuo,
por dentro de sus llamas me manejo
y en ellas, si ardo más, tanto más vivo?

¿En dónde está mi cuerpo, que aún reposa,
cuando la noche ofrece a mi fatiga
lecho de sombra y sueño iluminado,
si por sus lentos párpados se olvida?

Me persigue la fuerza que me acaba
y más la miro por que me acompañe.
Si más me aprieta, más alegre pido,
que apriete más por que el dolor me salve.
. . . .

Hallo mi piel y en ella mi destino,
y al encontrarlo más mi temor crece: (I,733)[32]

For the 'yo', there is a certain self-discovery and rest in the circumstances of war. There is an awareness of an identity which has for so long escaped him. Relieved of the burden which the need to flee from the body had imposed on him, he is able to experience a reality apart from the dream, even though it would seem to be the dark reality of death:

Hoy mi sombra, por la tierra,
siguiéndome me acompaña
y mi soledad sostiene:
libre mi cuerpo, ya tiene
amiga que no la engaña. (I,683)

In the same poem, he adds:

Cruzan mis pies por la guerra
despegándome del sueño
que antes, en la paz, fue dueño
de lo que mi cuerpo encierra.

For the moment, at least, he no longer feels any need to have recourse to the dream, to the channels of escape which characterise *Tiempo* and *Cuerpo perseguido*.

It is this intensely personal interest which governs the distinctive structure of many of the poems. Many of them can be divided into two parts. One might contain more comments of a general kind, referring to pain and anguish: and in the other there are more specific references to war. The poem 'Llegada', written on the death of Lorca, begins with lines dealing with a 'dolor personal'. The pain cannot be distinguished, in nature or expression, from that of earlier work. There is no reference to the dead poet:

Alamedas de mi sangre.
¡Alto dolor de olmos negros!
¿Qué nuevos vientos lleváis?
¿Qué murmuran vuestros ecos?
¿Qué apretáis en mi garganta
que siento el tallo del hielo
aún más frío que la muerte
estrangular mi deseo?
¡Qué agudo clamor de angustia
rueda corazón adentro

golpe a golpe, retumbando
como campana de duelo,
. . . . (I,568)[33]

In the course of the lines which follow, the familiar leit-motifs of the dream, persecution and the 'cinco llamas agudas' re-appear. For the most part the subject of the poem is the protagonist, 'perseguido de enemigos pensamientos'. The note of mourning is present, but it has a dual connotation.

The 'Encuentro' section of the poem 'Estancia en la muerte', referred to earlier, has a similar structure. Also written on the death of his friend, it opens with these lines:

Basta cerrar mis ojos para entrar en mi muerte,
que el mundo ha terminado su límite en mis ojos.
Basta cerrar mis ojos: vuelto de espalda al tiempo me imagino
hallarme nuevamente con la vida que pierdo.
. . . .

Basta entrar en mi muerte para salir de nuevo.
Basta cerrar mis párpados para entrar en mi cuerpo. (I,664)

It is '*mi* muerte' which is at the heart of the poem: the search for Lorca is a metaphor of his search for himself. In marked contrast with more objective poems on the same subject, like Alberti's 'Elegía a un poeta que no tuvo su muerte' or even Manuel Altolaguirre's sensitive 'Elegía a nuestro poeta', such material displaces almost exclusively reference to the poem's original point of departure.[34]

'Llanto de octubre' published as the second part of *Llanto en la sangre*, reflects in its structure a similar division of interest. Its opening poem builds up to a climax of invective. But as far as those lines dealing with the 'astillas del río' are concerned, the poem could just as easily be referring to the central figure's private situation. It is his undefined 'miedo', his 'sangre' and his 'angustia' which are important:

¡Ay, ni las tejas me cubran,
que a sangre me huele el techo
y el sol me sabe a locura
y a amargo dolor el sueño!
¡Ay, que no encuentren reposo
las corrientes de mi cuerpo!; (I,517)

Not only, then, in the ideas contained in the poems, but also in their presentation, the personal dilemma of the protagonist, inseparable from that of *Tiempo* or *Cuerpo perseguido*, is given prominence.

The quest for fertility and the life-giving death

Attention will now be drawn to two themes which, like some facets of *La voz cautiva* and *Andando, andando por el mundo*, recur in later poetry—further demonstrating how difficult it is to separate these poems from the main body of Prados's work.

Firstly, it is evident that the war brings to light once again the abiding theme of the quest for fertility. Images of fertility appear in many different contexts. Given that the war has suspended the hostility which his infertile, abnormal body has caused between himself and fellow-members of society, it is not surprising that such imagery can refer to the life of the community as readily as to that of nature. The common striving and cooperation of man is seen as a fertilising process as organic in the factory as is the co-working of the forces of nature. This is the ideal he sees in other socialist states, as he explains in 'Existen en la Unión soviética':

> millones de hombres que han sembrado el vigor de sus
> músculos y de sus voluntades
> y ya germinan sonrientes limpios y venturosos
> bajo cielos labrados en nueva inteligencia (I,451)

Even the factory motor of 'La ciudad', the third of the 'Tres cantos en el destierro', is described in terms of its 'fecundo engranaje' (I,676). The salvation of the 'yo' will lie in absorption into the fertile processes of the natural world. In the daily round of common effort, there is a foreshadowing of that absorption.

Identification with the fertility of nature is also pre-figured in 'Meditación en la noche'. Addressing war he argues:

> Así, deja, abandona tus potencias,
> que el mundo marcha con la luz del día:
> mira otra vez la tierra; mira el agua
> fecundando de nuevo sus semillas.
>
> El hombre acude con su lento arado
> . . . . (I,652–3)

The antithesis of war, as far as the 'yo' is concerned, is not peace but fertility. It is this which is distinctive to his nature poems. In a poem from the same *Destino fiel* collection, 'Cuatro tiempos', the whole point of the fourth of its tableaux is the contrast between the flowers, the ripening olives, the grain and the presence of war. It meets opposition there: 'en los campos la guerra / no halla descanso' (I,705). Above all else the war is seen as that which disturbs the fertile course of nature. It has upset the dream of the ordinary tiller of the soil, as these lines from 'Meditación en la noche' show:

> ¡Cuánta ventura en sus ligeras hoces
> soñaba con los mares de sus trigos!
> Pero tú, guerra, ¿qué veneno impulsas? (I,654)

The extent of the central figure's interest in the theme of fertility is considerable. It is seen as an over-riding power which cannot but emerge victorious from the ravages of war. Here, as he will do in future books, he places his confidence in its abilities, and the strength of those who trust in it:

> ¡Mira a los bellos hijos de la Aurora!
> Termina, guerra, que no en vano canto
> la paz que anuncia espigas de victoria.

The second of these important themes is that of the life-giving death. Prados was by no means alone in his involvement with this theme. Serrano Plaja's 'Federación de los Trabajadores de la Tierra' contains these lines:

> Cesarán los sollozos.
> Ya los muertos en guerra
> sucederán, eternos, en los pueblos,
> los hombres en trabajo:
> la lenta perfección que sólo alcanza
> la humilde libertad trabajadora
> descansará en los hombres convirtiendo
> su fatiga en reposo.[35]

The underlying preoccupation of Manuel Altolaguirre's 'Última muerte' is with 'insinuaciones de verdor y vida' growing from all-pervading death, with the 'multiplicada vida' to which it gives birth. According to Lechner, Prados's work, however, is outstanding in the emphasis it lays on this motif.[36] Again, what has already been discovered in the central *persona* of earlier poetry helps us to understand why this should be the case. As Lechner establishes, the death of the individual is seen as the beginning of a process in which the body returns to the earth and takes its place in the endless cycle which begins there. Death and pain are inevitable if birth is to take place. The absorption of the body into death will bring about life. It is the principle universal to the natural world:

Con dolor rompe la fuente
la tierra para nacer,
y con dolor, nuevamente,
se vuelve el agua a perder.
. . . .

Si tu cuerpo da en llorar
y por su dolor te olvida,
¿qué fuente podrá elevar
la oscura luz de tu vida? (1,690)

In this sense there is no death. And in such a context the central figure needs no longer regard his 'dead' body with such contempt.

There are other manifestations of this particular kind of dying. In certain of the commemorative poems the individual's death is seen in terms of the organic life of the entire fighting force. In the 'Fragmento de carta . . .' he notes:

. . . el que por nosotros muere,
no muere, sino que nace;
no tengo hermano que caiga
que una espiga no levante. (I,562)

The death of a member of the body is part of its renewal and re-birth. The same point is made about Antonio Coll, the first 'cazador de tanques'. Even though he has been killed, 'Cada cuerpo late en ti / y vives en cada cuerpo;' (I:574). Hans Beimler's death is treated in the same way. His death signals a return to Mother Earth; but it is to that same earth which sustains the army of the Left:

Dicen que vas muerto, hermano,
pero tu vida no acaba
porque se sequen tus venas
y se hiele tu garganta.
. . . .

No es esto morir, hermano,
sino dar vida y hallarla,
que la muerte, cuando es muerte,

de la tierra nos separa
y tú te quedas con ella,

. . . .

. . . la Muerte, en España
te hizo nacer en su tierra
para ganarte a su patria . . . (I,590–1)

Death heralds re-birth into the life of a people. The setting up of this pattern is of great relevance to the later poetry.

The abiding problem

It has been suggested, then, that though these poems are bound up with the tragedy of Civil War, there are other underlying strains, notably the reflection of personal problems and private dilemmas. Gullón made this general comment in discussing Prados's poetry: it is 'poesía . . . alejada de la contingencia histórica'.[37] The theme of the body, the quest for fertility, the theme of death are never far away. The final poem chosen for the *Llanto en la sangre* section of the anthology indicates the extent to which all this poetry is related to a personal struggle.

Instead of a poem dealing with some particular event it deals entirely with the condition of the central figure. The final 'llanto' deals with the unhappy position of a 'yo' who, though, thanks to the war, is temporarily shielded from his own sterility, realises that in reality he has no part in the natural cycle:

Lo que dice el sol, lo dice
lo que dice el mar.

. . . .

Y el mar
dice lo que dice el sol,
que eterno vuelve a cantar
lo que canta el mar eterno.

Yo me acerco por mirar
lo que de este canto entiendo
pero no puedo olvidar
que estoy dentro de mi cuerpo
y en mí me vuelvo a ocultar.

¡Pasen estos malos tiempos! (138:I,751)

He is still alienated from the fertility he seeks. The essentially limiting and deadening presence of the body is still with him. Alberti's 'Madrid-Otoño' provides us with a telling picture of a city at war, and of his hopes for the future:

> Bajo la dinamita de tus cielos, crujiente,
> se oye el nacer del nuevo hito de la victoria.
> Gritando y a empujones la tierra lo inaugura.[38]

But Prados's 'Ciudad sitiada' goes beyond even such identification. Its besieged city is the 'yo' himself. When the gunfire of war has ceased, the protagonist will still be threatened by a different, but equally devastating antagonist:

> ¡Ay, ciudad, ciudad sitiada,
> ciudad de mi propio pecho:
> si te pisa el enemigo,
> será para verme muerto!
>
> Castillos de mi razón
> y fronteras de mi sueño:
> mi ciudad está sitiada,
> ¡entre cañones me muevo! . . .
>
> ¿En dónde empiezas, ciudad,
> que, no sé, si eres mi cuerpo? (136:I,579)

1 L. Cernuda, 'Los que se incorporan', *Octubre*, 4/5 (October 1933), p. 37.
2 'Ponencia colectiva', *Hora de España*, VIII (August 1937), pp. 81–95
3 C. Blanco Aguinaga, *Vida y obra*, p. 66.
4 J. Lechner, *El compromiso en la poesía española del siglo XX* (Parte primera) (Universitaire Pers Leiden, 1968), p. 193. In these notes, Lechner's study is indicated by I, the anthology by II.
5 A. Serrano Plaja, 'Virginia, el amor en la guerra', *Hora de España*, XVII (1938).
6 J. Gil-Albert, 'El otoño', *Hora de España*, XI (1937).
7 M. Altolaguirre, 'Ultima muerte', 'Ejemplo' and 'Canto de vida y esperanza', *Hora de España*, III (1937), pp. 31–6. For a note on the publication of these poems, see J. Lechner, II, p. 102.
8 In *Octubre*, no. 4/5 (October–November 1933), pp. 20–1.
9 M. Hérnandez, *Obras completas* (Buenos Aires, 1960), p. 320.
10 In *Octubre*, no. 1 (June–July 1933), pp. 14–15.
11 César M. Arconada, *Vivimos en una noche oscura* (Valencia, 1936).
12 J. M. Quiroga Plá, 'Una mujer está cantando', *Hora de España*, XII (1937); A. Serrano Plaja, 'Federación de los Trabajadores de la Tierra ', *ibid.*; C. M. Arconada, 'Creo en ti, Pueblo', *Op. cit.*
13 R. Alberti, *El poeta en la calle* (Madrid, 1978), pp. 102–3.
14 A. Machado, *Obras: poesía y prosa*, p. 203. It is perhaps significant that Prados came to work as typographer to an edition of Machado's poetry: *Obras completas de Antonio Machado* (México, 1940).

15 C. M. Arconada, *Op. cit.*

16 R. Alberti, *El poeta en la calle*, pp. 118–19.

17 B. Clariana, 'Emilio Prados: *Llanto en la sangre*', *Hora de España*, X (October 1937), pp. 74–5.

18 This poem appeared in *El mono azul*, no. 13 (November 1936), p. 4. In this chapter poems which first appeared in individual magazines are given a full reference. Poems which appeared as part of a book (or a projected book) are given their reference in the *Poesías completas*.

19 'Tránsito' first appears in *Hora de España*, XIII (1938), pp. 61–4.

20 These poems first appear in *Hora de España*, X (1937), pp. 81–94.

21 A. Serrano Plaja, 'Federación de los trabajadoes del mar', *Hora de España*, XV (1938).

22 J. Lechner, I, p. 193.

23 'Darín', *Octubre*, no. 3 (1933); Pla y Beltrán, *Octubre* 4/5 (October 1933); R. Alberti, *El poeta en la calle*, pp. 29–30.

24 R Alberti, *ibid.*, pp. 114–5.

25 A. Machado, 'En el entierro de un amigo', *Obras: presía y prosa*, p. 58.

26 J. Lechner, I, p. 177.

27 See L. Cernuda's *La realidad y el deseo*, p. 41 and Alberti, *Poesías*, p. 322.

28 J. Lechner, *loc. cit.*

29 In *Hora de España*, VII (1937), pp. 49–54. Another version, slightly different, appeared in *Homenaje al poeta Federico García Lorca* (Valencia, 1937), pp. 31–7.

30 A. de Albornoz, *Poesías de guerra de Antonio Machado* (Puerto Rico, 1961).

31 'Dos poemas íntimos', *Hora de España*, XVIII (June 1938), p. 21. These poems, which do not appear in the *Poesías completas*, are not to be confused with the 'poemas íntimos' Lechner reproduces in his anthology (p. 224). They appear in Appendix VI, p. 324.

32 Originally this poem was published in *Hora de España*, XX (August 1938), pp. 25–9.

33 'Llegada', *El mono azul*, no. 4 (17th September 1936), p. 4. It is re-printed in *Verdades*, in an issue (no. 34) dedicated to Lorca in 1937.

34 Lechner gathers together poems written on the death of Lorca (Antología, pp. 251–61). For the Alberti poem, see *El poeta en la calle*, p. 109.

35 In *Hora de España*, XII (1937).

36 J. Lechner, I, p. 175.

37 R. Gullón, 'Septiembre en Chapultepec', *Ínsula*, no. 187 (1962), p. 1.

38 R. Alberti, *El poeta en la calle*, p. 93.

CHAPTER FIVE

The Re-birth of the Child

The things which I have seen I now can see no more.
. . . .

Heaven lies about us in our infancy!
(William Wordsworth, 'Ode: Intimations of Immortality from Recollections of Early Childhood')

. . . The glamour
Of childish days is upon me, my manhood is cast
Down in the flood of remembrance, I weep like a child for the past.
(David Herbert Lawrence, 'Piano', *Rhyming Poems*)

Introduction

The *Penumbras* section of the anthology contains only two poems. Nevertheless, it sheds much light on the central figure's thinking. As the overall title suggests, it stands as a kind of watershed, a point of transition—'Cuando era primavera' looking back on earlier, happier days, 'Vuelta a México' anticipating a better future. The total disruption of the thirties had, as far as Prados was concerned, ended in exile—the 'vivencia única de millares de exilados'.[1] Little wonder, then, that the poetry of *Penumbras* should, albeit briefly, turn attention away from an unsettled present.

In the lament of 'Cuando era primavera', however, there is not simply the 'eco de la voz común' of which Blanco writes. Its nostalgia runs deep: but it is more than an uncomplicated longing for the fatherland—just as the poetry examined in Chapter 4 was more than the tortured cry of a nation at war. Whatever exile might or might not have meant for Prados, it is certain, from examination of the poems in the context of earlier and later poetry, that *Penumbras*, and 'Cuando era primavera' in particular, reflect a far more fundamental change in the protagonist's view of himself and his environment—a change which took place long before he left Spain. Parallels with Cernuda have been established in earlier chapters. Cernuda shares a retreat into the dream, a vague yearning and an interest in the dawn and the dusk. *Penumbras* takes these comparisons further. In *Ocnos* Cernuda laments his childhood thus:

> Atrás quedaban los día soleados junto al mar, el tiempo inútil para todo excepto para el goce descuidado, la compañía de una criatura querida como a nada y como a nadie.[2]

The experiencc, recorded in 'Cuando era primavera', 'frente al mar', is one which can be related to those feelings expressed in *Ocnos*.

The importance of 'Cuando era primavera' and 'Vuelta a México'

The very inclusion of a section in the 1954 *Antología* entitled *Penumbras* is enough in itself to suggest that its poetry is of some significance. In his bibliography Blanco provides the following note on the use of this heading. Referring to the 1939–41 group, he writes:

> "Penumbras" es el título que da Prados en la *Antología* a ciertos poemas de transición entre libros. Éstas son las primeras 'penumbras' propiamente dichas. Ahora Prados usa el título para todo grupo de poemas de transición.

Records of such groups of poems, often unpublished, are to be found in the *Lista de los papeles de Emilio Prados*. A reading of this document confirms the information Blanco has already given: that there are several transitional groups of poetry collected under the title 'Penumbras'.[4] In view of the evolutionary nature of Prados's work such groups, standing between the progressive steps marked by each publication, are not without importance. Yet, as far as *Antología* was concerned, they were completely ignored. Such a decision—unless the view is adopted that the anthology is a random, haphazard compilation of his work—places *Penumbras, 1939–1941* in a pivotal position within it. It suggests that, rather than draw attention to a number of intermediate stages of development between the anthology's main sections, he has chosen to emphasise the most important division in the protagonist's experience—a division which implies that there is a radical difference between poetry included from *Tiempo* to *Llanto en la sangre* and that found under the titles *Mínima muerte, Jardín cerrado* and *Río natural*. The record of the central figure's adult experience, as described in the first half of the anthology, has been far from untroubled. The vision captured in *Penumbras* sets him upon new paths of discovery, where the chances of achieving contentment are much higher.

'Cuando era primavera'

Before 'Cuando era primavera' can be seen to have any relevance to the on-going process of the development of the 'yo', its crucial message needs to be identified precisely. That it is a record of intense regret and nostalgia is apparent from the closing lines:

> Pero, ¡ay!, tan sólo
> cuando era primavera en España.
> ¡Solamente en España,
> antes, cuando era primavera! (143:I,766)

The exact nature of the experience for which he hungers needs to be recognised. The distinctiveness of some of its features will lead to a mistrust of a straightforward equation of its sadness with the grief of the patriot in exile.

One of these features is the extent to which images of fertility figure in the expression of his sadness. Sea and water are mentioned throughout. The bliss once enjoyed by the 'yo' was inseparable from them:

Cuando era primavera en España:
frente al mar, los espejos
rompían sus barandillas
y el jazmín agrandaba
su diminuta estrella,
. . . .
Cuando era primavera en España:
junto a la orilla de los ríos,
. . . . (141:I,764)

These lines appear in the first and second stanzas. The third further establishes the sea's importance:

Cuando era primavera en España:
todas las playas convergían en un anillo
y el mar soñaba entonces,
como el ojo de un pez sobre la arena,
frente a un cielo más limpio
que la paz de una nave, sin viento, en su pupila. (141–2:I,764)

Even in the fifth stanza, where the land rather than the sea is being remembered, room is still found for reference to the 'agua humilde / de un arroyo que empieza . . .' (142:I,765).

In all these allusions to water is the implication that the land was, equally, fertile and life-giving. The fourth stanza describes the processes of nature, an integral part of his memory of these better days:

Cuando era primavera en España:
los olivos temblaban
adormecidos bajo la sangre azul del día,
mientras que el sol rodaba
desde la piel tan limpia de los toros,
al terrón en barbecho
recién movido por la lengua caliente de la azada.
¡Cuando era primavera!

In the stage of his development represented by *Tiempo*, sexual symbols—the fish, the bird—gave rise to great discomfort. During the period to which he is now looking back, at least, such symbols—the sun, the bulls, the plough—have little disconcerting effect. This will prove to be an important clue to the true meaning of the 'spring' on which the poem sets such store.

But not only does the protagonist feel at home in a fertile environment. He also, in this now lost estate, enjoyed a strong sense of harmony with the infinite. The first and third stanzas, already quoted, with their references to the star, the perfect ring formed by the beaches, to the eye of the fish, all suggest that the veil which has largely covered his vision of the infinite so far is as yet transparent. In *Mysterium coniunctionis*, Jung shows that the eyes of the fish belong to a group of symbols, the *Scintillae*, which are suggestive of the ceaseless vigilance of what Prados would take, to judge from later poetry, to be a divine principle. Jung wrote: 'The fish's eye is always open, like the eye of God.'[5] There was in *this* Spain an effortless awareness of and communion with the infinite natural world around him:

Cuando era primavera en España:
yo buscaba en el cielo,
yo buscaba
las huellas tan antiguas
de mis primeras lágrimas
y todas las estrellas levantaban mi cuerpo
siempre tendido en una misma arena,
al igual que el perfume, tan lento,
nocturno, de las magnolias . . .
¡Cuando era primavera! (142–3:I,765)

The sigh of the last line quoted reminds the reader that though this awareness, expressed by a sense of peace in the presence of images of fertility, was once his, it is now lost. It is becoming apparent that the poem expresses a nostalgia not simply for Spain, but for specific characteristics of a kind of life he used to lead there. The protagonist himself limits it to a restricted period of time:

Pero, ¡ay!, tan sólo
cuando era primavera en España.
¡Solamente en España,
antes, cuanda era primavera! (143:I,766)

There is the strong suggestion that even while he was in Spain this consciousness of harmony and peace were not always his. It is vital to establish what the 'spring', in which the eternal and fertile seemed so close, represents. Though, of course, it obviously refers to the pleasure of spring-time, an idyllic picture of the cherry-trees in flower, the tilling of the soil and the perfume of the magnolias, nevertheless certain aspects of the poem and Prados's work in general lead to the conclusion that as far as the 'yo' is concerned, the spring has more private connotations.

Much of the content of the poem, for example, has little direct bearing on the spring. Many of the activities it describes could equally have taken place at other times of the year. The stanza which follows is typical of this:

> Cuando era primavera on España:
> todos los hombres desnudaban su muerte
> y se tendían confiados, juntos, sobre la tierra,
> hasta olvidarse el tiempo
> y el corazón tan débil por el que ardían . . .
> ¡Cuando era primavera!

Though his delight in gazing up at the infinite sky above him may have been particularly pleasurable during the spring, it is unlikely that such activities were exclusive to it:

> yo buscaba en el cielo
> yo buscaba
> las huellas tan antiguas
> de mis primeras lágrimas

Indeed, much of the stress of the poem falls, as Blanco notes, on one word—'antes'—which in the last stanza is used to summarise all the longing which has preceded. The poem is a wistful plea for the return, not of spring—which is anyway still to be enjoyed—but for the return of an earlier period in his life. It is he, rather than the season, which has changed, thereby putting the kind of experience outlined in the poem out of reach.

Examination of other references to spring in Prados's work confirms the suspicion that he is dealing with a specific period in his life and suggests that this period is associated with childhood. The important prose poems, *Las tres noches del hombre*, make significant mention of the spring. In the second of the 'nights' the protagonist is still in the pre-adolescent state: he has yet to learn what love or the purpose of the body are. From the point of view of 'Cuando era primavera' it is interesting to note that the period of late childhood, when he is intended to be engaged in the delightful discovery of his true nature, is set in the spring:

> Es casi atardecer. Una rama de un árbol cercano vierte sobre el nombre la sombra de sus tallos en primavera. El adolescente ve que entre las hojas, en la sombra, un pájaro canta junto al nido . . .[6]

Just as, in the natural cycle, the spring represents new life, yet to mature, so in *Las tres noches del hombre*, it signifies that time when the beginnings of awareness of the mystery and infinite nature of life come upon the individual. It is also, of course, a stage where the unwelcome characteristics of the central figure's body have not yet impressed themselves on him.

For this reason spring and April, in Prados's poetry, are never unwelcome. The 'Cinco de abril' section of the original *Memoria del olvido* arrangement of *Cuerpo perseguido* contains the poem 'Adolescencia'. A sense of wonder and emergent life fills it. This is the *Antología* version:

¡Qué deshojar de pájaros!
¡Qué silencios de fuente! . . .

. . . Y, al fin, de un salto al agua.
¡Qué nupcias transparentes!

(El río, entre tus brazos,
contigo al lecho vuelve.) (92:I,340)

Later poetry supports this evidence of a connection between April, the spring and the central figure's childhood. The lines quoted below illustrate the link in his mind between the sea and the child, the child and the infinite, and the child and the spring. 'Memoria de un alba', for example, is punctuated by references to childhood from the mature protagonist's standpoint. As in 'Cuando era primavera', the prevailing mood is one of nostalgia, and the setting the infinite fertility suggested by the sea:

"¡En Abril las aguas mil!"
(¿Memoria de Abril nací?)

Sobre Abril vive cantando.
Del Tiempo de Abril me salgo.

Canta el sol: "¿Duerme en un niño
la carne y voz de mi olvido?"
. . . .

(Florece el árbol de olvido
de Abril del niño florido . . .) (II,489)

For the moment the meaning of these lines in the context of *Río natural* is unimportant. But the connotation of spring in the protagonist's mind is clear. The tree of oblivion, a blessed condition of mind, derives from the consideration of the child, and is defined as an 'olvido de Abril'. The association of the sea with the child and the experience of childhood underline links with Lorca and Cernuda. Lorca writes, in 'Gacela de la huída':

> Muchas veces me he perdido por el mar,
> como me pierdo en el corazón de algunos niños.[7]

And in *La realidad y el deseo* it is the 'muchacho andaluz' who is asked:

> ¿Eras emanación del mar cercano?
> Eras el mar aún más
> Que las aguas henchidas con su aliento,
> . . . .[8]

Such allusions further help us to identify this 'spring' with the central figure's childhood.

In the context of the post-adolescent problems which faced the central figure as outlined in *Tiempo* and *Cuerpo perseguido*, it is not surprising that the 'primavera' of *Penumbras* is so cruelly missed. It was after this happy childhood things went radically wrong. If he gained knowledge about the physical role of the body, he did not gain attributes needed to live it out. If he realised that a relationship with 'the other' was the norm, he was unable to form one. The 'tú' was nowhere to be found—as in this poem, 'Cristal del universo':

> Tus sienes sin fronteras
> se enredan en mis dedos.
> Mi corazón te aprieta
> como un puño de viento . . .
>
> Sin tactos y sin nombres
> andamos como ciegos.
> ¿Son acaso tus labios
> esta idea? . . .
> ¡Silencio! (78:I,342)

'Growing up', for the 'yo', has meant a painful and undesirable acquisition of a body which refuses to respond in the normal ways. For Cernuda, it was the intrusion of time which put an end to the bliss of childhood. While in the Eden of pre-adolescence he enjoyed, as Silver puts it, 'timelessness, innocence, and a feeling of oneness with the world.'[9] Cernuda himself wrote in *Ocnos*:

> Llega un momento en la vida cuando el tiempo nos alcanza . . . ¡Años de niñez en que el tiempo no existe![10]

'Cuando era primavera' suggests that all this was equally true of Prados. But if in Cernuda's case it was the intrusion of time which led to the disruption of the harmony he enjoyed with the natural order, in Prados's it was the sudden and disquieting discovery of the limitations of his body.

It is now possible to define more clearly the sense of the poem. The adult 'yo' longs for a return to a childhood in which the body was not a limitation, in which there was no discrepancy between desire and reality and in which there was no need for escapism. The poem is a more comprehensive form of the idea expressed in *Cuerpo perseguido*:

> Quisiera estar por donde anduve
> como la rama, como el cuerpo;
> como en el sueño, como por la vida; (70:I,269)

The central *persona* wishes to be where he once was.

Other references to nostalgia bring out the extent of the adult protagonist's longing for earlier days. In the following extract from *Río natural*, oneness with the infinite sun, sky, sea and dream are directly linked with childhood:

> ¡En la nostalgia de un tacto
> mi pensamiento ha brotado!
>
> En él estoy . . .
> ¡Verde y nácar
> es el cuerpo de mi alma!
>
> Lento es el mar; lento el cielo,
> lento el sol, lento mi sueño.
> . . . .
>
> ¡Mi hueco—mi verde nácar,
> el cuerpo de mi nostalgia—:
>
> Alma es del niño y del cielo,
> del mar y del sol eternos! (II,403–4)

The child was infinite, eternal, without limitations, the 'yo' of the south, the sky, the sea. Now, just as exile has separated him from the warmth of Málaga, so the hateful awareness of the body has resulted in alienation from the infinite, from the 'norm' and, consequently, from other people. Once, as 'Cuando era primavera' states, he felt a kinship with all that was around him:

> todos los hombres desnudaban su muerte
> y se tendían confiados, juntos, contra la tierra (143:I,765)

Now, his body has set him apart. The reality is that of *Andando, andando por el mundo*:

> Estoy cansado de ocultarme en las ramas;
> de perseguir mi sombra por la arena;
> de desnudarme entre las rocas,
> de aguardar a las puertas de las fábricas
> y tenderme en el suelo con los ojos cerrados:
> estoy cansado de esta herida. (125:I,403)

The 'yo' was, in fact, in 'exile' long before he left the shores of Spain.

When 'Cuando era primavera' is considered with these thoughts in mind, the references it contains to the body are less puzzling. During this 'primavera' the body is accepted more readily than at any point in the *Antología* so far. One of his chief complaints in *Cuerpo perseguido* was the unreality of the body: it concerns apart from his 'real' self, while his lips were 'labios ciegos'. There was a time, however, when this was not so, and it is recorded in 'Cuando era primavera':

> los cerezos en flor
> se clavaban de un golpe contra el sueño
> y los labios crecían,
> como la espuma en celo de una aurora,
> hasta dejarnos nuestro cuerpo a su espalda,
> igual que el agua humilde
> de un arroyo que empieza . . . (142:I,765)

There was a naturalness in his relationship to his body, a body as inseparable from his 'real' self as is one part of the natural cycle from the other. The same comment applies to the second main reference to the body in the poem. Far from cutting him off from the eternal, as it now does, it shares the nature of the stars above him:

> . . . todas las estrellas levantaban mi cuerpo
> siempre tendido en una misma arena,
> al igual que el perfume, tan lento,
> nocturno, de las magnolias . . . (143:I,765)

The reality of the physical, the tangible, was as unquestionable as the eternal life-force he sensed behind them. His banishment from that realm, resulting from his 'fall' into the post-adolescent state, provokes the intense nostalgia of the poem. In a study of the poetry of Cernuda, Derek Harris discusses the experience recorded in 'Bellez oculta' and 'Palabras antes de un lectura':

> This is the perfect harmony between self and world, between *realidad* and *deseo*, that is Cernuda's ideal state of existence. His experience of this condition during his adolescence explains the importance this age assumes for him in later years.[11]

Such a statement reflects accurately much of what might be said of the 'spring-time' of the central *persona* of Prados's poetry.

The ambivalence of Prados's poetic vocabulary

As this is a poem of retrospection, it is interesting to compare the use of certain words in the poem with their use in earlier poetry. This will serve both to review what has been discovered about the adult 'yo' and, at the same time, show how fundamentally the nature of his body has affected his appreciation of the world.

It has already been suggested that certain words seem to have a dual meaning. In one context they have a welcome, 'positive' connotation: in another their connotation is unpleasant, 'negative'. In dealing with *Cuerpo perseguido* it was shown that the dream was a way of transferring the units of experience they represent from the 'negative' to the 'positive' realm. The main factor there was the body: the removal of the body from consideration meant freedom from frustration and limitation. It follows, then, that many elements of his experience which have a 'negative' aspect in his waking adult life should have 'positive' associations during childhood—when there is as yet no need to be rid of the body.

In *Tiempo*, for example, the sea was representative of the unhappy condition of the protagonist. There the fish and the boats reminded him of his own impotence. It was often contrasted with what the 'yo' considered to be the 'higher' level of the soul. At the beginning of 'Espejismos' he asks: '¿Barco en el mar o en el alma? . . .' (20:I,386), while 'Perfil del tiempo' closes with the narrative detail: '(Resbala el barco en al alma / y el pensamiento en el agua . . .)' (20:I,117). The sea of 'Cuando era primavera', however, is very different. There is found something associated with fulfilment, freed from limitation:

> . . . el jazmín
> agrandaba
> su diminuta estrella,
> hasta cumplir el límite
> de su aroma en la noche . . . (141:I,764)

The measure of the extent of the body's intrusion on his childhood enjoyment of life can also be judged by reference to the moon. In *Tiempo* it played a sinister role. It represented sterility and death: it was a reflection of what he felt about his own body: '. . . veo, dibujado en la luna / . . . mi cuerpo sin imagen.' (16). In *Penumbras*, by contrast, the moon seems to have a role, even though indirect, in the fertility process: 'las grandes mariposas de la luna / fecundaban los cuerpos desnudos / de las muchachas' (141:I,764).

The fish of the *Tiempo* era was a malicious reminder of his inadequacy. It was sometimes, as in *Canciones del farero*, portrayed as a heartless spectator of the young sailor's shame. In the first chapter a poem from *País* was quoted where the demise of the boat (the sexual failure of the protagonist) was greeted with amusement: 'Mi barco se derretía . . . / (Los peces se sonreían).' In 'Cuando era primavera' attention is drawn rather to the eye of the fish, a symbol, as has already been established, related to the infinite, the eternal. The context suggests that his response to it then was entirely favourable:

> . . . el mar soñaba entonces,
> como el ojo de un pez sobre la arena ,
> frente a un cielo más limpio
> que la paz de una nave, sin viento, en su pupila.
> (142:I,764)

The 'yo' of *Tiempo* was a creature of the evening and the dawn. The night and the day were inhospitable. In the selection for the anthology few poems relating to the day were included. The sun brought with it painful reminders of his inadequacies. One pocm links the sun and pain together:

> . . . y el sol . . .
> . . . más sol en la arena . . .
> (Mi corazón se levanta
> y cruza, inmóvil, mi pena.) (I,368)

The presence of the sun is essential to the later poem:

Los olivos temblaban
adormecidos bajo la sangre azul del día,
mientras que el sol rodaba
desde la piel tan limpia de los toros (143:I,765).

Here there is a happy acceptance of its warm and fertilising power.

As the preceding section of this chapter demonstrates, it was the painful discovery of the adult body which resulted in such marked changes of attitude. Where there is peace in the physical realm, then the way is open for harmonious relations with the world about him. Where there is not—and this has been the problem of the mature 'yo'—there is that anguish which drives him to the escape of the dream of *Cuerpo perseguido*—or indeed to the nostalgia of 'Cuando era primavera'.

The new vision

It is in this very nostalgia that the protagonist seems to experience something entirely new—indeed new enough for *Penumbras* to merit their pivotal place in the *Antología*. It seems to offer the protagonist a way out of both his nostalgia and his obsessive awareness of his body's inadequacy. The main characteristics of this new pathway, explored more fully in *Mínima muerte*, will be noted here, to await more detailed attention in Chapter 6.[12]

Blanco fixes for us a moment in Prados's life which corresponds to the experience recorded in 'Vuelta a México'.[13] It involves an unusual degree of illumination—a quality of timelessness in which past, present and future are one:

¡Todo el campo era una joya !
¡Era un futuro recuerdo
que se empezaba a formar! . . . (143:I,780)[14]

It seems that time has been halted; a moment of equilibrium has been reached. The night is 'parada, / como un milagro, encendida!' (143:I,780). The pines seem to have caught fire but as the day does not turn to night so do they remain unconsumed. Fire and water, the most contradictory elements, are reconciled: 'el agua una llama viva'. In his 1973 study Harris refers to the critical view that Cernuda found in Mexico 'a paradigm of the Andalusia of his childhood.'[15] There is a strong basis for believing this to be true of Prados.

But despite the intensity of this vision, or perhaps because of its intensity, expression is difficult or impossible:

Busqué—para darle nombre
a mi nuevo huésped—guía,
en mis campos interiores . . .
Vacío encontré mi centro
y lejos mi soledad,
y me dio miedo el silencio.
. . . .
¿adónde podré buscar
la voz de este pensamiento
que, en mí, formándose está? . . . (144:I,781)

This is the task which he has set himself in *Mínima muerte*, and, to a large extent, in the rest of his poetry. For the moment all he can say is that he feels there is a link between this experience and the exceptional consciousness of nature he knew as a child. For a while it remains half-lost in the memory:

(Otro paisaje, en mi pecho,
iba encendiéndome el día,
también a medio lograr
por mi memoria perdida . . .)

The main problem addressed in the poem is how to return to this position. His momentary vision has left him, and he is 'vacío'. The childhood awareness departed from him some time ago: 'lo que tuve huyó'. His latest experience is too recent and novel for him to be able to repeat it:

. . . lo que tuve huyó
y está tan nuevo el presente,
que no sale a recibir
lo que tan bello se ofrece:

It remains a 'pensamiento' which has not been properly expressed (and which, therefore, according to platonic thought, he has gone but half-way towards understanding).

Two further points need to be mentioned in view of their importance in future developments in the poetry. Firstly there is the significance of the attraction the city irresistibly but inexplicably holds for him:

. . . la ciudad tendida
sobre un lago de metal,

frente al ocaso dormía . . .

Yo a la ciudad caminaba
ni sé a qué, ni para qué;
era el tiempo el que mandaba.

At first sight this would seem to be a strange match. The city, supposedly hard and impersonal (here, 'tendida / sobre un lago de metal') would seem to offer the materialistic existence which Lorca condemned. It is on the sub-conscious level, however, that its appeal can be more readily understood. It is in this way, too, that the poem foreshadows a major theme of *Mínima muerte*. Jung wrote of the city: 'The city is a maternal symbol, a woman who fosters the inhabitants as children'.[16] The desire to return to the childhood state and to the mother figure is strong. The return to the womb, to the mother and to the unity of nature they represent will be dealt with in the next chapter.

The second main characteristic of the experience of 'Vuelta a México' is the necessary presence of death. The death of the sun is to be the beginning of something new and important:

Yo sé que, esta luz que, el campo
hoy me da, como aderezo,
en las manos del ocaso:
ha de ser principio, en mí,
de lo que mi pensamiento
anda rondando en su fin.

But until he is able to give it a 'name' ('la voz de este pensamiento' (144:I,781)) then he will never truly know what that something is. There is no balance between the inner landscape of the soul and the outer landscape which the senses now perceive:

Paisajes de fuera y dentro
—puntos de un mismo compás,
platillos de una balanza
que mi vida han de pesar—:
¿dentro los nombres se pierden;
fuera los nombres se van,
sin apenas conocerme? . . . (145:I,782)

Ultimately it is only death which will remove the imbalance which the presence of the body, the senses, creates. In death the eternal and the central figure will be synonymous:

Y un día acabaré

al igualar mis silencios:
¡la muerte será mi fiel!

The only way to achieve something approaching this in life is to find a means whereby this principle of death is brought to bear on his experience.

Mínima muerte is, in part, a record of the search for this principle. 'Cuando era primavera' looked back to happier times over the débris of intervening years. The world of the central figure has, thus far, proved fragmented and isolated, culminating in the splintered chaos of *Llanto en la sangre*. Each section of the 1954 anthology, in fact, has recorded the protagonist's various attempts to come to terms with the problems his body poses. Chapter 1 described the 'corazón diario' of the central figure—an exposition, possibly therapeutic in intention, of his dilemma. *Cuerpo perseguido* marked an alternative escape route into the world of the dream. In *La voz cautiva* the 'yo' had become disenchanted with such an approach and was seeking the permanence which he associated with the inner 'voz'. If in the realm of the body he was weak, in that of this 'voice' he was not—a line of thought which also finds its echo in *Mínima muerte*. Finally, in both *Andando, andando por el mundo* and *Llanto en la sangre* the central figure used some aspects of the social reality—the struggles of the rejected minority or the turbulence of a nation at war—as a kind of camouflage, a protection from the discomfort which his own apartness and inner conflict had bequeathed him.

But the root problems remained. From *Mínima muerte* onwards, more radical techniques are brought into play in order to be reconciled to his body and thus find a place in the universal scheme of things. And they involve the two principles hinted at in 'Vuelta a México'—that of an inner death, a mortification of the senses (already glimpsed also in *La voz cautiva*) and a deliberate return to Cernuda's 'juventud pasada', to the coherent unity he knew as a child.[17] In other words, there is the beginning of an attempt to abandon his efforts to be what he is not and can never be in a physical sense—a normal adult man. This is to be a lengthy process—but one in which his own natural development, as well as the 'techniques' mentioned above, will bring him to the joyful freedom of *Río natural*.

1 C. Blanco Aguinaga, *Vida y obra*, p. 68.

2 L. Cernuda, *Ocnos* (Mexico, 1963), p. 185.

3 C. Blanco Aguinaga, *Vida y obra*, pp. 111–12.

4 C. Blanco Aguinaga, *Lista de los papeles de Emilio Prados*, pp. 18–19. Several sets of *Penumbras* are classified under Caja 6.c. These include the 'Tránsito de penumbras de *Jardín cerrado* a *Río natural* (6.c); 'Tránsito de penumbras de *Río natural* hacia *Circuncisión del sueño*' (6.g, 6.j).

5 C. G. Jung, *Mysterium coniunctionis*, p. 51.

6 Appendix III.

7 F. G. Lorca, *Obras completas*, p. 493.

8 L. Cernuda, *La realidad y el deseo*, p. 107.

9 P. Silver, *'Et in Arcadia Ego'* (London, 1965), pp. 56–7.

10 L. Cernuda, *Ocnos*, p. 29.

11 D. Harris, *Luis Cernuda, A Study of the Poetry* (London, 1973), p. 23.

12 It should be not surprising that *Mínima muerte* and 'Vuelta a México' should have much in common. Though *Mínima muerte* follows *Penumbras*—and therefore 'Vuelta a Mexico'—in the anthology, its dates suggest that it was written during very much the same period. *Mínima muerte* was written in 1939 and 1940, 'Vuelta a México' is dated 1941. The introduction to Chapter 6 discusses the point more fully.

13 C. Blanco Aguinaga, *Vida y obra*, p. 68.

14 There is possibly another Platonic echo here—the concept of knowing or learning as a process of remembering what has been 'forgotten'.

15 D. Harris, *Luis Cernuda*, p. 14.

16 C. G. Jung, *Psychology of the Unconscious*, translated by B. M. Hinkle (London, 1915), p. 231.

17 L. Cernuda, *Ocnos*, p. 55.

CHAPTER SIX

In Search of the Infinite Rose

Time past and time future
Allow but a little consciousness.
To be conscious is not to be in time
But only in time can the moment in the rose-garden,
The moment in the arbour where the rain beat,
The moment in the draughty church at smokefall
Be remembered; involved with past and future.

(Thomas Stearns Eliot, *Four Quartets*)

She is the Queen of all spiritual flowers, and therefore she is called the Rose for the rose is fitly called of all flowers the most beautiful. But moreover, she is the *Mystical*, or *hidden* rose; for mystical means hidden.

(John Henry Newman, *The Mystical Rose*)

Introduction

From the point of view of the 1954 anthology's structure *Penumbras* and *Mínima muerte* are the most interesting of its sections after the first, *Tiempo*. They provide clear evidence that the *Antología* was carefully planned, and that the reader is intended to perceive some kind of pattern in the central figure's development—even though some of the poetry's characteristics seem designed to cloud rather than clarify aspects of that development. Two features of the arrangement of *Penumbras* and *Mínima muerte* testify to the poet's care with regard to the overall shape of his anthology. A consideration of them must preface any accurate assessment of the relevance of *Mínima muerte* to the general pattern which has begun to emerge from Prados's poetry.

The first of these features concerns the order in which the sections appear in the anthology. Prados would seem to have ignored the sequence in which they were originally written. According both to the dates given in the anthology and Blanco's bibliography, 'Vuelta a México' was composed after the poetry contained in the *Mínima muerte* selection. 'Vuelta a México' is autographed: '(Desierto de los leones, 1941.)'. *Mínima muerte* is dated 1939–1940. In discussing *Penumbras* it was suggested that it presented a watershed in the central figure's experience. The effect of the disruption of the chronology of Prados's original output mentioned above is to confirm this view. The group of poems chosen serves as a rapturous continuation of the progress made in 'Vuelta a México', where: '¡Todo el campo era una joya! / ¡Era un futuro recuerdo / que se empezaba a formar! . . .' (143:I,780). The reader is to gain the impression that the new vision enjoyed there is carried over into the group of poems which follows.

This leads to the second indication of Prados's intentions in framing his anthology. The poetry of the *Mínima muerte* group has been chosen not in order to represent all the shades of experience which the book *Mínima muerte* expressed: rather has it been chosen to reinforce the reader's sense of progression and, indeed, achievement in the experience of the protagonist. In every poem selected the emphasis is on peace and harmony. In poem I he writes: 'Y el silencio es todo fiel: / alma feliz de la hora.'. Poem II ends with these lines: 'Todo era luz de misterio. / La Eternidad sonreía . . .'.

Poem III expresses contentment and rest. Poems IV, V and VI celebrate the perfection of the rose, hailed in these jubilant terms: '¡En todo está! / ¡Con todo palpitando: / destino fiel, / amor, / feliz presencia, / olvido . . .!' (156:I,809). Later analysis will suggest that poems VII and VIII, equally, denote a high level of satisfaction on the part of the 'yo'.

The tone of the original *Mínima muerte* itself is far less constant than this. There are poems—including, notably, 'Tres tiempos de soledad', which express doubts, fears and questionings. Without exception they are overlooked or, as in the case of 'Tres tiempos . . .' transplanted to an entirely different section. They have been sacrificed not, it would appear, simply to obscure the possibility that the 'yo' met with problems after the Mexico experience—otherwise such poems as 'Tres tiempos de soledad' would have been omitted altogether—but rather to maintain a sense of movement and progression in the anthology's overall plan. The graph of the protagonist's experience is straightened out: instead of the vagaries of such sections as *Cuerpo perseguido* there is—for a while at least—a consistent accent on stability and peace.

If this study were confined to the anthology's structure, then the poetry of its *Mínima muerte* section would provide a satisfactory basis for inspection. But if its aim is still to be the identification of the emotional context in which the 'yo' appears in Prados's work, then it must cast its net wider. In referring to the book *Mínima muerte*, we shall discover its poetry to be typical of nothing more or less than the protagonist's instinctive and habitual attempts to counter profound personal problems in a world which his writing creates for him.

'Tres tiempos de soledad'—the plight of the central figure

The 1944 publication begins with a long and involved review of the protagonist's situation, aims and personal history, entitled 'Tres tiempos de soledad'. Its three sections are directed towards 'soledad':

> Soledad, noche a noche te estoy edificando,
> noche a noche te elevas de mi sangre fecunda
> y a mi supremo sueño curvas fiel tus murallas
> de cúpula intangible como el propio universo. (197:I,795)

It is the meditation of the protagonist which gives birth to 'soledad', which can be seen as a state of extreme introversion (imposing its 'murallas' on him) in which the central figure can enjoy to the full what he calls his 'supremo sueño'.[1]

As the stanza quoted indicates, the main purpose of 'Tres tiempos de soledad' is to examine this 'solitude' and what the central figure hopes to discover about himself in it. In the course of this examination, there are several descriptions of the protagonist. These descriptions provide important insights into his view of himself. They are important particularly, from the point of view of this study, in that they share many characteristics with those of the 'yo' of pre-*Penumbras* poetry. It was in those terms that Laing portrayed the 'divided self': '. . . the individual cannot take the realness, aliveness, autonomy and identity of himself for granted . . .'. This state of affairs has drastic consequences.

> . . . he has to become absorbed in contriving ways of trying to be real, of keeping himself or others alive, of preserving his identity, in efforts, as he will put it, to prevent himself from losing his self.[2]

'Tres tiempos de soledad' is both a reminder that the 'divided self' of *Cuerpo perseguido* lives on and that the poetry of *Mínima muerte* was, once again, an effort made by the 'yo' to achieve a sense of reality, of 'identity'.

He continues, 'Tres tiempos de soledad' reveals, to bemoan the instability of his relationship with his body. He comments:

> Por buscar me he perdido y sin buscar no encuentro
> ya posible la forma que antes me equilibraba
> con la forma del árbol, ejemplo de mi vida,
> mitad buscando al cielo y medio entre las sombras.
>
> Ni bajo el tiempo mismo podré ya situarme
> para saber la estancia precisa de mi cuerpo: (199:I,798)

Several phrases used here are keenly reminiscent of those found in *Cuerpo perseguido*. He confesses that 'me he perdido'. He is lacking in 'forma'. He is finding it difficult to 'place' himself ('situarme'). And, perhaps the most obvious confession, he is unsure of 'la estancia de mi cuerpo'. Later in the poem he still trying to 'fix' or 'situate' himself, unable to discern 'la dimensión ni encaje preciso en que me busco' (200:I,799). If Cernuda's abiding preoccupation was with time, it is to the question of the body that Prados finds himself returning.

The poem also reminds us of the feeling the 'yo' used to convey about himself: that he was able, in a curious way, to observe himself entirely objectively. Here, again, he is addressing 'soledad':

Soledad, noble espera de mi llanto infecundo,
hoy te elevan mis brazos como a un niño o a un muerto,
como a una gran semilla que en el cielo clavara
junto a esta misma luna con que alumbras mi insomnio.

Yo que te elevo, abajo quedo absorto e inmóvil
viendo crecer la imagen de mi propia existencia,
el mapa que se exprime de mi fiera dulzura
y el doméstico embargo que mi crimen contiene.

A ti yo vivo atado, invisible y activo,
como el tallo del aire que sostiene tus torres.
Bajo mis pies contemplo tus cuadernos en tierra
y arriba la imprecisa concavidad del cielo. (198–9:I,796)

He is able to speak of 'la imagen de mi propia existencia'. He lifts up a 'soledad' to which he feels himself to be inextricably linked ('atado') and yet at the same time 'abajo quedo absorto e inmóvil'. The real 'yo' observes another self which lives independently from him. The 'Tres canciones', which follow 'Tres tiempos de soledad' in the complete *Mínima muerte*, corroborate these findings. In the first he talks of a separate world existing apart from him and yet 'a mi lado':

y llevo un mundo a mi lado
igual que un traje vacío
y otro mundo en mí guardado
que es por el mundo que vivo. (I,802)

In the third he describes himself as a phantom, another reminder of the language of *Cuerpo perseguido*:

Y entre mis dos soledades,
igual que un fantasma hueco,
vivo el límite de sangre
sombra y fiel de mis deseos. (I,804)

There is another way in which 'Tres tiempos de soledad' are reminders of earlier problems. The central figure describes himself as someone who exists in an unstable and ill-defined time-scheme. Laing writes that the 'unreal man' may lack the experience of his own temporal continuity'.[3] The poem's title in itself suggests something of this. Past, present and future exist separately rather than as coherent aspects of his experience. The following stanzas, parts of which have already been quoted, illustrate this:

> Ni bajo el tiempo mismo podré ya situarme
> para saber la estancia precisa de mi cuerpo:
> que tres hojas dividen la luz de mis palabras
> y entre las tres no entiendo cuál es la más presente.
> . . . .
>
> Al presente más miro, tratando de fijarme
> como fiel de balanza que muestre mi existencia;
> pero al hallar su centro, no encuentro en la penumbra
> la dimensión ni encaje preciso que me busco.
> (199–200:I,798–9)

The three leaves, the past, the present and the future, 'divide'—they constitute an aggressive and upsetting factor. Even the present is unsatisfactory: it is indistinct, it does not provide a context sharply defined enough to allow him to enjoy normal life, within that 'encaje preciso que me busco'. Part of the protagonist's reaction to this predicament is reflected in the technique used by Prados in certain poems. A lack of a sense of 'presentness' results in a tortuous leap-frogging of past over present, present over future and future over past, a desperate attempt to secure an answer to the question of his present identity:

> Pensaba lo que iba a ser,
> dejando, al pensar, de serlo
> antes de ser . . .
>
> Otra vez no lo pensé,
> y nunca supe que estaba siendo,
> por dejar de ser,
> lo que antes pensaba ser
> para ser.
>
> Ahora quisiera saber:
> ¿qué seré cuando no pueda
> pensar lo que pensaré? (I,831)

But as 'Tres tiempos de soledad' indicates, mere verbal manoeuvring of this kind brings little permanent satisfaction.

It is only against this background that the significance of the poetry of the *Mínima muerte* selection can be properly appreciated. The poems chosen are best understood when related to these problems—rather than to those to which Blanco refers: '. . . la oscura crisis espiritual que caracteriza, en su fondo más silencioso, a todos los emigrados de España'.[4] The irresistible attaction of the infinite flower, which will now be examined, is directly consequent upon those inadequacies and fears adumbrated in *Mínima muerte* as it originally appeared.

The attraction of the rose

It is in '¡En todo está!' that the rose's significance to the protagonist is most obvious. The opening lines demonstrate the close links between this poetry and that of 'Vuelta a México':

> ¡En todo está! ¡por todo va la rosa
> perenne y fiel en dar su fugaz símbolo
> al clamor de lo eterno . . .
> ¡En todo está! ¡por todo va pasando,
> visitadora dueña maternal,
> la rosa! (155:I,809)

The rose of this poem enshrines two of the fundamental principles sought in *Penumbras*. It embodies firstly the paradox of the living death. In 'Vuelta a México' he foresaw a time when the experience of the infinite would always be his—but only at the price of death to the outer world of the senses:

> Y un día me acabaré,
> al igualar los silencios:
> ¡la muerte será mi fiel! (145:I,782)

The ephemeral will give way to that which is eternal. The rose is continually undergoing a process involving both life and death. It is both 'perenne y fiel' and a 'fugaz símbolo'. It is, to quote another *Mínima muerte* poem, 'la flor que tanto dura'.

There is another way in which the rose extends lines of thought first apparent in 'Vuelta a México'. Part of the attraction of the rose lies in its potency as a maternal symbol. For the rose, just as much as the city in 'Vuelta a México', represents an irresistible haven in the shelter of which the protagonist may return to the blissful state of childhood. It is the 'visitadora dueña maternal'. In explaining the flower's significance Jung commented that it is a comfort for the man who feels a longing for re-birth, who is conscious of ageing and who grieves for his childhood:

Hölderlin exemplifies this path in his poetry and his life. I leave the poet to speak in his song:

To the Rose

"In the Mother-womb eternal,
Sweetest queen of every lea,
Still the living and supernal
Nature carries thee and me.
"Little rose, the storm's fierce power
Strips our leaves and alters us;
Yet the deathless germ will tower
To new blooms, miraculous."

The following comments may be made upon the parable of this poem: The rose is the symbol of the beloved woman ("Haidenröslein", heather rose of Goethe). The rose blooms in the "rose-garden" of the maiden; therefore, it is also a direct symbol of the libido. When the poet dreams that he is with the rose in the mother-womb of nature, then, psychologically, the fact is that his libido is with the mother. Here is an eternal germination and renewal . . . This is also perceived by Hölderlin as the enviable prerogative of the gods—to enjoy everlasting infancy.[5]

The kinds of problems observed in 'Tres tiempos de soledad' emerged as the protagonist left his infancy behind. Part of the attractiveness of the rose lies in its ability to draw him back to a time when such difficulties did not exist. Cernuda wrote in *Ocnos*:

¡Ah, tiempo, tiempo cruel, que para tentarnos con la rosa de hoy destruiste la dulce rosa de ayer![6]

Though Prados expresses an underlying concern with the body, rather than time, there is, especially in *Mínima muerte*, a common search for the lost rose of yesterday.

In discussing the lengthy 'Tres tiempos de soledad', it was noticed that the central figure still regarded himself as unstable, ill-defined and lacking in a sense of 'temporal continuity'. The rose of '¡En todo está!' is marked by its constancy and by its innate self-confidence:

¡En todo está! ¡por todo va quedando,
sin salir, sin entrar, sin ser apenas:
viajadora constante
de un tiempo corporal hueco de rosa! . . . (155:I,809)

Time for the rose is so real that it is 'corporal': its presence and existence, unlike that of the protagonist, are unquestionable: '¡por todo va quedando,'. The principle noted above is again at work: the rose attracts because it offers those qualities which the 'yo' would covet for himself.

The remaining stanzas of the *Mínima muerte* poem further explain why such emphasis should be placed on the rose as an object for the central figure's contemplation. The fragmented, divided self finds in it a symbol of totality and unity:

¡En todo está! ¡con todo va llegando
la rosa a ser la rosa
y todo es ya, como su luz varada,
figuración de mundo en pensamiento!

¡En todo está! ¡de todo está llegando
la rosa a ser y todo es ya la rosa!

¡En todo está! ¡por todo va flotando
su aurora descuajada:
incendio, herida, estela de la rosa!

¡En todo está!
¡Con todo palpitando:
destino fiel,
amor,
feliz presencia,
olvido . . .! (155–6:I,809–810)

He is fascinated by the rose's seeming omnipresence, mesmerised to such an extent that he sees it taking over the entire universe: 'todo es ya la rosa'.

When it is conceded that these poems are written against a backcloth of considerable self-doubt and insecurity, then the emergence of the rose as the virtually exclusive object of the protagonist's attention is not hard to understand. The 'yo' is divided. The rose is, according to Cirlot:

> . . . a symbol of completion, of consummate achievement and perfection. Hence, accruing to it are all those ideas associated with these qualities: the mystic Centre, the heart . . . the garden of Eros . . . the paradise of Dante . . . the beloved . . . the emblem of Venus . . . and so on.
>
> . . . the golden rose is a symbol of absolute achievement. When the rose is round in shape, it corresponds in significance to the mandala.[7]

Jung's research also suggests a link between the rose and the mandala. A work of his editing, *Man and his Symbols*, observes:

> Abstract mandalas also appear in European Christian art. Some of the most splendid examples are the rose windows of the cathedrals. These are representative of the self of man transposed onto the cosmic plane. (A cosmic mandala in the shape of a shining white rose was revealed to Dante in a vision.).[8]

That the rose should possess the properties of the mandala is of great significance to a study of the central figure. For the mandala—the rose in this case—represents the self that its observer would wish to be—unified, whole. In *Man and His Symbols* is found a definition of the circular or spheroid aspects of the mandala—shared, of course, by the rose of '¡En todo está!':

> Dr. M. L. von Franz has explained the circle (or sphere) as a symbol of the self. It expresses the totality of the psyche in all its aspects, including the relationship between man and the whole of nature. Whether the symbol appears in primitive sun-worship or modern religion, in myths and dreams, in the mandala drawn by Tibetan monks, in the ground plans of cities, or in the spherical concepts of early astronomers, it always points to the single most vital aspect of life—its ultimate wholeness.[9]

The central figure's admiration of and attraction to the 'estela de la rosa', so lavishly praised in this poem, is, then, two-fold. It has found the secret of those central principles outlined in 'Vuelta a México'. And its very nature, replete with those eternal and infinite qualities which the protagonist desires, makes it an inevitable and totally satisfying object of contemplation. From the point of view of his overall development, it is interesting to compare the 'boat' which stood for the central *persona*'s unhappy experience of his body in *Tiempo* with the rose of '¡En todo está!'. For the rose is described as a boat. It is 'varada'; its 'aurora descuajada' is seen 'flotando':

> ¡por todo va flotando
> su aurora descuajada:
> incendio, herida, estela de la rosa! (156:I,809)

In the penultimate stanza it is 'navegando' (156:I,810). The boat of *Tiempo* was ineffectual, a travesty. The 'boat' to which he now looks is majestic, powerful and all-consuming.

The process of contemplation

'Rosa interior' describes the experience of the 'yo' as he meditates upon the rose. The mood of the entire poem is one of calm, blessedness. It is marked by the gentleness of its progression from one stage of contemplation to another. Its vocabulary is restricted to expressions of tranquillity: 'quieta estancia', 'última paz', 'duerme el amor', 'el alba en reposo' all appear, for example, in the first two stanzas alone. In establishing this mood the protagonist refers, inevitably, to the rose:

> Mínima flor. Quieta estancia . . .
> La que el pensamiento busca.
> Última paz donde el tiempo,
> desbaratado, se ajusta! (149:I,860)

From the first it is apparent that he is dealing with an extremely elevated level of experience. The use of the epithet 'mínima' is enough in itself to suggest this. A clue to its meaning in this context is to be found in Poulet's *The Metamorphosis of the Circle*. There he argues that the concept of eternity involves the presence of apparent opposites. 'Absolute circularity' is impossible without 'absolute centrality'. (The concentric form of the rose, of course, lends itself particularly to consideration along these lines.) The same is true of 'maximum' and 'minimum', as this extract suggests:

> God is a point, because He is a centre, not only of the Universe, but of the soul. The synderesis, l'apex mentis, the Seelengrund, the fünkelein, all these expressions profusely employed by the mystics, signify that the maximum is the minimum, the infinity of the divine sphere is in the infinite minuteness of the centre, and that this centre is indeed that of the soul.[10]

It is the 'minimal' flower because it is the 'maximum' flower, eternal, all-pervasive and, as an object of contemplation, the key which the protagonist hopes will open the door into that infinite experience which he seeks himself. And it is by the same token, and by virtue of the paradox implicit in the principle of the life-giving death to which 'Vuelta a México' points, that the 'mínima muerte' will lead to the blessedness of the *vita minima*.

The effect of meditation over this 'mínima flor' is described in the rest of this first stanza. It creates a peace which is 'la que el pensamiento busca'. This is a statement of some importance when read in conjunction with the poem's closing lines, where the 'hora del alma feliz' is decribed as 'la que el pensamiento busca: / ¡mínima flor de su fin!. In the process of meditation, thought is working towards its own extinction. It is able to take the protagonist only so far in the road towards the infinite experience. The sight of the rose effects a willingness in him to renounce the intellect.

Other poems make this point more clearly. In 'Canción perdida' the 'yo' resolves that his epistemology will be based on 'muerte' rather than 'pensamiento':

Para saber lo que he sido
y ver lo que quiero ser,
tan sólo la muerte pido.

¿Es un descanso el olvido?
¿Es olvido caminar?
¿Es caminar, empezar
a olvidarse del olvido?

¡Nada me enseñe el pensar!

Para saber lo que he sido,
tan sólo la muerte pido. (I,837)

The experience described in 'Rosa interior' has a similar basis, in the quietness and absence of intellectual effort which observation of the rose induces.

It is also in this 'última paz' that 'el tiempo, / desbaratado, se ajusta.'. The central figure's view of time as a divisive force was a feature of 'Tres tiempos . . .' His attitude to it here is plain: it is 'desbaratado'. But as he contemplates the 'rosa perenne', time, which was so out of focus in the experience described in 'Tres tiempos . . .', ceases to perturb him. In the later poem, even when he concentrated exclusively on the present, the result was unsatisfactory:

Al presente más miro, tratando de fijarme
como fiel de balanza que muestre mi existencia;
pero al hallar su centro, no encuentro en la penumbra
la dimensión ni encaje preciso en que me busco. (200:II,143)

The use of the verb 'ajustarse' suggests that this sense of imprecision and of a lack of definition, of an 'encaje preciso', is to some extent countered.

The main feature of the second stanza of 'Rosa interior' is the emergence of the 'sueño':

Duerme el amor, toda el alba
en reposo entre sus labios
y toda el alba del sueño
de este reposo manando . . . (149:I,860)

The world of nature surrounding the rose and the 'yo' is at rest. 'El amor', an expression Prados uses in the next poem of the selection to signify the harmonious, unwitting co-operation of the natural elements, is lost in sleep. It is from this repose that the dream emerges, flooding the protagonist's consciousness, to judge from the extravagance of the language used ('*toda* el alba del sueño', 'manando').

The emergence of the dream from a state of total repose is also illustrated in the long poem, 'La rosa y el hombre'. Death, the elimination of the senses, is again the essential pre-requisite of this dream:

> Pesa lo eterno.
> El jardín,
> poco a poco halla equilibrio
> dentro de otro nuevo ser:
> dentro de otro nuevo ver.
> . . . .
> Hoy sólo admiro el momento,
> con la hermosura de ayer
> y el nuevo conocimiento.
> Hoy sólo admiro el no ser.
> Pesa lo eterno.
> El jardín
> va navegando en el sueño,
> sueño que es flor de un morir.
> . . . . (I,816–7)

The dream here is specifically defined as the 'flor de un morir', blossoming from 'el no ser'. The order is exactly that of 'Rosa interior': the 'última paz', the 'reposo' of death to the finite, followed by the experience of 'toda el alba del sueño'.

The equation of 'sueño' and 'lo eterno' in 'La rosa y el hombre' is a further reminder of the elevated level of experience which 'Rosa interior' is describing. The dream which he has entered is that area in which he may experience the infinite. 'Death', total 'repose', opens the way to infinite life. And, as in 'La rosa y el hombre' the 'sueño' principle is one which affects both the 'yo', the observer, and the surroundings which he is observing.[11]

The third stanza introduces us to a further step:

> Se abandona a la Belleza,
> aprisionado, el olvido

y en dos luces, la balanza
divide, de su equilibrio.

Within the realm of the dream, 'olvido' is abolished. Two stanzas from 'La rosa pensamiento' underline that the state of 'olvido' disappears when the dream comes upon the protagonist. Indeed, this is one of the prime motives for entry into 'sueño'. In the lines which follow, the 'yo' finds himself encumbered by it: it is for this reason ('por eso') that he ventures towards the dream:

Aun sentimento de olvido
soy de lo que quiero ver,
para poder luego ser
la verdad de lo que he sido.

Por eso al sueño reclamo
lo que en él sin sueño existe
y sobre su espalda viste
la forma de lo que llamo. (I,836)

What does this 'olvido' represent? From what we read in 'La rosa pensamiento' and 'Rosa interior' it is certainly an undesirable state. In the lines quoted above it is something to be removed: in 'Rosa interior' it is something which needs to be imprisoned.

Reference to *Cuerpo perseguido* helps to explain this particular use of 'olvido'.[12] In the true platonic sense, the imposition of the body has meant the 'forgetting' of the self's divine nature. As far as the 'yo' is concerned this imposition took place when he became an adult. The adult is, because he has been born into a body (and, in the case of the 'yo', acutely so) at a stroke excluded from a sphere of the infinite. For Plato, therefore, to learn is to remember—to rescue from oblivion. And for the 'yo' to experience the infinite is to recall that which he lost when he left childhood—in accordance with the situation outlined in 'Cuanda era primavera'.[13]

Some of the characteristics of contemplation are strongly reminiscent of the experience of the dream recorded in *Tiempo*. Perhaps the linking of 'sueño' and 'alba' in the second stanza is the most notable example of this. The development which follows the suspension of 'olvido' belongs to the same category. Although the syntax of the stanza is abstruse, one thing does emerge clearly: the recurrent motif of equilibrium. The higher state is marked by a sense of balance, of the removing of tension by converting what is, in this case, a negative force, 'olvido', into a neutralised and peaceful element of the experience. What is described as 'la balanza

. . . de su equilibrio' is divided 'en dos luces'. The next stanza celebrates the fact:

> Y el silencio es todo fiel:
> alma feliz de la hora.
> Con tantas luces en vuelo
> mínima muerte es la sombra. (149:I,860)

The darkness into which he voluntarily cast himself, 'la sombra', is in reality no darkness: it is that 'mínima muerte' which promotes what might be called the 'vida máxima'—life on the eternal infinite level. The process of which San Juan spoke, quoted at the outset of *Mínima muerte*, where the protagonist is 'sin luz y a obscuras viviendo', yields ultimately a higher and richer light.

The sense of wholeness implicit in the symbol of the rose, referred to earlier, is reflected in the last stanza. There is a deliberate blurring of the experience. The 'yo' is obliged to use precise, finite words. But he is determined to use them in the most ambiguous way open to him, arranging them in shifting patterns and contexts. The silence in stanza 4 was the 'alma feliz de la hora'. In the fifth stanza the same words are related to an entirely new idea:

> Hermosura, soledad:
> hora del alma feliz.
> La que el pensamiento busca:
> ¡mínima flor de su fin!

The effect is to stress the total union of experience around the protagonist. The protagonist's 'alma feliz' is sharing the same life as the perfect silence of the dream. The 'yo' is engaged in the infinite process of 'recollection', to which further reference will be made in later analysis.

The re-assessment of 'pensamiento'

In discussing 'Rosa interior' attention has been drawn to the rejection of 'pensamiento'. In the 'Canción perdida' the central figure avows: '¡Nada me enseñe el pensar!' (I,837). The experience of 'Rosa interior' is, according to its final lines, 'La que el pensamiento busca: / mínima flor de su fin!' (149:I,860). That tranquillity which the central figure seeks lies above the level of the workings of the mind—or so it would seem.

One of the poems in *Mínima muerte*, 'Estaba la rosa en nieve', (originally entitled 'La rosa desdeñada') appears to bear this out. The poem consists of the interweaving of two parallel narratives. The first concerns the rose. The second concentrates on a man as he passes by it. The events surrounding the rose are quoted below:

Estaba la rosa en nieve.

¡Ay rosa,
la rosa fría!

La rosa sin cuerpo:
el hueco de la rosa
ya sin vida . . .

. . . .
La rosa de hielo
se deshacía.

. . . .
La memoria de la rosa,
sin nombre, el olvido hundía . . .

. . . .
Todo el dolor de la rosa
se fue cuajando en el día.
Todo el olor de la rosa
sonaba a tierra perdida.

Estaba la rosa muerta . . .

¡Ay, rosa,
la rosa fría!

La rosa sin viento:
el sueño de la hermosura,
sin vida . . .

. . . .
Estaba la rosa abierta.

¡Ay rosa,
la rosa viva!

Todo el color de la rosa
se hizo razón de su huída . . . (153–4:I,818–19)

The overall direction of this narrative is clear. It records the progress of the rose through death into eternal life. At the beginning of the poem the rose has reached a state of 'neutrality'—as the 'yo' did in 'Rosa interior': it is the 'rosa en nieve . . . rosa fría'. The paleness of its colouring is an emblem of its separation from the finite world of passion and feeling. Indeed, it is 'sin cuerpo': the finite level has been entirely removed. The rose is undergoing the same process which the 'yo' of 'Rosa interior' underwent. Further finite aspects of the rose are eradicated: 'La memoria de la rosa, / sin nombre, el olvido hundía . . .'. It is 'muerta . . . sin viento'.

It is at this point that a dramatic change takes place. As the rose dies, so the poem celebrates its new and imperishable life: '¡Ay, rosa, / la rosa viva!'. The dead rose is now 'abierta'. It has found new brightness which justifies its abandonment of its original colour: 'Todo el color de la rosa / se hizo razón de su huída'.[14]

However, the poem's main point is not to show how the rose reaches this lofty and desirable condition. The poet's intention is to contrast the way of mortification, leading to life, with the way that the human figure in the poem has chosen, that of thought. Here are the lines which, scattered amongst the 'rose narrative', characterise his activity:

> Pasaba un hombre . . .
> . . . .
> El hombre no la [la rosa] miraba:
> iba pensando en su dicha.
> . . . .

The last couplet is repeated twice in the course of the poem. While the rose moves forward to a deeper experience, the man remains 'pensando en su dicha'. He had passed by, completely missing the point which the rose, in its death, is making. He is still attempting progress on the level of 'pensamiento'. The structure of the poem, concentrating as it does in the final stanzas exclusively on the exalted state of the rose, makes it clear that it has left him far behind. Once again, as it was in 'Rosa interior' and 'Canción perdida', intellectual thought would seem to have been dismissed as unprofitable.

It is this which, at first sight, makes such a poem as 'Rosa de la muerte'—the seventh in *Antología*—puzzling. It describes the imposition of night on the day. The central figure is an essential part of the process. The death of the day finds its echo in the death of the protagonist:

> Yo estaba soñando:
>
> El cielo se destejía
> para dar paso a la sangre.
> Todo el espacio fue sangre.

Todo el universo, herida.

La luna vino a posarse
sobre la sangre.
La tierra
en sangre se hundía . . .

Todo el tiempo se hizo sangre.
Mi corazón, su agonía. (156–7:I,820)

The day is bleeding to death: the moon hovers in the night sky to underline the threat of death which pervades the poem. The landscape is dying—just as the rose of 'La rosa desdeñada' was.

But, in contrast with the passer-by of that poem, the human figure of 'Yo estaba soñando' does not shut himself off from the principle which the natural world is trying to teach him. He allows himself to 'die'. His heart experiences, as the last line quoted above illustrates, the death of time—it ceases to have any significance for him. The remainder of the poem finds the 'yo' himself as a flower, as the rose. His experience is totally identified with that of the rose which the other, 'thinking' man had ignored:

Toda la muerte fue sangre.
Todo el misterio fue espina . . .

Fui deshojando mi cuerpo
sobre la sangre del día.
Fui perdiendo la memoria
con tanta sangre perdida . . .

Again, the level of the body is removed. The figure of the flower is continued. It is the 'leaves' of the body which are shed. In 'La rosa desdeñada' we read: 'La rosa de hielo / se deshacía.' (153:I,818). The 'yo' loses his 'memoria '. The rose in the earlier poem enjoyed a similar experience: 'La memoria de la rosa, / sin nombre, el olvido hundía . . .'.

The central figure, then, has followed what he takes to be the same life-giving path of the rose, the 'rosa de la muerte'. The final couplet of the poem, therefore, comes as something of a shock:

Yo estaba soñando:
yo estaba pensando.

In view of the earlier rejection of 'pensamiento', the equation of 'pensando' with this higher level of experience acquires a certain dramatic force. What is it that distinguishes this thought from the undesirable 'pensar' of other poems we have examined?

The key factor is the intervention of the principle of death. In previous chapters the connotation of certain words, such as 'cuerpo', 'barco', or 'mar' varied: the same word was used to represent entirely different units of experience. Outside the dream, their presence was unwelcome: within it—that is, outside the realm of the physical body—they were welcome. In *Mínima muerte*, it is the introduction of this 'death-principle' which brings about such radical changes. The difference between the man in 'La rosa desdeñada' and the protagonist of 'Rosa de la muerte' is that the latter's 'pensamiento' has been touched by his willingness to withdraw the activity of his finite mind. The 'Yo estaba soñando' poem is full of references to death: 'agonía', 'sangre negra', 'muerte', 'espina' all figure in it. He is therefore taken out of the finite realm of time ('Fui perdiendo la memoria / con tanta sangre perdida . . .') and reaches that 'sueño' referred to in 'Rosa interior'.

There is a close parallel in this with the thought of Plotinus—a philosopher with whom the protagonist has already been seen to share some interesting characteristics. McKenna explains that in Plotinus's work the faculties of thought—memory, hearing and so on—can either belong to the desirable spiritual realm or to the undesirable finite realm. He points out that imagination and memory, for example, may belong either to:

> The intellectual element of sensation, presenting sensations, as it were, to the higher faculty for judgment and for the uses of the semi-divine life of Philosophic Man.

or to:

> The sensible (or sense-grasping) imagination and sensible Memory, the appetites rooted in the flesh . . .[15]

The value of 'pensamiento', in the same way, can be dual: on the ordinary waking level its value is limited, negative, while on the level of the 'sueño', in which the principle of death has begun to play a part, it is engaged in a higher and infinite contemplation:

> This vision achieved, the acting instinct pauses, the mind is satisfied and seeks nothing further; the contemplation, in one so conditioned, remains absorbed within as having acquired certainty to rest upon.[16]

Re-integration

Some of the reasons why the rose should be so attractive to the central figure of 'Tres tiempos de soledad' have been established. It is not surprising, therefore, that several poems are the expression of a desire to 'become' a rose. The 'death-principle' is the key to such an experience, as the fifth poem of the *Antología* group shows:

La rosa tuvo tres muertes:
la que vino a ser la rosa,
la que se fue y la presente . . .

Luego la rosa nació
del anillo de sus muertes,
sobre la mano de Dios.

¡Feliz quien su rosa siente! (154–5:I,813)

In this poem, one where the similarity in technique and vocabulary to Miguel Hernández's *Cancionero y romancero de ausencias* is marked, the 'yo' accords to everyone that possibility of giving birth to the eternal, the infinite, the rose, within themselves.[17] Happy is the man who has made this discovery and who thus feels himself to be whole and unified, re-integrated, born 'del anillo de sus muertes', like the rose.

The ring mentioned in this 'Canción' is central to the expression of that integration which the protagonist lays hold of as a result of the experience of the 'sueño'. The structure of both 'Amor' and the poem following it in the selection, 'Mirando al agua', is entirely circular. 'Amor' presents the picture of a satisfying chain of inter-relationships. It can be divided into three sections. Each ends with a variant of this refrain:

Todo era calma,
silencio . . .
La Eternidad sonreía . (150:I,861)

The juxtaposition of the remaining material illustrates how the pattern of the natural cycle is an entirely harmonious and dove-tailing one:

La luna estaba
en el alba.
No lo sabía . . .

Le dejo la luna
al agua:
—Mira,
la flor, con mi luz,

parece alma de mi luz:
¡el alma mía!
. . . .
El sol mojaba
a la luna
y una rosa parecía.

Le dijo el agua
a la flor:
—Mira,
la luna sobre mi espejo
parece el alma de mi luz:
¡el alma mía!
. . . .
La rosa estaba
en el alba.
La luna no lo sabía.

Le dijo la rosa
al viento:
—Mira,
la luna bajo mi aroma
parece el alma de mi olor:
¡el alma mía!

Each of the natural elements in the poem—the moon, the water, the rose—is in conversation with the other. The moon talks to the water, the water to the flower, the flower to the wind. Each senses something of the other in its own light: nothing is separated, all is at peace:

Todo era luz de misterio.
La Eternidad sonreía . . .

This is in sharp contrast to the deceptive, apparent circularity of 'Bosque de la noche' (56:I,242) analysed in Chapter 2. The protagonist here observes nature as he did when a child—as a perfect cycle, characterised by the 'amor' of the poem's title. Just as in 'Cuando era primavera', where the childhood experience is recorded—'todas las playas convergían en un anillo'—it is to the circle that he turns in order to convey his awareness of its wholeness.

Another poem in the selection describes a circular pattern in terms of its structure. It consists of single lines inserted between repetitions of this lengthy refrain:

Mirando al agua
la rosa
y junto a la rosa
yo, mirando al agua. (151–2:I,855)

In itself this is a picture of rest and fulfilment: the activity of the 'yo' is exactly that of the rose. He has acquired, as he always wished, something of its nature.

It is the interspersed single lines which lend a sense of circularity to the poem. The complete time-cycle from dawn through the night and to the dawn again is traced through them:

. . . .
(La luz era el alba.)
. . . .
(El sol era un ascua.)
. . . .
(La tarde empezaba.)
. . . .
(¡Qué noche tan larga!)
. . . .
(¡Qué estrellas tan bajas!)
. . . .
(¡Qué azul vuelve el alba!)

There are no missing links. So long as he is like the rose—that is, in some way experiencing that death which the rose continually experiences—then there is no time which he need fear. He has been liberated from time, and the circle is the poetic image of that liberation. The feeling of temporal discontinuity which earlier troubled him is gone. In his private papers Prados spoke of an eternal present which: 'no es mitad pasado y mitad porvenir sino presente total . . .'.[18] It is this which 'Mirando al agua . . .' records.

The most complete expression of the integration of the 'yo' within a world which once seemed to reject him comes in the poem chosen to close the *Antología* group. The dependence of one element—including, most significantly, the 'alma', representing the protagonist—on the other is total. They are indistinguishable the one from the other:

El agua es vida de luz,
aunque el agua es vida
sin luz . . .
Pero el agua
es luz de la vida

y la vida es luz
y la luz es vida
en el agua . . .
Mas la vida
es agua de luz
y la luz es vida del alma . . . (157:I,858)

The poem's climax is reached in the expression of the realisation that just as light is contained in water, and water in light, so death is meant to inhabit life, and life death. This discovery has always been central to his investigation of the rose, which appears dramatically in the poem's closing line:

Mas el alba es el agua del alma . . .
Mas el alma no es alba del agua . . .
Mas el agua es el alma del alba . . .

Mas el alba: ¿no es tiempo de luz?
Mas el tiempo: ¿no es vida del alba?
Mas la muerte: ¿no es alba de luz?
. . . .
¡Una rosa florece en la Nada!

The poem ends on an exultant note. The chant-like repetitions create a mood of ecstasy, and it is thus the arrangement of the anthology material ends. Before going on to deal with *Jardín cerrado*, it is necessary to complement this overall impression of joy and fulfilment with a reference to less satisfactory experience recorded in the original *Mínima muerte*.

Guilt and fear

It was stated at the outset that *Mínima muerte* was an interesting section from the point of view of the overall shape of the *Antología*. It was claimed that less welcome experiences played an important part in *Mínima muerte*, but were overlooked in the selection in order to stabilise its overall tone and development. Reference will be made, then, to a poem which suggests that, though the 'sueño' experience of *Mínima muerte* is in itself satisfactory, it is not a complete answer to the protagonist's problems:

Siento que un saber me tira
y como de un pozo saca
toda el agua de mi ser
a otra vida.

Pero también sé que siento
que si me doy a este ser,
lo que comienzo a saber,
por saberlo, se me olvida . . .

Y pues que sólo escondida
la verdad puedo tener,
nada podré conocer
en esta constante huída. (I,829–30)

He is complaining of the same 'constante huída' of which *Cuerpo perseguido* complained. The exclusion of the body—necessary for 'sueño'—can always only be temporary. Herein lies the inadequacy with which the 'yo' is to battle in *Jardín cerrado*. As long as the body is excluded there can still be no resolution of the basic problem afflicting him—his relationship with his body. He complains in another *Mínima muerte* poem: 'Sin cuerpo / nada tendré' (I,848). Seward's opinion of the function of the rose is clear: '. . . no other symbol than the rose could have better filled the complex modern need for affirmation, integration and universality.'[19] This has always been its attraction to the central figure. But, equally clearly, there are in *Mínima muerte* suggestions that the rose has not proved itself to be the ultimate answer to the problems facing him. He has yet to arrive at an experience where he finds contentment in normal, waking life.

1 That 'soledad' involves a process of introspection is also suggested by these lines from the third of the 'Tres canciones': 'Me pierdo en mi soledad / y en ella misma me encuentro, / que estoy tan preso en mí mismo / como en la fruta está el hueso' (I,804). There is a loss of consciousness of what is without, and a discovery of that which is within.

2 R. D. Laing, *The Divided Self*, pp. 42–3.

3 *Ibid.*, p. 42.

4 C. Blanco Aguinaga, *Vida* y *obra*, p. 72.

5 C. G. Jung, *Psychology of the Unconscious*, pp. 435–6.

6 L. Cernuda, *Ocnos*, p. 101.

7 J. Cirlot, *A Dictionary of Symbols*, p. 263.

8 C. G. Jung (editor), *Man and His Symbols* (London, 1964), p. 241.

9 *Ibid*, p. 240.

10 G. Poulet, *The Metamorphosis of the Circle*, trans. by C. Dawson and E. Coleman (Baltimore, 1966), p. xiii.

11 There is, of course, nothing original in this process of the mortification of finite experience. In *What is Mysticism?* Knowles outlines a similar method of enjoying mystical experience in connection with the sixth century figure, Denis the Areopagite: '. . . the ascent of the soul to God was achieved by a series of negative resolutions by which all

sight and sound at every level of the external world were progressively blotted out of the mind'. (D. Knowles, *What is Mysticism?* (London, 1967), p. 111). Denis followed the neo-platonic school both in terminology and ideas: Plotinus gives similar advice to the soul seeking this higher level of experience. It can only be attained by 'disengagement': 'Disengagement means simply that the soul withdraws to its own place. It will hold itself above all passions and affections'. (Plotinus, *The Enneads*, p. 34). The importance of the dream to Prados is clear from this difficult quotation from the Prados papers: '. . . el sueño es comunicación a través de nuestra sangre entre la vida y la muerte'.

12 *Cuerpo perseguido* also contains many references to 'olvido'—though there its meaning is to be related to the first lines of the anthology selection's opening poem: 'Yo me he perdido porque siento / que ya no estoy sino cuando me olvido;' (69:I,279), where 'olvido' seems to be part of the escape-process which constitutes the dream of that section. This, indeed, is one difference between the dream of *Mínima muerte* and that of *Cuerpo perseguido*. In the former he is seeking something which cannot be reached other than by the method of meditational dream which he adopts, i.e. the infinite. In the latter he seeks something through the dream which is normally—and perhaps best—reached outside it, i.e. the 'tú'.

13 It is not only the 'yo' who finds himself in 'olvido', however. The rose seems to undergo a similar experience in 'La rosa desdeñada' (153:I,818): 'La memoria de la rosa, / sin nombre, el olvido hundía'. Its new consciousness (its 'memoria') rids it of the unwanted 'oblivion' in which it lies. There is perhaps some value in drawing attention to a slightly different usage of the word 'olvido' with reference to the dream: 'Three stages . . . may be distinguished: first, the borderland fantasies . . . then the sudden plunge into Oblivion . . . thirdly, the dream state . . .' (W. Allen, *The Timeless Moment* (London, 1946), p. 106). Here oblivion is seen more as part of the process of meditation than as a state from which meditation elevates the individual who practises it.

The heavy personalisation of the rose leads us to the conclusion that it is being used to represent that type of man who is capable of attaining this higher experience—though it is by no means inconceivable that the 'yo', with his strong feeling for the potential life of any organism, might mean this narrative to apply specifically to the rose.

Plotinus, *The Enneads*, pp. xxx–xxxi.

Ibid., p. 244. 'Pensamiento' is not the only word which the 'yo' uses in opposing ways in *Mínima muerte*. Both 'memoria' and 'olvido' have such a dual sense. 'Memoria' is initially regarded as 'negative'. The loss of memory in 'Yo estaba soñando . . .' precedes the higher dream. This is in keeping with Plotinus's view that: 'No memory, therefore, can be ascribed to any divine being . . .' (*The Enneads*, p. 281). At the same time, it would seem that there is a desirable 'memoria'. In 'La rosa pensamiento' the life of the soul is unsatisfactory without it: '. . . el alma, al saberse / presente, carne es de gloria, / pero, ciega y sin memoria, / jamás podrá conocerse.' Once the finite life has been left behind, memory becomes a vital faculty, akin to Fausset's recollection: 'To "recollect", in its essential meaning, has nothing to do with memory, unless it be to remember a condition of unified being which we may have enjoyed in some heaven we have forgotten. It is to unite thought and feeling in a creative or imaginative act . . .' (H. Fausset, *Fruits of Silence* (London, 1963), p. 167). A similar pattern can be traced in the use of 'olvido'. We have already seen that it often has a negative sense: it refers to the way in which the human being, once born into the body, is immediately plunged into a 'forgetting' of his divine origin. In 'Rosa interior', 'olvido' has to be neutralised before the 'hora del alma feliz' can be enjoyed. But other poems speak of a happy 'olvido' which overtakes the 'yo' and banishes the miserable state of 'olvido' in which he finds himself. In 'La rosa en el sueño', the rose asks itself: '¿Es que de olvido cubierta / soy del olvido olvidada / y, de esta forma, entregada / a la memoria más cierta?' (I,841). This abandonment of the lower 'olvido' for the higher is also described by Plotinus: 'The loftier [soul], on the contrary, must desire to come to a happy forgetfulness of all that has reached it through the lower: for one reason, there is always the possibility that the excellence of the higher goes with a baseness in the lower, which is only kept down by sheer force. In any case the more urgent the intention towards the supreme, the more extensive will be the Soul's forgetfulness, unless indeed when the entire living has, even here, been such that memory has nothing but the noblest to deal with: in this world itself, all is best when human interests have been held aloof; so, therefore, it must be with the memory of them. In this sense we may truly say that the good soul is the forgetful. It flees multiplicity; it seeks to escape the unbounded by drawing all to unity, for only there is it free from entanglement, light-footed, self-conducted'. (Plotinus, *The Enneads*, p. 287).

17 In the ninth poem of the *Cancionero . . . (1938–1941) Hernández writes: 'Llegó con tres heridas: / la del amor, / la de la muerte, la de la vida. / Con tres heridas viene: / la de la vida, / la del amor, / la de la muerte. / Con tres heridas yo: / la de la vida, la de la muerte, la del amor.' (M. Hernández, Obras completas* (Buenos Aires, 1960), pp. 363–4). The enigmatic, repetitive variants reflect much of what Prados wrote in *Mínima muerte*.

18 Taken from Caja 19.1.

19 B. Seward, *The Symbolic Rose* (New York, 1960), p. 6.

CHAPTER SEVEN

In Search of the Lost Garden

Meanwhile the mind, from pleasures less,
Withdraws into its happiness.
(Andrew Marvell, 'The Garden')

¿Te volveré a besar, en tu belleza
de abril, tierra lejana?
(Juan Ramón Jiménez, '(Desde el tren)', *Amaneceres*)

Introduction

In *Mínima muerte* the rose is the centre of the protagonist's mental activity. As he concentrates on it, his sense of his own personal fragmentation and inadequacy disappears: he enjoys an experience of the infinite, of being freed from the limitations imposed by the body and time. The rose of *Jardín cerrado* plays a far more restricted role. Instead of occupying a pre-eminent position it is, rather, a part of the wider setting of the garden, thus echoing the pattern Seward notes in the rose's literary history:

> Queen of the flowers in classified Glysium, it became the chief flower of the Garden of Paradise.[1]

In the course of this long and involved work, entry into the 'jardín cerrado' will confer a new status upon the 'yo'. He is to learn the secret of a far more sustained, accessible and, increasingly, 'natural' apprehension of the infinite than that described in *Mínima muerte*. Instead of involving an abrupt transition from finite to infinite, from 'vida' to 'sueño', the 'vida sin límites' is to be consistently closer to hand than it has hitherto been. What is felt within the garden is more robust and lasting than the fruit of the fragile, vulnerable relationship with the rose. *Jardín cerrado* charts the journey towards these new developments and the reasons for them.

In at least one important respect *Jardín cerrado* bears a strong resemblance to almost all the poetry studied thus far. The progress it marks is grounded in those expressions of private grief which underlie the poetry from *Tiempo* to *Mínima muerte*. Some critics have emphasised the universal nature of the sentiments it contains. Cano talks of the poet's 'nostalgia española'.[2] With Leopoldo de Luis, he emphasises the markedly Andalusian character of the verse. Luis described *Dormido en la yerba*, a selection from *Jardín cerrado*, in these terms: 'un libro muy andaluz éste de Prados'.[3] Larrea, having recognised the existence of a deeper significance to the book goes on to make a similar point:

> . . . puede concluirse que el fenómeno poético vivido por el poeta Emilio Prados no es el de un individuo sino el propio del pueblo o Verbo hispánico . . .[4]

If, as has been repeatedly suggested, there is an over-riding unity in Prados's work, then such comments must miss the mark. Though less personal struggles might be involved, the poems are essentially private, concerned above all with vital steps in the journey of the central *persona*.

One further point needs to be made. A single chapter could never provide space sufficient for a full discussion of all aspects of *Jardín cerrado*.[5] This chapter's main objective is, therefore, having established the abiding dilemma facing the 'yo', to concentrate on those poems which represent specific advances in his attitude towards himself, his body and towards the infinite. We shall be interested above all, as in previous chapters, in the unfolding of the account of the central figure's 'cuerpo perseguido'.

Jardín perdido

The titles of poems included in *Jardín perdido* are full of references to 'nostalgia'. The opening group of the selection is called 'Nostalgias y sueños', and itself contains a poem 'Tres nostalgias del jardín perdido'. Something which was once the experience of the central figure has been lost: it is now a 'jardín perdido'. The analysis which follows is an attempt to identify the exact nature of this loss.

The exposition of persistent problems

The first poem in both the original book and the selection made from it, 'Árboles', is an indication of the extent of the problems facing the central *persona*. Its opening lines comprise a single, complex sentence:

> En pie, delgado, altísimo
> nivelador de vientos,
> el material suspiro
> de mi oculto silencio,
> dejándome vacío
> sobre la calle, expuesto
> por falta de equilibrio,
> al fácil atropello
> del asalto de un grito
> o del cruzar de un beso,
> cansado, se ha evadido
> del largo cautiverio,

desatándose al río
interior, de mi cuerpo. (161:II,29)

The statement could be simplified and compressed in the following way: 'el material suspiro de mi oculto silencio . . . se ha evadido del largo cautiverio . . . de mi cuerpo.' The 'evasion'—which seems to be so important to the idea of nostalgia for the 'jardín perdido'—can be understood by more detailed reference to this framework.

The nature of the 'material suspiro' is disclosed by further reading of the poem. Its closing quatrain identifies it with the tree itself:

En pie, delgado, altísimo
nivelador de vientos,
es el árbol, suspiro
de mi oculto silencio.

But what of the 'oculto silencio'? Some lines from *Tiempo* shed light on this mystery:

¡Cierra el silencio al día!
(¡Mi cuerpo es el silencio! . . .) (20)

The concept of silence reflected his body's inability to respond to normal sexual stimulus, an impotence which had resulted in a crippling awareness of limitation and exclusion from the fertile, infinite pattern of the natural world. The phrase 'el material suspiro de mi oculto silencio' refers, then, to the tree as a tangible symbol of a reality which his body has prevented him from enjoying. The tree now stands apart from him, the tantalising object of his admiration:

Sólo un árbol me llama,
nivelador de vientos
sobre el jardín . . .
sus ramas:
índices hacia el cielo.

It is the 'apartness' of the tree which these opening lines lament.

It is noteworthy that the tree has not always been distant from the 'yo'. This consideration allows a more precise identification of the 'jardín perdido'. The very fact that the tree has 'escaped' at some specific point in the protagonist's private history implies that at some earlier stage it was one with him. It does not seem unreasonable to conjecture that there has been a time—now past—in his experience when he shared the characteristics symbolised by the tree, and that this is the 'jardín perdido' referred to in the section's title. The past history of the 'yo' leads to the conclusion that there has only been one time during his life when the fertility and infiniteness of the tree have been his: during childhood. The tree and the 'yo' were one only in those far-off days when he was at one with himself, humanity and his environment and when time did not seem to exist, when 'era primavera en españa' (142:I,765). It is the timeless quality—something the central figure associates with his childhood—which accounts for the unusual expression regarding the departure of the tree: '. . . se ha evadido / del largo cautiverio,'. In the Paradise of infancy it seemed that his links with the infiniteness of the tree were going to be endless. Such hopes have not materialised. The protagonist of 'Árboles' is, like Cernuda, lamenting the loss of that continuous, untrammelled communion with the eternal enjoyed by the child as the 'Cuerpo perfecto en el vigor primero'.[6] The loss of the tree stands as a graphic expression of the 'fall' into adulthood, and marks the moment of his exile from the 'jardín cerrado'. It is also, therefore, the event which marks the transformation of the blessed 'garden' of childhood into what Alberti calls the 'paraíso perdido'.

The remainder of the poem endorses such a view. If the 'jardín perdido' and childhood are one and if, in the language of 'Árboles', the presence of the tree within the protagonist is a token of that childhood, then the poem's description of him apart from the tree should match what is already known about his adult condition. In fact, it would be difficult to imagine a more comprehensive catalogue of those ills which adulthood has bestowed upon him. *Andando, andando por el mundo* contains these lines:

> Estoy cansado.
> . . . .
> Estoy cansado de ocultarme en las ramas;
> de perseguir mi sombra por la arena;
> . . . .
> Un amigo me dice:
> "Hay cuerpos que aún se ofrecen
> como jugosas frutas sin sentido" . . .
> Otro amigo me canta:
> "¡Vuelan las aves, vuelan!" . . .
> Yo quiero huir, perderme lejos,
> allá en esas regiones en que unas anchas hojas
> tiemblan sobre el estanque de los sueños que inundan. (125–6:I,403)

The sense of tiredness, of persecution, of vulnerability, the insensitive advice of friends are all reflected in the opening lines of 'Árboles', where the departure of the tree leaves him:

vacío
sobre la calle, expuesto
por falta de equilibrio,
al facil atropello
del asalto de un grito
o del cruzar de un beso,
cansado . . .

Lorca wrote:

No hay noche que, al dar un beso
no sienta la sonrisa de las gentes sin rostro.[7]

His anguish runs parallel to that of Prados.

The stanzas which follow list difficulties intimated in earlier poetry. The intrusion of the finite has impaired his intellectual faculty:

Pesada está mi frente . . .
Tal vez mi pensamiento,
voluntario, sus alas
ha fundido con el tiempo.

He is unable to express the infinite which he glimpses in the dream. He is earth-bound, limited:

No sé qué ardor de fuera,
como un sol de desiertos,
me aprieta en la garganta
la voz seca del sueño . . .

Mis pies, como dos sombras
larguísimas, al suelo
peligroso y urbano,
del día, están sujetos.

He is exposed, unable, because of the restrictions of society, to express affection in the way he would like:

Todo el hablar seguro
de mi dolor, deshecho . . .
Los caminos, cerrados
para mi amor abierto.

Como un carbón inútil,

que ardió en inútil fuego,
cansado de mí mismo
mi soledad entrego.

The sense of futility which such early books as *Canciones del farero* betray is shared by these later statements. They reflect the same set of circumstances—the protagonist's plight consequent upon his discovery of the nature of his body. And it was as he left the garden of infancy that this took place.

To the adult protagonist, then, the 'jardín perdido' is also in one sense a 'jardín cerrado'. He has been cast out from it. Just as Jiménez's 'parque viejo' lay under the spell of a 'nostáljico sueño', so the 'jardín cerrado' is the object of his nostalgia.[8] To be one with the tree would be to re-establish the paradise of childhood. Of *Jardín cerrado* Larrea writes:

> . . . la humanidad está buscando su cuerpo, aquel jardín que dícese perdío al ser condenada a muerte en el remoto y proverbial Paraíso donde crecía el árbol de la vida.[9]

In terms of this analysis, it is the 'yo' who is seeking to repair the harm which was done when he became aware of his body, and to overcome the death to which that awareness sentenced him. It is for this reason that the tree, symbol of what was once his, exercises such a strong attraction:

En pie, delgado, altísimo
nivelador de vientos,
es el árbol, suspiro
de mi oculto silencio.[10]

The opening stanza of 'Árboles' described the tree as 'desatándose al río / interior'. As it extricated itself from the central *persona* it entered a mysterious 'inner river': a level of experience beyond his own. *Jardín cerrado* is in part an effort to come to terms with this re-alignment and to recapture the mystery of the eternal garden which the tree, unlike the body, refused to abandon.

But 'Árboles' is by no means the only poem in this section to deal with the nature of the problems facing the central *persona*. 'Llanuras de sol', a short poem from the group 'Tres nostalgias del jardín perdido', provides another example. It begins peacefully. The central figure, bathed in sunlight, is observing the open stretches of the countryside: 'Campo, campo y más campo . . .' (165:II,34). However, interspersed between three repetitions of this line, are questions which significantly alter its originally restful tone. They introduce a deepening sense of nostalgia and grief. He is conscious of some deficiencies in the landscape:

—¿Y el olivar?
(Mi corazón, soñando.)

Reference to 'Cuando era primavera' explains the significance of the absence of the olive grove. It is particularly mentioned in the earlier poem as an outstanding memory of childhood:

Cuando era primavera en España:
los olivos temblaban
adormecidos bajo la sangre azul del día . . .

Its absence reminds him that he is no longer a child, that he is afflicted with an adult body, and an abnormal body at that. Those feelings of persecution to which we have so often referred re-assert themselves:

(¿Qué me persigue, Dios,
qué me persigue? . . .)

Another question immediately suggests itself:

—¿Y ¿dónde el mar?

The sea, the setting for the idyllic childhood picture of 'Cuando era primavera' is another conspicuous absentee. There, '. . . el mar soñaba entonces, / como el ojo de un pez sobre la arena,' (142:I,764). But the fertile, infinite sea is, like the garden, no longer his domain. It is not surprising that the final description of the protagonist is a sad one:

—¿Y ¿dónde el mar?
(Mi corazón, llorando.)

The final repetition of 'Campo, campo y más campo' has become the dirge of a weeping heart, celebrating only the fact that he must look upon the beauty of the natural world as an outsider. The day when he was a part of it, when he too was in the garden, has long since gone.

Another poem, 'Bajo la alameda', serves as a more explicit summary of the estranged position of the 'yo' in exile from the 'jardín perdido':

Ayer, tan cerca el jardín.

Hoy, ¡qué lejos!

Me voy perdiendo de mí,
para buscarme en lo eterno . . .

—¿Hoy? . . .
¡Qué lejos! (167:II,40)

What was once the protagonist's everyday experience is now distant from him. That these feelings should be so acute while he is 'bajo la alameda' is perhaps not without significance. It has been argued that exclusion from the garden, adulthood—that is, consciousness of the abnormality of his body—has meant the impossibility of a normal sexual relationship. It is of such a love that the poplar-grove is a traditional symbol.[11] For those to whom 'normality' is denied it can only be a place of unhappiness. Lorca, unable to respond to the presence of his 'morena', finds himself weeping there:

Me encontrarías llorando
bajo los álamos grandes.
¡Ay morena!
Bajo los álamos grandes.[12]

For Cernuda (another exile from the Edenic paradise, as Silver demonstrates) it is also a place of wistful longing, rather than the fulfilment of love:

Cuán lejano todo. Muertas
Las rosas que ayer abrieran,
Aunque aliente su secreto
Por las verdes alamedas.[13]

Love for our protagonist, as well as for Cernuda, was a secret which, if the poplars knew, they also kept. Love in a physical sense—or, for that matter, as poems such as 'Canción' (138:I,751) illustrate, in the sense of the loving unity of the natural order to which Blanco Aguinaga refers—has been denied to him. And it is a denial which makes the 'ayer', the loss of the paradise of childhood, all the more bitter.

Two more poems which show the connection between childhood and the 'jardín perdido' by their exposition of the central *persona*'s adult problems and by their sense of nostalgia for an earlier, happier time are '¿Luna sobre el olivar?' and 'Rincón de la sangre'. Before tracing his steps towards re-entry into the garden these poems need to be analysed.

'¿Luna sobre el olivar?' is the opening line of a short poem in the group called 'Tres nostalgias sin tiempo'. The attitude of the 'yo' to the moon confirms that the nostalgia is being dealt with from the view-point of adulthood. It is exactly that attitude which a realisation of the post-adolescent nature of his body has always inflicted upon him. As early as *Tiempo* it became clear that the protagonist found in the moon, a symbol of death and sterility, a reflection of his own dilemma, a 'port' to which his 'boat' (the body) most naturally tended, 'el puerto más cercano' (10). That it still performs the same function at the time of the writing of *Jardín cerrado* is evident from the middle section of '¿Luna sobre el olivar?':

> (Se oye en el mar un quejido,
> luego, el latir de una sombra,
> más tarde, sólo un suspiro) . . . (172:II,54)

The wind, the symbol of fertility missing from the troubled night of *Tiempo*, is again virtually absent—an ineffectual sigh, barely sufficient to disturb the surface of the sea. There is a note of desperation in the repetition of the poem's opening question, this time in the form of an apostrophe: '—¡Luna sobre el olivar!'. The presence of the moon and the absence of the wind are chilling reminders of his 'fall' into adulthood and of its aftermath, exclusion from the blessedness of youth.

'Rincón de la sangre' appears in a group entitled 'Otras nostalgias del jardín perdido'. It is one of the most poignant in its expression of the acute sense of loss from which the protagonist suffers. Part of its effect stems from the dramatic change of mood effected in its final lines. Here are the opening four stanzas:

> Tan chico el almoraduj
> y . . . ¡cómo huele!
> Tan chico.
>
> De noche, bajo el lucero,
> tan chico el almoraduj
> y, ¡cómo huele!
>
> Y . . . cuando en la tarde llueve,
> ¡cómo huele!
>
> Y cuando levanta el sol,
> tan chico el almoraduj
> ¡cómo huele! (175–6:II,59)

The picture would seem to be happy one. The flower's fragrance fills the observing protagonist with a glad astonishment.

But because he is in exile from childhood, when his enjoyment of the flower was total, the joy must be tinged with sadness. From the perspective of adulthood, even happy experience, when it evokes memories of childhood, is painful:

> Y, ahora, que del sueño vivo
> ¡cómo huele,
> tan chico, el almoraduj!
> ¡Cómo duele! . . .
> Tan chico.

Departure from the garden has meant dependence on the dream as a means of finding what he once found as a child—hence the confession: 'del sueno vivo'. It also means that even those moments in his maturity when the eternal seems as real as the flower's scent can give rise only to the piercing nostalgia which this poem records. Harris notes that at least initially Cernuda's garden was a private world protecting his dreams from 'the incursions of reality'.[14] For Prados, the garden is the reality he enjoyed in childhood. What the protagonist seeks is a radical change in his attitude to himself and to what surrounds him, a change which would bring him back to the position he consistently occupied as a child.[15]

El dormido en la yerba

The title of this section is an interesting one. Its importance is suggested by its use in several other poems, such as 'Cantar del dormido en la yerba' and 'Dormido en la yerba'. It is to be expected that recurrent references to grass are to be related to the symbolism of the earth—fertility, renewal.[16] As analysis will show, the central figure is again engaged in a search for those things which from *Tiempo* onwards he has felt himself to lack. As he 'sleeps' on the grass he hopes to absorb some of the qualities it represents. In one sense the section title is in itself a confession of failure: in another it is an indication that he is on the brink of major steps forward towards permanent presence in the enclosed garden.

A new attitude towards the body

In 'Cantar del dormido en la yerba' are given clear indications of what the central figure is learning and absorbing from the earth, from the natural order. The poem suggests that it is to the jasmin that he has turned in particular. In the second half of his reflections on death—the poem's main concern—we read:

> . . . el jazmín, no pregunta
> desmayado en la sombra:
> —¿Adónde irá el lucero
> que mi nieve ha perdido? . . .
>
> Si ha de morir: su aroma
> es muerte; su flor muerte,
> . . . . (183:II,100)

He has discovered that the secret of this flower's infinite quality is the presence within it of the principle of death—a presence which it joyfully accepts. He realises anew, as he did in *Mínima muerte* that some kind of 'dying' must precede the experience of the eternal. If he is to be like the tree of 'Árboles' then it is through such a process that he must go. The description of the 'jardín cerrado' which closes 'Cantar . . .' underlines the necessity for this 'death':

> . . . la tierra húmeda
> del cerrado jardín
> de mi alma, es carne
> de la muerte también:
> ¡Luz! ¡Fúlgida memoria!
> ¡Eje de un universo
> nuevo, que va a nacer
> sin niebla, al fin, de olvidos!

Death is aligned with light, renewal, clarity. It is not to be feared. This discovery (though, of course, not entirely new to him) has important repercussions in the central figure's thinking about himself.

In particular it affects his attitude towards his own 'cuerpo pálido'. In earlier poetry the 'yo' hated his body for its 'deadness'. Death, sterility, the moon, silence and fear together attended the protagonist's body in *Tiempo*. 'Cantar del dormido en la yerba' presents this 'dead' body in a new light. Its very 'deadness' means that it is already in tune with the kind of pattern which will bring about the return of the 'jardín cerrado'. Thus though the body is still seen as related to death, now that relationship is one which endangers peace, light and 'redemption':

La muerte está conmigo;
mas la muerte es jardín
cerrado, espacio, coto,
silencio amurallado
por la piel de mi cuerpo,
donde, inmóvil—almendra
viva, virgen—, mi luz
contempla y da la imagen
redimida, del fuego. (182:II,99)

This passage's slow-moving phrases, its leisurely lists—'cerrado, espacio, coto'—and its use of apposition—'—almendra / viva, virgen—',—succeed in dissolving the tension implicit in the opening statement: 'La muerte está conmigo;'. That which before barred him from entry into the garden and entirely disrupted his communion with the eternal—the 'deadness' of his body—is becoming rather that which above all else fits him for a sustained experience of the 'jardín perdido'. The renewal of this 'fúlgida memoria' within him can now take place without there being any artificial technique involved. The 'sueño', so fragile until now, is rendered obsolete. This 'new universe' is to be enjoyed: 'sin niebla, al fin, de olvidos'. He has found a new use for a body which was, as far as activity in the finite realm went, a failure: it is the framework, the walls within which the 'yo', no longer feeling the need to flee from his body and therefore into unreality, can re-live the Lost Paradise.[17]

A new attitude to normality

Throughout the poetry studied so far the 'yo' has been regarded by people and personalised objects and animals around him as 'abnormal'. He has been viewed with mocking curiosity by the fish; he has drawn a parallel between himself and the isolated lighthouse keeper; he has described himself in *Jardín cerrado* as: 'expuesto / por falta de equilibrio, / al fácil atropello / del asalto de un grito'; and he is outside the fertile normality shared by the natural world. This abnormality has always worried him. He has always wanted, in some sense, to be 'normal', to be 'como el mundo' (69:I,279). He admits that he is, unlike the majority, infertile: but there is always the hope that some compensating factor will bridge the gap between himself and the outside world.

The despondency of such poems as those of *Jardín perdido*

indicates that such a reconciliation has not taken place. The central figure will never be normal. He has only felt normal in childhood (as 'Cuando era primavera' shows) or in times where personal problems were both mirrored and forgotten in shared external experience. The 'jardín cerrado' he enjoyed as a child will remain remote so long as the tensions of being 'abnormal' continue to afflict him.

It is then a major advance towards permanent re-entry into the garden that he should begin to shun the values and advice which the majority have to offer. The poem 'Dormido en la yerba' describes the reactions of an old man—old enough to be able to ignore the seeming wisdom which the more materially minded would impose upon him:

> Todos vienen a darme consejo.
> Yo estoy dormido junto a un pozo. (191:II,123)[18]

His behaviour leaves others baffled:

> Todos se acercan y me dicen:
> —La vida se te va,
> y tú te tiendes en la yerba,
> bajo la luz más tenue del crepúsculo,
> atento solamente
> a mirar cómo nace
> el temblor del lucero
> o el pequeno rumor
> del agua, entre los árboles.

Why, with death closer than ever, does he not make the most of the life remaining to him?

> Y tú te tiendes sobre la yerba:
> cuando ya tus cabellos
> comienzan a sentir
> más cerca y fríos que nunca,
> la caricia y el beso
> de la mano constante
> y sueño de la luna.

The counsel of convention is rejected. Indeed, in the last stanza, he seems to be rejoicing in his 'abnormality'. He prefers to seek the company of 'algún amigo', to embrace him and to undertake with him that mysterious journey 'al borde, juntos, del abismo,':

> Sólo, si algún amigo

se acerca, y, sin pregunta
me da un abrazo entre las sombras:
lo llevo hasta asomarmos
al borde, juntos, del abismo,
y, en sus profundas aguas,
ver llorar a la luna y su reflejo,
que más tarde ha de hundirse
como piedra de oro,
bajo el otoño frío de la muerte.

The protagonist has replaced the involuntary isolation which abnormality produced by a voluntary solitude: he has ceased to compete with the norm. Another barrier to a sustained experience of the 'jardín cerrado' is being removed.

A new attitude towards the moon

This sense of reconciliation to what had previously been regarded as bitter disappointments is further illustrated in a changed attitude towards the moon. The symbol of death and sterility, it has also been the symbol of his body—in it he most readily found 'el puerto más cercano y el agua más serena . . .'. But now, as the 'yo' increasingly accepts his body, he also begins to view the moon with less distaste. The previous quotation from 'Dormido en la yerba' is in itself proof of this. The 'yo' is depicted as being in sympathy with the moon. The same can be said of four closing sections of 'El cantar del dormido en la yerba'. The distinction between the 'negative' moon and the 'positive' sun is entirely lost:

Como tú, luna, sí;
el sol, como la luna. (184:II,100)

Now he rejoices in the fact that his body is akin in nature to the moon:

—Y, aquí, dormido, está,
tembloroso, en la tierra,
pensando en que, al ser hombre:
alma fiel es del centro
candente de su espera . . .
—¿Luz? . . . —¡Luz, igual que sombra!
¡Cuerpo igual que tú, luna!

He is equally happy to lie in the light of sun or moon:

(Bajo el sol o en la noche,
centro soy del jardín:
sombra, cuerpo yacente,
figura del reposo.)

The protagonist's advance towards the 'jardín cerrado' is due, in large measure, to this new sense of harmony and repose.

Umbrales de sombra

El dormido en la yerba, despite the progress it recorded, contained poems—often of great beauty—such as 'Cantar triste' (186:II,108) and 'Bajo la alameda' (II,128) which cast long shadows. The title *Umbrales de sombra* suggests that the 'yo' is on the threshold of a major and permanent break-through in his search for a consistently higher level of experience. It is concerned particularly with the trend apparent in the previous section: a sense of resignation, a readiness to adapt to what he had before taken to be weakness. With this more detailed account of his new-found acceptance of his body and death, he comes nearer to the joyous fulfilment related in *Sangre abierta*.

Further acceptance of the body

In the early poem 'Noche en urna' the night's presence had an unsettling effect on the protagonist. His nocturnal activity was furtive, lonely and anxious. He was quick to take refuge in the dream:

Ahueca sus caudales y, en cáscara de barco,
se le va el corazón por mapa de recuerdos
—pirata de albedríos por él mismo apresado
en alta mar del ansia sin cadenas del cielo— . . . (15)

A fantasy world of 'recuerdos' is infinitely preferable to the discomfort of facing up to the reality symbolised by the night and particularly the 'corazón de su mundo', the moon. It is 'bajo la luna' that 'Cantar triste' is sung: while 'Bajo la alameda' identifies the night with the loss of love, and with an awareness of the 'hojas secas' of infertility.

Viewed in this light, 'Media noche', from the 'Noche humana' section of *Umbrales de sombra*, assumes great significance. Until now the night has been virtually shunned because it reminds the central figure of what is true about himself. It has been an unwelcome reminder of his inability to conform to the norm; of what has been in the past an awesome gulf between desire and reality. The night of 'Media noche' is entirely different. It belongs to someone who has abandoned normality—one who is 'dormido en la yerba'.

No longer is the night to be the object of his antagonism. Rather is the 'yo' beginning to see it as a kindred spirit. Like him she is mocked, feared, misunderstood, irrationally, cruelly. She begs him to have mercy upon her:

> La noche, perseguida, se entró por mi ventana:
>
> —Méteme por tus ojos, escóndeme en tu olvido;
> aun tu cuerpo, entreabierto, puede muy bien guardarme,
> antes de que se entregue al cerrado abandono
> que ya está desciñendo tu ardiente vestidura.
>
> Antes de que en el sueño sin voluntad de origen
> la razón se te pierda solamente en el goce:
> ocúltame, me buscan, traigo el olor a sangre
> y tal vez el delito y la muerte es mi sombra . . .
>
> Ocúltame, la tierra que hoy es carne y te invade,
> casi mi piel sostiene, pero es tumba y memoria.
> Yo voy desordenada y hasta el suelo me siguen
> donde llevo mi aurora y su puñal agudo.
>
> Pero mis sueños huelen al sudor de los hombres,
> a sus crímenes ínfimos y a sus manos en llamas.
> No pueden perdonarme que mi beso, en el lodo,
> llegue donde no encuentra la ley su pensamiento.
> Me acerco dolorida, no niegues tu desvelo. (206—7:II,63)

The attitude of the night towards humanity is most revealing. She feels herself to have been hounded, blamed, used as a scapegoat for the evil which is in fact within society. This is the authentic tone of the social outcast of earlier poetry. The poem is based on the parallel between the pressures undergone by the night and those undergone by the central *persona*. The night represents a clearly defined aspect of his personality—the dark, unacceptable side, those tendencies and deficiencies which, as 'Árboles' showed, have made of him an oddity, a figure of contempt.

The description of the protagonist following the night's plea underlines this. It summarises the way in which the abnormalities of his nature have left him rejected and persecuted:

(Mi cuerpo estaba huyendo; buscando a la noche
la falsedad de un ángel que fingiera un reposo;
. . . .
Mi cuerpo estaba huyendo; por las desiertas calles
de una ciudad sin suelo resbalaba impreciso,
deteniéndose al paso vulgar de la inocencia
y escapando al contacto con ella, por mi angustia.[19]

If contact with the girl represented by 'la inocencia' is impossible, so too is any relationship with the prostitute suggested in the lines which follow by images of putrefaction and corruption:

Junto al olor caliente del pescado podrido,
de la fruta marchita y el vinagre, en acecho
la mujer entregaba su cabello constante
herido por las uñas y la ardiente saliva.

The fish of *Tiempo* is by now 'podrido'. His activities excite only denunciation:

Mis manos se enredaban a la piel de los hombres
que, abiertos, derramaban sus entrañas sin fuego;
mis voces se mezclaban a la luz del cigarro
y a ese rumor más hábil que engendra la denuncia.

In the face of such difficulties the 'yo' almost succumbs to despair. The moon is again for the moment ominous:

Y la luna, gimiendo, se clavaba en el árbol,
con la burla precisa del nivel de su tiempo.
Golpe a golpe sonaban las plumas de mi espalda
y su navaja el aire, por mi espalda, blandía.

But the new spirit of the 'yo' is quick to assert itself. A remarkable outcome transpires. He and the night turn to welcome one another as lovers. She becomes, indeed, that which he had always sought:

Mi cuerpo estaba huyendo. Sonaba una cadena
y en la puerta del cielo mis manos golpeaban:
—¡Abrid, abrid, las sombras por dentro me persiguen
y las sombras de fuera mis manos acuchillan! . . .

Desperté estando muerto: Mis sábanas sangraban . . .

—¡Abrid, abrid! ¡Las sombras! . . .

(La noche, perseguida, se entró por mi ventana y era a la noche misma, a quien yo perseguía.)

In the context of the whole poem, such an ending suggests a growing acceptance of those sexual tendencies which have cut him off from others and hence been resented by him. He embraces the nature with which he finds himself endowed.

In 'Sobre la tierra' the very lifelessness of his body is regarded as grounds for hope. Death—the death of the physical—is anyway the grounds for true life. Before now there has been a conscious and artifical process of mortification: he refused to reconcile himself to the sterility of his body. At this stage, however, he is coming to terms with a death which is his 'by nature' and which he does not need to produce artificially—a characteristic which will be seen to have great significance in relation to the permanence of his experience of the 'jardín cerrado'. He addresses the earth:

Pienso en mi cuerpo y veo,
sólo un ojo de sombra oscura, y dentro,
tu misma muerte;
un sueño igual, tan fértil y tan puro,
como el hondo nacer
del agua, que, en tus venas
desconocidas, cruzan
por refrescar la ardiente pulpa
que ya como penumbra
—medio muerte—rodea
el hueso incandescente
—luz cautiva, alma acaso—,
vida de tu manzana.

Todo lo muerto, en ti puede dar vida:
el trigo, el agua azul,
el cuerpo pálido del hombre, el fuego . . .
(209–210:II,179)

Instead of fleeing from the body as he once used to, the 'romántico de huídas' is starting to see the body as a necessary receptacle for the 'jardín cerrado'.

'En la media noche' confirms this pattern. He is explaining why he feels so rejected and dissatisfied. It is 'porque no es justo acariciar lo que se ama'. The line appears at the close of each stanza except the last. The clear implication is that it is the abnormality of his behaviour which has brought about such a rejection. The second stanza shows how he has been forced to keep the real nature of his affections hidden:

Hubiera preferido, nacer
con los labios fundidos,
como las aguas
que nunca han de brotar
y profundas se mezclan
al corazón obscuro de la sombra,
a no sentir mis besos
bajo el olvido deshacerse
y esconder perseguidos
el ardor de su carne,
entre las hojas del recuerdo,
porque no es justo acariciar lo que se ama. (214:II,194)

He feels himself to have been deprived of true love. The bitter tone of such writing is matched by that of Cernuda's 'Diré como nacisteís':

Extender entonces la mano
Es hallar una montaña que prohibe,
un bosque impenetrable que niega,
un mar que traga adolescentes rebeldes.[20]

For Prados's 'yo', to have been born beyond the void would have been more acceptable:

Hubiera preferido, nacer
tras el vacío superior
de la Nada: en su sueño,
bajo el ancho misterio
de la campana silenciosa
y densa de su espacio,
a no sentir la flor del azahar
como una herida incandescente
en el hueso del alma,
y ver la roja fruta
del naranjo, en sazón,
amarga sobre el suelo
frente al lucero que tapada la mira,
porque no es justo acariciar lo que se ama.

Neither the natural world (represented by 'la flor del azahar') nor sexual love ('la roja fruta / del naranjo, en sazón,') are his. What does align this poem with his new attitude to the body is his reaction to such frustration. His answer is no longer to sleep. It is rather to take refuge in the night 'con los ojos abiertos'. This is a very different kind of sleep from that of *Cuerpo perseguido*:

Porque no es justo acariciar lo que se ama:
duermo y duermo, ya siempre
con los ojos abiertos,
como la luna nace
sin saber si ya es beso de la sombra
la luz de su cuchilla,
o es sólo su reflejo de oro,
nueva herida en el cielo,
con la que ha de salvar
la noche misma en que duerme.

He now lives in the light of the reality, ambiguous and suspect thought it may be, of the dark forces within him which the moon represents. In 'Nocturno fiel' the night brought a stifling death. In the stanza quoted above the 'yo' is not afraid to draw a comparison between himself and the moon—not as he did in *Tiempo* where their relationship was a sinister one, but in a way which suggests that he would be happy to share something of its nature. For this moon is spoken of in 'positive' terms: it is the moon which is able to 'redeem' the night—'ha de salvar / la noche misma en que duerme.' 'En la media noche' has, in the main, presented a dark picture of the protagonist's attitudes: but even here there is the hope that in the acceptance of what he is 'con los ojos abiertos' there is a way of making good the apparent waste and death of earlier years—a hope which can only be realised when, as he does here, the central figure comes to terms with, rather than ignores, his true self.

The necessity for the body

In discussing 'Jardín cerrado', it became apparent that unless the body were involved in the experience of re-entry into the garden, then such an experience was invalid—it had not involved the central figure's total self. Poems mentioned so far have seen a new sense of reconciliation on the part of the 'yo' to the body in which he finds himself. Some poems from *Umbrales de sombra*, however, go further than this, according the body a vital role in the re-creation of the 'jardín cerrado' experience. 'Cielo de bautismo', illustrates this point well, and in a manner which clarifies some developments in *Jardín cerrado*.

The poem looks back on the central figure's past attitudes towards himself. Once, he confesses, he tried to be like glass, transparent, so that he would not affect the passage of the infinite (the 'tú' or the 'amor' of the section-title, *Otro amor*, in which the poem first appeared) through him:[21]

> A la puerta de mi voz
> tu cuerpo estaba llamando
> y mi voz era tu nombre:
> tú, nombre andabas buscando.
>
> Quise ser cristal, espejo
> a tu amor no quise darle,
> por miedo a que te perdiera
> la hermosura de tu imagen. (II,243)

This is exactly what was seen in *Cuerpo perseguido* where the 'yo' tried to make himself into 'un vaso limpio / de agua pura, / como un ángel de vidrio / en un espejo.' (70:I,270), or where he felt he was 'unreal' unless he allowed his body to 'fly' away from him (69:I,279). He had stripped himself of everything finite—including, of course, his body. Again in 'Cielo de bautismo' he writes:

> Quise ser cristal, por miedo
> a que, al contemplar tu imagen
> tan encajada en tu nombre,
> en tu imagen te quedases.
>
> Y al quitar, dentro de mí,
> por mejor acomodarte,
> todo lo que, al no ser tú
> ni era mío ni de nadie:
> sin tu presencia, apagó
> mi cielo interior su carne.

He removed everything which did not belong to the 'tú'. But he was not rewarded by the kind of fulfilment for which he had hoped, as the final couplet of the above quotation suggests. Without the momentary presence of the infinite secured by such self-denial there was a distressing vacuum within himself, dark and hopeless.

The stanza which follows presents his revised position. Instead of making himself like glass, he is to allow his body to act as the substantial mirror, trapping the image of the infinite rather than allowing it simply to pass through him:

> Un chorro de sombra alcé
> a la puerta en que llamaste
> y espejo te vine a dar
> y en él, luna en que quedarte.

This leaves him in an invulnerable situation from which he cannot be 'awoken':

¡Qué umbral de desesperanzas
fue mi esperanza esperándote!
Hoy, nadie se acerca a mí;
nadie viene a despertarme.

The presence of the 'sombra', the 'luna'—the involvement of the protagonist's body—means that the experience will not slip away on his return to some more 'normal' level of experience.

This is but a re-statement of a process already observed. The refusal to flee from the 'luna' of his own body means that the higher experience is no longer escapist. It can be enjoyed and savoured as a lasting, permanent feature of life in which the old waking/sleeping distinction is no longer relevant. The body is to play the same role as the one in which Jiménez saw it, that which anchors the eternal and relates it to the individual:

Dormidos, nuestro cuerpo
es el ancla
que nuestra alma deja
en el fondo del mar de nuestra vida.[22]

It is to provide the 'muralla' for the garden.

The overall trend of *Umbrales de sombra* is, then, encouraging. The opening poem of *Jardín cerrado* seemed to offer little hope that the gulf between the lofty tree and the protagonist could ever be bridged. It was the 'material suspiro de mi oculto silencio'. 'Huída' indicates a change in direction. He is already drawing closer to the tree:

(Búscame despacio,
estoy en el árbol.
Búscame despacio,
te estoy esperando). (227:II,254)

Final re-entry into the garden will be marked by his total identification with the tree.

The re-appearance of the child

'Insomnio en el jardín', one of the final poems of the *Noche humana* section of *Umbrales de sombra*, provides further evidence of the progress being made by the central *persona*. It has already been shown that he regards his childhood as the original 'jardín cerrado'. The enclosed garden is the term he now uses to refer to a renewed experience of the limitless life he knew as a child. 'Insomnio en el jardín' underlines the affinity between this enclosed garden and childhood. But it also goes further: it suggests that as a result of the kind of changes in his attitudes outlined above there is taking place within him the rebirth of the child he once was. It is a development which is central to one of the section's main concerns, the re-creation of the lost Paradise of infancy.

The title is in itself important. The protagonist is not asleep. Indeed he cannot sleep. And yet this does not discomfort him: the poem is full of references to 'paz', 'mi paz dulce' and 'mi paz en la sombra'. He has chosen 'insomnio' deliberately in order to emphasise the fact that this peacefulness, hitherto obtainable only in the escape of sleep, is now being experienced in the normal waking state. The level of repose he now knows outside sleep or any kind of artificially produced awareness is quite new. Reconciliation to himself and withdrawal from competition with the norm are responsible for it:

No tengo voz;
estoy despierto y mi memoria
sobre la concha nácar del olvido,
cubre a mi corazón lo que no entiende.
Sólo tengo sentido
de mi paz en la sombra.

Un vértigo, me hace girar el alma,
me hace girar el alma:
redondo y negro mar
tendido frente al cielo.

Y brotan de este mar de mi alma en giro,
el canto de mi paz dulce en silencio:
toda mi voluntad perdida,
cuerpos de realidad,
figuras de mi sueño. (219:II,208)

If there were any doubt whether or not the 'yo' has returned to the kind of bliss he knew as a child then the stanzas which follow place it beyond argument:

El centro de mi alma,
como un clavo de luz,
fija la imagen de mi vida al mundo

y la seduce y guía,
hecha reposo y savia
de mi continua vocación de espejo.

Y siento,
como al moverse dócil de los años,
suena el otoño su oro, entre los árboles
de una vida vulgar
de un cuerpo dolorido
de un hombre que se aleja . . .

Luego, queda en la sombra
un niño por la arena;
inocente verdad
sobre una playa dócil,
tímida en la hermosura
junto a un eterno mar incomparable . . .

The man gives way to the child. There is an unforced enjoyment of the welcome figure of infancy:

¡Imagen de mi vida!
Como el calor de la memoria, subes;
como el sueño a mi sangre,
como el dolor, silencio de mi sombra.

Its appearance has become as natural to him as pain and suffering have been.[23]

It is the very deadness of his body which qualifies him supremely for the re-birth of the child within him. In 'Sobre la tierra' the 'yo' addresses the earth:

. . . lo muerto en mí, busca su vida.
Lo sé, porque soy hombre
y hoy temo, en este estío,
tierra, al dolor.

Y por eso te busco
y en tí me duermo, tierra, como un hijo,
el más pequeño, el último;
pero el más parecido también
a tu presencia, madre:
a la verdad augusta
que encierra tu regazo. (210–11:II,179–180)

Because he has recognised that the 'verdad augusta' of the earth—namely the primacy of the principle of death—also exists within himself, and recognised it to a far greater degree than the normal person, then he is the one most likely to become her son, to become again the child he has wanted to be. As so often in *Jardín cerrado*, these lines suggest that only in physical death will this process be complete. But, as the section also indicates, recognition and acceptance of the lifelessness of his body has brought about an anticipation of that death which makes the 'jardín cerrado' a possibility in the present. The desire for a return to the mother-figure, to the womb, to the rose of *Mínima muerte*, is taking a more precise form.

Two angels

The use of the figure of the angel was not exclusive to Alberti in the poetry of the 1920's. In *Cuerpo perseguido* Prados's protagonist compared himself with 'un ángel de vidrio'. Something of the association of the angel with that which is asexual, outside the realm of physical response, was noted there. In *Umbrales de sombra* the word is used in a similar way. But in the different contexts of the two poems to be mentioned, the effect of the presence of the angel varies widely.

In 'Puñal de luz' the angel is regarded with animosity. It is a sinister 'ángel negro'. It entered his life as an unwelcome intruder. Interestingly enough, from the point of view of earlier analyses, its arrival coincided with the discovery of his body. Here are the poem's opening lines:

> Este cuerpo que Dios pone en mis brazos
> para enseñar a andar por el olvido,
> no sé ni de quien es.
>   Al encontrarlo,
> un ángel negro, una gigante sombra,
> se me acercó a los ojos y entró en ellos
> silencioso y tenaz igual que un río. (221:II,215)

When the 'yo' discovered his body, he discovered sterility, deadness—represented by the angel. Referring to the angel—but in terms which describe equally well what has been discovered about the protagonist's post-adolescent state—he records:

> Todo lo destruyó con su corriente.
> Los íntimos lugares más ocultos
> visitó, alborotó, fue levantando

a otro mundo en los bordes de mi beso:
única flor aún viva en el espacio.
Luego en mi carne abrió sus amplias alas
—alas de luz y fuego de tristeza—,
clavándole sus plumas bajo el pecho,
todo temblor y anuncio de otras dudas . . .
. . . .
Soy un templo
arruinado, desde que vino a mí:
farol vacío, como puerta cerrada de lo eterno . . .

In spite of spasmodic progress this angel continues to afflict him:

Más ya, por fin, he detenido al día;
le he destrozado el corazón al tiempo,
aunque dentro de mí, como una daga,
siento al ángel crecer que me atormenta.

Sterility has proved to be, in the main, the only hallmark of his body prior to *Jardín cerrado*.

However there is another poem in which the attitude to the angel is far from hostile. The contrast between the effect of the presence of these two angels in his experience demonstrates clearly the kind of advance marked by *Jardín cerrado*. The 'ángel negro' of pre-*Jardín cerrado* days brought only pain. Sterility was associated with failure, anguish. But, as has been noted, the protagonist has ceased to equate sterility, death in the realm of the body, with failure. He has accepted it—just as he has accepted the night in 'Media noche'. Indeed this second angel is dubbed the 'ángel de la noche'. The angel continues to symbolise sterility, the death of the body: but the protagonist's attitude to that sterility has radically altered. Closer examination of 'Ángel de la noche' shows that the poem is a restatement of the central idea of 'Media noche': the growing acceptance and welcoming of the central *persona*'s physical weakness.

It begins by decribing the protagonist's condition prior to the advent of the 'ángel de la noche'. Not unexpectedly, it corresponds to the kind of instability and isolation chronicled from *Tiempo* on:

Yo no me conocía.
Estaba solo, en medio de la cumbre
alta y plana del mundo;
debajo de una noche
tan honda, tan lejana,

que, casi parecía
ser, noche en un espejo reflejada,
más que verdad segura
consentida del tiempo y permanente. (235:II,291)

His body was without function or purpose:

Y, más agudo, el corazón
clavado en mis entrañas se metía,
tan fino y afilado,
que, al no ser ya mi carne transparente
también, como una noche hueca
en un espejo reflejada,
me hubiera parecido
entrar por el dolor
tan lejos en la muerte,
que la vida dejada atras,
fuera cristal inútil,
donde sólo mi nombre, y, para nadie,
quedara escrito, sin amor, en lo eterno.

But, in a way very similar to that recorded in 'Media noche', he undergoes a vital change:

Pero ante el vidrio frío,
en este invierno,
ante mis ojos empañados,
el calor de unas manos invisibles
fue borrando la bruma de las noches:
¿dentro? ¿fuera? . . .
¡A la vez!

The illuminating reference to 'invierno' confirms a possible explanation for all the new ways of thinking found in *Jardín cerrado*. The 'yo' has passed through the spring of childhood, where there was no disparity between desire and reality; through the summer and autumn of adulthood, when such a conflict did exist; and is now entering the winter of old age when, once again, there is no tension between desire in the realm of the body, which has by now waned, and the reality he can achieve. The work of the angel is described in the lines which follow. It enables him to live in the presence of those things which had previously most disturbed him: 'el corazón' (his unusual emotional condition) and 'la luna suspendida' (the threat imposed by his finiteness and by the darker, socially unacceptable side of his personality):

Y así encontré: que, mano contra mano
y palma contra palma
y cielo contra cielo
de eterno contra eterno,
ángel o transparencia fue limpiando
mi piel,
dejándome vivir
frente a mis dos abismos:
en uno el corazón iluminado
sobre la plaza de mi sueño
y allá arriba, la luna suspendida
derramando en la rosa,
delante de mis ojos.

The angel is best understood, in this context, then, as a symbolic agent, effecting the kind of transformations in the protagonist's attitudes which have been so prominent in *Jardín cerrado*.

The result of this removal of sources of disturbance is as it has already been in *Jardín cerrado*, presence within the enclosed garden in a way which he knew as an infant:

Y la inocente verdad del niño,
me vuelve a defender y me acompaña,
para sentir—más cerca que una lágrima—,
diminuto, en la rosa,
el brote de rocío
que la noche le da
como insignia, a lo Eterno. (238:II,294)

Cernuda wrote:

Sólo vive quien besa
aquel cuerpo de ángel que el amor levantara.[24]

Our protagonist, too, has learnt to embrace what he once regarded as a tragic hindrance to presence in the garden. He can now describe himself as:

un sollozo de Dios
puesto en el mundo
y como el mundo, en pena
sólo por el amor
del cuerpo más perfecto. (240:II,295)

La sangre abierta

In themselves the titles of the sub-sections into which *La sangre abierta* is divided suggest a large degree of fulfilment. The first, *La voz es un río*, contrasts with the bleak *Cuerpo perseguido* statement that 'mi cuerpo no es un río'. The third is called 'El germen que se cumple'. 'El cuerpo en el alba', the fourth, suggests a contrast with the unhappy situation in *Tiempo*, where sunrise brought a flight from the realm of the body. They share a note of triumph. *La sangre abierta* is, as Blanco puts it, 'la revelación final'.[25] From now on—and throughout the books that remain, the body is a 'río natural', by means of which and within which the central figure is to have dealings with the infinite.[26]

Further resolution of doubt

In one of the group's opening poems, 'Cantar sonámbulo', there is a repeated question: '¿Es mi cuerpo una caracola?' (241:II,303). The protagonist wishes to know if the nature of his body is akin to that of the shell. The shell's chief characteristic as far as he is concerned becomes clear from the second stanza:

> Estoy en el jardín. Mi pensamiento
> se va alejando de la rosa.
> Ir a la mar es su deseo.
> ¿Es mi cuerpo una caracola?

There is a re-directing of his attention. The rose of *Mínima muerte* ceases to interest him. Even the fruits of such a meditation are inadequate. His concern now is with the sea. Referring to his thought, he explains: 'Ir a la mar es su deseo'. His object is total union with the eternal, with what Jorge Manrique described as 'la mar que es el morir'.

The repeated question in the poem, then, might be expanded in the following way. The shell contains within it the sound of the sea (symbol of the eternal) to which it irrevocably belongs. The protagonist asks: does my body carry within it the eternal, the potential for total union with the eternal when death finally comes? The central figure closes his eyes in search of an answer to his question:

> Cierro los ojos. Voy a dormir.
> (Toda mi sombra está en el sueño.)

Siento mi corazón latir.

(Retumba el mar contra el silencio.)
¿Es mi cuerpo una caracola?

En la noche oscura de abril,
mi cuerpo duerme frente al cielo.
Baja la luna hasta el jardín
y pisa el nácar de mi pecho . . .

—Cerca de ti . . . Cerca de mí . . .
Lejos de aquí . . . (repite el eco).
Sobre la tierra obscura de abril,
duerme mi corazón, hueco.

(Mi cuerpo, es una caracola.)

The assurance that his body is, indeed 'una caracola', comes in the context of reminders of the kind of development marked by *Jardín cerrado*. He is, firstly, in the garden—thanks to an inner peace denied him in earlier years. Secondly the setting is the 'noche oscura de abril'—the spring, the time associated above all others in the mind of the 'yo' with childhood, a childhood to which, because of his new-found freedom, he is able to return. And thirdly, the moon's touch is a blessing rather than a curse: he has nothing to fear either in the realm of the body or in death—to which he can now look forward eagerly. The return to the 'jardín cerrado' of which these things are evidence is sufficient to persuade him that such moments of heightened experience will not simply cease when he dies.

The centrality of the body

'Cantar sonámbulo' demonstrates something of the function which the body has assumed. Just as the shell is the receptacle for the sound of the sea, so is the body the receptacle for the tokens which he now receives of a future eternal life. In 'Cruz del cuerpo' the protagonist explains:

Es mi cielo la tierra;
mi cruz el cuerpo;
mi lanzada la luna,
mi muerte el sueño. (243:II,306)

It is there, in the body, as the use of the language of the Passion suggests, that the death to life process is carried on.

But the closing section of the book has more to say about the body and its new-found status. 'Árboles', drew a strong contrast between the nature of the tree and that of his own body. It represented the kind of fertility and infiniteness which he longed for. The 'Árboles' of *La sangre abierta* reveals the extent to which his attitude towards his own body has changed. In the first 'Árboles' the tree looked down upon him with lofty disdain. The second 'Árboles' describes his adoption by it—the acceptance of his body by a symbol of life and of the infinite.

The poem begins with the 'yo' walking amongst a group of trees, feeling them, allowing a sense of their oneness, their wholeness, to overtake him:

Y, acaso un árbol solo
es toda la alameda.
(¡Qué oscura voz de Estío
bajo las hojas secas!)

—¿Un árbol?—¡Sólo un árbol! . . .
Y mi mano se acerca
para tocar el tronco
o el sueño que la asedia. (245:II,319)

He continues to move among the trees until finally he takes refuge in the shade of one of them:

De árbol en árbol voy
formando mi alameda.
Del cielo entré en su sombra :
ahora soy sombra en ella.

¿Sombra en ella? . . .
¿Y mi cuerpo? . . .
(Un álamo, sus ramas,
húmedas por la luna,
hacia mis hombros baja.)

The outcome of this is that his body becomes identified with that of the tree, which now moves its arms freely, having 'absorbed' the presence of the body of the 'yo', leaving behind 'tan sólo mi ausencia':

Un árbol y otro y otro
y ninguno, son todos
los árboles que llaman . . .
(Pero . . . ¿y mi cuerpo?)
El árbol,

mueve libre sus ramas.

Cae una flor. (El viento
la ha soltado.)
Y cruza,
ya tan sólo mi ausencia.
(Sube al cielo la luna.)[27]

The tree, by now, recognises a kindred spirit in the central figure.

A similar process—but one in which there is a clearer identification between the 'yo' and the tree—is outlined in 'Un árbol nace'. It traces his mood through despair to rapture. The opening lines are filled with doubt and questioning. Is the garden itself real after all?:

Pero el jardín, tan cerrado,
¿en dónde está?
Ni sus muros
dan la sombra—seña
de su retiro—; ni el agua
correr se siente,
ni el rumor de la alameda
levanta al sueño,
ni el ciprés vierte
su llanto de pena o luna
sobre el temor de la fuente. (248:II,336)

What is the evidence for the garden's existence? The remaining parts of the poem set out to resolve the problem.

It is in its fourth part that the answer emerges:

¡La luz!
¿Sin nombre la luz? . . .
—Pero la luz será el nombre.
Nombre de luz de la luz,
el Nombre.
La luz, el hombre.

(Jardín cerrado: tu voz
se empieza a ordenar . . .)

It is in the presence of man that establishes the reality of the garden, because it is man who is able to bestow upon it its 'nombre'. And it is, furthermore, specifically the body of that man which lends it this reality:

—¿Sin nombre el jardín? . . .

La luz, sin nombre, esperando
el cuerpo del hombre: ¡Luz!

The protagonist's body is again the mirror, capable of retaining and, here, assimilating and ordering the image of the infinite as it approaches him.

The central figure's body now occupies an elevated position in the garden. It has as much right to be there as the tree. Indeed, the 'yo' now begins to regard himself as being not in or in the shade of the tree, but as himself being a tree:

Jardín cerrado: ¡tus muros
filtran el tiempo! . . .

—Semilla soy, fecundada
del tiempo, en la tierra eterna . . .

—Semilla, no, cuerpo y luz
hacia arriba . . .
¿Y árbol ya? . . .
¡Árbol!

There is no limit to the activities in which the 'yo' in this condition can engage:

—¿Tan alto el árbol?
¡Arriba!
¡Hacia arriba!

(Cuidado con el lucero . . .)

—¡Más alto el árbol!
¡Arriba!
Aún más arriba . . .

(Tras el lucero, la luna . . .)

¡Arriba!

(Y, tras de la luna, el cielo . . .)

—¡Hacia arriba! . . .
. . . .
(¿Sin nubes, el sol? . . .)
¡Más alto!
¡Hacia arriba! . . .

The end of effort

It is with the lengthy poem 'El cuerpo en el alba', that the book ends. In the earlier poetry of *Tiempo*, apart from during certain moments of equilibrium, the protagonist could not bear to be conscious of the sun. In *Jardín cerrado* the presence of the sun does not mean the withdrawal of the body. He is now as he was when a child, in a natural, unthinking harmony with the universe. His body has again become like that of a child:

> . . . hoy, me abrís los brazos,
> cielo, tierra, sol, piedra,
> igual que presentí de niño
> que iba a ser la verdad bajo lo eterno.
>
> Hoy, siento que mi lengua
> confunde mi saliva
> con la gota más tierna del rocío
> y prolonga sus tactos
> fuera de mí, en la yerba
> o en la oscura raíz secreta y húmeda. (256:II,352)

Such statements prepare the way for the pantheism of later books.

The poem further emphasises the contrast between 'antes' (pre—*Jardín cerrado* days) and 'ahora' (in the light of new attitudes and feelings about himself). The arduous methods once needed in order to achieve an awareness of the infinite are contrasted with the natural spontaneity of his present experience. The third stanza depicts the laborious artificiality of previous efforts:

> Antes, el alma vi nacer
> y acudí por salvarla,
> fiel tutor perseguido y doloroso
> pero siempre seguro
> de mi mano y su aviso.
> Ayudé a la hermosura
> y a su felicidad,
> aunque nunca dudé que traicionaba
> al maestro, el discípulo,
> más, si aquél daba forma
> en su libertad,
> al pensamiento de lo bello.
>
> Y así vistió su ropa
> mi hueso madurado,
> tan lleno de dolor y de negrura,
> como noche nublada
> sin perfume de flor,
> sin lluvia y sin silencio . . .

Sólo el cumplir mi paso
aunque por suelo tan arisco,
me daba luz y fuerza en el vivir.

Though not without its rewards, this kind of life was taxing and negative. He was forced to root out anything in the realm of the finite because the alternative was consciousness of his body's infertility. His existence was dutiful rather than joyful.

By the latter stages of *Jardín cerrado* he has come to terms with a world of sky, earth, sun and stone. His body shares the same character as that of the natural world, and is appreciated as a vital part of the 'misterio de amor' which informs it:

Ahora sí que ya os miro
cielo, tierra, sol, piedra,
como si al contemplarlos
viera mi propia carne. (255:II,351)

No longer does he need to hide from his body:

Hoy, sí, mi piel existe,
mas no ya como límite,
que antes me perseguía,
sino también como vosotros mismos,
cielo hermoso azul,
tierra tendida . . . (256:II,352)

It is still the 'piel', the 'carne'—the body—which is at the heart of Prados's work.

In the light of this Blanco's assertion about 'El cuerpo en el alba' must be questioned. He sees the problem facing the 'yo' in these terms:

> . . . a la realidad de los paisajes interiores redescubiertos tan vivos le falta aún su cara complementaria: la de los paisajes de fuera.[28]

As earlier poetry has shown, the central figure is in reality saying that because of his body's sterility he had been forced to hide from the natural world. 'Paisajes de fuera' were denied him because they caused too much pain. But the situation has changed. He is now like the tree, fertile, infinite. He no longer feels that emptiness which once assailed him. His body has a part in the divine body of the total universe:

Ya soy, Todo: Unidad
de un cuerpo verdadero.

De este cuerpo que Dios llamó su cuerpo
y hoy empieza a sentirse
ya, sin muerte ni vida,
como rosa en presencia constante
de su verbo inacabado y, en olvido
de lo que antes pensó aun sin llamarlo
y temió ser: Demonio de la Nada.

The measure of fulfilment attained can be gauged from the conjunction of the flower, the rose and the sun—implicit in the poem's dawn setting. Seward writes:

> The ancient integration of sun and flower was intended to symbolise simultaneously the sexual union of male and female creative forces, the physical fertility of all natural things, and the spiritual attainment of ultimate harmony.[29]

He has found his place in the eternal, fertile world system. He has discovered, moreover, that he is essential to it. It is he (as later books emphasise) who 'names' it, who is able in an unique way to recognise and appreciate its existence. It is to be this creative act which will continue to lift him to the eminence of the once-envied sun and tree whose presence, now the partaker of their nature, he no longer fears.

1 B. Seward, *The Symbolic Rose*, p. 19.

2 J. L. Cano, 'La poesía de Emilio Prados', *Ínsula*, IX, no. 97 (1954), pp. 6–7.

3 L. de Luis, 'Dormido en la yerba', *Poesía española*, no. 25 (1954), pp. 24–5.

4 J. Larrea, 'Ingreso a una transfiguración', foreword to *Jardín cerrado* (Mexico, 1946).

5 The reader of *Jardín cerrado* may well take courage from the following comments made by Antonio G. de Lama, writing in an article entitled 'Poesía y verdad: El mismo Emilio Prados': 'El libro tiene un defecto capital aunque no esencial: es excesivo. Con la quinta parte de sus páginas se hubiera hecho un libro delicioso. Así, como viene, profuso, abundantísimo, resulta pesado y monótono.' (*Espadaña*, Revista de poesía y crítica, no. 38 (1949), p. 1.

6 L. Cernuda, 'Oda', *La realidad y el deseo*, p. 35.

7 F. G. Lorca, *Obras completas*, p. 493.

8 J. R. Jiménez, *Tercera antología poética*, p. 29.

9 J. Larrea, 'Ingreso a una transfiguración', pp. 13–14.

10 We have already referred to Laing's book *The Divided Self*. Another book of the same title provides equally fascinating insight into aspects of Prados's work. The autobiography of W. S. Stewart, a schizophrenic, it contains the following poem he wrote which records feelings not unlike those of the 'yo': 'Yew tree / Shut out the sunlight like a dunce's cap. / Safety I felt in the amber twilight, / Cloaked by the yew tree, / Covered from Fear, / Free from aimlessness, / Free from wandering— / I was a child then. I could be comforted / By umbrellas of trees / Extinguishers of loneliness. / How on the bare earth / To small cones the trees have shrunk, / Ineffectual to hide me, / Taller am I than the

yew tree of my childhood, / Naked on a plain am set, / Fear—a wind—blows there.' (London, 1964), p. 42. Despite the enormous differences in the poems, the association of the tree and the relative happiness of childhood is interesting.

11 D. Alonso and J. M. Blecua include in their *Antología de la poesía española lírica de tipo tradicional:* 'De los álamos vengo, madre, / de ver cómo los menea el aire. / De los álamos de Sevilla de ver a mi linda amiga, / de ver cómo los menea el aire. / De los álamos vengo, madre, / de ver cómo los menea el aire.' ((Madrid, 1964), p. 47). Here the poplars and love are clearly linked.

12 F. G. Lorca, *Obras completas*, p. 275.

13 L. Cernuda, *La realidad* y *el deseo*, p. 17.

14 D. Harris, *Luis Cernuda*, p. 30.

15 Stewart's comment on a slightly different topic, the death-wish, echoes the mood of 'Rincón de la sangre': 'Behind the death-wish, the longing for annihilation, the rejection of the limitations of oneself, there is something positive, or so I see it to be. "Our souls have sight of that immortal sea which brought us hither." I know of no better way to describe it. It is quite true, as Wordsworth says, that a child is capable of this experience, though he cannot express it. I myself, in childhood and adolescence, have had it many times, and more rarely as an adult. One pays dearly for such glimpses of reality in a consequent sense of loneliness and desolation when they are withdrawn.' (W. S. Stewart, *The Divided Self*, p. 16). It will be noted that the interpretation offered in this chapter differs from that of other critics, for example Cano, who writes that the garden of the poetry's title 'es para el poeta unas veces el alma y otras el cuerpo.' (J. L. Cano, 'La poesía de Emilio Prados').

16 Chevalier has this to say of 'les herbes': 'Symbole de tout ce qui est curatif et revivifiant, les herbes redonnent la santé, la virilité et la fecondité' (J. Chevalier, *Dictionnaire des Symboles* (Paris, 1969), p. 401). Though, of course, 'les herbes' and 'l'herbe' are not one and the same, it would be surprising if this interpretation were entirely irrelevant. Referring more precisely to 'l'herbe', the entry compares its symbolism to that of the fountain. Interestingly enough, under 'Fontaine', we find that it suggests: '. . . non pas l'immortalité, mais un perpétuel rajeunissement . . . Qui y boit s'affranchit des limites de la condition temporelle et obtient donc par une jeunesse toujours renouvelée la longévité . . .' (*Idem.*, p. 365). The implicit association of grass with the desire for youthfulness is not without relevance in the context of the 'Cantar del dormido en la yerba'.

17 In the pages which follow we show that the 'yo' finds peace by turning away from those conventional standards of behaviour in the light of which he had been found wanting. The discovery of the presence of death within him, however, brings him into the realm of the normal: there is perhaps even some consolation for him in the fact that if he is to die, that in this at least he will be as other men—that death will indeed prove the leveller which he seeks. The traditional theme of the presence of life in death must have deeply impressed itself on the mind of the well-read poet. He would have been conversant no doubt with Quevedo's sonnet: 'Signifícase de la propia brevedad de la vida sin pensar y con padecer salteada de la muerte', where we read: 'Azadas son la hora y el momento, / que, a jornal de mi pena y mi cuidado, / cavan en mi vivir mi monumento.' (*Obras completas, I*, edited by J. M. Blecua (Barcelona, 1963), p. 5). The intimacy of the tone of Prados's poem is reminiscent too of Juan de Mairena's: '. . . la muerte es un tema de la mónada humana, de la autosuficiente e inalienable intimidad del hombre. Es tema que se vive más que se piensa . . .' (A. Machado, *Obras*, p. 425). Both these comments share with Prados's poem a consciousness of the presence of death in life. Nor is it unlikely that Prados was acquainted with Rilke's statement: 'Pues sólo somos la hoja y la corteza. / La gran muerte que cada cual lleva en sí es el fruto / alrededor del cual da vueltas todo.' *(Obras de Rainer Maria Rilke*, translated by Jose María Valverde, (Barcelona, 1967), p. 157).

18 In the light of the past history of the central figure, it is not surprising that he should be

found 'junto a un pozo'. In J. M. Aguirre's article 'El sonambulismo de Federico García Lorca' we find a reference to the 'aljibe'—'símbolo de pasión sin salida, estancada, muerta.' (*Bulletin of Hispanic Studies*, XLIV (1967), p. 283). Such a symbol has immediate relevance to the 'yo' of *Tiempo* or 'Árboles'.

19 We have already quoted in Chapter 2 Laing's view on the concurrence of persecution thoughts and homosexual tendencies (*The Divided Self*, pp. 146–7). It is significant, perhaps, that as the sense of persecution strengthens in such lines as those reproduced here, so there is reference to 'la falsedad de un ángel' (to be linked with 'amor angélico'?).

20 L. Cernuda, *La realidad y el deseo*, p. 68.

21 There are reasons for interpreting the 'tú' in this way. Firstly, as we have seen in *La voz cautiva* and will see more clearly in *Río natural*, the infinite is always closely involved with the concept of the voice—and in 'Cielo de bautismo' this 'tú' is 'A la puerta de mi voz'. Secondly, in his private papers, Prados refers to man as being like a lens, traversed by the rays of the infinite in a way similar to that described in this poem (Caja 19.1).

22 J. R. Jiménez, 'Puerto', *Tercera antología poética*, p. 758.

23 It is interesting to compare this child with the one who appears in Cernuda's: 'A un muchacho andaluz'. He is there described in these terms: 'Eras tú una verdad, / Sola verdad que busco, / Más que verdad de amor, verdad de vida;' (*La realidad y el deseo*, p. 108). Prados's 'imagen' is far more narcissistic—and perhaps more closely related to the schizoid tendencies mentioned earlier. In this context Stewart's reference to the role played by a childhood friend in his own experience is noteworthy: 'It was as though this boy became so much a part of me, so closely identified in spirit and mind, that we were one, not two, . . .' (*The Divided Self*, p. 19).

24 L. Cernuda, *La realidad y el deseo*, p. 97.

25 C. B. Aguinaga, *Vida y obra*, p. 85.

26 The overall title of the section would appear to be a play on the juxtaposition of the ideas of 'el jardín *cerrado*' and 'la sangre *abierta*'. Jiménez's poem 'Descanso' contains a similar paradox: 'Basta. El jardín cerrado / es lo mismo que abierto'. *Tercera antología poética*, p. 592). Why Prados's protagonist should choose the symbol of the blood in particular is not altogether clear. It is traditionally linked with love. Chevalier notes that it may be regarded as 'le véhicule de l'âme' (*Dictionnaire*, p. 673). In earlier poetry, however, it can be sometimes equated with 'consciousness', as in 'Signo de la luz' (57:I,249): '¡Cómo se va saliendo por mi frente, / clara, serena, toda mi memoria / y, huyendo por el cielo derramada, / libre su anhelo cambia en cuerpo vivo! . . . / Sangre al fin de la tarde, arriba queda, / igual que un agua en tránsito, desnuda, / ya de la limpia estrella companía / y hondo espejo sin carne del silencio'. In this case *La sangre abierta* might be paraphrased as 'liberated consciousness'—an expression which does not seem too far removed from the content of the section.

27 The disappearance or 'fading away' of the 'yo' which this poem seems to recount can be compared perhaps with that of the old man in Aleixandre's 'El viejo y el sol', *Obras completas* (Madrid, 1968), p. 725.

28 C. B. Aguinaga, *Vida y obra*, p. 79.

29 B. Seward, *The Symbolic Rose*, p. 10.

CHAPTER EIGHT

A Sense of Fulfilment

Con tu luz tú me unes a ti, sol;
tú me unes a todo lo que luces.
Por tu luz soy más grande que todo lo que veo.
(Juan Ramón Jiménez, 'Con tu luz', *Una colina meridiana*)

No sólo estás entre los hombres,
dios deseado; estás aquí también en este mar
(desierto más que nunca de hombres)
esperando su paso natural, mi paso,
porque el mar es, tan olvidado,
mundo nuestro de agua.
(Juan Ramón Jiménez, 'De nuestros movimientos naturales', *Dios deseado y deseante*)

Introduction

In the course of this study Prados's work has been analysed in terms of development in the relationship between the central *persona* and his body. The preceding chapter suggested that with the onset of maturity and with the adoption of a voluntary attitude of withdrawal from competition with the norm, the problems posed by the body were steadily being resolved. *Río natural* bears witness to an even more permanent reconciliation to what had been the 'cuerpo de mi hastío'. New fields of enquiry begin to occupy the liberated protagonist. Prados himself wrote:

> En *Río natural*, el poeta, libre de sus límites individuales, se plantea el problema: ¿qué es el nombre?[1]

The reader should not, however, be misled into viewing *Río natural* as an entirely new and separate stage of development. Blanco describes *Río natural* as a book in which:

> . . . el poeta se adentra totalmente en la realidad a cuyo umbral le habían llevado los últimos poemas de *Jardín cerrado*.[2]

The 'reality' with which *Río natural* is concerned cannot be understood apart from that which has constantly concerned the central figure—his relationship with his body. When viewed in this light, Blanco's is a useful summary of the role played by *Río natural* in the poetry's overall pattern.

In view of its being selected by the poet himself, a number of references have been made in passing to the 1954 *Antología*. The choices made for the selection's final section are as careful as those made for its first, *Tiempo*. The original publication has undergone considerable pruning and re-organisation. Prados has gone further than merely to reduce the number of poems. The original *Río natural* consists of five sections. Their content can be sketched as follows: an exposition of the dichotomy in the central figure's experience between moments when he is engaged in the 'infinite' creativity of writing and moments when he is not ('En voz vivo'); the record of a search for an equilibrium which might remove this unhappy dichotomy ('Luchas dídimas'); a meditation on childhood and on the re-birth of the child within himself ('Dudas de abril'); poems of fulfilment ('En los cuerpos de un hombre'); and further poems of celebration ('Río natural'). The anthology selection, however, begins with a lengthy poem from 'Luchas dídimas', 'Sangre de Abel', and completely ignores the concluding *Río natural* selection of the original book.

As a result the final section of the anthology assumes the character of a culmination and resolution of all that has gone before. All fifteen poems end on a triumphant note, with such closing lines as these:

> . . . esclavo del silencio
> de Dios, vivo en su tierra . . . (271:II,449)
>
> "¡Vengo en la espuma del mar,
> a ser caracol besado!") (273:II,411)
>
> Oigo que murmura el agua:
> "¡Hacia el árbol voy contigo!" (274:II,412)
>
> ¡Hoy, vivo en razón de un sueño! (276:II,437)
>
> ¡Cante en mí, mi nuevo fruto! (277:II,468)

To the last Prados, in making his selection, has an eye for the overall shape of his *Antología*. If the journey of his hero has been an arduous one, it is nevertheless to be presented as ultimately victorious. As this study is particularly concerned with poetry written up to and including *Río natural*, particular attention will be given to poems chosen to appear in *Antología*.

'Sangre de Abel'

Prados chooses to open his selection with an involved poem based on the story of Cain and Abel, originally narrated in the fourth chapter of *Genesis*. Five verses of this account are reproduced here:

> And Cain talked with Abel his brother: and it came to pass, when they were in the field, that Cain rose up against Abel his brother, and slew him.
>
> And the Lord said unto Cain, Where is Abel thy brother? And he said, I know not: Am I my brother's keeper?
>
> And he said, What hast thou done? the voice of thy brother's blood crieth unto me from the ground.
>
> And now thou art cursed from the earth, which hath opened her mouth to receive thy brother's blood from thy hand;
>
> When thou tillest the ground, it shall not henceforth yield unto thee her strength; a fugitive and a vagabond shalt thou be in the earth.

As one might expect by now, Prados's treatment of this simple—though profound—material is far from straightforward. 'Sangre de Abel' is something other than a re-telling of the biblical narrative.

The fact that it found a place in *Antología* provides us with an initial clue to its interpretation. In making his choice Prados meticulously excluded any poem not concerned with the 'yo', either in the context of the 'tú', of the 'multitudes', or of the natural world. There is not a single poem where some third person is at the centre of interest. Deviation from a policy so ruthlessly implemented throughout the anthology would, at this advanced stage, be inconsistent and surprising. It is far more likely that the poem was included there on the basis not of its faithfulness to the *Genesis* account but rather of its relevance to the protagonist's condition.

Examination of the poem bears this out. It is the 'yo', rather than Cain and Abel, who is central to it. Before any reference has been made to the two brothers it is the situation of the central figure which is brought to the reader's attention:

> Cantando estoy llenando
>
> ¿Muerte es mi voz? . . .
> (La muerte,
> por mi palabra es muerte.)
>
> Llenando estoy mi vida
> con nombres de mi muerte . . .
>
> (Mi cuerpo estoy llenando
> de muertes que he salvado.) (261:II,440)

And again, at the close of the poem, it is the voice, well known to the reader by now, of the central *persona* which speaks:

> Y otra vez reflejado
> hacia mí de mí mismo,
> vivo el desierto doble
> de un sueño abandonado. (270:II,448)

The structure of the poem underlines the centrality of the 'yo'. It is set in the form of speeches made by Cain and Abel in the hearing of the protagonist. It is he who acts as a point of unity. Indeed, as section 5 of the poem demonstrates, he acts as a stage or setting for the events recounted in the poem, for its 'historia dialogada':

> Mientras llega la lluvia
> a mi espejo tendido,

—a mi cuerpo, sembrado
sin voz ni sombra, en tierra—:
la historia dialogada
que me dará el futuro,
antes de que me pierda
por él, miro en mi alma . . . (263:II,441–2)

Such lines as these provide the context for what Cain and Abel have to say. Similarly, following a speech by one the brothers (who will later be identified as Cain) in section 6, section 7 is entirely taken up with its effect not on the other brother, but on the central figure:

. . . Un acorde de nubes,
suspende sobre el cielo
al rumor intocado
de la voz que termina.
Todo el azul, presenta
su belleza, ante el fuego
que va a nacer . . .
(¿Contemplo
a Dios? . . .)
¡Vuelvo a mi alma! (265:II,443–4)

It is, then, the 'yo' who is, as commentator, spectator and participant, at the centre of 'Sangre de Abel'. Cain and Abel are important only insofar as they represent some kind of division or struggle which has existed or is existing within him.

The question which then arises is an obvious one: what aspects of the protagonist are represented by the two scriptural characters? When the poem is considered in a wider context their true identity becomes less mysterious. In dealing with *Cuerpo perseguido* a fundamental division in the protagonist's experience was noted. Sometimes this was expressed by the use of 'yo' and 'tú'. At others he made use of the more conventional 'body–soul' division. Many poems contain references to such categories. In 'Formas de una huída' we read:

Sorbió la fuga al cuerpo
y se quedó la ausencia
en pie cerca del agua . . .
Se fue acercando el alma
hasta entrar en la ausencia. (77:I,330)

Referring to the 'tú' of 'Resurrección' he writes:

La sombra, quedará abajo,
presa dentro de tu cuerpo,
igual que al dormirte ahora
queda sobre ti . . .
¡Qué espejo,
prendida tu alma en tu sangre,
dentro de ti irá encendiendo! (80–1:I,306)

Poetry as late as that of *Jardín cerrado* bears witness to similar ways of thought. In the example which follows, from 'Tres canciones de despedida', the sense of opposition between the 'cuerpo' and the 'alma' is particularly apparent. It is as though they can never co-exist without some kind of an artificial pact within his experience of the world:

Muerto mi cuerpo, en mi alma
vivirá el mundo conmigo.
El mundo muerto, en mi alma
se alzará mi cuerpo vivo. (230:II,274)

The central figure has been seen repeatedly to reject the level of the body in favour of that of the soul (or 'pensamiento', as it is sometimes called). It was this artificiality which *Jardín cerrado* began to abolish. 'Sangre de Abel' is, in fact, also concerned with the final reconciliation of these two warring factions within the divided self, the 'body' and the 'soul'.

The language of the poem is confirmation of the fact that it is concerned with the body–soul distinction. Those sections which introduce, punctuate and comment on their speeches are strewn with references to 'cuerpo' and 'alma'. Section 12 contains six references to 'cuerpo': sections 5, 7 and 9 respectively end in the following manner: 'miro en mi alma . . .', '¡Vuelvo a mi alma!', '¡Escucho / a su espejo en mi alma!'. It would not, therefore, be unreasonable to use as a model the view that the poem deals with the latest developments in the relationship between what the protagonist has viewed as the counterproductive parts of himself, the soul or the 'real self', and the body, and that, in some way, Cain and Abel represent them.

Specific evidence exists in the poem to support such a view. Reference to the biblical narrative links the voice of the brother who sings in section 6 with Cain. In Genesis he was left to wander as a vagabond on the face of the earth. The voice of section 6 is 'peregrina y errante'. Less obvious, but of equal importance, is the fact that the lines preceding Cain's words associate them directly with the realm of the soul:

la historia dialogada
que me dará el futuro,
antes de que me pierda
por él, miro en mi alma . . .
6
Canta una voz, por ella,
. . . . (263:II,442)

Furthermore, in the course of section 6, Cain has this to say:

Buscando estoy tu muerte
que derramé en la tierra.
Labrando estoy tu cuerpo,
hermano, con mi lengua . . . (264:II,442)

The other brother, Abel, is referred to in terms of the body, 'tu cuerpo'—aligning Cain, by implication, with the contrasting 'soul'. The confusion of the biblical roles, so that Cain is identified with the 'good' soul and Abel with the 'evil' body, is less than surprising in the light of the central figure's new attitude to his body—or for that matter in the light of the kind of liberties taken by contemporary poets such as Cernuda with the scriptural original. The voice, that of Abel, which replies in section 8, is aligned with the body. These are the lines which introduce it:

Inmóvil en su tierra
una sombra ha cantado.
Una sombra—conversa
de sombra—está penando . . . (265–6:II,444)

The reference to 'penando' suggests the traditional 'cuerpo en pena del alma' (which has already been mentioned in *Tiempo* in the poem 'Noche en urna' (15)). And in the course of his speech (in section 8) Abel refers to himself in these terms: 'Soy tu sombra esperando / de pie sobre la tierra' (266:II,445). He is the visible form of the invisible soul—the body. For the purposes of his poem, then, Prados has cast Cain as soul and Abel as body.[3]

Having established something of the poem's framework, it is now necessary to see what light it sheds on the important question of the protagonist's attitude to what have been in previous years the two separate realms of his experience. In the past, the over-riding tendency of the central figure has been to obliterate the level of the body and to make much of that of the soul (sometimes referred to as 'pensamiento' or even, in some cases, 'sueño'). 'Sangre de Abel' maintains the trend, already asserting itself in *Jardín cerrado*, towards a recognition of the necessity for the body and towards an acceptance of its nature.

Nowhere is this more in evidence than in Abel's speech in section 9:

> Canta la sombra:
> "Hermano,
> alégrate en mi culpa.
> No huyas de ti, sostenme,
> yo mismo me he matado . . .
> ¡Aleja ese dolor
> de causa inexistente!
> En ti, me quedé muerto,
> para poder cantarme:
> ¿quién como tú, mi hermano,
> sangre de mi palabra? . . . (266:II,444)

At first sight his assumption of guilt—including his statement that he in fact killed himself—is indeed unexpected. But in the light of the central *persona*'s past and present attitude to his body it is less than surprising. Cain experienced guilt because he murdered Abel. The protagonist's 'alma' has also come to feel guilty for suppressing what it found inconvenient and disagreeable—the body. Abel is now reassuring Cain that he need feel no guilt: he allowed himself to be killed 'para poder cantarme'. Similarly the central figure's body is telling his soul to forget the guilt feelings which have come to cloud his attitude to the body. If it is true that the body has been neglected, allowed to 'die', then it need be true no longer.

The 'yo' has come to see that no experience from which the body has been excluded is valid. Both Cain and Abel confess their total interdependence. Abel declares:

> No me alejes de ti,
> que soy mudo destierro.
> Soy, tu sombra esperando
> de pie sobre la tierra:
> ¡La nación preparada
> fácil, para gobierno
> del cuerpo que sembramos
> los dos bajo la muerte!
> . . . .

¡Cántame, hermano!, y libra
mi guarda, por cantarme.
Temor tengo a mi nombre,
aunque en ti se redima.
¡Soy mitad tuya! ¡Espero
tu voz, para mi canto! (266–7:II,445)

Cain has already confessed his need of Abel:

"Mitad mía, mi hermano,
mi equilibrada sombra.
. . . .
Mi vida, está acabando
sin ti, mi misma sombra. (263–4:II,442)

Without the body the soul is insubstantial, unreal:

Tu muerte estoy penando
por no encontrar mi muerte . . .
De la luz en futuro
del alba que he parado;
del resplandor que piensa
venir a levantarte
desde el pueblo escondido
destinado a tu sueño
—espuma preparada
en flor para habitarte—:
sólo soy voz en vuelo
ausente y sin palabra.
Hermano, dale nombre
al brillo que padezco: (264–5:II,443)

By the end of section 8 the pleas for reconciliation are completed. Cain and Abel have admitted that they must not exist separately. If it is true that this represents the end of the protagonist's negative, suspicious attitude towards his body, it should follow that such a reconciliation will be expressed in terms of his, rather than the brothers', feelings. This is in fact the case. Section 9 describes the elevation of emotion produced by the new attitude towards his body. There is a particularly significant reference to a 'cuerpo nuevo':

Vuelvo al cielo mis ojos . . .
—Las nubes se han perdido.—
Un blanco acorde suena
sobre el cielo sin nubes.

Un sitio. Un cuerpo nuevo.
Una eterna armonía . . . (267:II,445)

As there was in 'Cuerpo en el alba', there is peace in the presence of the sun:

(Bajo el azul misterio
que vivieron las nubes,
un diminuto sol
comienza por sus llamas . . .)

¡Cruje el tiempo!
(Los huecos
contemplados, se prenden . . .
El sol invade el sitio
de las nubes.)
¡Ya es alba!

(¿Contemplo a Dios? . . .)
¡Escucho
a su espejo en mi alma!

The effects of such a new unity of experience are far-reaching. Section 11 records the emergence of the 'voice'. His ability to write, to create, is acquiring a new status—it enables him to commune with what he calls 'Dios':

¡Entro a mirar la sombra
de mi voz!—¡La que viene
a cantarme! . . .
(¿En ella vivo?)

"¡Cantando estoy llegando
de Dios!", mi voz me canta. (268:II,446–7)

Section 12 describes his state of mind having returned from the intense climaxes of section 9 and 11:

Despacio, y ya en silencio,
vuelvo a mí de mí mismo
—a mi cuerpo sembrado
sin voz ni sombra en tierra—.

There is now a sense of inner peace: he is at one with himself:

Desnudo, en mí, la historia
que he de tener conmigo
y, al hablar de otro tiempo
de mí, me llamo hermano . . . (269:II,447)

He speaks to his body, the 'cuerpo . . . de mi tiempo', the limited, physical body 'en que he vivido'. In the past so separate has it been from him that he calls it 'tu cuerpo': but now, as these lines show, he neither can nor desires to be apart from it:

Mírame, por ti he muerto
—a mi tiempo le digo—:
mi herencia está en mi lengua,
recógela al cantarme
tu cuerpo, en que he vivido.
Canto sólo a tu cuerpo;
sólo tu cuerpo escucha,
sólo llego a tu cuerpo
por verme en ti cantado . . .

Once the unhappy nature of his body meant that only in the dream was any joy to be found. Now this happiness has burst out of the confines of the dream and has invaded all levels of his experience. Both 'body' and 'soul' inhabit the lofty planes through which he once travelled only by means of the dream:

¡Alza tu guarda! El sueño
rompió su piel . . . Hoy, libre,
los dos somos el sueño.

His awareness of the infinite has been strengthened:

¿Resucitó infinita
nuestra lucha al cantarlo? . . .
¡Nuestra madre infinita
vivimos bajo el sueño!:
Dentro de una canción
de su cuerpo habitamos . . .
¡Sangre de Dios y muerte
de Dios, por Dios vivimos!"

Section 13 ends on a similar note:

(¿Llego a Dios? . . .)
¡Me contemplo
en Dios, muerto y cantado! . . . (270:II,448)

'Sangre de Abel' began with fundamental questions about the central figure. He wants to know what is the nature of his 'voice', what is his relationship to death: '¿Muerte es mi voz? . . .', '(¿Muerto, desde mí, nazco?)', '¿Soy esclavo de muerte, / en la muerte sembrado? . . .' (261–2:II,440–1). The settling of such questions has involved analysis of his relationship towards his body and what has been called his 'soul'. From the final fourteenth section it would seem that a complete solution has yet to appear:

> Ni sé qué mundo vivo,
> ni qué mundo me deja
> lo eterno en lo infinito
> que, en mi sangre, despierta.
>
> ¿Siempre desconocido
> dentro de mí o por fuera,
> caminaré esta sangre
> —sangre mía y ajena—? . . .
>
> Penando bajo el cuerpo
> que visito por ella,
> extranjero y errante
> de mí soy en mi lengua . . . (270–1:II,448–9)

But the closing couplet indicates the extent of the progress achieved:

> Y esclavo del silencio
> de Dios, vivo en su tierra . . .

Despite lingering doubt and uncertainty, one thing stands firm: the knowledge that the whole level of his experience has been raised to a point where, to use the language of *Jardín cerrado*, he is no longer in exile from the sense of the divine which permeated his childhood. In addition, the mature 'yo' is now in a position, thanks to his 'voz' or 'palabra' to effectively record and re-live what he experiences.[4]

Further steps towards the uniting of the 'divided' self

An 'En voz viva' poem, 'Soledades', is based upon a contrast between his past and present attitudes towards the 'caracol'.[5] Both time levels are in evidence in the opening stanza:

> ¡Caracol lejos del mar:
> estoy haciéndome luz
> y, tal vez, por no ser tiempo
> justo, que sin ti he perdido.
> ¡Te contemplé! ¡Te sentía
> pesada de mi tristeza!
> ¡Juntos frente a frente y solos! . . .
> Y sin poder habitar
> —huecos de sangre y de nácar

señales de nuestra ausencia
la figura que nos dimos,
cuando pensamos los dos
vivir sólo un universo. (271:II,409)

In the past, the shell and the 'yo' have been separated from one another—'¡Juntos frente a frente y solos!'. To share the same life—'vivir sólo un universo'—was an impossibility. Both were engulfed in the 'solitude' of the poem's title.

This is not to say that they have remained entirely apart. There has been some kind of rapport. But it has always been incidental, passive:

¡Me acompañabas!
Yo, en ti,
descansaba cotidiano,
de mi qué hacer siempre inútil:
de preguntar por mi ser
aquí y allí; no encontrarlo
y cavar más hondo: abrirme
de arriba abajo y caer
como en dos valvas—sin cuerpo—
en tiempos que nunca he visto. (271–2:II,409)

The 'caracol' has been nothing more than an unobtrusive companion. The 'yo', almost entirely ignoring it, has been too engrossed in his search for what he considered to be his 'real' self, 'por mi ser'.

The description of this 'qué hacer siempre inútil' identifies it with the kind of quest for a consistently heightened level of experience which from *Tiempo* onwards has obsessed the central *persona*. It shares, in particular, the major weakness of such investigations—a repeated failure to recognise that the body, for all its abnormality, must be involved if such a quest is not to prove artificial and, ultimately, fruitless. In 'Soledades' he describes himself as falling '—sin cuerpo— / en tiempos que nunca he visto'. His body, like the 'caracol', was being overlooked. The poem records his dismissal of the shell's attempts at communication:

. . . me decías:
"¿Por qué no vives conmigo? . . ."
Yo jamás te di respuesta.
Sólo escuché tu nostalgia
sonora. ¡Tu hermosa vida!
Tu descansada belleza
ante el papel de mis ojos.

La geometría de paz
interna, bajo el espacio
constante que te perdía . . .

It is merely the object of aesthetic admiration or of nostalgia, a reminder of a better day when the 'yo' was a creature of the sand and the sea in childhood.

If one were to take the 'caracol' to refer simply to the type of ornament which finds its way onto work-desk or mantelpiece, then the developments contained in the rest of the poem would indeed assume an air of unreality. For the new relationship with the 'caracol' brings about fundamental changes in the protagonist's condition, as the last stanza indicates:

Caen marchitas las paredes
de mi soledad cantando:
"¡Vengo en la espuma del mar,
a ser caracol besado!") (273:II,411)

It can safely be assumed that the shell is representative of some more radical feature of his experience. A *Jardín cerrado* poem, to which reference has already been made in this section, clarifies the point. 'Cantar sonámbulo' begins with this question:

¿Es mi cuerpo una caracola?
Cierro mis ojos para el sueño:
toda la sombra está en silencio.
¿Es mi cuerpo una caracola? (241:II,303)

The conclusion it reaches is a significant one:

En la noche oscura de abril,
mi cuerpo duerme frente al cielo.
Baja la luna hasta el jardín
y pisa el nácar de mi pecho . . .
. . . .
(Mi cuerpo, es una caracola) (242:II,304)

The equation of the body and the shell is the basis for an understanding of 'Soledades'. His neglect of the shell represents his neglect of his body.[6]

The remainder of the poem describes the reconciliation of the shell and the central figure. In terms of the evolution of his relationship with his body, it represents the cementing of the process whose beginnings were seen in *Jardín cerrado*. The body is acquiring a status previously denied it:

Pero en nuestra intimidad
—¡vivimos juntos tan solos!—:
un día, en el mismo cuarto
que habitamos, un secreto
doloroso, desnudaste
de ti, cuando yo caía
abierto y más desolado
que nunca, en nada saber.

Pude escucharte en la voz
que no es tuya y en ti hablaba
y, sentí, por escucharte,
que mi secreto desnudo
era tu mismo dolor:
amor de ti, mi alegría
de amor que tú en mí gozabas . . . (272:II,410)

In earlier years the 'yo' had seen in the body only an enemy, a distraction—a drain on his energy. He has now come to believe that it shares his own pain and his secret desire to know more of the eternal life which the sea represents. The 'caracol', then, is aggrieved because of its separation from the sea—from the infinite 'alma' of the central figure: and the protagonist himself, in turn, longs for the ultimate release which death (the 'espuma' of the closing stanzas) will afford. The barrier between what the protagonist considered to be his 'true' self and his body is broken down:

Y por eso me hago luz:
para encontrarte aquel tiempo
oculto, en que fui tu amante,
caracol lejos del mar
infinito en sangre y nácar.

¡Dejé mi qué hacer inútil,
por vivir en ti conmigo! . . . (273:II,410)

He decides to live *in* the body (the 'caracol') rather than in isolation from it. There is to be a re-living of the blessed infancy he knew beside the sea of 'Cuando era primavera', when he was the 'amante' of his pre-adolescent body. The sense of mutual fulfilment which results carries them forward towards the sea where their common desire lies. He has a foretaste of the blessing, the 'kiss' of the infinite to be enjoyed to the full in death:

¡Mira mis ojos! Mi cuerpo

—espiral de ti—es el mar
que no eres tú y te buscaba:
¿se oye en ti mi voz de mar?

(Entra mi cuerpo a la espuma
que se desnuda en mis brazos.
Dos soledades, ajustan
nácar y sangre a mis labios . . .

Caen marchitas las paredes
de mi soledad cantando:
"¡Vengo en la espuma del mar,
a ser caracol besado!")

A new confidence

'Canción' is another poem which makes use of the symbols of *Jardín cerrado*. Here it is the tree, rather than the shell, which is the focus of interest. In *Jardín cerrado* the protagonist's relationship to it, by virtue of its connotations as a symbol of fertility and infiniteness, was an index of the extent to which he had laid hold on such qualities for himself. One of the climaxes of that section comes in 'Un árbol nace', where the central figure asks what his nature is:

—¿Y árbol ya? . . .
—¡Árbol! (252:II,340)

To judge from the opening of 'Canción' it would seem that the whole question has been re-opened: '¿Soy árbol? . . .' (273:II,412). So great is his sense of insecurity that he is reduced to asking this of the shadow cast on the ground by his body:

(Miro a la sombra
de mi cuerpo en árbol vivo.)

¡Hablando estoy con mi sombra
para saber de mí mismo!

This is the kind of question which haunted *Cuerpo perseguido*—and of which 'Soledades' is reminiscent. It is the reality of his experience of himself, the reality of his body, which is at issue.

None of the steps taken in order to reach some kind of conclusion are satisfactory. He is first advised by his shadow to look more carefully in its direction—advice which the 'yo' foolishly accepts:

Me dice la sombra: "¡Acércate
más, al brocal de tu olvido!"

Me acerco y pierdo la sombra . . . (274:II,412)

The more closely he tries to observe his shadow, which should act as proof positive of the fact that he exists, the more quickly does such evidence lose its force. Now (presumably) lying on the ground he looks back to where he took his body (the 'tree' of the poem) to be. It is, of course, no longer there:

Vuelto hacia el árbol le digo:
¡Nos salvamos! . . .
Miro al árbol
y, el árbol, también se ha ido . . .

However contrived this conceit might seem, it does nevertheless bring back into sharp focus the introspective and tormented questioning and self-doubt of earlier poetry.

What is new is the way in which such doubts are resolved. Puzzlement is laid to one side. Instead he looks upwards, outside and beyond himself:

(Cruza un pájaro sin sombra
en diagonal de infinito.)

Oigo que murmura el agua:
"¡Hacia el árbol voy contigo!"

There is a simple re-directing of attention. He follows the course of the bird in its upward path towards the infinite. He allows the considerations outlined in 'Soledades', his natural affinity with the eternity symbolised by the sea, to permeate his thought. It is to be the water of the 'río natural' now within him which promises him that he will eventually appropriate that fertility and infiniteness of which the tree is a symbol. There is no trace of the 'divided self' hinted at in the poem's opening question. As the protagonist concludes in 'Mayo es abril':

Amante es mi cuerpo,
que ha sido en la flor
amante del viento. (278:II,475)

The importance of the poetic act

It has been obvious in 'Sangre de Abel' and 'Ventana al sur' that an increasingly high value is being set on the ability to express his new-found joy in the form of poetry. The establishing of the 'nombre exacto de las cosas' is co-equal, as far as the 'yo' is concerned, with an experience of the infinite. Two poems dealing with this point will now be discussed.

The first of these is 'Canción mínima'. As so often in Prados's work, the poem's sense emerges from implicit rather than explicit contrasts which the reader is to deduce as each strand of the narrative unfolds. At first sight the opening stanzas seem to be purely descriptive:

Sobre la playa: tú, piedra,
¡chinita blanca!

Y sobre el cielo: la noche
que pasa y pasa

y te mira,
¡chinita blanca!

La sombra que pasa
y pasa . . . (274:II,414)

Only as the poem develops does the significance of the repetition of the word 'pasa' emerge. The stanzas which follow introduce a new factor:

Está el silencio contigo,
chinita blanca;
pero no con el olvido.

¡Alguien que te vio
te canta,
chinita blanca!

The night and the shadow can only pass by the stone. But there is someone who is able to do more than simply pass by; someone who is able to 'name', to 'sing of' the stone.

The same pattern is then repeated. Three stanzas register the night's inability to record in any lasting way the experience of observing the 'chinita'. The night sings, yes, but continues on its way, leaving behind nothing tangible or concrete:

Y pasa la noche y pasa,
estrella a estrella
y te mira,
¡chinita blanca!

Y se va la noche
y canta.

Y pasa el mundo contigo,
chinita blanca.

There is a further contrast with the reaction of 'alguien':

Pero el que te vio,
te canta:
"¡Chinita blanca,
en ti vivo!"

It is the 'yo', the poet alone who is able to name the insignificant little stone and bring it to life:

Y en su voz
tu muerte acaba . . .

¡Tu sombra que pasa
y pasa!

The stone, a symbol, according to Cirlot, of the inert, is made to live. By the same token the 'voice' of the central figure confers on him a new status: he is now creative, fertile—vital to the pattern of the natural world around him.[7]

The two final stanzas of the exultant 'Sueño y canción' re-affirm this. The poem's opening follows a pattern similar to that of 'Canción': doubts as to the nature of the body followed by an upwards, rather than inwards glance. He asks of himself :

—¿En dónde estás?,
pregunto en mí.
Y al callar,
Como un espejo en voz baja,
me repite:
"¿En dónde estás? . . ."
Alzo los ojos. (280–1:II,510)

Again it is the voice, though dormant, which is continually ready for us, abolishing the difference between the sleeping and waking state:

Delante de mí, mi voz
duerme en mi espalda, soñando.
Mi voz sueña, que es mi voz,
soñando que he despertado.

¿Canción soy?: ¡Canción he sido! . . .
¡Y para ser canción vivo!

The life of the poet is becoming more and more inseparable from poetry. Jiménez wrote these words in connection with the subject of the 'anthology' (a topic particularly relevant to Prados):

> La verdadera selección poética sería aquella—¡qué imposible!—que representara sintéticamente la serie de los sentidos más bellos de cada poesía; es decir, de los instantes mejores, más agudamente bellos de la vida de un poeta.[8]

It is towards this kind of equation of life and poetry that Prados is moving.

The end of dependence on the dream

Throughout the course of this poetry the dream has had a part to play. It has been both a means of escape and, in varying degrees, a means of discovery. However, it has rarely been entirely welcome as part of his technique for reaching those moments of heightened experience which *Tiempo*, for example, describes. The 'sueño' has been regarded as a necessary evil. The central figure has disparagingly referred to himself as the 'romántico de huídas': he has expressed regret that he only feels himself to exist 'cuando me olvido'. Even in *Jardín cerrado*, where the 'yo' feels less of a need to flee from the body to the dream, 'sueño' remains as a key to entry into the garden.

Río natural marks an advance on this. The protagonist feels he has reached a high-point of development. In 'Espejismo' he announces: '¡Maduro estoy! Mis racimos / de lágrimas doy al mar.' (276:II,467). This maturity is reflected in his view of the dream. There is a blurring of the distinction between the dream and life, expressed in a poem entitled 'Copla' in the anthology, 'Trinidad' in the original *Río natural*:

> Sin pensar que estoy viviendo,
> voy saliéndome de mí
> a llenar mi pensamiento.
>
> ¡Ya estoy en él! ¡Ya estoy lleno! . . .
> Sin saber que estoy pensando
> vuelvo a meterme en mi cuerpo.
>
> ¿Y vuelvo a pensar? . . .
> ¡No sé!
> ¡Hoy, vivo en razón de un sueño! (276:II,437)

In the full presence of the body, the 'pensamiento' process (identified in *Mínima muerte* as the activity of the higher 'alma') continues to take place. The entire life of the central *persona* is now carried out on the level which once belonged only to the dream. It is in this sense that Cano is correct when he comments that: 'Mientras el cuerpo sueña y ama, el cuerpo es camino, es río—río natural . . .'.[9]

At times this seems to take the protagonist by surprise. In consequence there is an ironic return to the technique much used in earlier poetry, such as *Cuerpo perseguido*, of repeated questions and enigmatic, unresolved statements. It is ironic because now, it is not a case of the 'yo' being at a loss to cope with basic questions about the reality of his own existence. He is rather overwhelmed by the immediacy and spontaneity of this certain experience of the infinite. This 'Canción', for example, finds him unable to decide whether he is alive or dead, awake or asleep:

¿Mis párpados
equivocan mi dormir
y el mundo vive soñando
y yo despierto por mí? . . . (282:II,455)

He is able, at this advanced stage, to eschew such problems with unprecedented confidence:

No quiero enmendar mi cambio;
porque el mundo que ahora miro
es el que viví buscando.

A similar abandoning of the attempt to distinguish between sleeping and waking, living and dying which informed so much earlier poetry is described in 'Juegos de canción'. Again the technique of tentative questioning finally swept away by a surge of confident, joyful statement is used:

Y me canso y me voy.
¡Sin vivir soy!

¿Dónde estoy viviendo?
¡Pregunto y no veo!
. . . .
¿Acaso estoy muerto?
¡Pero no lo veo!
. . . .
¡Todo lo recuerdo!
¡Me canso y me voy!

Todo lo recuerdo . . .
¡Sin vivir soy! (282–3:II,518)

Without the need for the conscious effort which once characterised his experience of the infinite, he now enjoys an effortless appreciation of his own reality—which, as far as he was concerned, had always been a major barrier to what he at least took to be an experience of the divine. The emphasis on 'playing' and on the sea ('jugaba en la playa') reminds us that this is a return to Cernuda's 'país perdido / Que abandonas un día sin saberlo', the childhood experience longed for in *Cuerpo perseguido* (where the central figure wrote of the 'niño / que cuelga de mis ojos'), in 'Cuando era primavera' and in *Jardín cerrado*.

A new body

In his study of Coleridge, McFarland comments that:

> In so far as the poet does feel the need for philosophical abstraction . . . his interest will tend, so this history of culture tells us, towards some variation of the pantheistic view.[10]

Prados's poetry is in measure a confirmation of this view. In earlier work nature was the object of the central figure's mistrust and fear—except when recorded objectively, as in *El misterio del agua* or in the context of childhood, as in 'Cuando era primavera'. By *Río natural* the body which has in adult life excluded him from a full enjoyment of the natural cycle comes more and more to partake of it, to belong to it, to share its nature. Its closing poems mark the culmination of the process by which he has become entirely reconciled to the nature of his body.

It is to two of the most important of these poems, 'Cuerpos de un nombre' and 'Nombre del mar', that reference will be made. The central figure's reaction to the presence of a number of factors which before harassed and unsettled him is in marked contrast to anything found in earlier poetry.

The first of these contrasts concerns his attitude towards the stream or the river which are so prominent in 'Cuerpos de un nombre'. The 'yo' has always shied away from identification with water, the symbol of fertility, life. Because of his ineffectiveness in the realm of the body he openly admitted in *Memoria del olvido*: 'Yo sé que mi piel no es un río'. A work as late as *Jardín cerrado* showed that the protagonist found it most natural to lie 'dormido junto a un pozo'—the well being a symbol of stagnation and inertness. In the *Río natural* poem the situation is radically different. He exclaims:

. . . El agua soy naciendo
arrancada de mí para mí misma
y no acabo ni quedo en mí ni estoy . . .
¡Fuente soy! ¡Fuente fui! ¡Fuente es mi arroyo!
"Agua de libertad sueño en mi fuente
—la fuente que por mí nació cautiva—
y agua en la fuente he sido y fuente soy
canta por mí la fuente que me canta." (283–4:II,512)

He restates the point in a flood of exuberant clauses piled joyfuly the one on top of the other:

¡Arroyo fui y arroyo he sido y soy!
Arroyo claro en mí, fuente serena . . .
Y nazco y nazco más: que soy el agua
y porque estoy porque me voy la vivo. (285:II,513)[11]

He is now living the same life as that of the youthful, ever-living stream.

In *Jardín cerrado* the section's starting-point was a comparison which the 'yo' drew between himself and the tree—another symbol of the fertile and the eternal. The comparison was in no sense favourable. It represented something which was his desire rather than his present experience, 'el material suspiro / de mi oculto silencio'. The closing poems saw the adoption of the 'yo' by the tree, thanks to the changes of attitude observed in the course of the section, so that by 'El germen que se cumple' the 'yo' *is* a tree. 'Cuerpos de un nombre' records a similar transformation of attitude, one which underlines the progress made in *Jardín cerrado*:

Espuma, espuma soy—¡golpes del agua!—:
árbol de espuma en ramos de corriente . . . (285:II,513)

His total identification with the potent tree-symbol is if anything bolstered by the image of the 'ramos de corriente'. He is now, in brief, both tree *and* river—whereas once he felt himself to be neither.

It has been our contention that the body, the physical reality of the central figure, has been—sometimes overtly, sometimes implicitly—the main concern of the work of Emilio Prados. It is, therefore, not surprising that the final poems of *Antología* should contain more direct references than those already mentioned to that body. A comparison between the 'cuerpo' of 'Nombres del mar' and that of earlier poetry is again revealing. An earlier 'Canción' read thus:

Y el mar
dice lo que dice el sol,
que eterno vuelve a cantar
lo que canta el mar eterno.

Yo me acerco por mirar
lo que de este canto entiendo
pero no puedo olvidar
que estoy dentro de mi cuerpo
y en mí me vuelvo a ocultar.

¡Pasen estos malos tiempos! (138:I,751)

It was the body (and for more reasons than those outlined in 'Canción') which kept him from the sea. One of the hallmarks of his expulsion from the infiniteness of childhood was his removal from the sea of 'Cuando era primavera', where 'el mar soñaba entonces, / como el ojo de un pez sobre la arena,' (142:I,764). 'Nombres del mar' is the final proof that the gulf has been bridged. In its third section the 'yo' finally claims affinity with the sea—but, most importantly, an affinity between his *body* and the sea:

Y el mar azul mis venas atiranta,
arrancando de mí sólo gemidos:
"¡Como el mar! ¡Como el mar!" . . . vibra en mi cuerpo
la soledad del mar que me ha pulsado. (290:II,528)

The concrete weight of this relationship between the 'yo', his body and the sea emerges from the closing stanzas of section 4. The 'voice' of the 'yo'—his ability to 'name' the elements of the natural world in poetry (as has already been seen, a central constituent of his mature appreciation of his role in the universe)—is in itself like the sea within him:

"¡Mar quiero ser! ¡Mar quiero ser!", le digo
al mar de voz que bulle en mi garganta.
"¡Mar quiero ser! ¡Mar quiero ser!", repite
dentro del mar, el mar por mí cantado. (290:II,529)

The name he is able to give it has the solidity and reality of rock. Furthermore, and more relevant to the comparison of early and late poetry, this rock is now blessed by what was once of all things insubstantial and unreal—the central figure's body:

¡Roca del mar, mi cuerpo te bendice,
—¡mi sueño—: un hombre en mí del mar cautivo! (291:II,529)

As these lines suggest, the uniting of himself and the sea is the realisation of the virtually life-long dream of the 'romántico de huídas'.

A final contrast between the outlook of the mature 'yo' and that of the 'yo' of earlier poetry can be established by reference to the symbol of the sun. In *Tiempo* he fled from its presence. 'Nombres del mar' re-affirms the extent to which the central figure's view of his body has changed. In *Jardín cerrado* he worked through to a position where his body could withstand the presence of the dawn. In 'Nombres del mar' the sun's presence is more than welcome—it is an integral part of his experience of his body and of the poetic activity described above. Without the sun, the eternal within him, the 'mar en mí', cannot be realised:

> Casi es Mayo en Abril
> y punza y punza el sol.
> Aguardo al mar en mí . . .
> ¡Y el mar no viene!
> Pero el sol—¡aún más sol!—se acerca y canta:
> "¡Llego del mar! ¡Llego del mar! ¡Me quema!" . . .
> Y salgo al mar. (Su cuerpo en mí levanto.)
> Beso en el sol. (Soporto en mí su beso.) (287–8:II,526)

In sections 4 and 5 of the poem the central figure rejoices in the presence of the very sun which he once feared:

> Blanca es mi voz y oscuro mi silencio.
> Al sol mi soledad en la luz canta
> y cubre en sombra el canto de mi olvido. (290:II,528)
>
> . . . .
> "¡Llego del mar! ¡Llego del mar! ¡Me quema!",
> vuelve a cantarme el sol.
> . . . ¡Y al sol me duermo!
> ¡Nazco otra vez, del mar tan deseado! (291:II,529)

The 'yo' sleeps in the light of the sun no longer in an attempt to avoid it: he sleeps with the tranquillity of one who has, he believes, nothing to fear from one to whom he is equal, and whose divine nature he shares. His own view, however misguided, is that he has succeeded in a task to which Plotinus, with his dying words, referred: 'Strive to bring back the god in yourself to the Divine in the universe.'[12]

1 Taken from Caja 19.3.

2 C. B. Aguinaga, *Vida* y *obra*, p. 88.

3 It must be borne in mind that at some points in the poem 'cuerpo' and 'alma' are not used simply in the sense of a division within the 'yo'. As was the case in *Cuerpo perseguido*, their meaning fluctuates. In section 9, where reference is made to 'Un cuerpo nuevo', then, as we shall see, a different concept altogether is involved.

4 The opening poem of *Río natural* 'Ventana al sur', dwells at greater length on the question of poetic expression. There the 'voz' is seen as the product of the protagonist's maturity—his 'estío', to adopt the language of 'Ventana al sur': '. . . entro a estío en mi voz: / ¡vivo en mi voz entera!' (II,391). The onset of this maturity, signalled by the emergence of the 'voz' brings—as it has brought in 'sangre de Abel', an end to the artificial dream/life dichotomy of earlier poetry: '¿Mi voz vive? . . . / Sí; vive / nivelando al sueño la realidad; . . .' (II,392). Possibly the act of poetic expression is coming to be that which perpetuates and provides permanent access to the moment of heightened awareness. The use of the word 'palabra' in 'Sangre de Abel' is interesting. It reflects the long-standing Platonic influence on Prados's work. In *Studies in Plato's Metaphysics*, R. C. Cross quotes from the *Theaetetus*: '. . . whenever then anyone gets hold of the true notion of anything without a logos his soul thinks truly of it, but he does not know it; for if one cannot give and receive a logos of anything, one has no real knowledge of that thing . . .' ('Logos and Forms in Plato', in *Studies in Plato's Metaphysics*, edited by R. E. Allen (London, 1965), p. 13). Thus the protagonist's maturity will come to be preferable even to his childhood. In childhood the experience of the infinite is his—but it cannot be fully his until he is in a position to express, to 'name' it. Only then is it truly 'his'. (This, of course, is another reason for the recognition of the need for the body as part of the experience of the eternal.) In 'Las tres noches del hombre' the child is presented in the context of such a weakness: 'El niño comienza a comprender pero algo se le resiste a la inteligencia. Le faltan elementos con los que poder comparar.' (See Appendix III).

5 The respective meanings of 'caracol' and 'caracola' would seem to be very close, as for example in *Vox, Diccionario general, Bibliograf* (1964). Under 'caracol' we find: '1. Nombre común a todos los moluscos gasterópodos de concha en espiral . . . 2. Concha de caracol . . .'. Under 'caracola': '1. Caracol marino grande, de forma cónica, que, abierto por el vértice y soplando por él, produce un sonido de trompa . . .'. As the idea of the shell is common to both words, and the idea of the mollusc within the shell at variance with the context, we have taken both words as used by Prados (here and in 'Cantar sonámbulo') to mean 'shell'.

6 We have already noticed that a feature of Prados's work is the use of the same word for two different units of experience. In *Cuerpo perseguido* such opposites as 'cuerpo' and 'alma ' were sometimes interchanged. The poem 'Fuentes de bautismo' contains the expression: 'en la carne del alma' (66:II,244). The opening of the third stanza of 'Soledades' contains a further example of this technique. The 'yo' is, as our interpretation of the poem suggested, 'sin cuerpo'. It seems at first sight inconsistent, then, that the shell, the symbol of the body, according to our interpretation, should also be 'sin cuerpo'—until we remember that it is quite possible for Prados to be referring here to a completely different kind of body, that of the 'body of the soul' mentioned in 'Fuentes de bautismo'. Read in this way, the lines are a simple statement of what we have taken to be the poem's central situation—the 'soul', the 'yo' apart from the body, and, as a result, the body distant from the soul, the protagonist.

7 The *creative* aspect of the poet's work is, as well, another form of the much-sought fertility to which we have so often referred. In a slightly different context Jung underlines the relationship between 'naming' and 'creating': 'The act of naming is, like baptism, extremely important as regards the creation of personality . . .' (*Symbols of Transformation*, p. 187).

8 J. R. Jiménez, *Tercera antología poética*, p. 626.

9 J. L. Cano, 'La poesía de Emilio Prados', *Ínsula*.

10 T. McFarland, *Coleridge and the Pantheist Tradition* (Oxford, 1969), pp. 121–2.

11 These lines are, incidentally, a significant confirmation of our view that the final stage of the protagonist's evolution involves a return to childhood—to the 'jardín perdido' of the preceding chapter. I am indebted to J. M. Aguirre for drawing my attention to this nursery song—from which these lines must spring and which thereby link this record of his adult experience with that of the child: 'Arroyo claro, / fuente serena, / quién te lavó el pañuelo / saber quisiera. / Me lo ha lavado una serrana / en el río de Atocha / que corre el agua . / Una le lava, / otra le tiende. / Otra le tira rosas, / y otra claveles. / Tú eres la rosa, / yo soy el lirio. / ¡Quién fuera cordón de oro / de tu justillo!' (words from the record: *En el patio de mi casa*, Coros de escuelas avemarianas.) The similarity cannot be coincidental. For Lorca's use of the same song, in addition to an alternative reference, see C. B. Morris, *A Generation of Spanish Poets*, pp. 49–50.

12 Plotinus, *The Enneads*, p. xliii.

EPILOGUE

This analysis has led to the conclusion that *Río natural* marks the end of a long journey of doubt and self-discovery. The central figure is entirely reconciled to the nature of his body; he is no longer reduced to meaningless escapism; he is aware of what he sees as the presence of the infinite around and, indeed, within him. Detailed comment on poetry Prados wrote after *Río natural* lies outside the scope of this survey. Brief reference will be made here, by way of a post-script, to aspects of poetic technique which serve to indicate that *Río natural* does indeed mark a climax of achievement and which suggest that remaining books are to be seen as a celebration of fulfilment rather than further steps toward it.

In his exploration of the poetry of Jorge Guillén Dr Havard argues the importance of the mandala symbol in the expression of the world-view of *Cántico*. He comments:

> Probably the most immediate impression that the mandala symbol conveys is that of totality.[1]

Such poems as 'Perfección del círculo' are quoted in relation to this theme:

> Misterio perfecto,
> Perfección del círculo,
> Círculo del circo
> Secreto del cielo.[2]

It is this preoccupation with the circle and the curve, the mark, according to the authorities Havard cites, of an experience of totality and fulfilment, which informs the symbolism of Prados's final work.[3]

The opening poem of *Circuncisión del sueño*, 'El presente feraz', is concerned with one of the most potent of mandala symbols—the sun. Its power, virile and cohesive, self-supporting, life-giving are captured in the poem's final stanza:

> Presente sin retiro, advenimiento,
> estancia: el sol—abierto al mediodía—

al Sur condensa un rayo y, por él, baja
—paloma en vuelo al nido—, luz continuo.
En torno a un trigo abandonado, en tierra
el sol, alumbra a un círculo de sombra . . .
Centrado a él, el trigo su luz abre . . .
¡Entre a su campo el sol bajo el olvido! (II,627)

This is the same central figure who once fled before the sun's appearance. The extent of his progress is immediately apparent and re-affirmed throughout later writings. The poem 'Torre de señales', from *La piedra escrita* contains these lines:

¡Gloria! ¡Gloria! ¿El laurel escapa? . . .
(Piedra y pájaro—inversos—lo cabalgan.)

Fuenta redonda. ¿Hacia qué cumbre,
herencia de un laurel, el día sube?

(Fuente redonda. Lo infinito
se asoma al día y cruza lo infinito.) (II,760)

A sense of unity and infiniteness pervades the section 'El cielo sin reposo'—and again images of circularity are prominent:

Invisible infinito:
redondo y ciego número
aumento atrás y alante,
nunca en cero, renuevas.
. . . .
Uno grande,
completo: el uno esfera
—mito que se pronuncia
solamente en la vida
total, . . . (II,799)

As described in the final chapter, the experience of the eternal he sensed as a child is once more to be enjoyed. In 'Cuando era primavera' he remembered that: 'Cuando era primavera en España: / todas las playas convergían en un anillo'. Once more his world-picture has become predominated by the completeness which that long-lost ring represents. His new-found appreciation of what *Signos de ser* calls the 'redondo abrigo' which the sun affords confirms the end of the fragmentation described in *Cuerpo perseguido* and an end to the infertility which has, since *Tiempo*, weighed on the poetry's central *persona*.

The image of the circle is part of the expression of that

contemplation of the natural world which marks the third section of *Signos del ser*, and which contrasts so strongly with the frustrated circularity of poems such as 'Bosque de la noche' (58:I,242). In poem XV we read:

> Las adelfas se inclinan sobre el agua.
> (¿No han sentido el lamento tan continuo
> de esta bandera en parto?) El agua inclina
> su cuerpo a las adelfas . . . ¡Todo es círculo! (II,966)

References to a universal fertility (where circularity is again implicit) abound:

> Ahora no hay yermo. En soledad el aire
> que te suspende y centra, y da su fruta
> de silencio aparente, es voluntad
> de una caricia fecundada. (II,971)

The old central figure would have fled such open contact with the fertile natural world. But the body, which has emerged as the major motif of Prados poetry, is no longer the problem it was. He writes in an earlier poem in the book:

> No tengo párpados . . .
> . . . .
> Sin límites, soy vida y sueño, en mí (II,931)

Dream and reality are one. The true purpose of the body is becoming more and more clear:

> En esta dalia azul, inacabada,
> tu cuerpo se completa, en su color,
> tus límites se apuran. El aroma,
> apenas perceptible en ti, ya es luz
> de otro planeta. Y va rodando lejos,
> sin tu sabor, la gota de rocío
> devanándose. Acude, toca el pétalo
> que acaricia al pistilo que lo engendra . . .
> Olvida en él tu cuerpo sin sentidos. (II,970)

The body which plagued him as the battlefield of his private 'guerra civil', the 'cuerpo sin sentidos' as far as fertility and the infinite are concerned, is no more. The 'yo' now has a sense of belonging to an all-embracing total system which, in his own view at least, has brought him, unfailingly, 'sin límites', to the eternal.

A further direct contrast with earlier work lies in a shift of emphasis in the poetry's distinctive 'voice', as observed at the close of Chapter 2. Insubstantiality and abstraction are replaced by a concrete solidity of image. Doubt gives way to affirmation. The question-mark typical of *Cuerpo perseguido* has already, by *Río natural*, become a vivid apostrophe, typified in this confident assertion from 'Cuerpos de un nombre':

¡Mi río es Dios! ¡El agua ha despertado!
¡Sueño en el agua por qué he sido
y bebo al cielo en mí que al cielo subo,
porque me voy, porque me voy del agua! (286:II,514)

Poems such as 'Libertad dirigida' (from *Circuncisión del sueño*) provide examples of this increased 'solidarity'—in the reference to specific months and times of years, in the use of everyday sayings. Though the overall sense remains dark, the texture of the poetry is more closely rooted in a shared experience:

¡Abril las aguas mil las aguas llueve!
Fiel de un reflejo intemporal, el agua
cruzó en la luz de un cielo sin espacio;
entró en Abril de Abriles mil desnuda,
y al cielo limpio, Abril los cielos mil,
sus lunas va clavando en altas noches
que, en nubes mil, el cielo le devuelve
deshecho en flor—en nubes mil—de lluvia. (II,647)

In addition to the echo of Machado's 'Son de Abril las aguas mil', Sanchis Banús rightly notes a tendency towards 'sintaxis saltarina, encabalgamientos, reiteración llevada a su grado máximo . . .'[4] The vigour of the poetry, far from waning, seems to gain strength—a vigour sufficient to distinguish it from the measured serenity of Jiménez's later years, to which, in terms of content, it bears a certain affinity. It could be said that the emphasis in Jiménez is on 'being'—reflected by the exclusion of verbs in the closing lines of 'Despierto a mediodía', from *Dios deseado y deseante*:

Y el pleno sol te llena, con su carbón dentro,
como la luna anoche te llenaba,
y cual eras la luna, el sol eres tú solo,
solo pues que eres todo.

Conciencia en pleamar y pleacielo,
en pleadios, en éstasis obrante universal.[5]

The final poem of *Circuncisión del sueño* is in contrast entirely taken up with action—specific, concrete, simple:

Tiré un trigo al cielo. El agua
lo desnudó de su cuerpo:
¡trigo es el cielo y me canta! (II,676)

Such exuberance of expression is a reminder that the dream, the escape from reality, the search for identity, the inhibiting awareness of infertility have passed away. The protagonist is at work in the centre of a new order of his own creating. If it is also, to the impartial observer, one of his own imagining, it is nevertheless an order in which he feels himself to be accepted, valuable, active and fertile.

1 R. G. Harvard, *Image and Theme in Jorge Guillén's 'Cántico'*, Ph.D thesis, University of Wales 1968, p. 40, in the National Library of Wales.
2 J. Guillén, *Cántico*, p. 80.
3 As well as the work of J. E. Cirlot, to which reference has already been made, see C. G. Jung, *The Collected Works*, vol. 12 (1953), pp. 91–8, where he writes on 'The Symbolism of the Mandala'.
4 J. Sanchis Banús, 'Temas y formas . . .', pp. 55–6.
5 J. R. Jiménez, *Tercera antologia poética*, pp. 983–4.

PUBLISHED WORKS OF EMILIO PRADOS

Tiempo. Veinte poemas en verso, Imprenta "Sur", Málaga, 1925.
Canciones del farero, Litoral, 1926.
Vuelta (Seguimientos-Ausencias), 5th supplement to *Litoral*, Málaga, 1927.
El Llanto subterráneo, Ediciones Héroe, Madrid, 1936.
Llanto en la sangre. Romances 1933–1936, Ediciones Españolas, Valencia, 1937.
Cancionero menor para los combatientes (1936–1938), Ediciones literarias del comisariado del Ejército del Este, Montserrat, 1938.
Memoria del Olvido, Editorial Séneca, México, 1940.
Mínima muerte, Tezontle, México, 1944.
Jardín cerrado, Cuadernos americanos, México, 1946.
Dormido en la yerba, Imprenta Dardo, Málaga, 1953.
Antología 1923–1953, Losada, Buenos Aires, 1954.
Río natural, Losada, Buenos Aires, 1957.
Circuncisión del sueño, Tezontle, México, 1957.
La sombra abierta, supplement to Ecuador O°O′O″, México, 1961.
La piedra escrita, Universidad Nacional Autónoma de México, 1961.
Transparencias, Colección cuadernos de María Cristina Caffarena, no. 12, Málaga.
Signos del ser, Ediciones de *Papeles de Son Armadans*, Palma de Mallorca, 1962.
Últimos poemas, "El guadalhorce", Málaga, 1965.
Diario Intimo, "El guadalhorce", Málaga, 1966.
Cuerpo perseguido, Editorial Lasor, Barcelona, 1971.
Poesías completas, edited by C. B. Aguinaga and A. Carreira, vol. I, Aguilar, México, 1975; vol. II, 1976.

GENERAL BIBLIOGRAPHY

(1) *Books*

Aguirre, J. M. *Antonio Machado, poeta simbolista* , Taurus, Madrid, 1973.

Alberti, R. *Poesía (1924–1967)*, Aguilar, Madrid, 1977.

El poeta en la calle, Aguilar, Madrid, 1978.

Aleixandre, V. *Los encuentros*, Guadarrama, Madrid, 1958.

Obras completas, Aguilar, Madrid, 1968.

Allen, W. *The Timeless Moment*, Faber and Faber Ltd., London, 1946.

Aub, M. *La poesía española contemporánea*, Imprenta Universitaria, México, 1954.

Bachelard, G. *L'Air et les Songes*, Corti, Paris, 1943 (reprinted 1950).

L'Eau et les Rêves, Corti, Paris, 1942 (reprinted 1956).

La Poétique de la Rêverie, Presses Universitaires de France, Paris, 1960.

Brown, C. G. *A Literary History of Spain: The Twentieth Century*, Ernest Benn Ltd., London, 1972.

Cernuda, L. *La realidad y el deseo*, 3rd edition, Tezontle, México, 1958.

Ocnos, Universidad Veracruzana, México, 1963.

Chevalier, J. *Dictionnaire des symboles*, Laffont, Paris, 1969.

Cirlot, J. E. *A Dictionary of Symbols*, translated by J. Sage, Routledge and Kegan Paul, London, 1962.

Debicki, A. *Estudios sobre poesía española contemporánea*, Gredos, Madrid, 1968.

Deck, J. N. *Nature, Contemplation and the One*, University of Toronto Press, 1967.

Durán Gili, M. *El superrealismo en la poesía española contemporánea*, Universidad Nacional Autónoma de México, México, 1950.

Fausset, H. *Fruits of Silence*, Abelard-Schuman, London–New York–Toronto, 1963.

Field, G. C. *The Philosophy of Plato*, Oxford University Press, 1969.

Freud, S. *The Complete Psychological Works*, translated under general editorship of J. Strachey, Vols. IV and V.

The Interpretation of Dreams, Hogarth Press, London, 1953.

Guillén, J. *Cántico*, first edition, Editorial Sudamericana, Buenos Aires, 1950.

Hamburger, M. *The Truth of Poetry*, Pelican, Harmondsworth, 1972.

Harris, D. *Luis Cernuda, A Study of the Poetry*, Tamesis Books Ltd., London, 1973.

Havard, R. G. *Image and Theme in Jorge Guillén's* Cántico, Ph.D thesis, University of Wales, 1968.

Jiménez, J. R. *Tercera antología poética, 1898–1953*, Editorial Biblioteca Nueva, Madrid, 1957.

Jung, C. G. *The Collected Works of C. G. Jung*, edited by Sir R. Head, M. Fordham, G. Adler, Routledge and Kegan Paul, London.

Vol. V, *Symbols of Transformation*, 1956.

Vol. XII, *Psychology and Alchemy*, 1953.

Vol. XIV, *Mysterium Coniunctionis*, 1963.

Psychology of the Unconscious, translated by B. M. Hinkle, Kegan Paul, Trench, Trubner and Co. Ltd., London, 1916.

Man and His Symbols, edited under C. G. Jung, Aldis, London, 1964.

Knowles, Dom D. *What is Mysticism?*, Burns and Oates Ltd., London, 1967.

Laing, R. D. *The Divided Self*, Pelican, Harmondsworth, 1970.

Lorca, F. G. *Obras completas*, Aguilar, Madrid, 1957.

Machado, A. *Obras, poesía y prosa*, edited by A. de Albornoz and G. de la Torre, Losada, Buenos Aires, 1964.

Poesías de guerra de Antonio Machado, edited by A. de Albornoz, Ediciones Asomante, San Juan, Puerto Rico, 1961.

McFarland, T. *Coleridge and the Pantheist Tradition*, Oxford University Press, 1969.

Morris, C. B. *A Generation of Spanish Poets, 1920–1936*, Cambridge University Press, 1969.

Rafael Alberti, Sobre los ángelos: *Four Major Themes*, Hull, 1966.

Surrealism and Spain, 1920–1936, Cambridge, 1972.

Newman, J. H. *The Mystical Rose*, St. Paul Publications, 1960.

Olson, P. R. *The Circle of Paradox: Time and Essence in the Poetry of Juan Ramón Jiménez*, The John Hopkins Press, Baltimore, 1967.

Piaget, J. *Six Psychological Studies*, translated by A. Tenzer, University of London Press Ltd., 1968.

Plato, *Symposium*, translated by M. Joyce, Dent, London, 1935.

Plotinus, *The Enneads*, translated by S. McKenna, Faber and Faber Ltd., London, 1962.

Poulet, G. *The Metamorphosis of the Circle*, translated by C. Dawson and E. Coleman, The John Hopkins Press, Baltimore, 1966.

Quevedo, F. de, *Obras completas*, vol. I, edited by J. M. Blecua, Planeta, Barcelona, 1963.

Rilke, R. M. *Obras de Rainer María Rilke*, translated by J. M. Valverde, Plaza y Janes, Barcelona, 1967.

Seward, B. *The Symbolic Rose*, Columbia University Press, New York, 1960.

Silver, P. "Et in Arcadia Ego": *A Study of the Poetry of Luis Cernuda*, Tamesis Books Ltd., London, 1965.

Stewart, W. S. *The Divided Self*, George Allen and Unwin Ltd., London, 1964.

Underhill, E. *Mysticism*, Methuen, London, 1957.

Wright, G. T. *The Poet in the Poem*, University of California Press, Los Angeles, 1960.

(2) *Articles*

Aguirre, J. M. 'El sonambulismo de Federico García Lorca', *BHS*, XLIV, no. 4, 1967, pp. 267–285.

'La poesía primera de Luis Cernuda', *HR*, XXXIV, 1966, pp. 121–134.

Cross, R. C. 'Logos and Forms in Plato', in *Studies in Plato's Metaphysics*, edited by R. E. Allan, Routledge and Kegan Paul, London, 1965.

Bibliography of Articles and Books on The Work and Life of Emilio Prados referred to in the text

(For a complete bibliography, see *Poesías completas*, Vol. I, pp. LXIX–XCV.)

Aleixandre, V. 'Emilio Prados, en su origen', *Insula*, no. 187, 1962, pp. 1–2.

'Emilio Prados, vivo', *Índice de Artes y Letras*, no. 168, 1962, p. 16.

Allué y Morer, F. 'El poeta Emilio Prados', *Poesía Española*, May, 1962.

Andújar, M. 'Primeras palabras en torno a Emilio Prados', *Ínsula*, no. 187, 1962, p. 3. Also in *Índice de Artes y Letras*, no. 168, p. 16.

Aparicio, F. 'La soledad in Emilio Prados', *Caracola*, no. 49, Málaga, 1956.

Blanco Aguinaga, C. 'La aventura poética de Emilio Prados', *Revista Mexicana de Literatura*, no. 8, 1956.

Emilio Prados: Vida y obra. Bibliografía. Antología, New York, 1960. Also in *Revista Hispánica Moderna*, XXVI, 1960, pp. 1–107.

Lista de los papeles de Emilio Prados, The Johns Hopkins Press, Baltimore, 1967.

Cano, J. L. 'La poesía de Emilio Prados', *Ínsula*, IX, no. 97, 1954, pp. 6–7.

'Presencia viva de Emilio', *Ínsula*, no. 187, 1962, p. 3.

Carreira, A. 'La primera salida de Emilio Prados', *Homenaje universitario a Dámaso Alonso*, Gredos, Madrid, 1970, pp. 221–30.

Cela, C. J. 'Carta truncada a un poeta en el cielo de México', *Papeles de Son Armadans*, XXV, no. LXXIV, 1962, pp. 115–18.

Ciplijauskaite, B. *La soledad* y *la poesía española contemporánea*, Insula, Madrid, 1962.

Ciariana, B. 'Emilio Prados: *Llanto en la sangre*', *Hora de España*, X, 1937, pp. 74–5.

Debicki, A. P. 'Unos procedimientos sintácticos en la poesía de Emilio Prados', in *Estudios sobre poesía española contemporánea*, Gredos, Madrid, 1968, pp. 307–20.

Díaz-Plaja, G. 'La luna y la nueva poesía', *La Gaceta literaria*, no. 61, July 1929, p. 6.

Diego, G. 'Emilio Prados: *Vuelta*', *Revista de Occidente*, XVII, no. LI, 1927, pp. 384–7.

Durán Gili, M. *El superrealismo en la poesía española contemporánea*, Universidad Nacional Autónama de México, México, 1950.

García Ascot, J. M. 'Para Emilio', *Ínsula*, no. 187, 1962, p. 2.

Landa, R. 'Emilio Prados como maestro', *Ínsula*, no. 242, 1967, p. 14.

Larrea, J. 'Ingreso a una transfiguración', in *Jardín cerrado*, Cuadernos Americanos, México, 1946.

Lechner, J. *El compromiso en la poesía española del siglo XX*, 2 volumes, Universitaire Pers Leiden, 1968.

Luis, L. de 'Dormido en la yerba', *Poesía Española*, no. 25, 1954, pp. 24–5.

'Emilio Prados', *Papeles de Son Armadans*, XXV, no. LXXV, 1962, pp. 333–5.

Monterde, F. 'Obra de dos poetas españoles en América', *Cuadernos americanos*, no. 3, 1955, pp. 284–6.

Morris, C. B. *A Generation of Spanish Poets, 1920—1936*, University Press, Cambridge, 1969.

Muñoz Rojas, J. A. 'Las caídas de Emilio', *Ínsula*, no. 187, 1962, p. 2.

Nuñez, V. 'Sobre *El dormido en la yerba*', *Cuadernos de Literatura*, no. 82, Madrid, 1953.

'Sobre Prados: *Río natural*', *Ínsula*. no. 142, 1958, p. 7.

Porlán y Merlo, R. 'Sobre *Tiempo*, Poemas de Emilio Prados', *Mediodía*, no. 4, 1926, p. 16.

Salazar y Chapela, E. 'Sobre *Vuelta*', *El Sol*, Madrid, Junc, 1927.

Sanchis Banús, J. 'Temas y formas en la obra de Emilio Prados', Sorbonne Thesis, 1959.

Souvirón, J. M. 'Sobre: *El dormido en la yerba*', *Caracola*, no. 12, 1953.

Zardoya, C. 'Emilio Prados, poeta de la melancolía', in *Poesía española contemporánea*, Guadarrama, Madrid, 1961, pp. 431–5.

'La obra poética de Emilio Prados', *Revista Hispánica Moderna*, XXII, no. 34, 1956, pp. 304–5.

APPENDICES

Appendix I: 'Apuntes para nada menos que una "Declaración estética" que le piden a un servidor de Vds'

Appendix II: Excerpts from 'Recuerdos de mi vida . . .'

Appendix III: 'Las tres noches del hombre'

Appendix IV: 'Retratos'

Appendix V: A Classification of Prados's output

Appendix VI: A group of unpublished poems

APPENDIX I

'Apuntes para nada menos que una "Declaración estética" que le piden a un servidor de Vds.'[1]

Para mí, la poesía, siempre es un secreto que no trato de descubrir sino que, como a una flecha, dejo que vaya ahondando más y más en mis entrañas; porque mientras esté el secreto clavado en ellas existirá conmigo la poesía, pero si me lo arranco, si lo descubro, presiento que la poesía se me convertirá, para siempre, en angustia.

La poesía, en mí, se precisa en su misterio. Y surge al entregarse.

El misterio de la poesía es su virginidad permanente.

La entrega de la poesía no significa la entrega de su misterio.

Yo no puedo impedir que en la poesía se despierta la reflexión; pero esta reflexión hago que se refleje el sujeto, no fuera, sino dentro de la poesía , en su secreto, ¿en su centro?

La poesía ama apasionadamente a los tiempos opuestos.

La herencia del Pasado y la del Futuro, en el sujeto reflejado dentro de la poesía—que los une—es la Trinidad que le da vida.

Por eso yo nunca estoy solo en mi poesía, si no es en sentido figurado.

Y si aparentemente yo en mi poesía conmigo oscila entre el ser y el no ser es por amor. El secreto de mi poesía es como un fiel de equilibrio al que se unen los cuerpos de un Futuro que todavía no ha proyectado en mí, desde una memoria, un nombre vivo y los cuerpos de un Pasado (que yo como al Futuro considero presente) y el que sólo me llega en símbolos vivos, también innominados, a través del sueño ¿o ensueño?

Al centro de su fiel en equilibrio, apasionadamente consumida por el amor, la poesía se hace palabra en la unidad de la cruz: nombre secreto, escrito en ella sobre el alma. Por eso si la poesía cumple alguna vez su fin es siempre sobrenatural.[2]

1 Taken from the Prados Papers, Caja 20.3.

2 These comments are undated. They are to be found, however amongst papers obviously written fairly late in Prados's life. This is no doubt why much of its content aligns it closely in tone with the post-anthology books. In *Circunsión del sueño*, for example, there is a very intense preoccupation with the question of time. Nevertheless its opening sentences, in their emphasis on 'el misterio de la poesía' have a relevance to Prados's work as a whole—as we suggest in the 'Introduction' and seek to confirm in the main body of the study.

APPENDIX II

Excerpts from the Autobiographical 'Recuerdos de mi vida (1899 . . .)[1]

Prados notes the effect on him of the journeys made around 1911 up the 'cuesta de la matanza' towards 'Los montes':

> A mí me sobrecogía enormemente, sin saber por qué, esta parada y ver a la ciudad [Málaga] cubierta como de una niebla plana y rojiza que parecía defenderla . . .
>
> . . . Después de "La Venta", la carretera seguía llana y bordeada de magníficos alcornoques de tronco color de sangre y hoja espesa—verde oscura. Toda esta parte del camino estaba tan llena de silencio y majestad que nadie hablaba. Yo, la verdad es, que sentía un miedo espantoso en ello, pero me callaba también y nunca lo dije.
>
> (dated October 1961)

On a less happy note we have this decription of life in the 'Instituto Nacional de 2ª enseñanza':

> El ambiente estudiantil era el reflejo de todo aquello. Las faltas a clase estaban considerados como un signo de virilidad. Alguna vez que intenté vencer al grupo que delante de la puerta de la clase obstaculizaba la entrada a ella fui arrojado por las escaleras a empellones, rodando hasta el patio en medio de los gritos de mofa y la risa general. Casi diariamente había algún incidente grave entre los compañeros. La moral no existía. Se debía faltar a clase o no se era hombre . . .

The folder contains more than one attempt at describing his early years. Here is how another begins:

> Nací en Málaga el día 4 de Marzo del año 1899. En Málaga pasé mi infancia y estudié mis primeras letras.
>
> Desde muy pequeño sufrí mucho a causa de mi salud y—quizá también por el mismo motivo—, con el concepto que me iba formando de un mundo, contrario en toda relación al mundo de los que me rodeaban. Premonición; lo que más tarde—ya sometido a tratamiento médico—me dieron a conocer con el nombre de "pavor nocturno", y el misterio de mi soledad, que poblé de elementos

1 These are contained in Caja 20.3 according to Blanco's classification, in the *Lista de los papeles de Emilio Prados.*

naturales para la observación y experiencia directa de la vida, fueron creándome, sin yo saberlo, ese concepto en el que, como lugar de apartamiento, yo me ocultaba para poder vivir sin oposición alguna el juego o sueño—terrible a veces—que tan extraño e invisible era para los demás.

Creo que a estos primeros años debo la formación principal de mis sentimientos. Y me parece recordarlos entre los cuatro y los ocho o nueve de mi vida.

Después de ellos, y en vista de que mi afección pulmonar no mejoraba, tuve que pasar algunos años en el campo, en 'los montes de Málaga' situados entre dicha provincia y la de Granada. La vida me abrió entonces con alegría a lo real, salvándome. Al contacto directo con la naturaleza no contemplada, sino vivida, aprendida en su cuerpo verdadero, las anteriores observaciones y experiencias de mi soledad, hallaron su verificación normal. Inconscientemente aún, pude sentir la unificación de mis dos mundos: el que ocultaba en mi refugio incomprendido, primero, y el de la verdad tangible que la realidad me entregaba en lo natural hacia mis doce años de edad. La impresión fue tan fuerte que, aún en mis poemas actuales 'Río natural', 'Circuncision del sueño', viven la misma tierra, el agua, el aire, y el cielo que comencé a sentir entonces.

Sobre esta base principal y real se fundamentó la poesía que, más tarde, nostálgica y ausente daría en mi palabra. Un punto solamente quedaba sin solucionar para mí entonces, y ese punto mismo vive sin solucionar en mí, hoy, haciendo que por él siga sintiéndome constantemente 'cuerpo perseguido'. (¿Acaso en ese punto está la unión invisible de los mundos de que hablo?) Casi podría afirmar que esta unidad—equilibrio inestable—es transparente de la premonición que temo y que deseo a un mismo tiempo, y de la que emerge siempre 'memoria del olvido', mi palabra poética.

Por sentirlo así me he detenido algo más en ello. Todo lo que posteriormente puede referirse a mi vida particular, lo considero como accidentes de mi persona, que unas veces borran y otras recalcan con mayor energía, el centro de mí mismo que nació sin saberlo dentro de aquellos años lejanos que aún me poseen.

The folder also contains this interesting account of his stay in the Residencia and the type of education received prior to it:

Llego a Madrid en 1914 (principios de la 1ª guerra mundial). Ingreso en Residencia de Estudiantes (grupo preparatorio). A causa del fallecimiento de D. Francisco Giner (1915) asisto con mi hermano a reuniones que en la Institución Libre de Enseñanza, se verifican en recuerdo del Maestro. Allí conozco a D. Manuel B. Casío, Sr. Ricardo Rubio (la hija del que, más tarde, se casara con mi hermano). Estas dos personas influyen mucho en mí, con su prestigio de fundadores de la Institución. En estas reuniones conozco también a los Machado y Juan Ramón. No recuerdo si allí también conocí a Unamuno; pero a éste le recuerdo más en la Residencia durante las charlas que tenía con nosotros por las noches, en el salón, después de la cena. En dichas reuniones de la Institución también conocí a Ortega Gasset, Fernando de los Ríos (que me ayudó más tarde mucho, para el curso de mis estudios literarios), Dr. Nicolas Achicarro, Dr Lafera, Vicente Viqueira y otros muchos nombres en los que por aquel momento, se centraba la atención intelectual de toda España.

Este ambiente anterior me hizo un gran bien y fue la cura principal que entonces tuvo mi espíritu adolorido por la incomprensión de los profesores y compañeros que en la 2ª de Málaga tanto daño me hicieron.

Nota (¿Tendré que recordar toda mi vida en la escuela, el Instituto etc. con el cúmulo de inmoralidades que la llenaban? Mala ensenanza, injusticia de ella (como en la Historia, Religión, Psicolõgía, Educación física, Literatura, Dibujo artístico etc.) y aún mayor la lucha con la perversión de los compañeros?—perversión sexual, poco deseo de estudio, mofa y golpes contra los que se negaban a seguirles en sus brutalidades) ¡Aquel instituto malagueño, antiguo convento, creo que de agustinos, en el que recuerdo a su entrada este lema 'Prima sapientia est vita laudabilis'! En ese patio, donde estaba la frase que cito, se golpearon el Dr. del Instituto y el padre del filósofo M. Gª Morente, al que después de sus estudios de Francia (en la Sorbonne) suspendieron en Málaga, únicamente por no conocer sus ideas (de entonces).[2]

El bien que me hizo el ambiente de la Institución, así como de la Residencia de Estudiantes (continuación de aquél) quedó roto con mi entrada a la Universidad Central, en Madrid, la cual era a su vez como una continuación de los que dejé en Málaga. Al mismo tiempo me sentía presa de una gran angustia al notar que incluso en la educación institucionista que venía recibiendo había grandes contradicciones entre lo aconsejado y las realizaciones más cumplidas, por mí, del consejo recibido. Si en Málaga (en la primaria) se me hablaba de caridad y yo la realizaba, se me llevaba a un médico, y si aquí (en plena adolescencia) mis relaciones amorosas las conducía según lo aconsejado, se me trató, a veces, de expulsar de la escuela. (¿Recordar a Mª Maeztu y mi amistad con Jimena Menéndez y otras muchachas de la Residencia de Señoritas en Fortuny).

A todo esto puso fin mi enfermedad y el tenerme que aislar obligatoriamente en Suiza, hizo que, después de una gran crisis llena

2 Between 'únicamente' and '(de entonces)' the original is not very clear.

de un sentimiento de culpa, ante una culpa inexistente, reaccionara a mi modo, en mi soledad salvándome y trazando los cimientos de la personalidad que me llevaría ya para toda la vida hasta lo que hoy continúo.

Entonces, al aclararse dentro de mí las cosas fue cuando decidí el dedicar mi vida a la filosofia, error que más tarde me harían comprender entrando con ello dentro del mundo mío poético en el que ya iba enriquecido por el conocimiento que adquirí en la Residencia debido a mis buenos maestros, Gª Morente, Landa, Millares, Santullano, Jiménez, Fráid etc. y al trato de otros que, como ya dije Unamuno, Juan Ramón, Ortega, Machado etc. (aparte de las personalidades de 1ª de otros países que nos visitaban frecuentemente) y de un grupo selecto de compañeros que en esa época vivieron conmigo en la Residencia (consultar para las conferencias "Vida en Claro" pag. 104).

Al comenzar mis nuevos estudios universitarios, empecé también a asistir al Centro de Estudios Históricos en el que trabajaba algún tiempo con Solalinde (Ricardo Oruela, Américo C., T. Navarro etc. dirigían en dicha época este Centro de Estudios).

APPENDIX III

Las tres noches del hombre[1]

Por tres noches oscuras, tiene que atravesar, para vivir, el hombre:

La primera es la infancia. En ella sólo alcanza a ver las cosas que le rodean, sin conocer sus nombres, sin poder comprender la esencia de ellas. Por eso, el hombre se pasma ante lo que contempla y aún no teniendo conciencia de sí mismo, se pierde de él, abriéndose amorosamente al universo que ama sin saberlo.

Es entonces cuando el universo comienza a hablar a su modo, con su presencia, removiendo dentro del niño todo aquello de más valor que trae, como herencia de luz, en su sangre.

Así, primeramente hablan las partes perdidas (átomos ya) de un nombre que fue tallado en la piedra. Ellos hablan como nostálgicos del cuerpo a que pertenecieron (como partes del todo que ellas suponen fue su cuerpo).

Esto lo hace sentirse cuerpo, por primera vez. Pero cuerpo en noche oscura, puesto que de él nada sabe.

Mira hacia los cuerpos que le rodean y siente la compañía y el calor de ellos, pero tampoco sabe en que se fundan.

Es el tiempo el que despacio le irá diciendo, primeramente, lo que es. Y, para ello utiliza igualmente que la primera materia consultada el nombre ante el cual el muchacho quedó primeramente sorprendido.

Quiere meditar sobre lo dicho por el tiempo el muchacho; pero le falta conocimiento para ello, y es el polvo, a través también, del nombre grabado el que le habla en nombre del *mundo* del cual él fue, aún es y seguirá siendo.

Ya casi comprende el niño lo que dice la voz del polvo, pero para hacerlo pensamiento propio le falta inteligencia.

Y, es entonces cuando habla el viento y ahuyentando al polvo del mundo le comienza a dar vida al espíritu, contando la historia suya (la del viento, como soplo de vida).

El niño comienza a comprender pero algo se le resiste a la inteligencia. Le faltan elementos con los que poder comparar.[2] ¡Tal

1 The words 'de mujer' have been lightly scored over.

2 An extremely important statement when considered in the light of our analysis of the protagonist's attitude to his body in the *Antología*.

vez dolor! Quiere preguntar al viento pero: ¿dónde está? . . .

Y es el rocío el que le habla de su fábula, y hoy, llena el hueco del nombre grabado en la piedra ante la que se encuentra el muchacho.

La luz suave de la Luna brilla sobre el rocío y calma la primera tristeza del niño que, aún sin conocerlo, ya presiente el dolor que le espera.

La 2ª noche del hombre es su adolescencia. Ella es casi como una continuación de la misma oscuridad de la infancia y únicamente el presentimiento, lleno de inquietud, la diferencia de ella.

Sí, tiene nuevos elementos y comienza a ver su inteligencia casi naciendo; pero ¿y los nombres de ella? A través, juntamente del nombre de mujer inscrito ante sus ojos comienza a sentir un impulso amoroso casi agradecido, ya que es, debido a ese nombre misterioso, a lo que él mismo va encontrándose.[1]

Y siente que la sombra se le va y, teme a la luz, pero no le resiste.

La noche lo abraza y le canta amorosamente, místicamente, su propia historia; pero se acerca el alba y se va sin terminar su canción.

La luz se acerca. Desde el sol resbala suavemente sobre montes, campos y llega al nombre inscrito en la piedra.

Habla de él, del nombre y, de lo que representa el sol y el día para el hombre; pero esta vez se dirige al adolescente cuyo cuerpo *no existe* aun en la verdad . . .[2]

Mientras el día existe el hombre adolescente, tan solamente puede sentirse con todo el poder de su alma innominada.

La luz le hiere si la mira de frente (mito de la caverna de Platón). Y, entonces, cruza la nube y canta, su historia y la del hombre. La sombra de la nube, llena el hueco del nombre inscrito.

Cae la lluvia y lo llena, fecundándolo:

Canta la lluvia su canción propia de fecundidad de la tierra.

Pero el sol aprieta y la nube se deshace.

La fuerza del fuego evapora al agua que al subir canta su canción de eternidad.

Comprende a medias el adolescente la canción del agua que no habla del nombre inscrito pero si del amoroso impulso que ella misma anima por la Vida . . .

Trata de comprender y mira al nombre inscrito ante sus ojos.

Es casi atardecer. Una rama de un árbol cercano vierte sobre el nombre la sombra de sus tallos en primavera. El adolescente ve que entre las hojas, en la sombra, un pájaro canta junto al nido . . .

Levanta la cabeza (su imagen) para mirarlo y, mientras la tarde cae:

Canta la tarde toda su historia de crepúsculos y de amor. (***romanticismo).[3]

Entra el adolescente en la 3ª noche del hombre.

La noche reanuda entonces su canción interrumpida por la fuerza del alba y hace junto con ello una breve historia de la vida del hombre.

La Luna, vuelve a salir y ahora sin referirse al hueco del hombre inscrito en la piedra, habla al hombre de amor, de fábula y belleza . . .

Al referirse al amor quiere situarlo en el corazón del hombre y al señalarlo, sólo ve una rosa blanca sobre un rosal joven.

La rosa canta y dice que sí es ella, el corazón del hombre: en ella está el símbolo de la vida, de la belleza, del amor y de la pureza.

Corta el muchacho en su movimiento inconsciente la rosa blanca y la coloca sobre el nombre inscrito en la piedra (¡cualquier nombre primero!) al que debe todo su conocimiento amoroso propio.

Al hacerlo se oye la voz del olvido que vive (ya sin serlo sobre el sueño) y la voz del sueño que a su vez vive por el hombre y canta al fin el hombre que sale del olvido (noche oscura en que estaba).

Hombre, sueño y olvido se acercan a besar la rosa blanca; pero la rosa blanca, se ha fundido amorosa sobre el hueco del nombre grabado en la piedra.

Sólo queda la piedra como página blanca frente al cielo.

En donde estaba el nombre y la rosa se unen los labios del Olvido, el Sueño y el Hombre en un solo beso de una sola persona.

Canta la esperanza desde la piedra blanca ya cumplido su ser encarnado de nuevo por la rosa (átomos que separaron de ella).

El hombre mira a su alrededor. No hay límites. Vive el espacio infinito en el cual todo lo ama. No hay muros en el jardín ni piel en su cuerpo.[4] Todas las cosas son su esencia viva eterna.

Es entonces cuando el hombre comprende sus nupcias . . . ¿Acaso con la muerte, puesto que un nombre de muerte era el que ante sí tenía y ya no ve?

Habla la muerte desde dentro del hombre y él, al cantar, canta al

3 *** The text is not clear here.

4 It is interesting that Prados chooses to associate all this very heightened level of experience with the garden.

universo unido: a la unidad del amor: al alma deseada y que en ella lleva el conocimiento de su *ser* alcanzado por el *amor* . . .

Y, ahora, de nuevo el hombre escucha como una llamada que desde los *cuerpos resucitados* le canta y hace ver que nada resucita en ellos puesto que sólo el pensamiento del hombre ha hallado, al fin, que la vida es continua: eterna.

Pero ¿cual será el nombre de esto? . . .

Todo se ha transformado por el amor, por entrega, y no no hay muerte . . .[5]

Pero ¿qué nombre nuevo ha de tener el mundo?

El hombre va a buscarlo: sale desde él mismo hacia el futuro en donde la luz lo recibe en temblor, disperso en átomos.

5 The repetition of the 'no' is in the original text.

APPENDIX IV

'Retratos'

'No estaba muerto . . .'[1]

No estaba muerto como todos creían , aunque ya todo el río le había cruzado el pecho; aunque se entraba hacia el atardecer en las iglesias sin quitarse el sombrero; aunque cruzaban las palomas de un lado a otro de su carne sin torcer ni una pluma; aunque se atravesara con alfileres como cera. Pero había comenzado a sepultarse, porque ya olía; porque ya no se reconocía él mismo en los espejos.

Un día al levantarse se olvidó de su piel, dormida entre las sábanas. Ya de vuelta, a la tarde trajo colgando de sus hombros como milagros de cartón, un árbol, cuatro barcos, un cuchillo, la luna, dos escapularios, tres niños, una piedra, y luego en su cuarto comenzó a podrirse despacio por las sienes.

Un día hacia el toque de laudes recibió el primer aviso de la paloma.[2] Resurrexit sicut dixit . . . y comenzó a abrirse su pecho como un libro. Pero el toque de prima no ya tenía memoria.

'Lo que a mí me pesa . . .'[3]

Lo que a mí me pesa es que me estoy sepultando. Eso es, que me voy hundiendo. Y en qué carne tan negra; en qué cartón tan duro. El rostro, arriba, se niega, tendido de perfil, plano, como una luna redonda de yeso. ¡Qué trabajo tan fuerte!

Me estoy sepultando como raíces, como cabellos en el agua, como orugas. Y me sepulto tembloroso, eléctrico, sonámbulo, deshilachado, colgando en hebras negras desde el rostro, parado terco en la corteza. Desde este rostro pegado arriba al fondo, como un plato vacío o como una charca de cera en la memoria.

1 The compositions which follow are to be found in Caja 1.7.
2 In the text, 'la l^{a} aviso'.
3 Like 'No estaba muerto . . .', taken from 1.7.

A mí no me importa podrirme; por eso estoy vivo. Pero mi rostro que siempre fue un horario en síntesis no quiere descomponer en sus cinco sentidos. Por eso se sostiene intacto en su negación sorda, sin podrirse, sin querer pasar a mejor vida, quedándose quieto en lo alto, muerto de perfil como una enorme moneda de yeso.

'Estábamos sentados . . .'[4]

Estábamos sentados frente a frente en mi cuarto. Apenas había luz. Nuestra conversación se había extinguido ya hacía rato y nosotros aun continuábamos mirándonos, pendiente uno de otro, como esperando que una palabra nueva viniera a deshacer toda la melancolía que nublaba nuestro pensamiento. Muy lentamente y en silencio siempre, me levanté de mi butaca y me dirigí hacia el extremo de la habitación. Una vez allí comencé a desnudarme totalmente muy despacio. Ya desnudo me tendí de espaldas con los ojos cerrados sobre mi lecho. Tú desde el mismo sitio en el que anteriormente te encontrabas me ibas siguiendo atentamente con la vista, sin comprenderme pero observando sin embargo mis menores movimientos. Me ardía el corazón. Aquella quemadura me escocía en el pecho como una lanzada. ¿Donde terminaría aquella herida? Pasé mi brazo por debajo de mi cuerpo como para cerciorarme que terminaba dentro de mi sangre, pero no pude hallar el límite de mi piel ni pude tampoco palpar la superficie del lecho sobre el que yo me creía estar recostado. Intenté abrir los ojos pero fue inútil todo esfuerzo. Volví a pasar una vez y otra mi brazo por debajo de mi espalda pero todo en vano: mi cuerpo había huído, quizá se había quedado muerto sin sentido; pero mi pensamiento todavía se encontraba allí sobre el aire inmóvil, intangible, flotando, como una nube, como un huso olvidado en el vacío.

La sombra cada vez más intensa me envolvía latiendo como un oleaje sereno. Me apretaba el silencio sobre las sienes y mi cerebro giraba terriblemente bajo mis ojos.

Abandonado ya por completo a aquel influjo misterioso, notaba yo como mi cuerpo iba ascendiendo despacio, despacio, igual que una burbuja por el agua . . . El escozor del corazón a cada momento se hacía sentir con mayor fuerza.

4 Taken from Caja 1.8.

El silencio era ya insoportable.

De repente me pareció escuchar un nombre, un nombre que se repetía una, dos, tres, cuatros infinitas veces.

Inmediatamente mi cuerpo comenzó a descender de prisa, cada vez más de prisa. El aire me zumbaba en los oídos, me arañaba en la cintura, bajo los tobillos, entre los brazos. Y yo seguía descendiendo, descendiendo, cada vez con mayor violencia, con mayor frío. La angustia me ahogaba. Ya no podía soportar más tiempo la quemadura del corazón.

De pronto un golpe seco bajo la nuca me hizo abrir de nuevo los ojos.

Mi cuerpo aun estaba tendido sobre mi lecho. La habitación toda presentaba su forma habitual, todo volvía a renacer como después de un sueño, únicamente tu cuerpo no se encontraba ya en su sitio de costumbre. ¿Te habías desaparecido quizá para siempre por llamarme? ¿Te habías filtrado bajo tu propia voz detrás del aire quizá por pronunciar mi nombre?

'Habían roto . . .'

Habían roto nuestra conversación de un golpe. Nos retiramos, como dos trozos de un elástico en tensión, que cortan, y nos quedamos recogidos, arriba en el recuerdo, medio apagados, por los aires rápidos, que el trajinar sordo de fuera, iba tratando de colgar a nuestra luciérnaga. Yo te había perdido ya; pero te tenía más así, a media entrega, casi adivinado . . .

Te había apartado con cuidado, sin forma ninguna tú, como un algodón de pensamientos, y te tenía, incubándote en tu ausencia, para seguir sin saltos nuestra conversación, cuando nos viéramos.

Nos movíamos para lo más inútil con verdadero afán de terminarlo todo a lo costumbre, para eludir preguntas, para poder abandonarnos al cuidado de nuestra crisálida anhelante, y llevarla, completada por nosotros mismos, silenciosa y cumplida en su trabajo para la reanudación .

Estábamos seguros de ella. Sabíamos ya que tendríamos que aguardar,—llenando—, un tiempo soso, sin alma apenas, que nos exigía a cada momento, tirándonos de todos nuestros miembros flojos, caídos, una mirada vacía, una mano sin calor, o un gesto sin forma; pero todo lo dábamos como si soñáramos que lo estábamos dando, seguro de que nos despertaríamos al fin, otra vez en la misma palabra que dejamos por terminar, en la misma sílaba de ella, en la misma letra sin enlace . . .

Íbamos y veníamos como hipnotizados. Yo fui el que llegué, primero, al lugar necesario, fijo, sin saberlo. Te esperaba, te esperaba . . . y de pronto apareciste.—¿por dónde?—frente a mí. ¡Me levanté! Tú sonreías. Nos saludamos mudos, nos sentamos juntos, uno al lado de otro, y comenzaste a hablar tú . . . No callabas, no te callabas nunca y no te entendía, no había ya medio de entendernos, habías cambiado de voz, de cara, de aire, de alma . . . Me volví contra el espejo, temeroso de ser yo, de haber llegado, yo, demasiado lejos, en mi espera de haberme salido del tiempo sin notarlo; pero no pude verme, no pude encontrarme ya por ningún lado . . .

Y tú seguías hablando, hablando extravagante, raro, irónico, descompasado; mientras yo veía, sin comprender, tus palabras, pasar de prisa como nubes por encima de mí, ya, como un río del recuerdo en huída . . .

Málaga 7.12.27

APPENDIX V

A classification of Prados's output[1]

I (Escritos en España)
1. Tiempo. (1923–1925)
2. El misterio del agua. (1926–1927)
3. Memoria de poesía. (1926–1927)
4. Cuerpo perseguido. (1927–1928)[2]

II
1. La voz cautiva. (1933–1934)
2. Andando, andando por el mundo. (1934–1935)
3. Llanto en la sangre. (1936–1938)

III (Escritos en México)
1. Penumbras. (1939–1941)
2. Mínima muerte. (1939–1940)
3. Jardín cerrado. (1941–1945)

IV
1. Río natural. (1950–1953)
2. Circuncisión del sueño. (1955–1956)
3. Sonoro enigma. (1956–1957)
4. La sombra abierta. (La primera parte de este libro fue escrita en 1947–1950, y la segunda en 1954–1955)

V
1. La piedra escrita. (1958–1960)
2. Signos del ser. (1960–1961)

Las fechas señaladas arriba, indican el tiempo en que los libros fueron escritos y no en el que fueron publicados.

Los cinco libros primeros forman el ciclo anterior los cambios sociales (y personales) y a la Guerra civil.

Los tres libros de la segunda parte, precisamente al desarrollo de estos cambios.

1 This interesting grouping made by the poet himself is to be found in Caja 2.5.

2 Prados originally included *Vuelta* in this section, as his comments on 'los cinco libros primeros' (cf. infra) indicate.

Los cuatro primeros de México o sea la tercera parte (ciclo tercero) a la adaptación al ambiente nuevo con la experiencia vivida.

Los cuatro del cuarto ciclo a la experiencia personal una vez sobrepasada lo que representa el ciclo tercero.

A partir de 'La piedra escrita' inclusive vencido lo meramente personal debe tener todo una profundidad sin límites tanto en lo personal como en los colectivo—universal de la vida.

APPENDIX VI

'Yo estoy no es la adolescencia'

No es la adolescencia
ese olvido que se presiente por primera vez bajo las axilas
y gota a gota llega a transparentar toda la lluvia.

Para devorar los hombres animan el sol y las escamas de los peces
esas moscas blanquísimas que poco a poco van horadando a través
de los muros
hasta lograr atravesar toda la sangre
lejos lejos lejísimo donde una lágrima es a veces más dulce que el
olvido;
donde una mano sobre los ojos basta
para que todo el sueño gire alrededor de un sólo dedo . . .

No es la esperanza la esperanza anima a las piedras,
salir lejanos donde una voz es el silencio,
donde no existe el aire pero todo presiente el caminar de un hombre
por la vida . . .

No es la adolescencia
ese dolor de las algas que se pudren sobre la arena;
esa humedad que enciende sus manos más allá de la nuca
esa inconstancia;
esa inocencia que nos imita,
que traspasa la frente para acabar desnuda entre plantas jugosas
sin sentido . . .

Es la indolencia,
el primer navajazo que un río nos desmaya,
la formación de un mapa y de un ejército,
la voz,
las persecuciones que trasmutan sus términos,
la tierra sin aliento que no será una estancia en un cuerpo seguro:
¡un grito!

En las primera hojas;
en los espejos:

yo estoy no es la adolescencia cuando una ciudad se ha abierto por
su base.

'Si yo pudiera . . .'

Yo pertenezco a esos anchos caminos donde los árboles se cuentan;
a ese dolor que el estambre abandona en sus ruedas hilo a hilo que
canta.
Me muevo entre mis brazos porque mi rostro solo no lo encuentro
en la miel, gota a gota, como el ganado que trashuma.
Vivo bajo esa lama de los estanques,
en la paz de los bosques que se ignoran.
Como la luna resbala por las piedras
vivo en las multitudes herrumbrosas que acampan junto a un río.

'Si yo pudiera un día, un día tan sólo,
como esta razón que mi genio anima,
abrir de par en par las puertas
de mi cuerpo y las granjas . . .'

Yo pertenezco al fondo de esas viejas lagunas,
de esos hombres que marchan sin conocerse sobre el mundo;
a esos largos racimos que duelen contra el cáñamo
que abandonan sus nombres como las hojas del aceite.

Yo pertenezco a ese pez que resiste cuando la nieve cae, como la
nieve cae;
a esas aguas tan duras que se alejan cantando
y que un día amanecen junto a la orilla, erectas.

'Si yo pudiera como esos seres en olvido que pasan y repasan su
soledad bajo la luna,
dejar sobre la tierra
todo el ardor del ansia que circunda mi frente . . .'

Yo pertenezco a esas largas llanuras que resuenan sin viento y se
extremecen;
a esos antiguos pozos olvidados donde unos ojos miden el albor de
sus huesos . . .
al rumor de los élitros sobre unas hojas tiernas . . .
A ese ronco mugido de los bisontes que galopan cerca ya de la
pampa . . .

'Si yo pudiera un día

abandonar sobre este ardor lejano,
como un blanco navío,
el altísimo témpano que apuñala mi angustia . . .'

Hay gotas de una lluvia que no encuentran, perdidas, los roces de su cielo
y hay pájaros que olvidan la plenitud de la distancia en que han sido engendrados.
Yo pertenezco a esos hombres que mueren.
Vivo aquí entre mis brazos, porque no encuentro el límite que los separa.
Pertenezco a la sombra de los más anchos ríos . . .
Como la luz difusa de esos últimos puentes.

'Si yo pudiera un día, un día tan sólo,
abandonar sobre la tierra enteramente
estos bueyes que hoy labran los bordes de mi sueño . . .'

'El llanto subterráneo'

Junto al mar, ese manto que la luz origina
y que repliega el aire, como a la dura arena en su costado;
donde los hombres miran y mueren contra el vino
y las cabezas de los niños lloran;
donde los ojos de los pescados lloran
y los cabellos de las mujeres se tienden en silencio hasta las nubes:

yo no puedo cantar como esas aves
que iluminan su voz bajo la espuma.
No puedo ya cantar como esas aves
que desconocen el dolor de la harina
y están sobre la nieve,
sobre la nieve vuelan y cantan dulcemente
entre sábanas largas mientras la luna sube.

Yo he visto y he volado
también, como esas aves en la bruma . . .
Y he pensado que he muerto . . .
Y he deshilado el río de los mapas
recostado en mi llanto como encima de un sueño.
Blanca estuvo mi mano en su dulzura;
mas no puedo cantar como esas aves.
Ya no puedo cantar. (Canta quien puede.)
Ya no puedo cantar como esas aves . . .

Ando en patios humildes;
ando en ropas nocturnas,
ando en seres que velan sus rebaños y el ansia de otros muertos.
Ando entre rostros míseros que a la luna dormitan o que tal vez se
mueren.
Ando con los cipreses que arrastran sus cadenas
y engrandecen su marcha, sin temor, en los puentes.

Bajo los grandes puentes donde duele la vida
y unos hombres se acercan a morir en silencio
—esos hombres que llegan sin amor y sin rostro,
uno a uno, millones desde los cuatro olvidos.
Desde los cuatro mares que los pescados lloran,
llegan y se arrodillan bajo los anchos puentes
—bajo esos anchos puentes donde duele la vida
y obedecen los muslos sin temblor y sin gozo
a la sombra que escupen de un ardor que no sienten.
Bajo esos anchos puentes donde acaba la luna
y se olvidan las conchas desde los cuatro vientos . . .
En esos anchos huecos húmedas como heridas que no duermen,
donde juntan sus bocas los hombres
uno a uno soñando sobre la misma arena:
uno a uno, millones desde las cuatro muertes
—desde las cuatro esquinas de la sangre que tiembla—
uno a uno han venido y han pedido mi rostro.
Hoy, sin él, me arrodillo bajo los anchos puentes.
Sin él canto y me encuentro más unido a mi sangre.

¿Soy otro peso errante sobre la misma esfera?
¿otro cuerpo que ofrece sus inútiles horas?
¿otra apesadumbrada voluntad que camina?
¿otro crimen reciente? . . .
'¡Tal vez! ¡Tal vez . . .'!
¿Quién canta? ¿Soy yo?: Tal vez soy yo. (Canta quien puede).

Ahora cantan de mí como esas aves . . .
Antes cantaba yo como ellas vuelan
sobre la blanca espuma. Mi voz, también cantaba . . .
Cantaba yo sobre la blanca espuma . . .
Volaba yo, volaba yo como esas aves . . .
Mas hoy perdí mi rostro; el pescado me duele,
toda la arena clava su espina en mi silencio,

y no puede cantar, tan sólo escucho . . .
Hoy no puede cantar, —canta quien puede— . . .
Ahora vivo y me arrastro sobre el llanto que escupo,
como el amor que digo, la sangre que no escuchan.
Blanca estuvo mi mano y ella misma me lleva.
Nadie me ve. Mi antigua forma ha desertado . . .
¿Cómo podré, como podré crecer sin manos bajo las filtraciones
dolorosas que mi oquedad hereda?
Junto al mar, ese manto que el silencio unifica:
dondc los ojos de los niños lloran,
donde los ojos de los pescados lloran
y las cabezas de los hombres miran y mueren contra el vino
y los cabellos de las mujeres se levantan gimiendo hacia las nubes!
he perdido mi cuerpo y no encuentro mi rostro . . .
Al fin puedo cantar: '¡Estoy bajo los puentes,
con los ápteros brazos de los viejos obreros!'
Porque he reconocido la amplitud de esa herida
en la que estoy sembrando lo que pedí a la muerte,
húmedos de un silencio que aguarda bajo tierra,
junto a mi sien se pudren un caracol y un mundo.

'Aquí estoy'

Cuando el cielo descubre su razón sin estrellas
porque el hermano ha herido el hermano en el pecho;
cuando la sangre asciende silenciosa y oscura
como un lamento de la nada que como piedra rige . . .

aún viven estas ramas tiernas que nos invitan
y aún florecen ingrávidas como un mundo que nace.
Las tiernas ramas que no conocen el quebranto
ni el espantoso choque de dos cuerpos en tierra.

Como el mar, como un sueño que se olvida,
como el sol en la arena mientras los nombres luchan,
ellas vuelan y agitan arriba entre las nubes
felices en la lluvia y en la luz que se exaltan.

Están las tiernas ramas y las hojas que mecen
mientras curva la tierra uniendo al horizonte.
Están las verdes ramas y están los tiernos tallos
sobre el dolor que envuelve siempre a los mismos aires.

Se sabe de unos hombres que mueren en la ausencia
mientras muerde la lluvia la arena enrojecida:
de unos hombres lejanos en la piel que resisten,
de unos hombres de cuerpo que obscurecen sus hojas.

Allí donde sin sangre las flores se enfurecen
y arde sobre las charcas la espuma enfebrecida,
hay árboles que esparcen felices su existencia
como las bellas nubes sobre el cielo que ignoran.

Están las tiernas ramas y los hombres que mueren
sobre la tierra que confunde sus llantos oprimidos.
Están las blancas manos de unos niños que quiebran
su tenue luz sin cielo bajo las flores que se olvidan.

Y están los ojos entreabiertos y está la espina estéril de la lluvia
y la piedra caliente de la noche estrellada,
donde las alas ínfimas del pájaro más bello
grita su luz y absorbe una flor de dos conchas.

Allí, junto al silencio, una voz ya permanente
que el pecho no retiene y en el sueño rezuma,
sube, se alza inflexible por su justicia al viento,
sin límite, insumisa, fuera de la memoria.

Por eso no abandono estas playas tan quietas ni la luz de su luna.
Cuando las flores giran dulcemente sus sombras
sobre la misma tierra que una frente domina
y es la noche tan sólo paño para el gemido.

Lejos, lejos las flores de una risa jugosa,
que aún se duerme sin límites detrás de la conciencia.
¡Que mis ojos desangren, profundos, sus corales!
¡Que un caracol retumbe doloroso en mi sueño!

Lejos las mariposas que un mapa disminuyen;
las diminutas sienes brillantes de los insectos;
las suspirantes hojas que una bruma sostienen:
esa música fácil que sin saberlo prende su olvido en la inocencia.

Donde el látigo aún rige sobre el marfil que mancha,
donde la inmensa noche con su calor alienta
la enfurecida arena contra los mismos cuerpos
que antes se imaginaba ser libertad gozosa . . .

Allí quiero vivir. ¡Oh sombra, sombra, elévate!
Un árbol crece inmóvil bajo los altos vientos.
Ignotos habitantes en su savia conversan.
Hablan, hablan sus astros: su universo conspiran.

Mientras giran las lunas, los llantos y las fuentes,
los pequeños gemidos en multitud alborada,
la quietud de los pozos, las pacientes hormigas,
el barco que se aleja lento sobre los mares . . .

Mientras pulsado el cáñamo que atiranta la angustia
canta bajo los puentes el hombre de los bosques,
la carne perseguida—playa del estampido—
y ese pez que se pudre diariamente en la arena . . .

Mientras los hombres miran y miran mansamente
al silencio que horada la sangre que aún existen,
esa humedad que empieza suavemente en la nuca
y acaba como un cuerpo que su orilla abandona . . .

Mientras todo el silencio florece en una aguja
y enciende la navaja su corona sin astros
junto al nácar pulido de la sangre que mana,
sueña, canta y sonríe como yerba muere:

me quedo en estas aguas y a la luz de esta luna,
que árbol tras árbol llega hasta que un árbol vuelve
y ya la tierra es curva, curvada por el tiempo,
y el árbol ya conoce las órbitas que aguardan.

Me quedo en estas playas hasta esperar que lleguen
de nuevo a ver mis manos la curva del espacio
y arrancarle la sombra para que el hombre pueda
tocar él mismo al cielo donde duermen los árboles.

Me quedo en esta tierra: Oh, tirad, tirad contra el pecho.
No es la muerte tan fácil como un niño que llora.
No es al fuego a la dicha que la semilla atiende.
¡Yo estoy con el olor caliente del estiércol en tierra!

Bello es el mar tan lento y el cuerpo que desnuda;
las misteriosas algas que profundas se enredan;
la amistad que unifica más allá del olvido,
ese otro ardor tan claro como un sol que lo enciende.

Es bella la inocencia y la piel que la alumbra;
dulce es la miel y el pan si en la paz se levantan,
pero sé de unos hombres lejanos y la sed en que excitan:
ahora sé de unos cuerpos de sangre que agonizan sin llanto.

Aquí, bajo estas ramas que esparcen felices su existencia,
mientras duermen las fieras sin temor en su sombra
y la espuma se agita por no herir a los astros,
hay hombres que se olvidan bajo el marfil o el oro que curvan sus espaldas.

Lejos, lejos las hojas de una música fácil:
no es tan blanda la vida como el sueño que cubre.
Oh, tirad, tirad contra el pecho, que el dolor de las balas
se perderá en el tiempo, pero quedan los árboles.

Sí, quedarán las ramas que al moverse me dicen
las manos por qué encienden y la tierra a que escapan.
Oh, tirad, tirad contra el pecho, que un árbol me sujeta.
Devastaréis mi sombra pero no evitaréis que penetre en cielo mi semilla.

'Un día . . .'

Un día la persecución será por fin abandonada
y marcharemos descuidados sin observar las sombras que nos escuchan.
Los ríos mansamente resbalarán sobre sus lechos sin temblores.

No se alzarán los muros lo mismo que ojos sorprendidos por la muerte, guardando entre sus sábanas estos cuadros terribles de un espantoso número.
Ni el cristal ni la piedra conocerán los ásperos sabores de sus límites.
Un salto será el grito de una rama de flores . . .
Pasear será un pájaro que volara sin cielo.

Habrá algunos hombres todavía tremolando toda su sangre extendida;
una sangre que no podrá nombrarse porque serán desconocidas las distancias;
una sangre sin dueño
que fluirá ya voluntariamente
como una voz aun trémola del tiempo . . .

Un día,
el vigor de los músculos será cambiado prudentemente como un deseo;
el corazón y el trigo brotarán juntamente para todos los ojos,
gota a gota esos hierros que hoy lloran las cadenas se irán
hundiendo en una tierra que no conocerá los nombres del delito.

Un día será el mundo
como un inmenso anillo abierto;
libre como ese anillo que hoy nos enseña el agua:
ese anillo potente de una sola sonrisa
lo mismo que una estrella.

Un día será el mundo lo mismo que una espiga,
un anillo de brazos unidos sobre la tierra,
lo mismo que un ejército invencible sin posible enemigo:
como un inmenso nombre que no conozca ningún cuerpo.

'Dos poemas íntimos'[1]

I
Sombra de abril

Mi cuerpo vive y casi lo conozco;
apenas percibir puedo su forma
y sólo cuando cruza por mis sueños
siento, por el dolor, que en él habito.

No sé cómo se llama, ni he sabido
cual es su nombre nunca, ni lo quiero;
su nombre ha de formarse en su memoria;
la memoria de mí, que nunca es mía.

Pero nacido estoy, casi ya viejo
después de tantos duros vendavales
y en él se afila entera mi ternura,
hoy por la guerra, al borde de la muerte,
igual que antes miedosa mi esperanza
se afilaba, al nacer, junto a mi vida.

¡Oh forma persistente que así enredas
mi pensamiento al giro de las horas!
¿adónde has de llevar mi eterna lucha
que siempre has de encontrarme desolado? . . .

Aun la sombra de abril a mí se acerca,
como otras veces cuando niño he visto
acercarse su ardor junto a mis nervios
a despertar su angustia por mi sangre.
Aun su amenaza inquieta mis sentidos,
como ayer inquietó mi triste infancia,
entre fantasmas, sueños y amarguras
de mi primera edad desamparada . . .

Igualmente me muestra sus auroras
e idéntica ilusión por mi desgrana.
Abril, en guerra o paz, siempre me encuentras
desconocido en medio del combate,
junto a las hojas de mi muerte, trémulo,
aguardando su eterna flor desnudo:
si como un árbol, bajo mi arboleda;
si débil hierba, entre mi compañía,
pero igual en la vida de mi suerte.

Siempre al llegar, ves que mi cuerpo sigue
la romántica forma de su ausencia,
que un desmedido afán le llama olvido.
Yo, siempre en mi dolor, sin conocerme.

¡Oh, primavera inquieta, que me ocultas,
lleno por tu ambición, mi propio cuerpo!
Abril, abril: ¡qué eterna adolescencia
mi renacer constante por tus ramas!

II
Sacrificio

¡Tan cercano el amor! ¿Y ahora dejarte
de nuevo? ¿He de perderte así logrado,
oh persistente sueño de mi angustia,
cuando entero me das lo que te pido;
mis labios te recorren plenamente
hecho incendio de carne en tu hermosura?

No quiero abandonarte, más te entrego
y consciente al dolor vivo tu ausencia
y el recuerdo de haberte al fin hallado:
sea mi culpa menor que mi desvelo.

Que el cuerpo nuevamente se deshaga
en tristes esperanzas y abandono
y de nuevo al dormir, mire el descanso
frágilmente poblado a mi deseo.

Otra vez en la noche vaya entrando,
como dulce ladrón de mi tristeza,
ya que la cerca de su huerto es fácil
y en su engaño mi azar ve su reposo.

Que tanto andar, es vano . . .
¿Por qué busco
lo que a mis manos niega su ternura,
si tan fugaz deleite, sólo el daño
de su verdad feliz deja en mi dicha?

En las candentes rosas de sus ascuas,
en la guerra, el amor más se ilumina
y más promete lo que nunca encuentra:
¡Oh, mi mano de ciego en su destino!

Quisiera retener mi pensamiento
y mi brazo, en las horas del presente
que tan feliz valor me da en tu premio;
pero el tiempo es veloz y en él pasamos
dejándonos detrás nuestra memoria . . .
Huye, amor, que yo sé que entre sus palmas
aún no hallaré el cobijo de su sombra.

Cumple, fiel tu misión y vuelve luego
cuando esté rota entera mi condena,
que como el dios antiguo voy cegado
y aún más, con sangre ardiendo entre los ojos:
huye, que yo te aguardo en mi retiro . . .

¿A qué vienes cercano a cautivarme
y ante la misma muerte levantado
si has de inmolarte entre sus negras brasas?
¡Tan logrado! ¡Y saber que he de perderte,
volviendo a mis delirios por buscarte! . . .

Tal vez este dolor me es necesario,
si en caminar contigo está mi vida
y he de alcanzar por ello nuevas glorias.

Huye, yo soñaré que estás llegando,
aunque en tu ausencia olvide mi alegría
y entre fantasmas viva mi esperanza.

No, no quiero perderte por no darte:
¡Huye y déjame hundido en esta guerra!

1 Taken from *Hora de España*, XVIII, June 1938, pp. 21–24.

Index to Titles and First Lines of Poems referred to in the Text